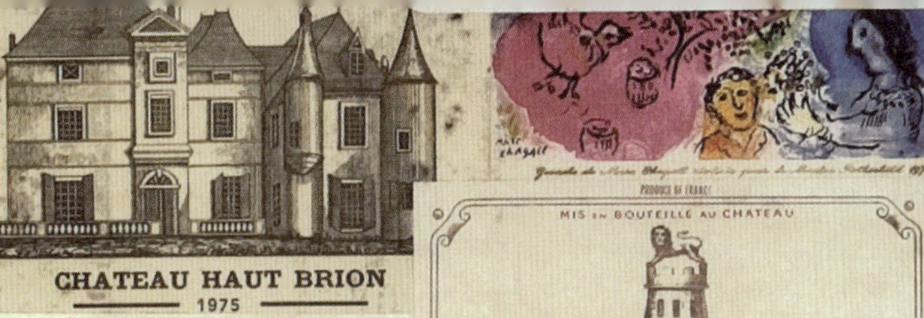
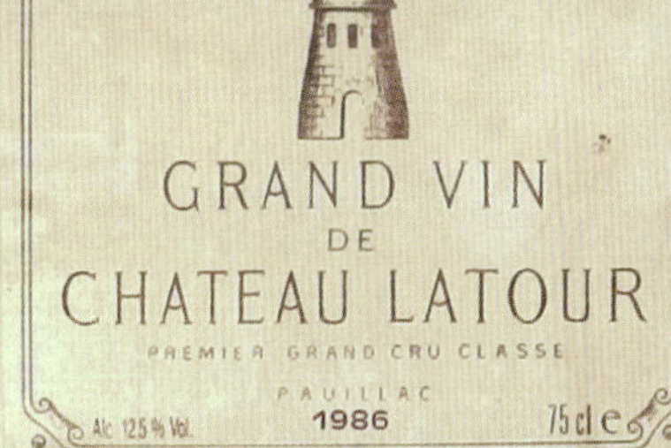

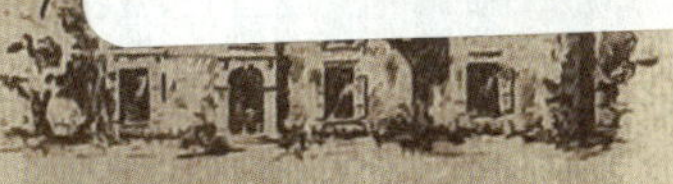
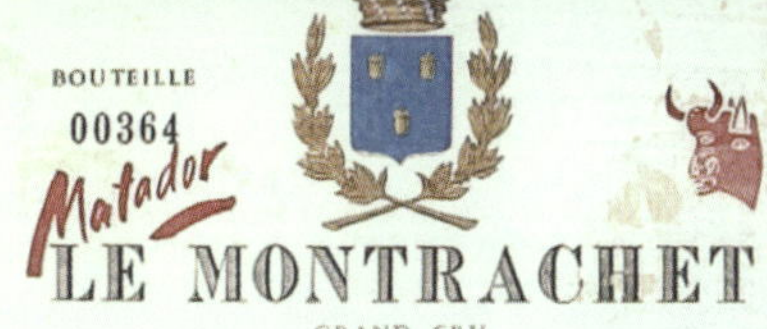

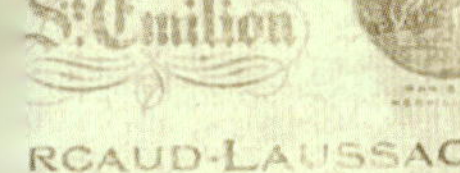
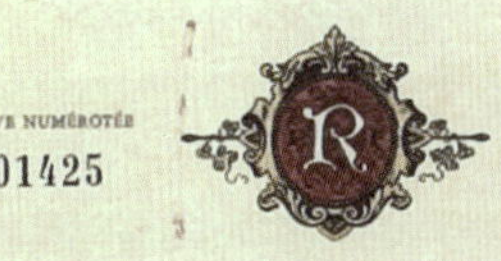
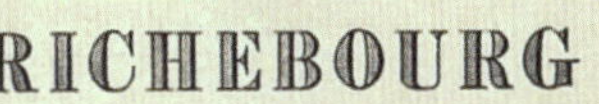
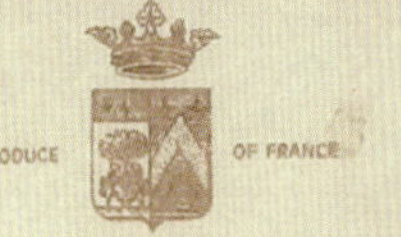

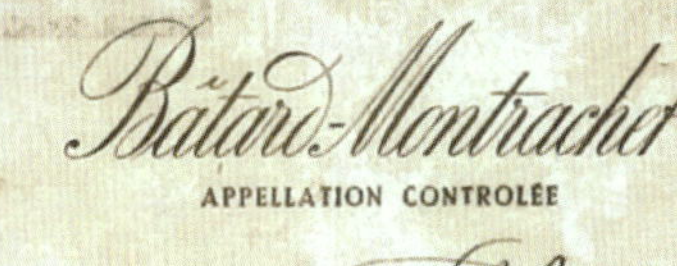
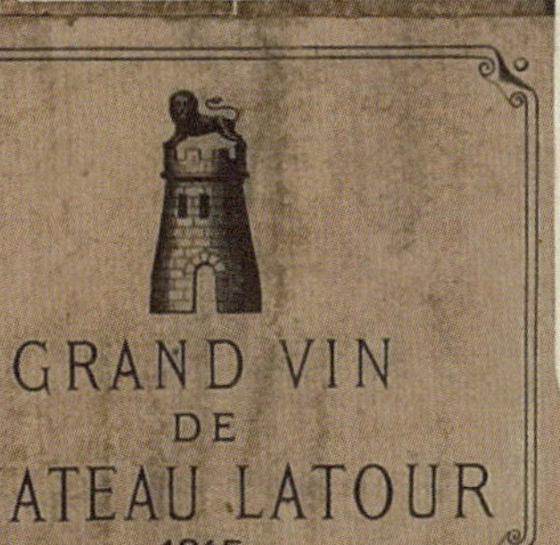
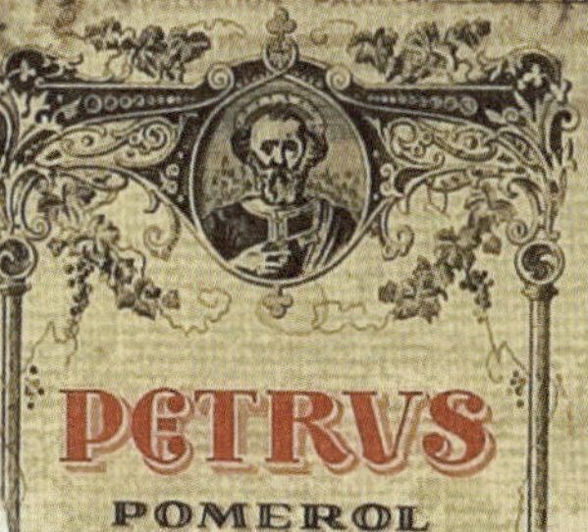
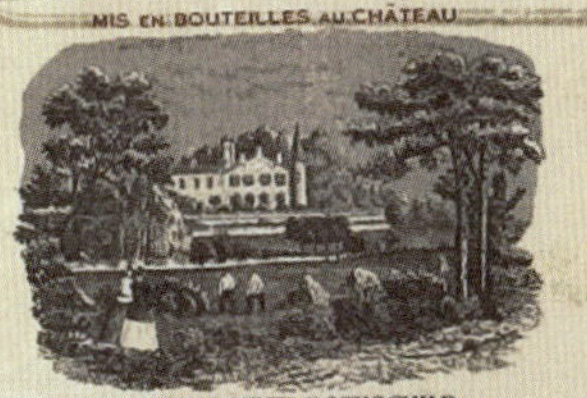
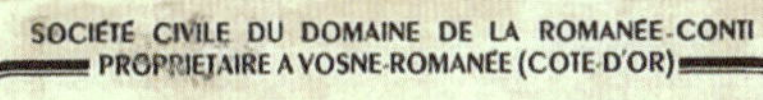
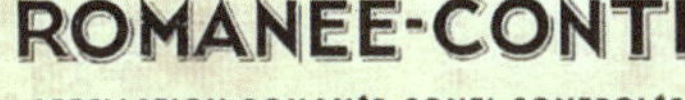
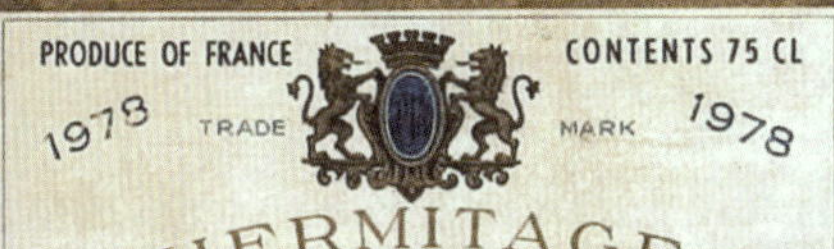

VICOMTE AMAURY D'HARCOURT
CHATEAU HAUT BRION
1975
Châteauneuf du Pape
1990
DELAS
GRAND VIN
DE
CHATEAU LATOUR
1986
CHATEAU HAUT-BRION
Premier grand crû classé
Malmaison Wines
HERMITAGE
La Chapelle
PAUL JABOULET AINÉ
LE MONTRACHET
REMOISSENET PÈRE & FILS
Château
Mouton Rothschild
Hospices de Beaune
1985
MEURSAULT-GENEVRIÈRES
RICHEBOURG
PETRUS
POMEROL
1975
CHATEAU PICHON LONGUEVILLE
1983
PAUILLAC
Bâtard-Montrachet
1945
ROMANÉE-CONTI
ANNÉE 1971
CHATEAU LAFITE ROTHSCHILD
1961

Things I Love

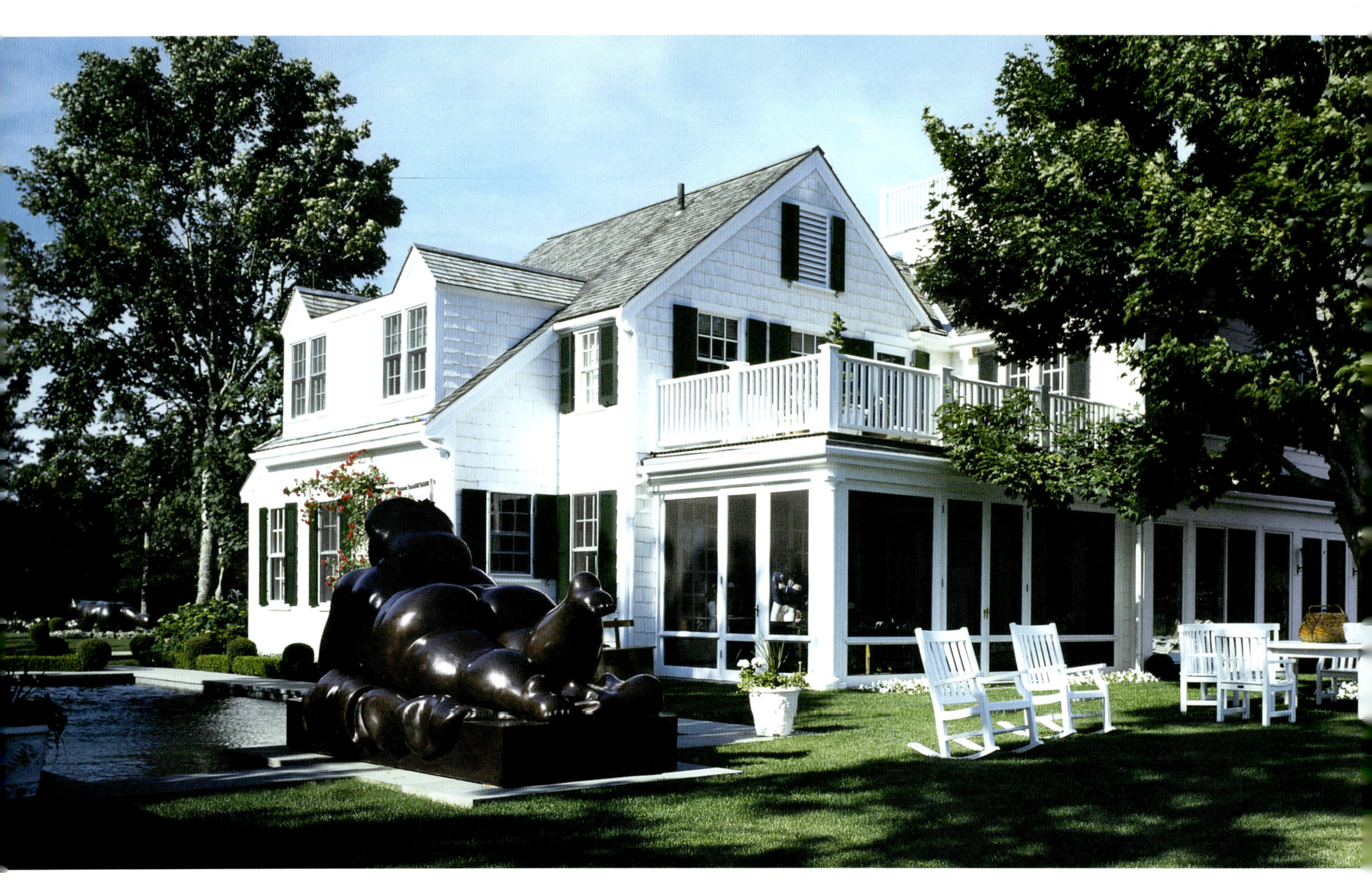

Things I Love

THE MANY COLLECTIONS OF WILLIAM I. KOCH

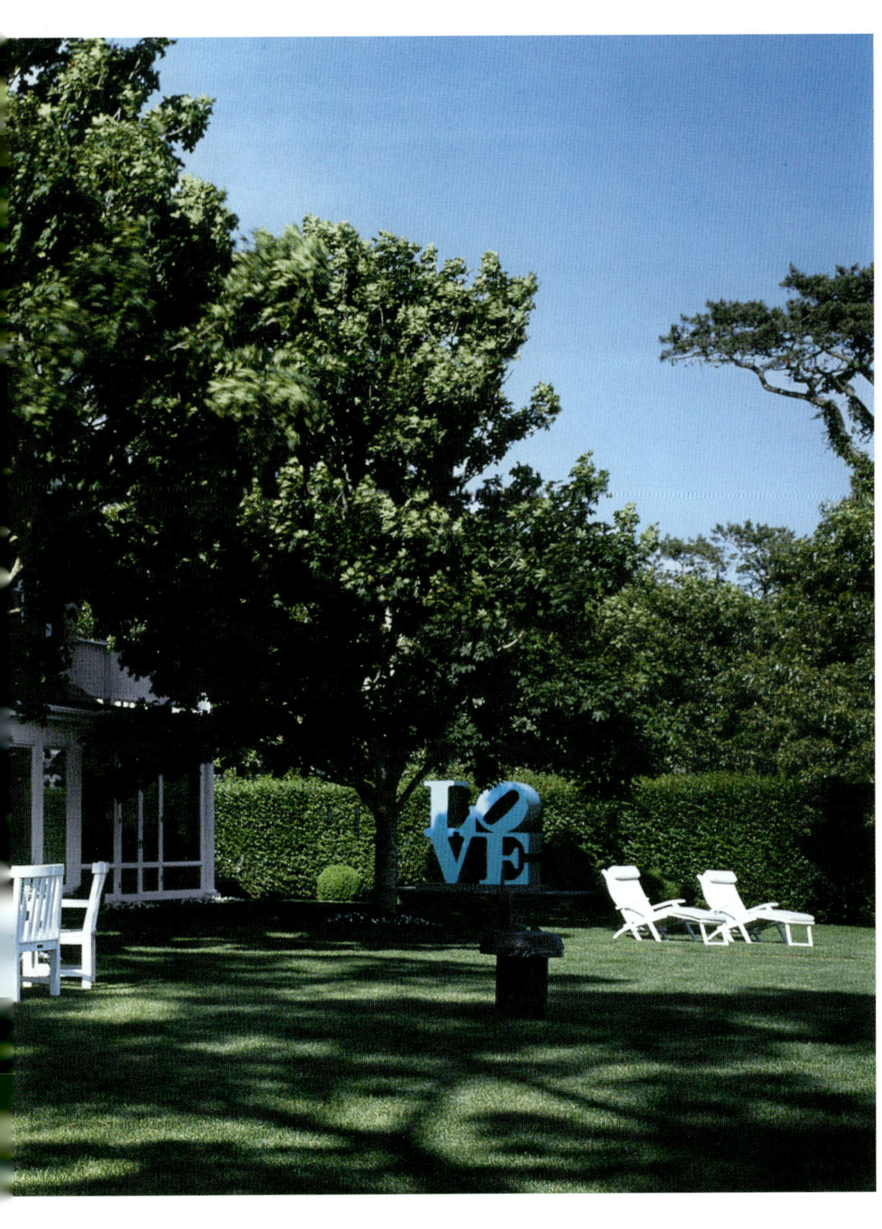

George T. M. Shackelford
and Elliot Bostwick Davis

With contributions by
Bob Fisher, Alan Granby, Janice Hyland,
Christine Kondoleon, and R. L. Wilson

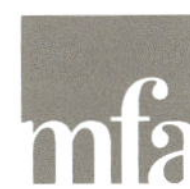

MFA PUBLICATIONS
a division of the Museum of Fine Arts, Boston

MFA Publications
a division of the Museum of Fine Arts, Boston
465 Huntington Avenue
Boston, Massachusetts 02115
www.mfa-publications.org

This book was published in conjunction with the exhibition "Things I Love: The Many Collections of William I. Koch," organized by the Museum of Fine Arts, Boston, from August 31, 2005, to November 13, 2005.

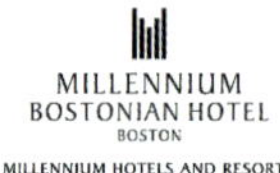

Millennium Hotels and Resorts is the exclusive hotel sponsor of the exhibition.

ISBN 0-87846-695-9
Library of Congress Control Number: 2005926792

Generous support for this publication was provided by William I. Koch.

For a complete listing of MFA Publications, please contact the publisher at the address at left, or call 617 369 3438.

Front cover: Amedeo Modigliani, *Reclining Nude* (detail), 1917 (p. 76)

Back cover: Frederic Remington, *Evening on a Canadian Lake* (detail), 1905 (p. 106)

Title page: The Koch residence at Osterville, on Cape Cod, Massachusetts

P. 204: The Koch residence at Palm Beach, Florida

Unless otherwise noted, all objects are in the William I. Koch Collection.

Measurements for three-dimensional objects are taken from a vantage point facing the subject head on.

Photography credits are listed at the back of the book.

Research assistance provided by Natasha F. Khandekar
Edited by Sarah E. McGaughey
Copyedited and proofread by Julia Gaviria

Designed and produced by Cynthia Rockwell Randall
Printed at Sawyer Printers, Charlestown, Massachusetts

Trade distribution:
D.A.P. / Distributed Art Publishers
155 Sixth Avenue, 2nd floor
New York, New York 10013
Tel. 212 627 1999 Fax 212 627 9484

FIRST EDITION
Printed in the United States of America.
This book was printed on acid-free paper.

CONTENTS

* * * * * * *

DIRECTOR'S FOREWORD

* * * * * * *

A QUARTER CENTURY AGO, William Ingraham Koch began buying paintings in earnest. Among his first great acquisitions was a painting he still cherishes, a view of a poppy-strewn field bordered by deep green trees. Painted by Claude Monet near the French town of Giverny in 1890, this work recalls, to Bill, the landscapes of his youth in Kansas. To him, as to every viewer, it seems to show a very pleasant place.

Whenever I talk with Bill Koch about his collection, I have the sense of a man deeply engaged with the art he lives with and loves very deeply. His reasons for loving a work may not always be the same as mine; that is part of the excitement of discussing art with him. A scientist, a businessman, a sportsman—Bill brings to his understanding of art a singular and intensely personal vision.

"Things I Love: The Many Collections of William I. Koch" celebrates the diverse and eclectic groups of objects and works of art that Bill has amassed over the past three decades. The exhibition was organized by George T. M. Shackelford, Chair, Art of Europe, and the Arthur K. Solomon Curator of Modern Art, and Elliot Bostwick Davis, the John Moors Cabot Chair, Art of the Americas, in conjunction with Christine Kondoleon, the George and Margo Behrakis Curator of Greek and Roman Art, Art of the Ancient World. They were assisted by Natasha F. Khandekar and by staff throughout the museum. The MFA is grateful for Millennium Hotels and Resorts' sponsorship of the exhibition and for their ongoing commitment to the arts.

An honorary trustee of the Museum of Fine Arts, Boston, Bill Koch is a wonderful supporter of the institution and a great friend to our city. We are grateful to him, above all, for his willingness to let us present his collections to the public. I hope that every visitor to "Things I Love" will come away with a sense of wonder at the vivid imagination and free spirit of the collector, and with thanks, like mine, for his generosity in sharing his treasures.

MALCOLM ROGERS
Ann and Graham Gund Director
Museum of Fine Arts, Boston

ACKNOWLEDGMENTS

* * * * * * *

FIRST AND FOREMOST, we would like to thank Bill and Bridget Koch for their warm hospitality and great generosity during the time that we have been working on "Things I Love." We owe them a particular debt for allowing us to visit their homes on many occasions. On Bill Koch's staff, Mark Curley, Steven Reinacher, Karen L. Rowe, Rick Burnham, and Peter Grubb have been a constant source of information and support, arranging meetings and photographic sessions and providing information about the collections. We would also like to thank Brad Goldstein and Gisela Garneau of the Oxbow Corporation for their assistance.

As with every exhibition, the final product is the result of the work of many people. It was Malcolm Rogers who first proposed the idea of doing an exhibition on this wonderful collection; we are grateful to him and to the Museum's management team for their support of our work.

Natasha F. Khandekar, Research Assistant, Art of Europe, has been unfailing in her contributions and assistance throughout the project. We also are very grateful to our co-curator Christine Kondoleon, George and Margo Behrakis Curator of Greek and Roman Art, for her expertise and guidance, and to Cornelius C. Vermeule III, Curator of Classical Art Emeritus. In the Department of Art of Europe, we would like to thank Kate Silverman, Brooks Rich, and Deanna Griffin; in the Department of Art of the Americas, we are indebted to Betsy Parkyn Cruikshank, Erica H. Hirshler, Croll Senior Curator of Paintings, Gerald W. R. Ward, Katharine Lane Weems Senior Curator of Decorative Arts and Sculpture, Patrick T. McMahon, Danielle Archibald, and Jessica Croll.

We also would like to thank Jennifer Bose for her supervision of the exhibition; Mark Polizzotti, Sarah McGaughey, Cynthia Randall, and Terry McAweeney for their work on this catalogue; Thomas Lang, Damon Beale, John Woolf, C. J. Walker, Daniel Forster, and Kim Sargent for the beautiful photographs of the Koch collections; Jennifer Riley, Debra LaKind, Sonia Janks, Haley M. Shaw, Christine Pollock, and Emily Malone for additional assistance with photography and rights and licensing; Keith Crippen, Jennifer Liston Munson, Poonam Sharma, Jaime Roark, Neal Johnson, and Michael Savona for the exhibition's design and installation; Patricia Loiko, Head Registrar, for her seamless loan coordination; Rhona MacBeth, Jean Woodward, Irene Konefal, Elizabeth Jablonski, Pamela Hatchfield, Roy Perkinson, Gail English, Andrew Haines, Gary Rattigan, Karen Gausch, and Meredith Montague for their conservation work; Dave Geldart and his staff for coordinating the installation; Gillian Shallcross for her help with interpretive materials; Dawn Griffin, Kelly Gifford, and Jennifer Standley for their assistance in publicizing the exhibition; Melinda Hallisey for her role in securing sponsorship for the exhibition; and Kim French, Janet O'Donoghue, and Jennifer Weissman for their marketing expertise.

GEORGE T. M. SHACKELFORD
Chair, Art of Europe, and Arthur K. Solomon Curator of Modern Art

ELLIOT BOSTWICK DAVIS
John Moors Cabot Chair, Art of the Americas

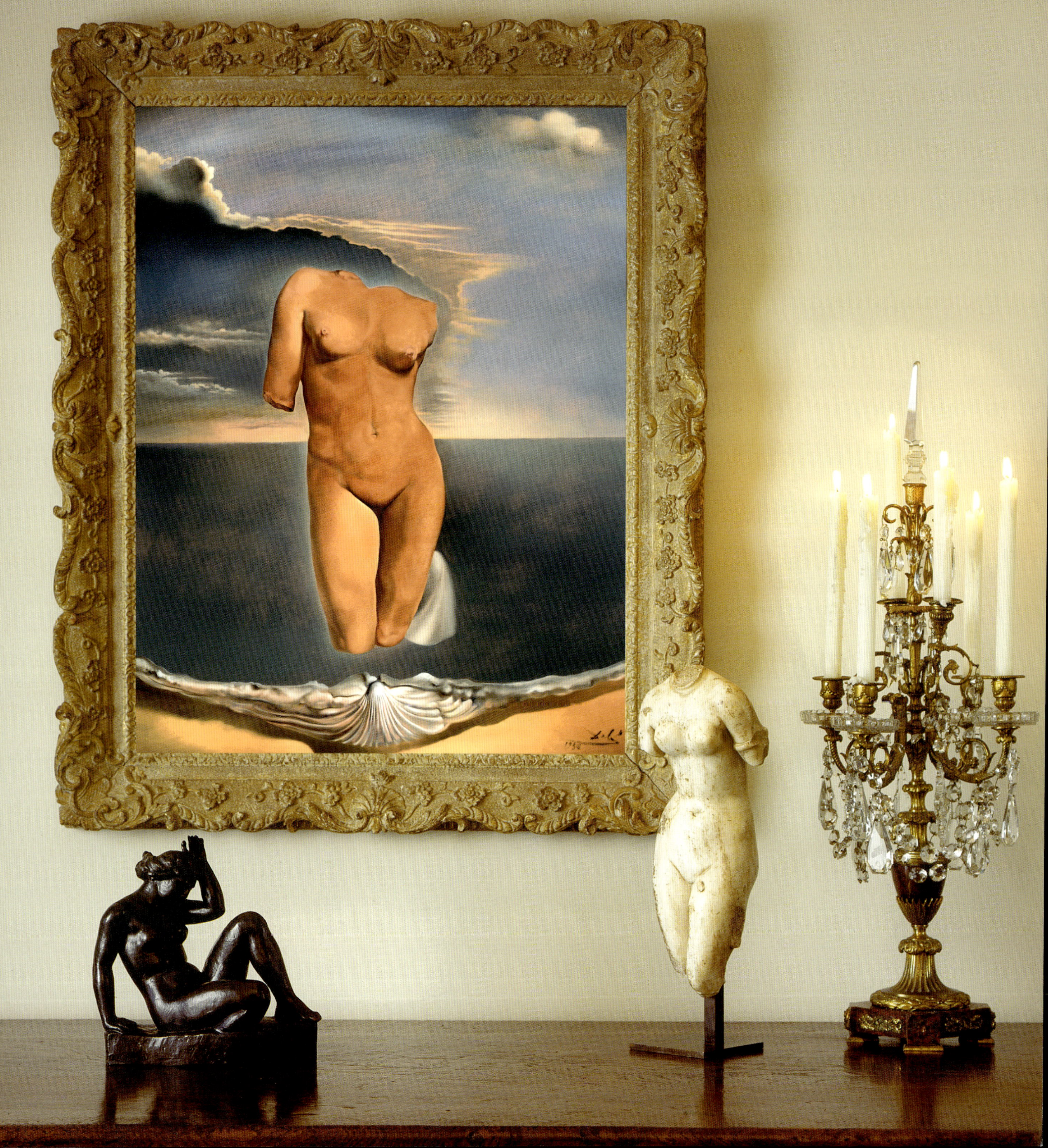

THE WORLD OF WILLIAM I. KOCH

* * * * * * *

The roots of William Ingraham Koch's diverse collections of European and American art dig deeply into the soil of his native Kansas, where he was born and raised in Wichita by parents with an eye for beauty. His father, Fred C. Koch, photographed the familiar landscapes of his ranches in Kansas, Montana, and Texas, and his mother, Mary R. Koch, was an artist and founder of the Wichita Art Association. They traveled to Africa on their honeymoon and later returned there with their son, who traces his first efforts as a collector to that trip and his purchases of African sculptures intended for the tourist trade. Over time, those first steps would find their stride in the lithe bronzes of Malvina Hoffman, whose statues *Shilluck Warrior (Nuer Tribe), Upper White Nile, East Africa* (p. 20) and *"Daboa," Dancing Girl of Sara Tribe, Lake Chad* (p. 21) are among the many sculptures in the Koch Collection.

Born in 1940, Bill Koch learned the value of taking risks at an early age. When the nation's oil companies sought to block his father's process for extracting more gasoline from crude oil by filing numerous patent lawsuits, the elder Koch stood up to them and prevailed. Fred Koch created what was to become Koch Industries in 1940, and by the late 1970s, it had grown to be the second-largest privately held company in the nation. Bill, the fourth and youngest son of Fred Koch—nineteen minutes younger than his twin brother, David—was educated in Indiana at Culver Military Academy and later at Massachusetts Institute of Technology in Cambridge, Massachusetts, where he received three degrees in chemical engineering, including a doctorate of science. Applying the strong work ethic he learned from his father, Bill was involved in various operations at Koch Industries. In the early 1980s he started Oxbow Corporation, whose main business was building and operating alternative energy power plants, and buying, transporting, and selling petroleum coke, a waste product from oil refining that is used as a solid fuel source. In 2000 Oxbow sold its geothermal power plants. Since then, the company has developed a 6.5-million-ton-per-year, low-sulfur, environmentally compliant coal mine in Colorado; found and developed a large natural gas reserve; and become the largest petroleum coke marketer in the world. The company has annual sales of more than $1.5 billion and operates facilities throughout the United States, Europe, the Middle East, Asia, and South America.

In establishing the Oxbow Group, Koch sought to create a company reflecting his own personal vision of corporate responsibility and to promote his belief in the power of self-initiative. Philanthropy is central to his philosophy, and he has dedicated himself to a variety of worthy causes. In addition to participating on the boards of schools, hospitals, and museums, Koch developed innovative ways to fight crime in his native Kansas, establishing the Koch Crime Commission in 1993. Art has played a major role in his sense of corporate responsibility. When he began forming his art collection in the early 1980s with the assistance of John Walsh, then the Mrs. Russel W. Baker Curator of European Paintings at the Museum of Fine Arts, Boston, Koch placed the artworks in a foundation that exhibited them publicly at the Museum. Since that time, he has changed the purpose of the foundation, yet remains deeply committed to providing public access to his collection at his main residence in Palm Beach, Florida. There, he annually welcomes about five hundred schoolchildren from the area to experience museum-quality works of art in their unique setting. He has worked closely with several Palm Beach Public Schools, helping to support art curricula and underwriting a student art guide produced by an advanced-placement art history class (at the Alexander Dreyfoos School for the Arts) entitled *Bill Koch's Art Collection: Presented for Kids by Kids*. Koch also lends works to museum exhibitions in the United States and abroad.

At first glance, the Koch Collection appears eclectic, spanning several continents (Europe, the Americas, Asia, and Africa), styles (antiquities to Pop Art), and categories (wine to model yachts). Bill Koch is at the core, and his strong personal associations and emotional responses bind together the myriad objects he has assembled. The many facets of his personality and interests are evident in the different rooms he has created for displaying his collections at his homes in Palm Beach and on Cape Cod, in Osterville, Massachusetts, where he spends the summer months. In both settings, the sea and the natural landscape are never

Fig. 1. Salvador Dalí's *Rhinocerontic Gooseflesh*, Aristide Maillol's bronze *The Mountain*, and a Roman torso of Aphrodite in the hallway of Koch's Palm Beach house

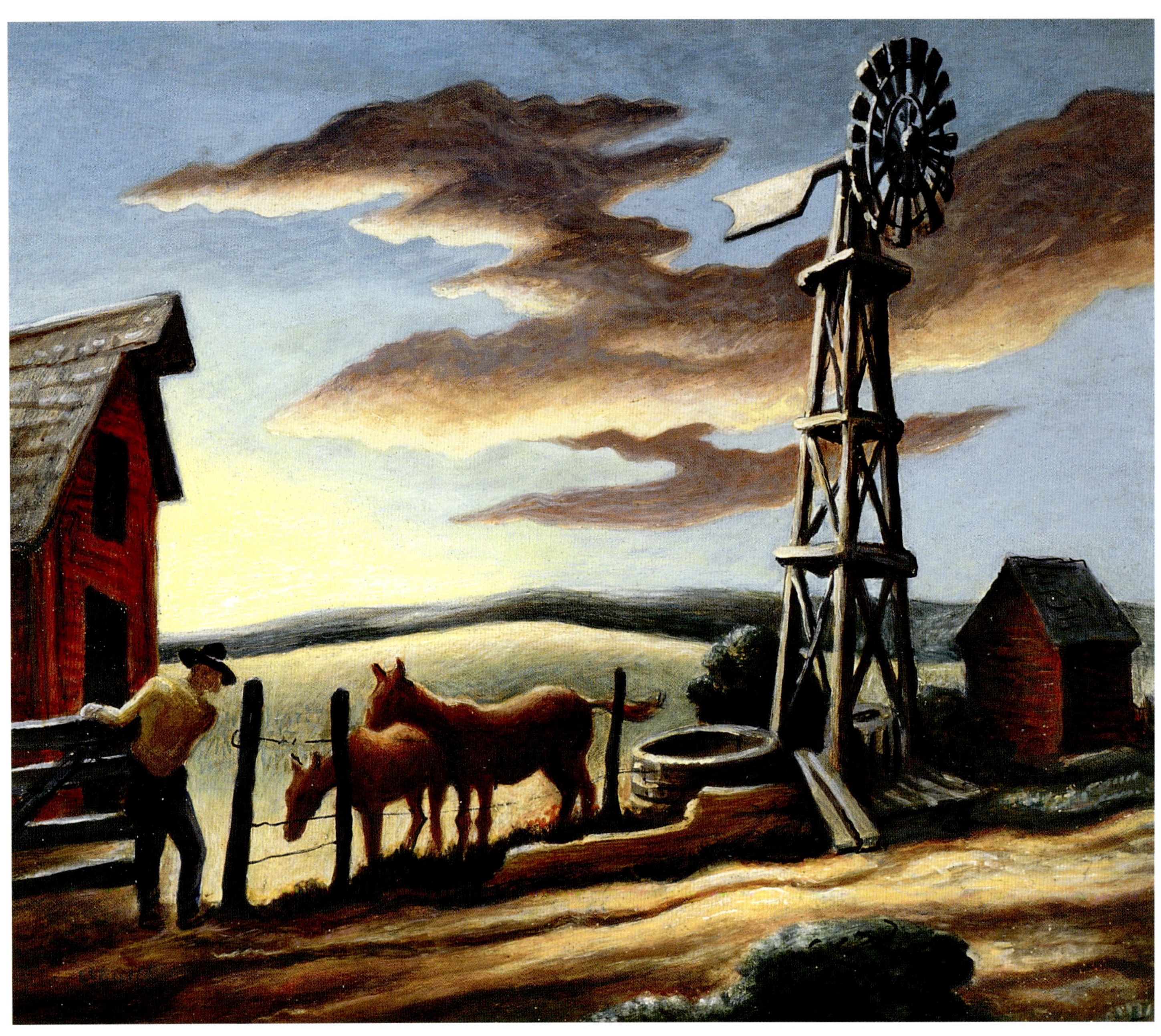

THOMAS HART BENTON

American, 1889–1975
Nebraska Evening, 1940
Oil and tempera on Masonite
15¾ x 18½ in.

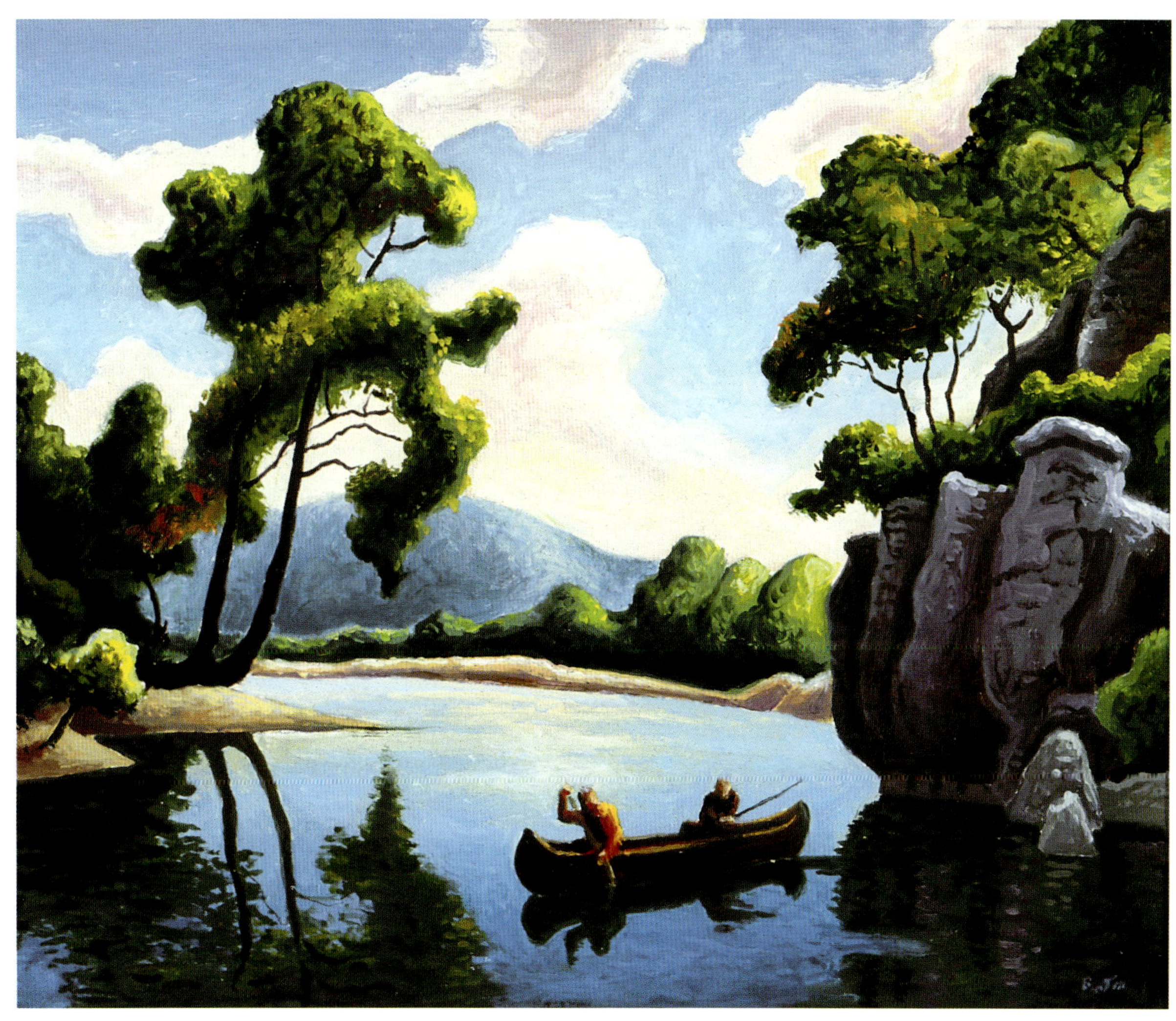

THOMAS HART BENTON

American, 1889–1975
Fishing in the Ozarks, about 1966
Oil on panel
9¼ x 11¼ in.

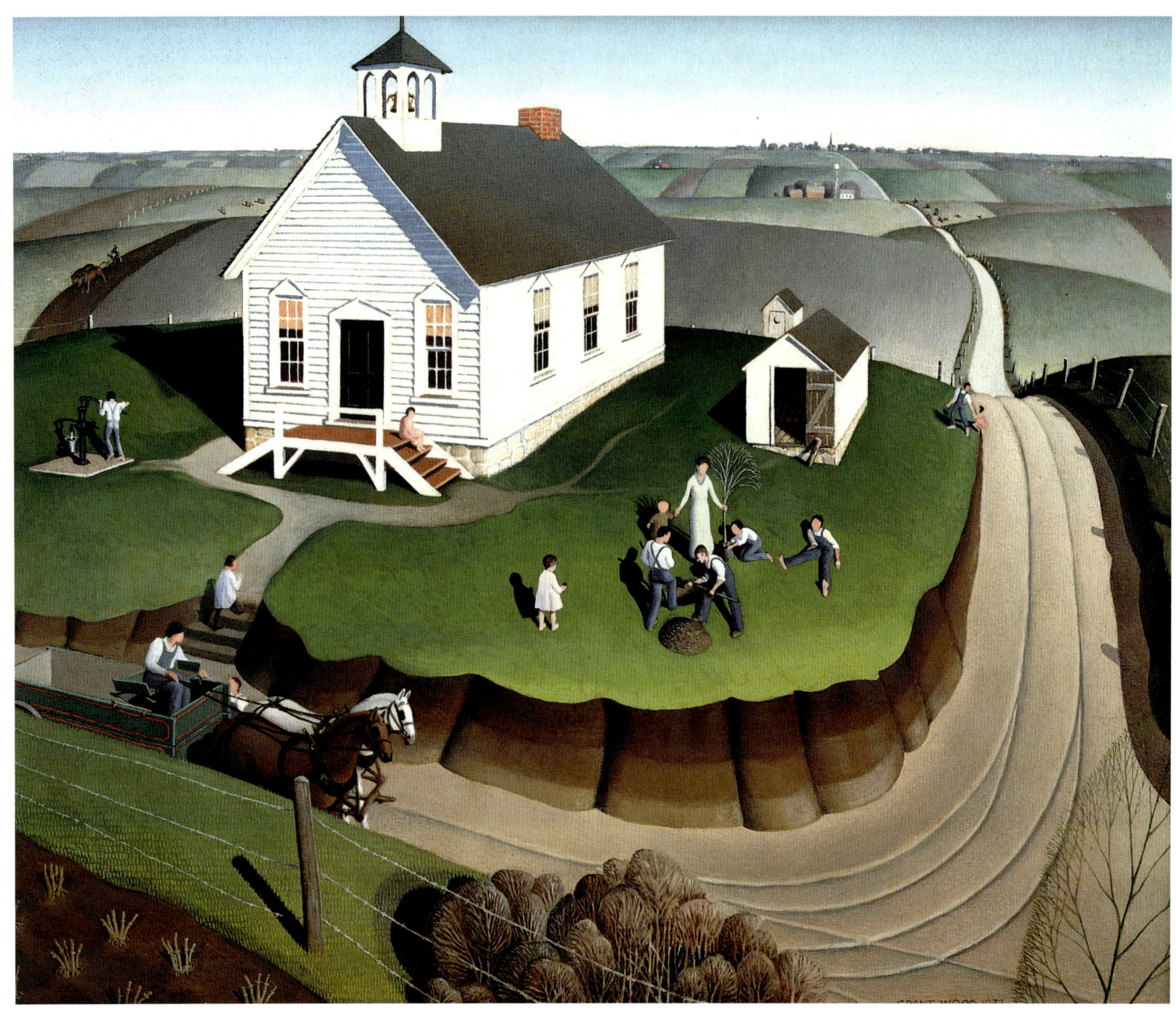

GRANT WOOD

American, 1891–1942
Arbor Day, 1932
Oil on panel
25 x 29⅞ in.

far from view outside the rooms. Inside, visitors may experience the gunpowder and drama of a naval duel in the dining room, the expansiveness of the western landscape in the Western Room, and the artful, unexpected combination of ancient and modern sculpture with a painting by Salvador Dalí in the foyer outside the living room (fig. 1). Koch carefully places each work of art himself, likening the process to solving an algorithm of shape, form, color, and geometry.

Some of the first paintings Koch bought, in 1983, were marine paintings documenting the exploits of his relative Captain James Lawrence, a naval hero of the War of 1812. While attending Culver's naval summer school, Koch developed a love for sailing. That experience, combined with his engineering aptitude fostered at MIT, fueled his passion for the sea and ultimately led him to win the coveted and prestigious America's Cup in 1992 at the helm of the specially designed boat *America*^{3}, one of a series of yachts he commissioned to race in the trials and finals. In contrast to prevailing wisdom at the time, Koch stressed working as a team over individual talent and developed a scientific, high-tech approach to boat design and construction. His pursuit of victory was decidedly unconventional: he made tobacco offerings to the Native American gods he had come to know through his youth in Kansas and the time he spent on his father's western ranches. He invited the head of the tribal council to christen the fourth boat to enter the America's Cup campaign "Kanza," or "People of the South Wind," after the name of a Native American tribe from lands along the Kansas and Oklahoma border. Koch would go on to sponsor the all-women's America's Cup team, which was edged out by a razor-thin margin in the 1995 competition.

At the time of the 1992 campaign, he began acquiring marine paintings by the foremost European and American artists, among them Robert Salmon, Fitz Henry Lane, and James Edward Buttersworth, who capitalized on the popularity of trans-Atlantic yacht racing and the America's Cup competitions. Koch also developed a passion for collecting related maritime arts, such as scale models of every challenger and defender to sail in the America's Cup; ship figureheads; and nautical furniture, including a desk from the ship's surgeon aboard the USS *Constitution* and an eighteenth-century China trade daybed belonging to the Brown family of Providence, Rhode Island.

His early life in Kansas also inspired an appreciation for American Regionalist painting and imagery of the midwestern heartland. As a child, Koch was familiar with Thomas

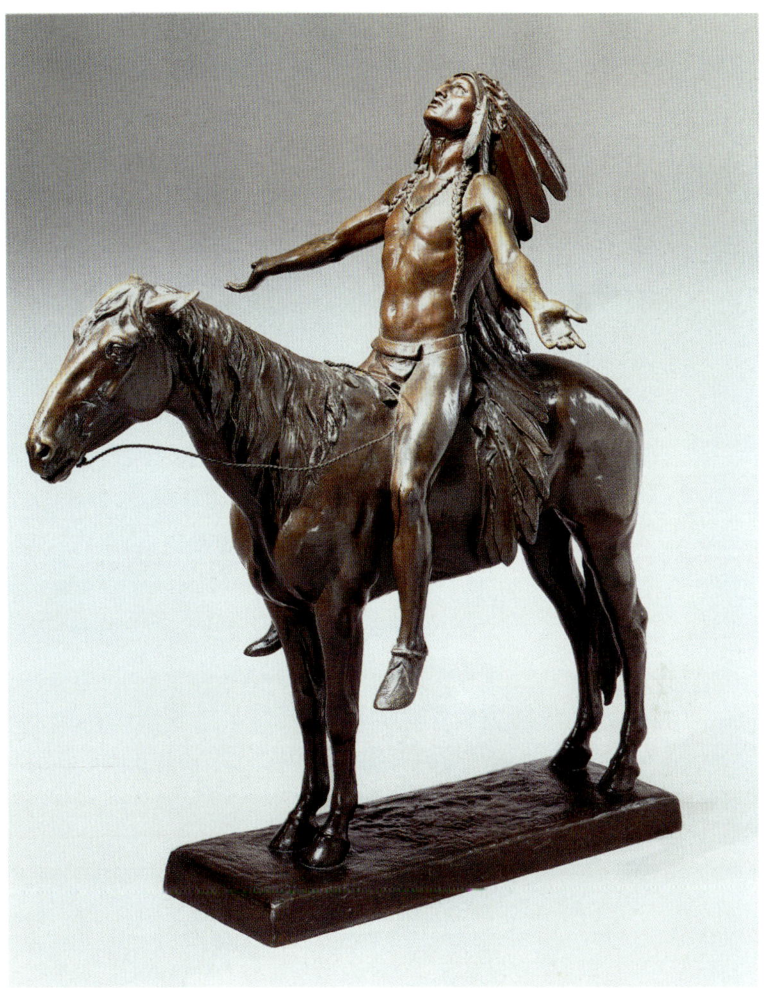

CYRUS EDWARD DALLIN, American, 1861–1944, *Appeal to the Great Spirit*, modeled 1912, cast 1918–28, bronze with dark red-brown patina, h. 39¾ in., w. 26¾ in., d. 38 in.

Hart Benton's well-known composition *The Music Lesson* from his parents' collection, and he later acquired two paintings by the artist. The earlier of the two, *Nebraska Evening* (p. 10), depicts a farmer visiting his horses in an expansive landscape, a scene that may recall Koch's youth on his father's ranches. Another painting in his collection, ensconced within the artist's beautifully carved frame, is one of the most memorable Regionalist images of the midwestern landscape: Grant Wood's *Arbor Day* (p. 12). The scene was painted during the depths of the Great Depression, yet it conveys optimism for the future in a carefully ordered world where children attend school within the comfort of fields resembling a patchwork quilt tucked over the swelling hillsides. (The painting is celebrated today in a detail reproduced on the back of the Iowa State Quarter, issued in 2004 as the twenty-ninth coin in the State Quarter Program.)

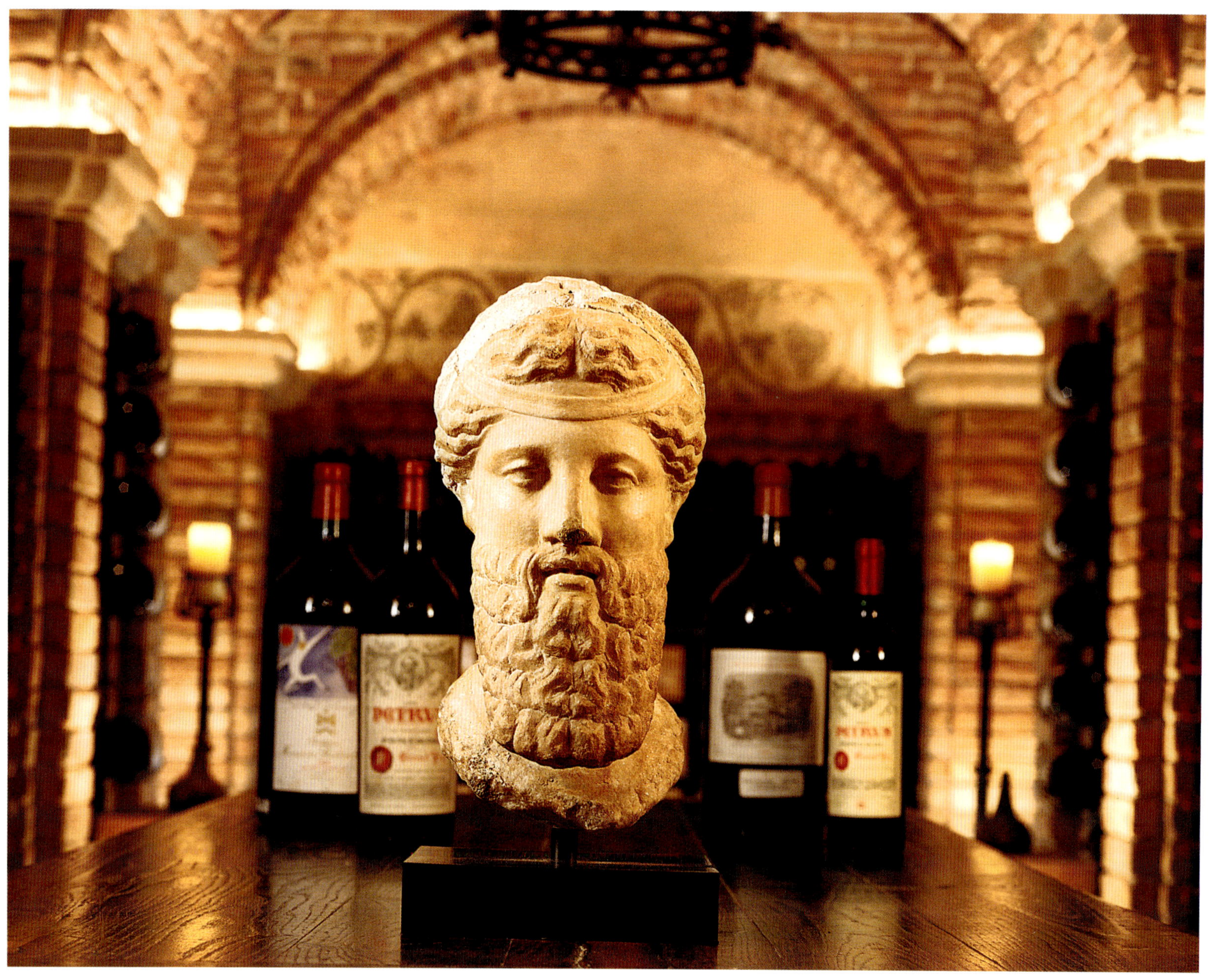

Roman
Head of the god Dionysos, about 2nd century A.D.
Marble with traces of polychrome; back of the head worked or reworked in stucco
H. 15¾ in., w. 7¾ in., d. 7½ in.

Opposite:
Greek
Attic red-figure kylix, about 470 B.C.
Ceramic
H. 8 15/16 in., diam. (without handles) 11⅞ in.

Roman
Portrait bust of a man, 20–50 A.D.
Bronze with green patina
H. 16½ in., w. 10¾ in., d. 10½ in.

Koch's experiences on the family ranches manifest themselves in his extensive collection of images and artifacts of the American West, including paintings, sculptures, guns, hats, branding irons, Native American pottery, clothing, rugs, toys, and other beadwork. Fascinated by the contradictions of western myths and the struggle between the white man and the Indian, Koch is drawn to the tension in Frederic Remington's nocturnes and the spirituality expressed by Native Americans in Charles Marion Russell's oils. Sculpture plays a major role throughout his collections, and some of the finest western bronzes by Remington, Russell, Cyrus Dallin, and others are displayed in his Western Room. One of the sculptures by Dallin, a mounted Lakota chief with arms outstretched entitled *Appeal to the Great Spirit* (p. 13), is familiar to Boston audiences as the signature piece in front of the MFA's Huntington Avenue entrance. The plaster for the over-life-size *Appeal* received a third-class (gold) medal at the Paris Salon of 1909, and the full-scale bronze was placed in the Fenway near the MFA by 1911. Dallin astutely retained the right to reproduce the sculpture, and by 1918 smaller-scale versions—including the rare half-life-size bronze in the Koch Collection—were as popular as replicas of Frédéric-Auguste Bartholdi's Statue of Liberty.[1]

The ancient artworks that Koch owns encompass a variety of media that date from early Greek through the Roman Imperial periods. Many of these works relate to themes that run through his entire collection, such as female sensuality (p. 82), the hero, and wine. A rare and inspired depiction of masculine strength versus feminine allure is found in a miniature Roman bronze (p. 19). The vignette shows Ares, powerful god of war, seated upon a rock while six playful erotes strip off his armor—a charming visualization of the warrior disarmed by his love for Aphrodite. One of the first ancient pieces Koch acquired was a Roman bronze portrait bust of a man of high position made in the fashion of Julio-Claudian emperors (right). The forthright treatment of the physiognomy and the forward gaze make a strong statement about the virtue of the Roman statesman. Koch's collection also includes a funerary relief depicting a young man on horseback (p. 19), which belongs to a group of such reliefs commemorating young heroes that were produced in Asia Minor and Aegean Greece during the time of the successors of Alexander the Great. Koch's example is inscribed with the name of the deceased—Diomedes.

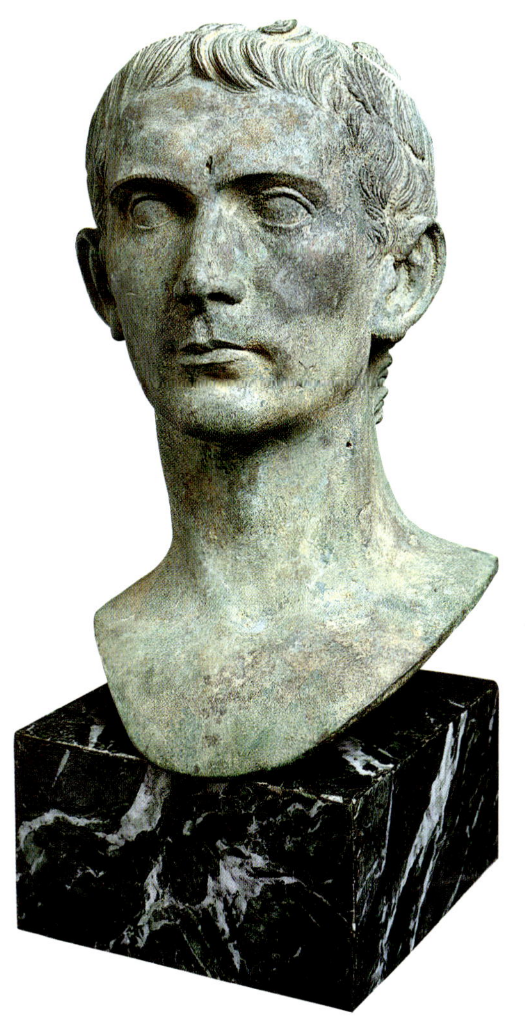

Heroes are again the subject of a fifth-century Greek drinking cup that is painted with scenes of warriors taking up arms and departing from family members (p. 15). Such vessels were used in all-male drinking parties called symposia, and their decorations expressed various aspects of male identity in Greek culture—the athlete and the warrior were most popular. No doubt ancient drinking vessels have a special resonance for Koch, who has one of the finest wine collections in the world. A monumental marble head of Dionysos is shown on page 14 presiding over Koch's famous cellar in Florida; the god of wine's identity is confirmed by the headband on his forehead. With more than thirty thousand bottles, most for consumption, Koch's collection is particularly strong in the great vintages of France. His cellar boasts 90 years of Château Petrus, 100 years of Château Latour, 120 years of Château Mouton, and 150 years of Château Lafitte. Indeed, his oldest bottle is a 1737 Château Lafitte. Koch is particularly proud of the bottles of Mouton and Lafitte thought to have been purchased by Thomas Jefferson when he was ambassador to France in the 1780s and engraved with the patriot's initials (fig. 2).

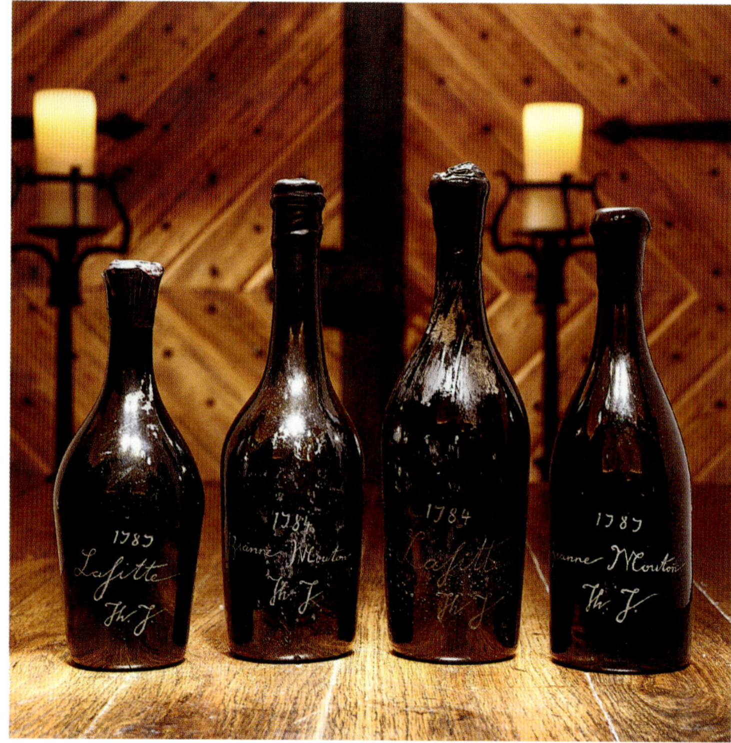

Fig. 2. Bottles of 1784 and 1787 Lafitte and Mouton reputedly purchased by Thomas Jefferson while he was ambassador to France from 1784 to 1789

Koch's collections of nineteenth- and twentieth-century European and American art are legendary. Great works by the Impressionists include early landscapes by Pierre-Auguste Renoir and Claude Monet, three masterworks from Monet's series paintings, as well as a superb Paul Cézanne still life and a ballet scene by Edgar Degas. A group of depictions of the female nude includes masterpieces by Pablo Picasso, Amedeo Modigliani, and Henri Matisse, among others. Koch's discerning eye also has led him to acquire major works by artists not so familiar to the general public, including a caricature of faces by the early-nineteenth-century French master Louis-Léopold Boilly, a tender, melancholy portrait of a child by the German Expressionist painter Gabriele Münter, and a haunting interior with a still life by the New York artist John Koch (p. 17)—the latter no relation to the collector.

Bill Koch's voracious appetite for life, his pioneer spirit, and his passion for excellence are everywhere reflected in his collection. The eclectic, the unpredictable, and the thrilling: these are, Bill Koch would say, the things I love.

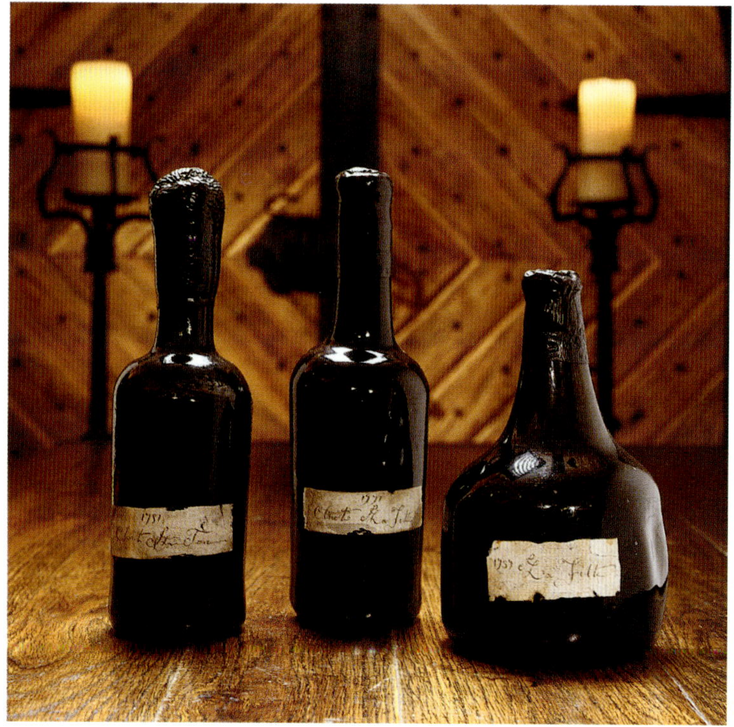

Fig. 3. Bottles of 1737, 1751, and 1777 Lafitte

1. Kathryn Greenthal, Paula Kozol, and Jan Seidler Ramirez, *American Figurative Sculpture in the Museum of Fine Arts, Boston* (Boston: Museum of Fine Arts, 1986), 276–78.

JOHN KOCH

American, 1909–1978
Still Life with Laurel, 1973
Oil on canvas
48 x 36 in.

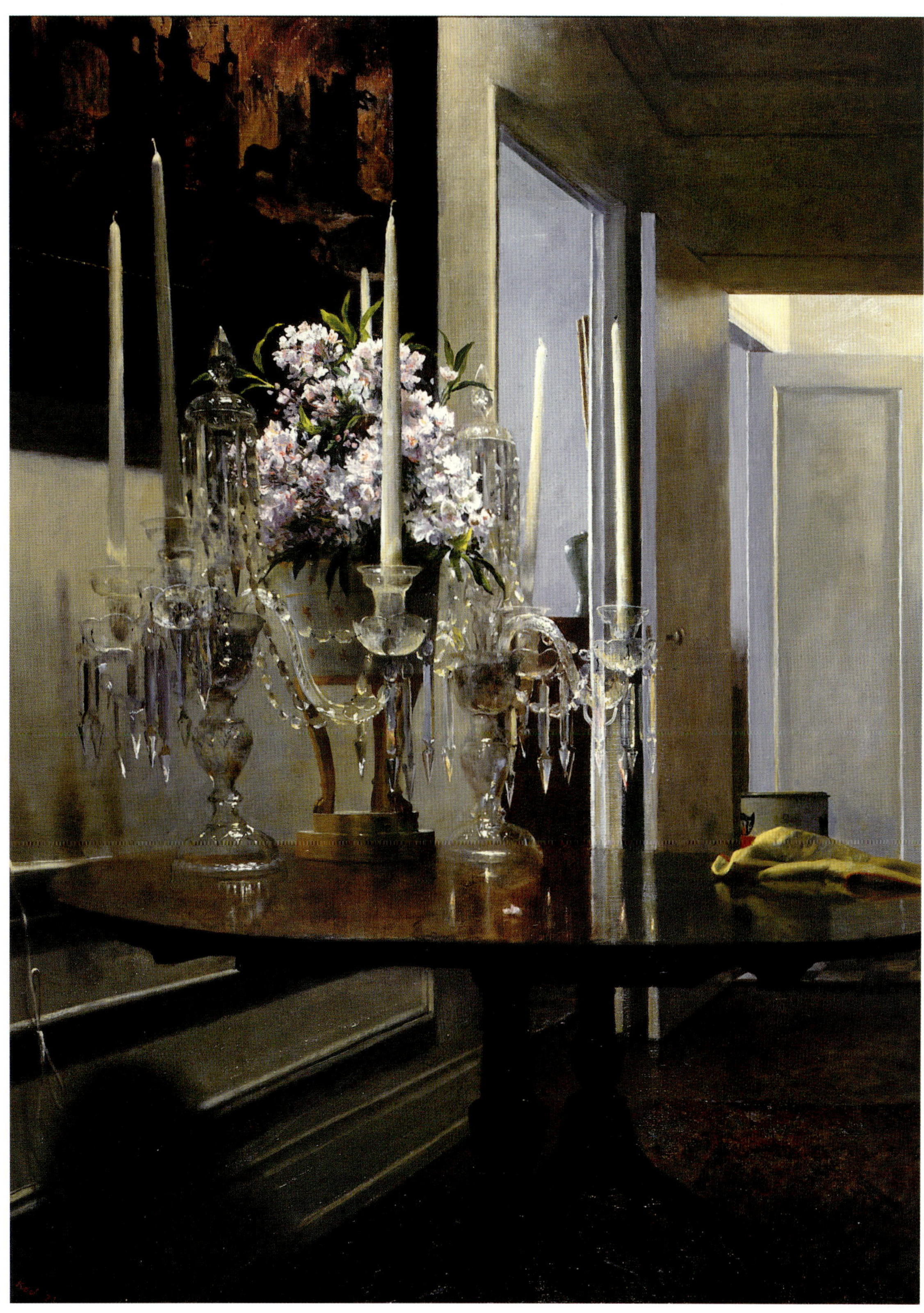

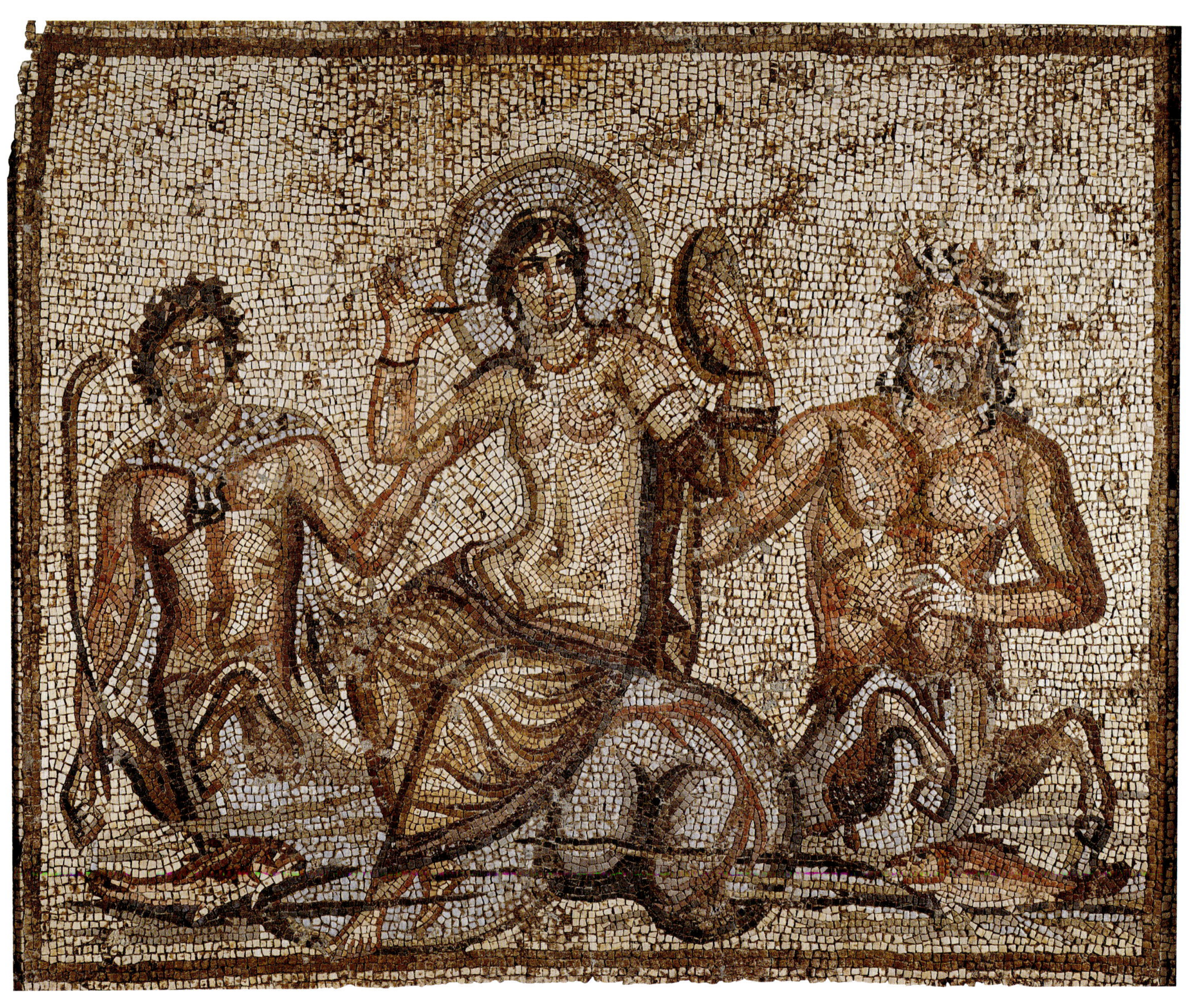

Roman
Triumph of Marine Venus,
about 3rd–4th century A.D.
Stone tesserae
H. 61¼ in., w. 75 in., d. 4½ in.

Greek
Hero relief of Diomedes, 2nd century B.C.
Marble
H. 13¼ in.

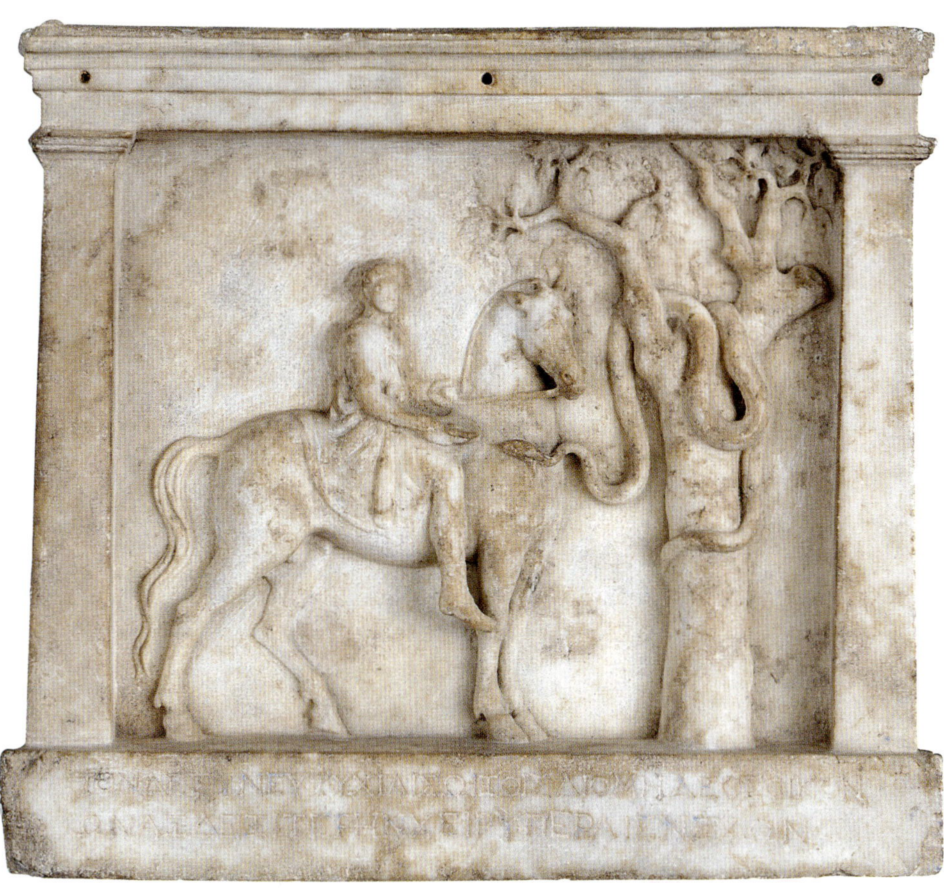

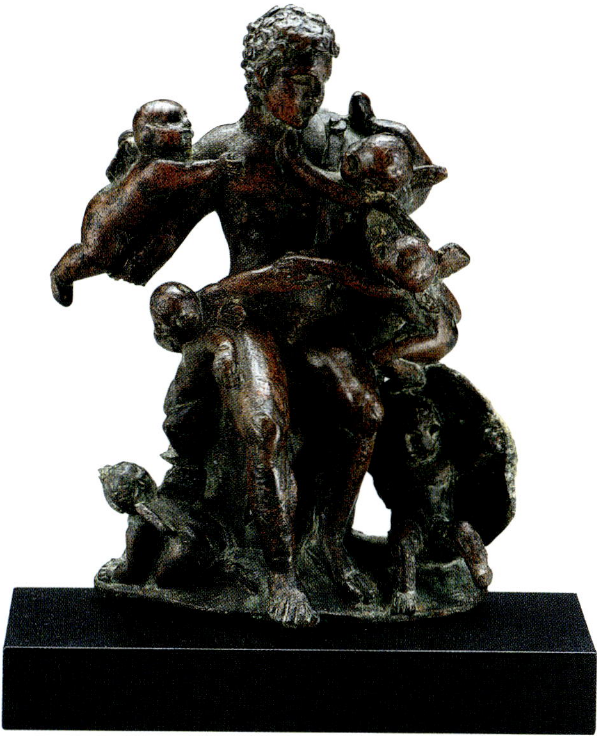

Roman
Ares overcome by love for Aphrodite,
about 2nd century A.D.
Bronze
H. 3⅞ in., w. 4¾ in., d. 2¼ in.

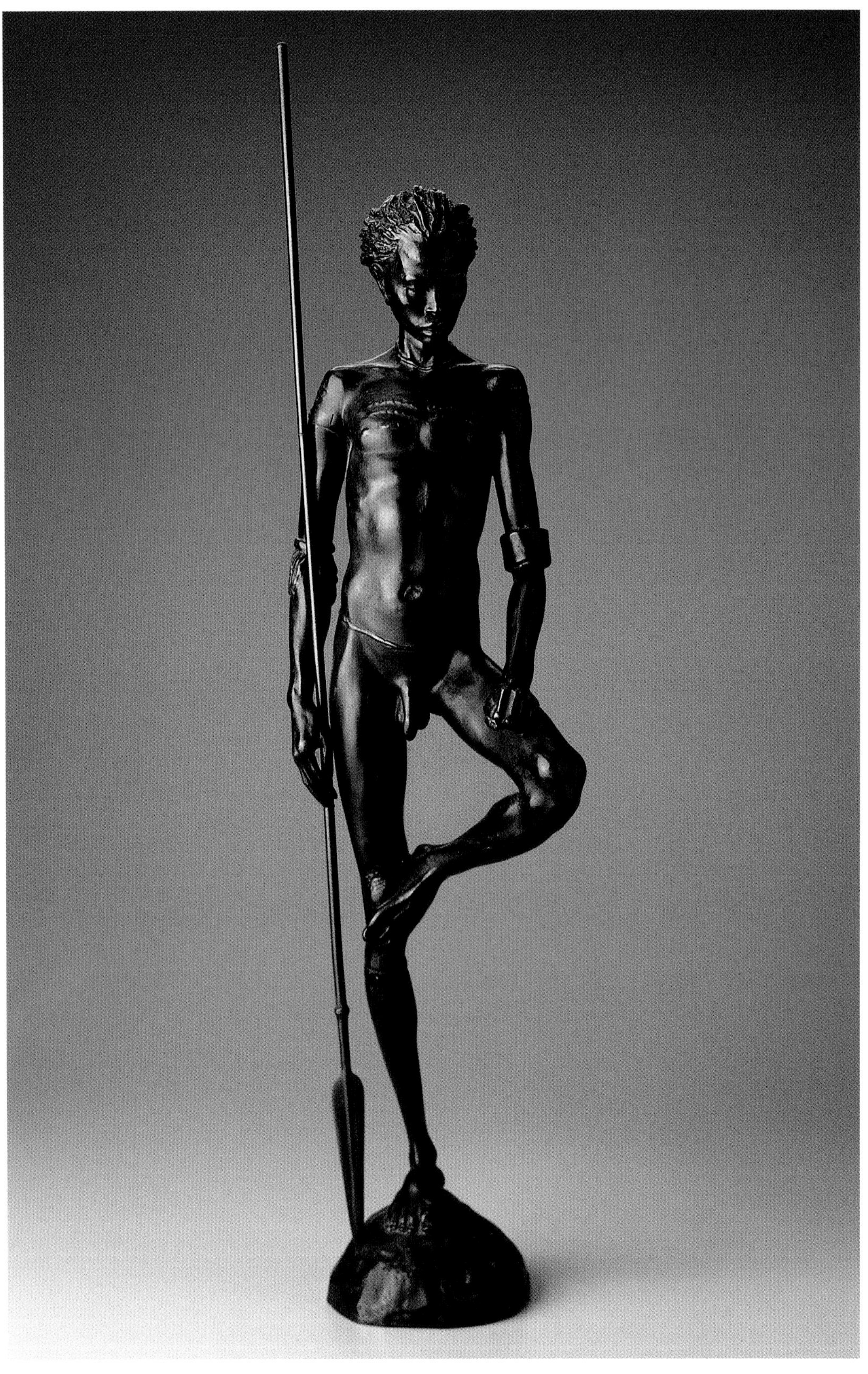

MALVINA HOFFMAN

American, 1885–1966
Shilluk Warrior (Nuer Tribe), Upper White Nile, East Africa, 1932, cast in 1934
Bronze with dark brown patina
H. 29½ in., w. 8 in., d. 5¾ in.

MALVINA HOFFMAN

American, 1885–1966
"Daboa," Dancing Girl of Sara Tribe, Lake Chad, 1930, cast in 1936 or 1937
Bronze with dark brown patina
H. 23¾ in., w. 6¼ in., d. 11¼ in.

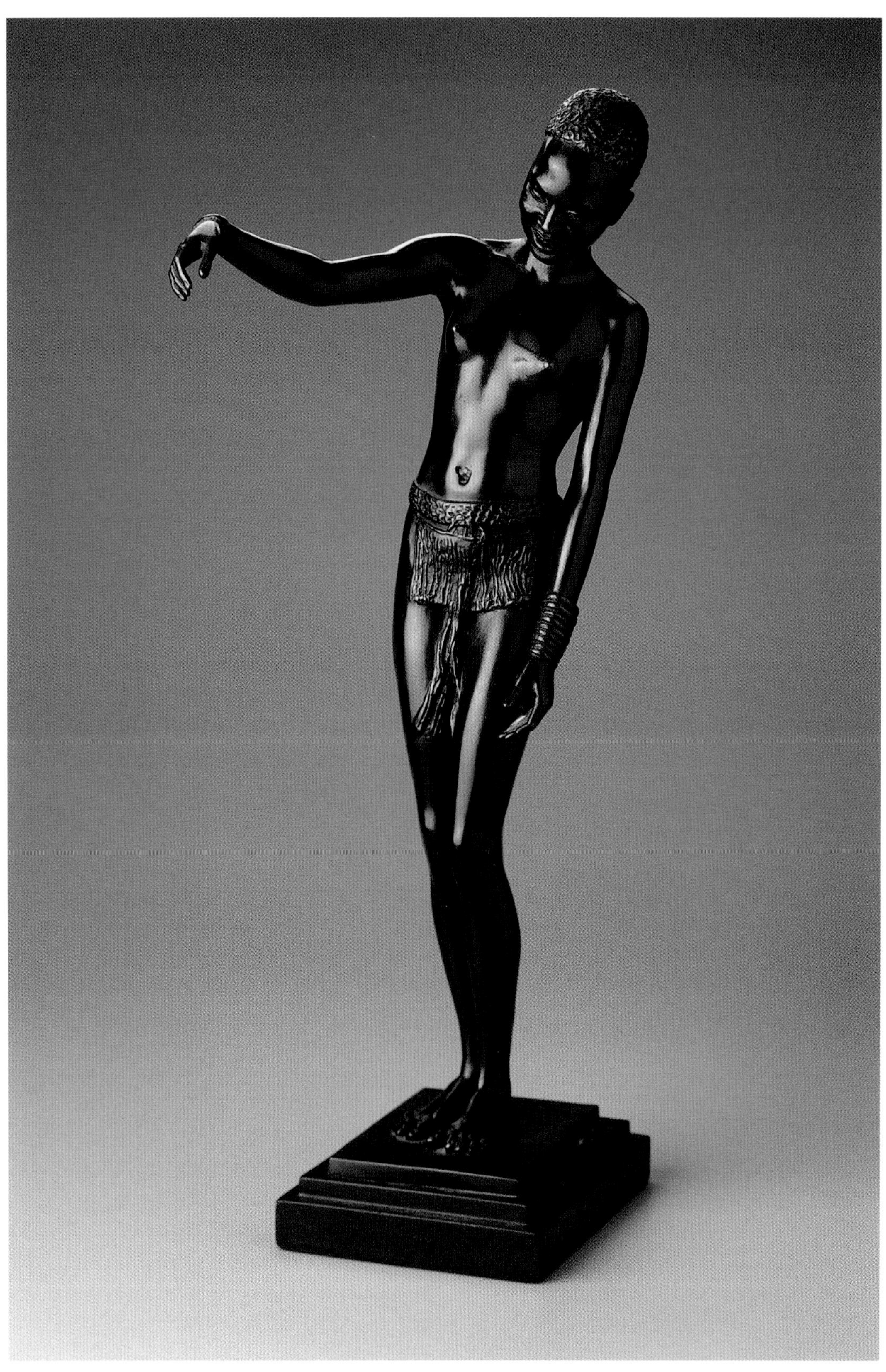

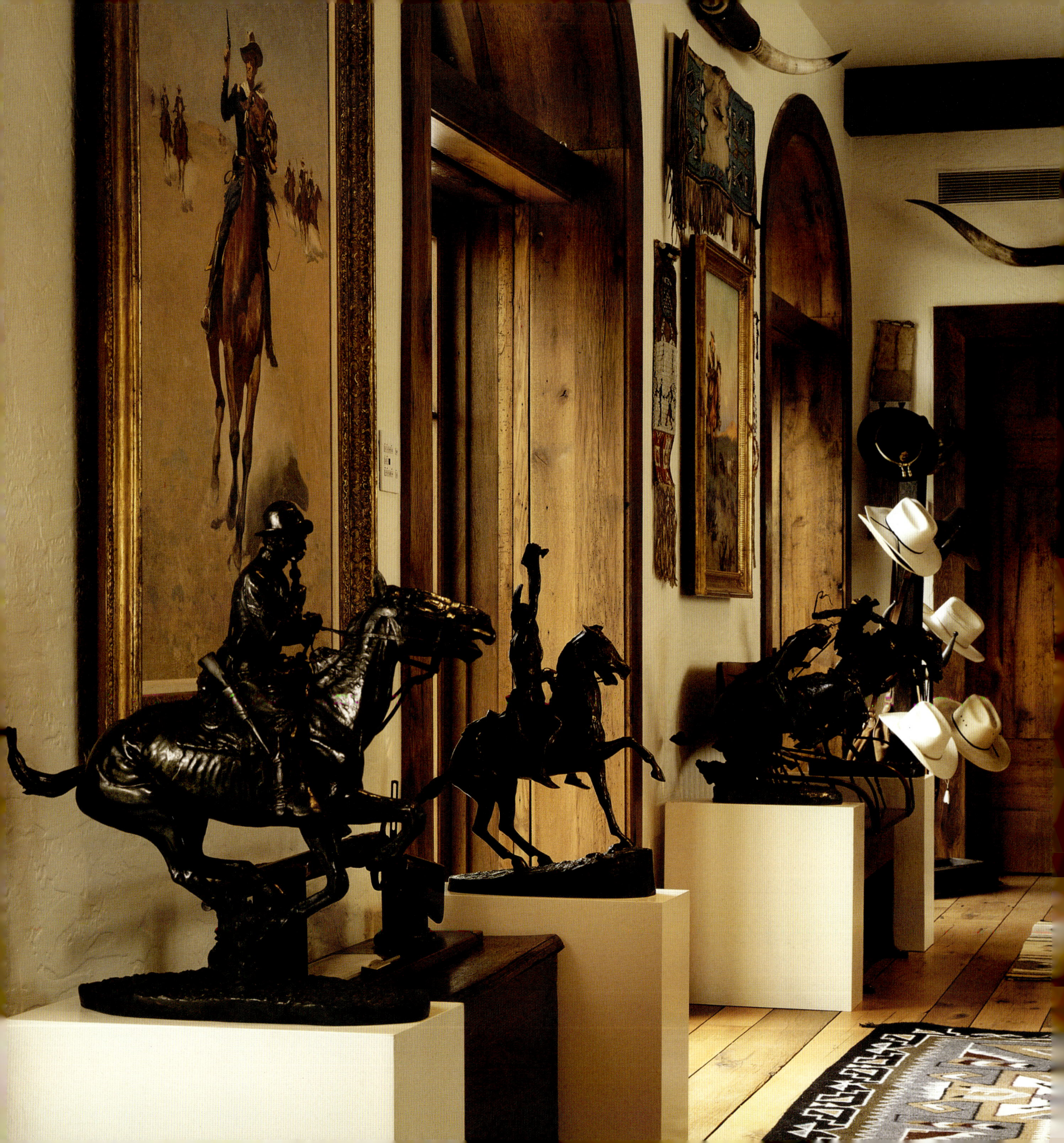

THINGS I LOVE

* * * * * * *

The following interview took place at William Koch's homes in Osterville, Massachusetts, and Palm Beach, Florida, in August and November 2004.

You and your personality are clearly at the heart of this entire collection, and I wondered if you could tell us about your early experiences. Did you begin collecting anything as a child—bottle caps, baseball cards? When did you discover that you're a natural collector?

Unfortunately, my attention span as a child was short, so I didn't form any real collections. I would collect one thing, then go on to something else, and then lose what I'd collected. At one point I collected toys and toy guns, but my mom threw them away when I got older.

When I was a student at MIT, I didn't have much time to collect. But I did start acquiring a few things, because I had my own space. On a trip to Africa with my parents in my early twenties, I bought some African sculpture—carvings that they sell to tourists. When I went back again later I bought more, and I still have some of them in my saloon.

Were your parents encouraging you as a collector at that stage in your life?

No, they'd throw everything out because I was such a pack rat. But I guess I gradually developed a collector's mentality as I got a little older. For a while I collected samurai swords and Greek coins, and I started collections of yacht burgees, models, sailing hats, cowboy hats, and branding irons. Then I got interested in art, and I decided this was something I really wanted to collect. My first serious girlfriend in college, Jackie Winsor (see p. 97), was an artist studying at Massachusetts College of Art, and she explained art to me. My mother was also an artist.

One of the boats you sponsored for the women's team in the America's Cup was christened Mighty Mary *in honor of your mother. Did the art she made at home have an impact on you?*

The art she created and the modest collection she encouraged my father to put together had a huge impact on me. My father owned a couple of Renoirs, a famous Thomas Hart Benton, and some other paintings. My mother made drawings of African natives and animals. Later, she became a silversmith and crafted lots of belt buckles, tie clasps, rings, bracelets, ashtrays, et cetera. She was an artisan, even though she started off as an artist.

Were her African drawings made during the trip you took there together?

No, she made them when my father took her on their honeymoon to Africa in the 1930s, before all the game was decimated. I grew up looking at them, along with my father's Renoirs and a few paintings by the Spanish artist Ribera. My father also had a small collection of swords that he picked up around the Middle East and Europe, and a collection of guns. The seeds of some of my own collections were actually planted by my parents.

I understand you have at least one brother who's also a major collector.

Fred collects castles and art that fits in his castles. I think it's great for him—it's beautiful. For example, he bought one of Archduke Ferdinand's hunting castles in Austria, and he's gone to the meticulous trouble of going to auctions and finding pieces that were originally in the castle, carefully putting it back together.

Can you elaborate on how you first became interested in the fine arts?

Well, first, I'm a very visual person. As an engineer, I can gain more information from looking at a graph than I can

Fig. 4. Bronze sculptures by Frederic Remington in Koch's Western Room, Palm Beach

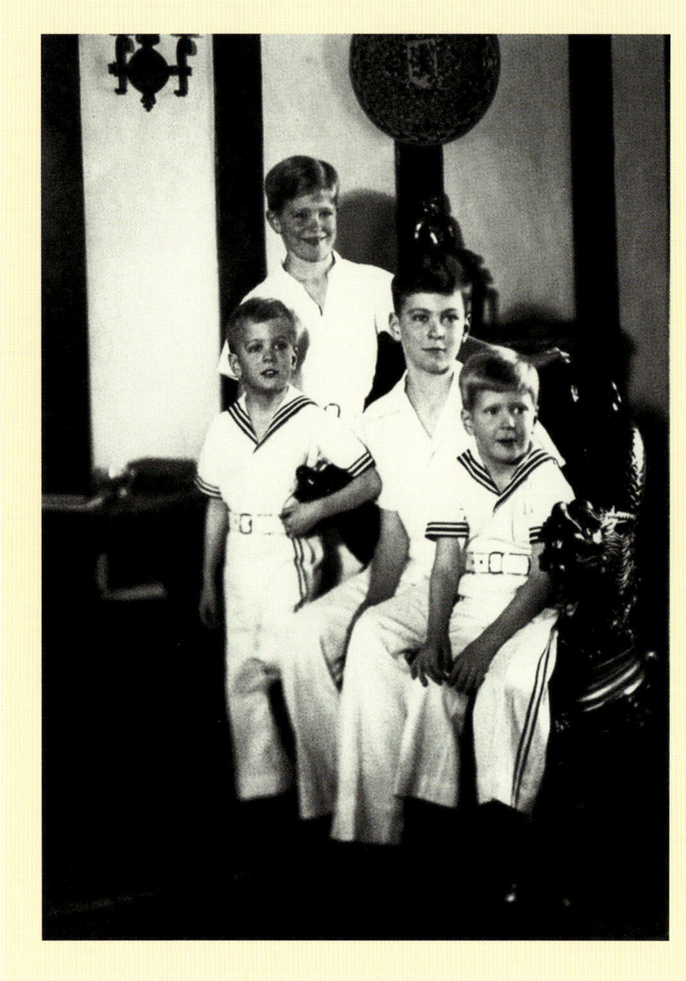

Fig. 5. Bill Koch and his three brothers (from left to right: David, Charles, Frederick, and Bill) at their father's house in Wichita, Kansas, in 1944

from reading a whole textbook. I'd always had an interest in art, and then my girlfriend started taking me on trips to museums. I saw some paintings that I just loved, and I said, someday I'd like to own some. I remember the one I was most attracted to, Monet's triptych of *Water Lilies* at the Museum of Modern Art, in New York. That was the most peaceful thing I'd ever seen.

I looked at other artworks and found some very hideous ones and some that were very peaceful to me. And I decided I'd like to have things around me that remind me of happy feelings—of happy moments in my youth—and make me feel comfortable, peaceful, pleasant. When I got enough money to start buying paintings, I bought the ones I really liked.

How do you respond to some of the pictures you own?

One of the first major paintings I bought was Monet's *Field of Oats and Poppies* (p. 60). I like it because it reminds me of a particular field on my father's ranch in Kansas where he used to take us picnicking as kids. It's the tree line and the height of the grass in springtime, and the wildflowers that grow in the grass. I just get a wonderful feeling looking at it. I'm less concerned with the esoterics of why Monet painted a certain painting at a certain point in time. That sometimes adds to the story, but I'm more interested in how people can look at many different works of art—from modern art to antiquities, and from cowboys and Indians to Impressionists—and get their own sense of beauty from them, and have their own emotional reactions. That, to me, is what's most important: the artist's ability to transmit an emotional experience to people.

Some collectors start with a Monet of a certain period and then need something earlier and then something later. Does that kind of thinking appeal to you?

I don't care about that at all. I currently have four Monets, but it's the impact of a picture on me that counts. It's the genius of an artist to transmit emotion to me, to transmit emotion in such a way that I can interpret it my own way. What I really love about paintings is, first of all, the work that the artist does, and, second, the emotion that it stimulates in me. Those are the two things about it that matter most.

Is the Monet the first really important picture that you bought?

Yes, I bought the *Field of Oats and Poppies* in the early 1980s. But my first major purchase of art was actually a sculpture by Auguste Rodin, the *Three Shades*. I kept that for several years but got tired of it because it wasn't a pleasant thought to me—three guys standing over the gates of hell, saying, "abandon hope, all ye who enter here." They were distorted, melancholy, and in agony. Now, I have a cast of Rodin's *Thinker*, which is also on his *Gates of Hell*, and he's contemplating his life and his sins before he goes into hell. I look at the cast now and I think I can understand how that guy feels. Before I go through a deposition or a lawsuit, or before I enter a big race, I'm thinking about everything pretty intensely. I can understand and sympathize with what he's going through.

How do you find works of art you want to acquire? Do you come across them at auctions, or does somebody propose a piece to you? Is there a particular person with whom you've worked most?

Well, it's a long story. I started off working with John Walsh, a former curator of paintings at the MFA, more than twenty years ago. I used to ask John's opinion, and he was the one I went to when I could first afford to buy paintings. I was a student at his throne; it was wonderful. John has exellent taste and can articulate what's good in a painting. By the time he left the MFA, he'd taught me the difference between good quality and poor quality. I said, I'll just do it myself.

In fact, by then I'd gotten enough confidence in my own taste that I didn't want anybody else's judgment or taste, I wanted my own. Now the only time I ask someone's opinion is when I am concerned about the physical condition of the work of art. Other people's opinions are nice, particularly if they're reinforcing, but the most important thing is what the work says to me.

There are three ways I find art for my collection: I go around and visit numerous dealers and see what they have; I look through auction catalogues, which is the easiest way because they give the most diversity; finally when dealers find out about my collection, they make me unsolicited offers of paintings. But to find what you really want, what really fits, the best way is to go out and do a lot of looking. I've probably bought about 60 percent of my collection from auctions and 40 percent from dealers.

What period of artwork did you start collecting with John Walsh?

It was nineteenth-century European. In addition to my father's collection and what I saw at the Museum of Modern Art, when I was traveling around Europe one summer in college, I went to the Louvre and saw several Monets, and I fell in love with the emotional sense that I got from each one. When I came back I decided that Impressionism was where I really wanted to start, and that's where John helped me a lot. He got me beyond Impressionism to a wide variety of painting styles.

Do you still discover artists that surprise you and interest you?

Yes, I do. I wish I had more time to go to all the galleries and look at modern works of art. It's very demanding and takes a lot of time. I just haven't had the time to study contemporary art, and the allocated space for my collection is already full. I've got four little kids and a big business to run, so I decided maybe I'd better settle for acquiring one or two paintings a year, rather than buying twenty or thirty a year as I did in the past.

Some of the Impressionists have gotten a little bit commonplace to me, but I still love the ones I have. And there are others out there that I would absolutely adore to have. Unfortunately, they're way out of anybody's price range now. I'd love to own a Gauguin and a Van Gogh, and I've been offered some, but the price/quality ratio is out of balance now.

But you have bought some Impressionist works in the last few years. The two later Monets are relatively recent purchases, aren't they?

Yes, I bought them in 2000. I purchased the Monet *Water Lilies* because, as I said, it reminds me of peace and contentment. I bought *Morning on the Seine* (p. 47), because that's also extremely peaceful. There's another work in that series that I missed buying early on—and actually like better—which was painted later in the morning and in which the light is more vibrant. But the one I have is still a wonderful painting that gives you a feeling of what early morning on the river is like.

That kind of calm pervades much of your collection. Even many of the western paintings, which are generally much more violent, are situated in a contemplative landscape.

Well, they look that way, but what's fascinating about them is that even if on the surface they look extremely calm and peaceful, there's something else happening. Take the nocturnal paintings, like the Remington canoe painting, *Evening on a Canadian Lake* (p. 106). It's peaceful, but if you look at the faces of the two canoeists and if you look at the dog, you note that his fur is up and his ears are up. They're all sensing danger. And you wonder what's going to happen next. It's that contradiction, which we all experience in life. If you look at the hunter and the canoe in *Coming to the Call* (p. 107), what's going to happen next—the killing of the moose—is very obvious. But that particular moment is extremely peaceful, even if the next instant there's going to be a lot of blood and gore.

Some of the paintings of women in my collection convey a similar tension. The Picasso nude (p. 67), for example, is in an awkward position, and you don't know whether she's angry or happy. She's unsettled and, particularly, unexplained.

I have a lot of fun with a parlor game, especially with the Modigliani (p. 76). When a group of people who've never been to my house wants a tour, as I take them around and show them the Picasso and the Renoir, I ask them, "Can you guess who the artist is?" Very few guess who painted the Picasso, and only the art experts guess who painted the Renoir. But when I take them to the Modigliani, I tell them, "The myth about Modigliani is that before he would paint a nude, he would make love to her. The real question is: Is this woman happy, is she bored, is she unsatisfied, is she satisfied, what is she? Look at her face: it's flushed." It's amazing. One visitor will raise her hand, an older woman, for instance, and say, "She's totally bored. She wants to get out of there." And at the end of it, I say to them, "Art isn't what the painter wanted you to see but what you see in it, and so you're telling me about yourselves." They get all embarrassed.

You talked about how the paintings present calm and are almost escapist. Do you see that as an antithesis to your own life?

My life is rarely calm. It's quite hectic and full of contradictions—as most people's lives are. Some of the paintings are escapist and some reflect that contradiction. The Remington paintings are very good at showing the contradiction. My Cézanne is, too. There's idealized fruit there but it's very flat, very abstract, and the fruit's going to be hard to get. It's inviting, and yet it pushes you away.

Even in the Altoon Sultan (p. 95), for instance, you see this beautiful barnyard scene but you think, that's a lot of work to keep up. I grew up on a farm and I know there are two things that are missing in that picture: cow dung and flies. Sultan has presented the farm as idyllic scenery. And yet it's a working barnyard, a twentieth-century farm with a big, blue, ugly silo and mud around the big, ugly, plastic feeder. It's the combination of the two facets that draws me to it.

Some of the American collectors of the late nineteenth century felt at home with early Renaissance works of art, because they felt like modern-day princes. There's a strong flavor of the West and the American landscape in many of your pictures. Do you feel a real sense of your upbringing in Kansas when you look at them?

Could you tell us more about your attraction to the western collection?

My father was a rancher and he had about five or six ranches when I was growing up. One was in Kansas, and he'd take my brothers and me there every weekend. One of my paintings—we call it the "Marlboro Man"; the guy smoking a cigarette, by Phillip Russell Goodwin (p. 112)—he bought to hang in his Kansas ranch house. Fortunately, I ended up with that painting. During the summers, my father would make all his sons work on a ranch to learn the value of hard work. We did every menial task you could imagine: fixing fences, shoveling out stalls, digging irrigation ditches, spreading manure, baling hay.

One summer I was lucky enough to be a cowboy on my father's ranch in Montana. I was sixteen or seventeen, and the work was hard. We'd start at 5:00 a.m. and quit at 6:00 p.m.; we were paid five dollars a day plus room and board; we slept in bunkhouses with no running water and had to use the privy outside; and we took a bath maybe once a month. When I think back on it, it was one of the best years of my youth. We were out in Mother Nature, in this very rugged wilderness area, and we were living a life that we saw in the movies—parts of it, anyway.

You must be quite a horseman.

I spent a lot of time on a horse. A friend of my father's was a big gambler and won a herd of Shetland ponies in a poker match; he didn't have a place to put them, so he made a deal with my twin brother and me that if we would take care of them on my father's place in Kansas, then we'd split the offspring and profits. David and I took care of the Shetland ponies for a year until my father had to feed them in a snowstorm that happened while we were at school. I went to Culver Military Academy, where I was in the cavalry and rode every day. I even rode in Eisenhower's first inaugural parade and caught pneumonia as a result. Later, I broke horses for Culver, got thrown and knocked out for a couple of days.

I have a very healthy respect for horses. I don't want to take care of them, I don't want to feed them, and I only ride them out West. That's where they're romantic. I have no interest in going over to Wellington, Florida, and riding around a horse park, paying to take care of them, or worrying about them. I only want to be on one out in the West looking at longhorns.

And, therefore, closer to the Remington and Russell experience. I've noticed that you have many beautiful Remingtons from the period when he was focusing on nocturnes. Were you particularly drawn to the nocturnes because of your western experience?

It was a combination of that and opportunity. The Remingtons came my way. Since I had done a lot of canoeing and kayaking in Maine, New Hampshire, Idaho, and Colorado, the canoe pictures appealed to me. The gunfighter picture, *An Argument with the Town Marshal* (p. 109), just appealed to me because it's a romantic version of the West. But *The Trooper* (p. 118) is a full-blown cavalry charge in broad daylight.

I love Remington's nocturnes. He's one of the few painters who could capture what it was like in the West at night. Night has its own beauty separate from the daytime, or from early morning or late afternoon. Similarly, that's the thing I like about Russell—the way he was able to capture light early in the morning or late in the afternoon. There are wonderful colors in the West.

Do you feel a particular affinity with Native Americans on account of having grown up out West? I was fascinated to read in one of the books produced about the America's Cup that you brought a crow feather on your boat America[3] *and you occasionally made some offerings of tobacco over the side, as well as arranged for a blessing of the boat by one of the tribes from Kansas.*

They were here first. I have an affinity for underdogs because I've felt like an underdog. The Indians had a very noble sense of life—their own code of honor, their own code of ethics, their own code of treating one another. If you define civilization as good treatment of one another, then they were a lot more civilized than the Euro-Americans. The white man found their culture primitive and subhuman and tried to wipe it out. They took all the land, simply because they wanted to.

One thing I really like about Russell is that he saw nobility in the Indians and their way of life. Remington just viewed them as savages; he was a bigot. His *Cheyenne* (p. 115) and *The Scalp* (p. 115) are all very primitive and fierce. Russell painted his subjects as much more refined, elegant, and religious—one with nature, respecting nature. And to me, as a kid, that was very appealing. Unfortunately, their culture could not compete with the Euro-American culture, which almost eradicated them.

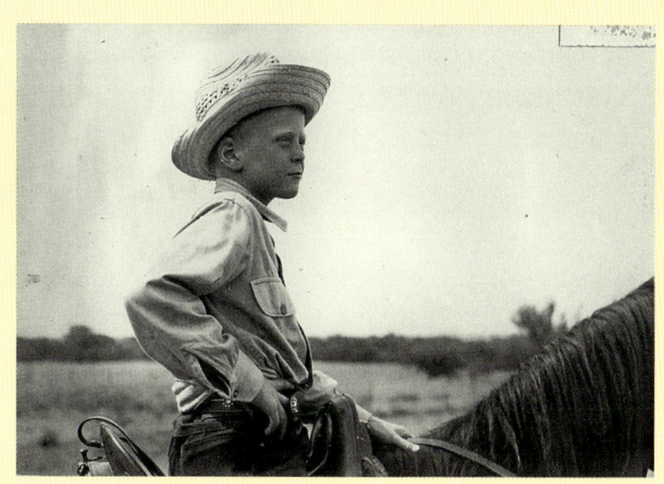

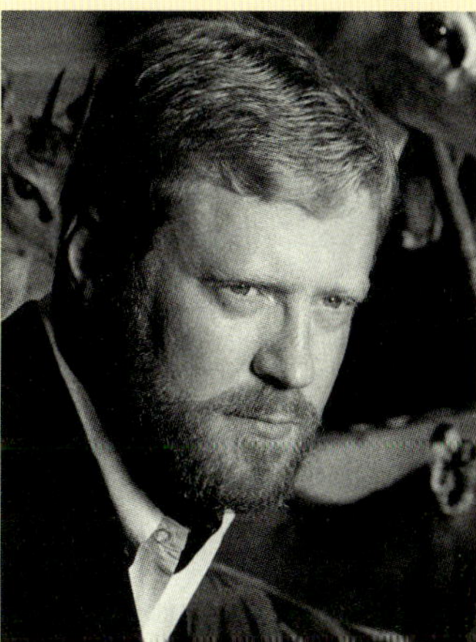

Fig. 6. Bill Koch at age eight on his father's ranch in Kansas, in 1948

Fig. 7. At age twenty-nine, while a graduate student at MIT, in 1969

Fig. 8. With his son, Wyatt, in San Diego during the 1992 America's Cup

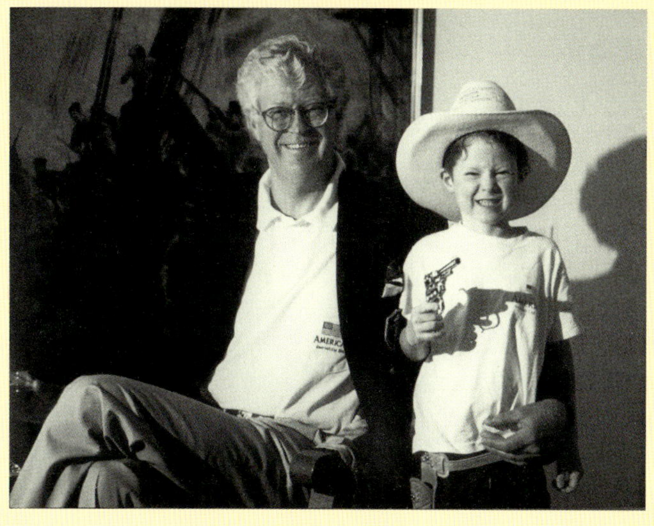

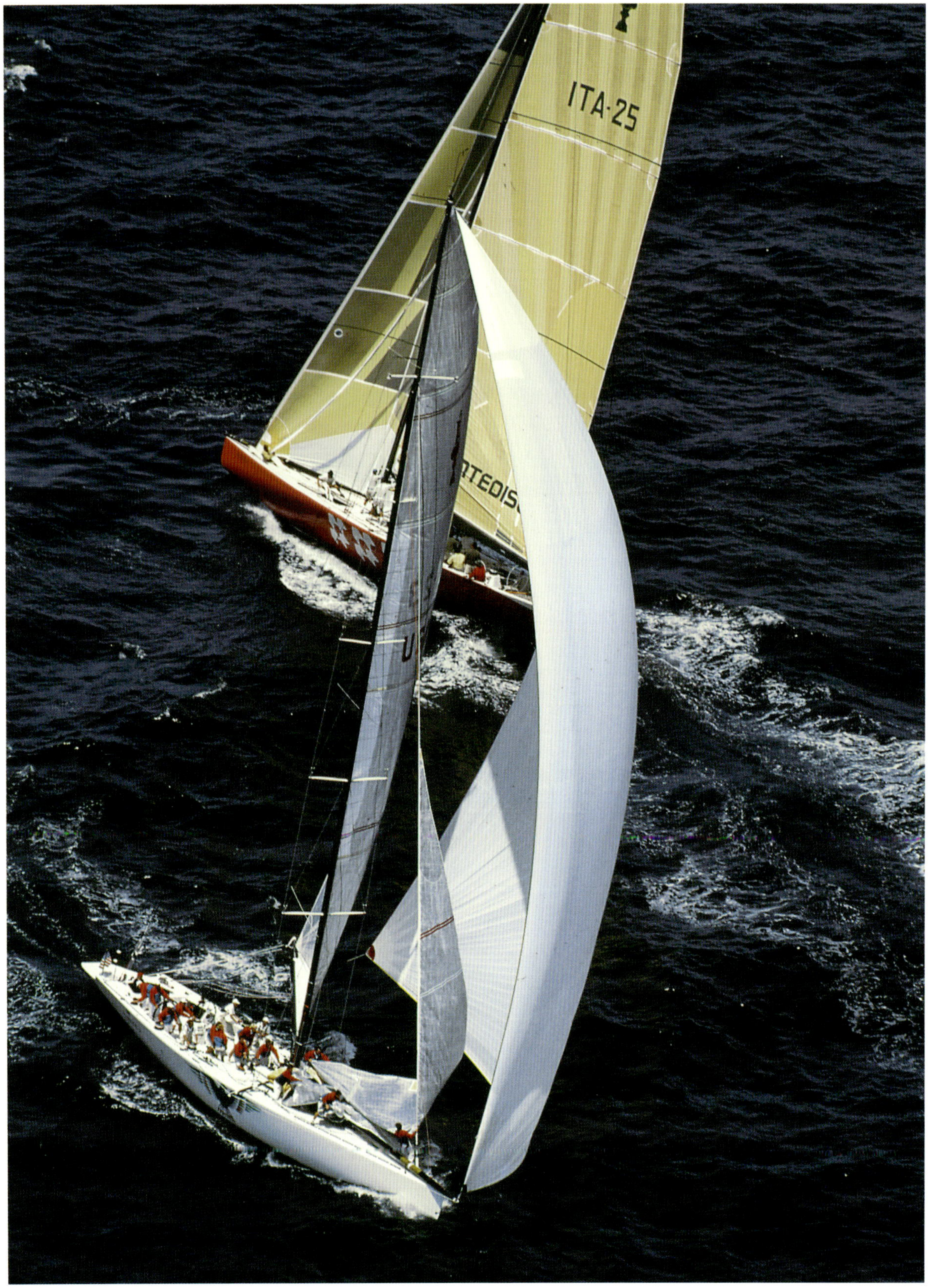

Fig. 9. *America*^{3} and *Il Moro* competing in the 1992 America's Cup. *America*^{3} has just rounded the windward mark

Did you feel that sense of struggle as an underdog in the America's Cup competition of 1992?

We were laughed and jeered at in the America's Cup campaign all the way up to the time we won. In fact, there were forty-five thousand articles written about us, and forty thousand were negative and five thousand were positive—and those five thousand occurred after we won. People were saying, "What nerve for a bunch of amateurs to compete in our august sport!"

How did the campaign for the America's Cup interact with your activities as an art collector? Did you stop during that time, or did you forge ahead?

I didn't have much time to look at paintings because I was so busy with the Cup. I did buy, immediately after the Cup, a Winslow Homer of three boys in a dory. I also took my art collection out to San Diego and displayed it in the house I rented.

The house was right on the bay, overlooking the yacht club. There wasn't room inside for all my sculptures, but there was a front lawn that went up to the water. Technically, this strip of lawn belonged to the port and was public property; I wanted to put a couple of statues out there. I had to get permission from the port authority, and because they were works of art, they gave approval.

Many people objected to Fernando Botero's sculptures on the front lawn where people walked. A couple of newscasts featured stories about them. One newscaster was interviewing people who were complaining about them when my son, who was five at the time, walked by. The newscaster asked him, "What do you think of these sculptures, young man?" And he said, "I think they're sumptuous." Fortunately, I believe I still have that on tape.

At the time, the neighbors called the Botero of a reclining woman "Roseanne," after Roseanne Barr (p. 64). I had her facing the yacht club, and one time when we were competing against Dennis Connor to see who was going to be the defender in the America's Cup, the San Diego crowd had a rally for Connor at 5:30 a.m. on my front lawn under my bedroom window. They put a brassiere on Roseanne and put flags on the sculpture reading, "Go Dennis." Yet I was there competing to help the San Diego Yacht Club. The next day, I threatened to turn her around so she'd moon the yacht club. I regret that I never did it. My priority, however, was not to snub my nose at the San Diego Yacht Club, but to win the Cup. It would have been fun to turn her around, but it would have taken a crane to pick her up over the house, and flip her around.

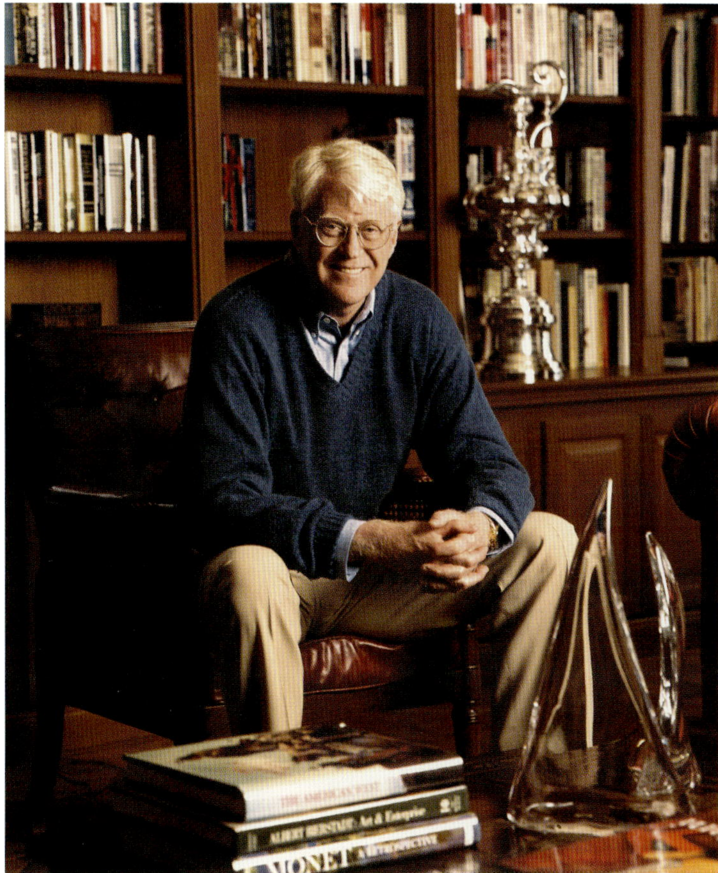

Fig. 10. Bill Koch in the library of his home in Palm Beach, in 2002. Behind him is an exact replica of the America's Cup made in silver by Garrard's of London, the makers of the original Cup

What I like about that sculpture is that if you look at her closely from the front, you can see a Buddha, which represents wisdom; you can look at her again and see the sphinx, which represents mystery; look again and you can see humor; and then you look again and you see independence; you look at her again, you see sensuality. Botero captured what I think of as the best in women: wisdom, mystery, sex appeal, humor, and independence.

The MFA owns a standing Venus by Botero. Our galleries of pre-Columbian art are nearby, and you can see how Botero fits quite neatly into a South American perspective. Although many muse-

um curators don't think highly of Botero, many collectors are really passionate about him. Maybe it's because collectors often are much more individualistic and daring with art than institutions can be.

Some of his works are very difficult. When he depicts a man in a business suit standing on a naked woman, that's a pretty tough subject. Other works of his are incredibly humorous.

I think perhaps people find him almost too enjoyable. And they're a bit leery of the distortion of the female figure, perhaps of the continual distortion—the "fattening up" of everything. But you and Botero have become friends, haven't you?

Yes. I asked him to paint a portrait of my eldest son, and he made a painting (p. 73).

You have a dozen or more pieces of his sculpture, representing a serious commitment to an individual artist. Where did you see the first piece?

I was walking down West 57th Street in New York and I saw the *Man and Woman* in front of Marlborough Galleries. I went in and tried to buy them. Unfortunately, they were already sold. I looked in auction catalogues and found a few other pieces, which I bought. I ended up buying only a couple of things directly from Botero.

I bought the man, the woman, the girl, the dog, and the cat from auction catalogues, and I put them all together as a family. When Botero came to visit me, he loved it, but he said he didn't plan them that way. He made them individually. If you look through my art, you see that some of it represents family. I have a version of an idyllic family.

When did your collection of maritime art really begin? Was it part of the America's Cup activity, or did it precede that?

It preceded it. I started that collection in 1983 because I always wanted to be a sailor. My father ran away to sea when he was eighteen years old and worked his way around the world on a tramp steamer. And my mother would tell me stories about my ancestor Captain Lawrence, the naval hero and captain of the *Hornet*, who sank the *Peacock* (see p. 161). I'd go out to my father's ranch in the prairies of Flint Hills, Kansas, and look at the rolling hills of tall grass blowing in the wind. The grass had a brown top, a blue stem, and a green base; you could see the colors change as puffs of wind blew. I would pretend that was the sea.

I went to summer school at Culver Military Academy in Indiana. I opted to enter the sailing school instead of the cavalry, because I was going to be in the cavalry in the wintertime. I fell in love with sailing. When I went to MIT, I sailed only once every other year or so. Later, when I got enough money, I bought the biggest sailboat I could find. I discovered that people wouldn't sail with me because I pushed too hard. Someone suggested I try racing because you push hard all the time.

I started buying nautical paintings along the way. I saw some paintings with my ancestor Captain Lawrence in them, and I decided to collect them because I have a connection with them.

It's unusual for anyone competing in a sport in their mid-forties to make it to the top of an international class in the matter of a few years.

I started racing in 1985 and won the America's Cup in 1992. That's why I was so controversial during the Cup, because I was competing against professionals who had sailed all their lives, who had fought their entire lives to get into the Cup, much less to win it. They thought it was presumptuous that this hick from Kansas could come in and compete in their sport and win it on his first try. It created a lot of controversy. I was called a nutty chemist, a buffoon, and so on. But that's only natural.

The other competitors went by old traditions, and fortunately I knew nothing of them. I studied the history of the America's Cup and found that only fast boats and crews that make the fewest mistakes win the Cup. The simple secret was to get a fast boat and train your crew so hard they won't make any mistakes. When I told this to Ted Turner he laughed at me and said, "Well, you give me a slow boat and I'll outsail the other guy."

Many of the sailors had that kind of macho attitude. The sailor was the key, and the boat was just the instrument. I thought, no, the boat's the talent, and the crew just has to put the boat in the right place. Boat speed is a function of aerodynamics and hydrodynamics and those are sciences. I put together an outstanding scientific team who designed through experimentation. They made the fastest boat in the world, *America*^{3}. All the other syndicates put yacht designers in charge of their development programs. Yacht designers are part artist and part scientist. They will design boats that look beautiful and look fast. I didn't care how the boat looked, only how fast it was.

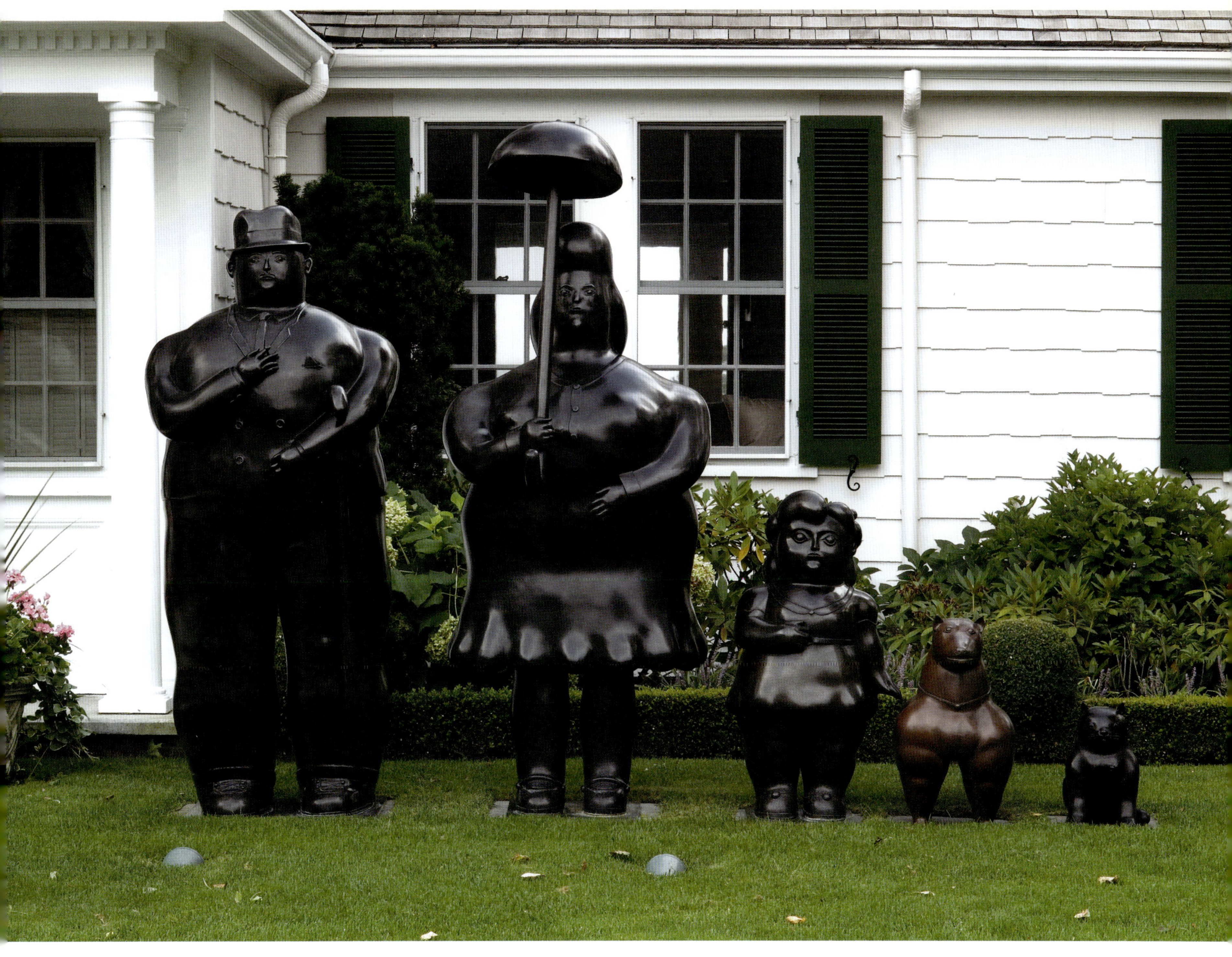

Fig. 11. Botero "family" next to the front foor of Bill Koch's house on Cape Cod,
© Fernando Botero, courtesy, Marlborough Gallery, New York

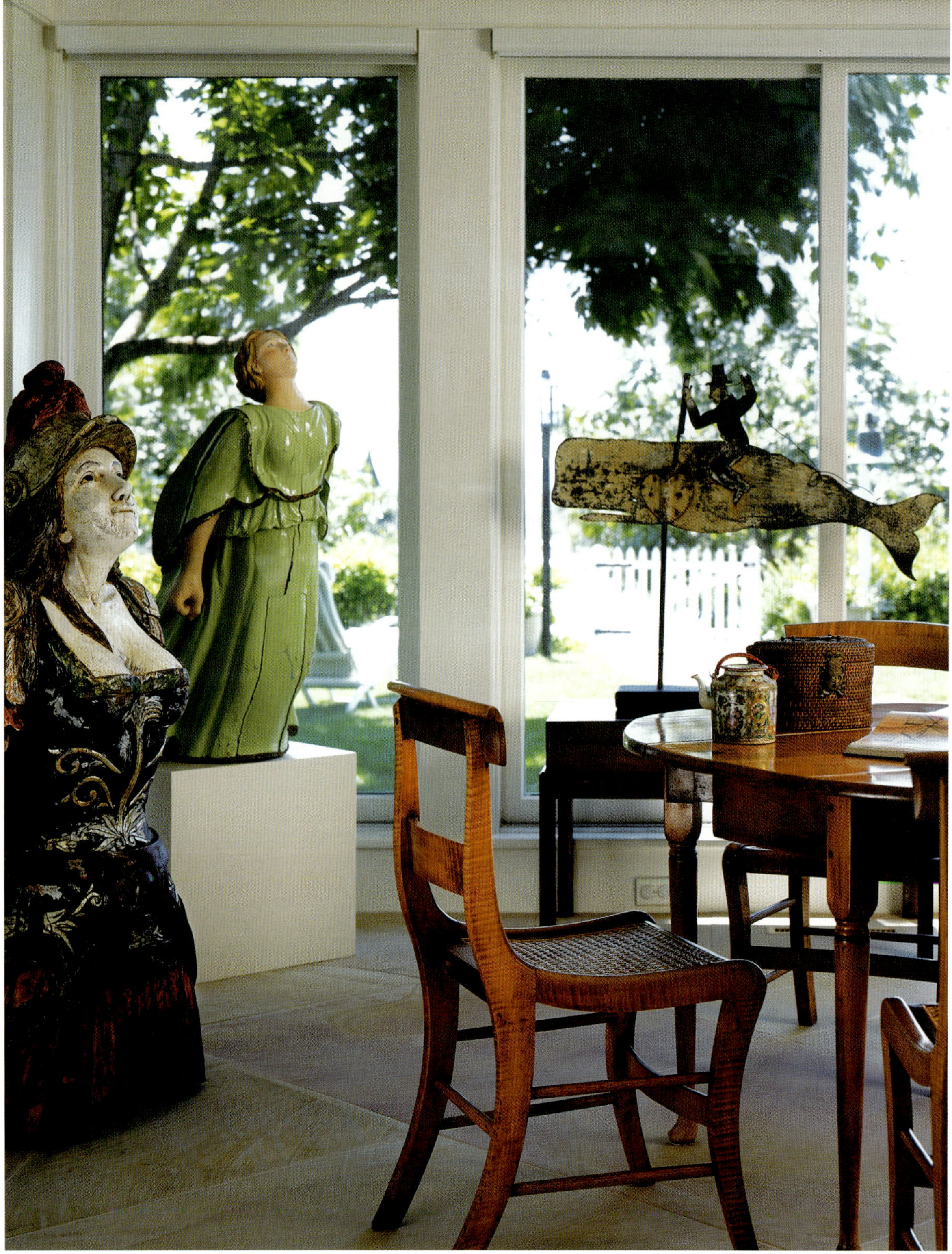

Fig. 12. Figureheads and an antique weathervane depicting a scene from *Moby-Dick* on the sun porch, Cape Cod

Our number-one competitor said if our boat was right, then all the rest of them were wrong. They were all very wide and we had a narrow boat. When a wide boat tips over, its form supports it; the water pushes it back up. But it goes through the waves much more slowly, since it has to push a lot of water out of the way. We designed a narrow boat, even though it would tip over more easily, because it would slice through the waves. We countered its tendency to tip over more by putting much more weight in the keel and making the hull structure very strong and light. It worked. Since then the competitors copied us.

You said that the race for the America's Cup in 1992 didn't allow you a great deal of time to build your collection of marine paintings, and that the maritime collection has grown painting by painting over time. Do you still add to it?

I add to it if a unique painting comes along. For example, the last maritime painting I bought was the Fitz Henry Lane (p. 185). It's a unique painting and has wonderful light and color. However, you can see that my walls for maritime art are full. I have a rule now that if I buy something new I have to get rid of something old. If I buy something it's got to be better than what I have.

Collectors sometimes break their own rules. John G. Johnson, who formed a major collection at the Philadelphia Museum of Art, loved Madonnas. He said, "Every week I'd swear off Madonnas, and then I'd swear back on the next week. And I found I had to intersperse Madonnas with Sabines!" He thought he could get over his taste for religious art, but in the end he couldn't. Do you think you'll stick hard and fast to your rule or do you think you might bend a bit?

No, you always bend, but I just traded four works of art for a single painting by Jacob Miller.

But I imagine you bought the Fitz Henry Lane for reasons that are different than the reason you'd buy a painting by Xanthus Smith, or indeed even by James Edward Buttersworth. You get a different quality of experience from Lane.

That's right. I love Buttersworth's paintings, because he's able to capture light on the water and feelings on the water that I've experienced myself. The Lane has a higher dimension than Buttersworth and the others. It's close to the epitome of Luminism, which I love. It's about coming home from a long voyage.

It's a wonderful complement to the Homer. One is very majestic and the other is very peaceful, quiet, and serene—the experience of the children in the boat. In fact, that sense of boyishness comes through in a number of pieces in your collection. Even if the sailing scene in the Homer isn't entirely true to the way you were raised, perhaps it's the way you'd like to picture your youth—out sitting on a dory in a harbor. . . .

Three kids are out in a boat; they're working, picking up lobster traps, but you can tell they're having fun by their positions in the boat (p. 57). It reminds me of my time working on a ranch and the camaraderie with other workers. You had to do the work, but you could interact and joke around while doing it.

It's interesting that you paired the Homer with the painting of an Italian terrace by Giuseppe de Nittis. Did you see the de Nittis and say, this is a great fit for my Homer, or was it just gut instinct?

I collect each painting individually, and I bought the de Nittis first. When I saw the Homer, I had no idea it would relate to the de Nittis. When you hang paintings, you have a three-dimensional problem to solve—an algorithm. The paintings have to fit geometrically in the room, on the wall; they have to balance one another; they have to reflect some of the colors in the room; they have to relate to one another somehow, through geometry, subject matter, and quality; and they have to evoke similar feelings. You put that whole equation together and you try different solutions. After a while, by trial and error, you find a solution that seems to work. I didn't have any preconception that the Homer would fit above the de Nittis.

But then you put it there and it looked right to you?

That's right. It felt good there; it had found its spot.

When I was hanging a Picasso I have on loan from a museum for a while, I went around the house and wondered, will this work on top of another painting? Will it work side by side with my other Picasso? We held them up, and I realized it had to stand on its own. Yet it works with the Gabriele Münter painting nearby. There's a child in that, there's a child in this; there's a gloominess in the Münter, there's a gloominess in the Picasso.

You also have a very playful attitude toward how you display your art—not strict at all.

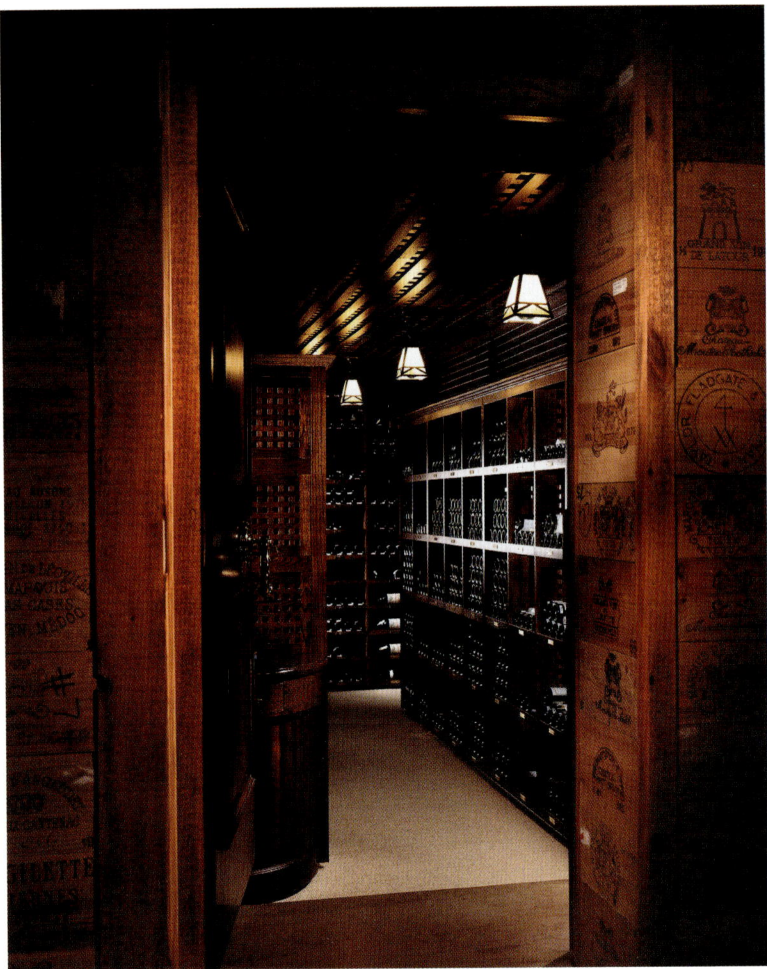

Fig. 13. The wine cellar at Osterville, Cape Cod

I hang all my own paintings. There was recently an article in the *Wall Street Journal* about how people hire experts from museums to hang their paintings. My staff will tell you, I'll hang it and rehang it, because I want it to mean something to me. When I go to museums I like to study a painting, move on, and study another one. But what a collector sees in his art is different than the purposes of a museum exhibit. Sometimes I hang three paintings stacked one above the other. I like to combine paintings with things you might not expect. I even have a bench in Florida, in what I call my Captain's Room, that came off a sunken ship.

I also hang guns right next to the paintings. I want that room to look like a lived-in ranch house, where you hang things for utilitarian purposes. Maybe it's a little cute to put the bear trap below the painting of a bear in the trap and hang the same rifle that's shown in the painting above it. But it seems to me that when you look at the bear in the trap in the painting and then you look down at the trap, you realize how big the trap is and that the bear is even bigger; then you look up and see the small rifle, and you get a good sense of what the whole scene is about.

A famous New York collector came to my house once, and his wife said, "Now don't tell Bill how to rehang his paintings and which ones to sell." Well, after touring the house, he sat down with a glass of wine and said, "Bill, if you hang this painting over here, if you hang that painting over there, and if you get rid of 60 percent of your artworks, you'll have the start of a wonderful collection."

Two years later, his secretary called to ask whether he could bring a friend to the collection. I said, "Sure, but tell him that he can't say what paintings I should sell or where I should hang them. It's my business, and if he doesn't like that, then tell him not to show up." Well, he came, brought his friend, introduced him to me, and then said, "Bill, I just have to go—I have to meet somebody somewhere else." He split because he knew he couldn't resist!

I think you said specifically that your collecting wasn't at all about art history.

Not at all. There's only one area in which I do try to collect systematically, and that's wine.

I should tell you first why I love great wine so much. Not only does it taste beautiful and wonderful and makes you feel great when you're drinking it—you can also really taste the love the vintner had in making the wine, which is an art form. That's particularly clear if you compare an outstanding wine to a mass-produced wine.

I have 90 years of Petrus, 100 years of Latour, 120 years of Mouton, and 150 years of Lafitte—going all the way back to 1737 with the Lafitte. I also have four bottles believed to have been bought by Thomas Jefferson. That is fun. I can display them all on the wall in my wine cellar, with all of the years in sequence, but I still have a number of years to fill in.

You don't collect art systematically, but it seems to me that you don't see the paintings as power pictures on the wall, either. Yours is a much more personal relationship.

It turns out my taste is such that I like the most beautiful and, therefore, in most cases, the most expensive things. That just reflects the fact that some of these artists are recognized as great not only by me but by so many other people that their prices have jumped way up.

You're a wealthy man, but art's expensive. Has there ever been a time when you've bought something and thought that you were stretching, that you couldn't justify the price?

Yes, lots of times.

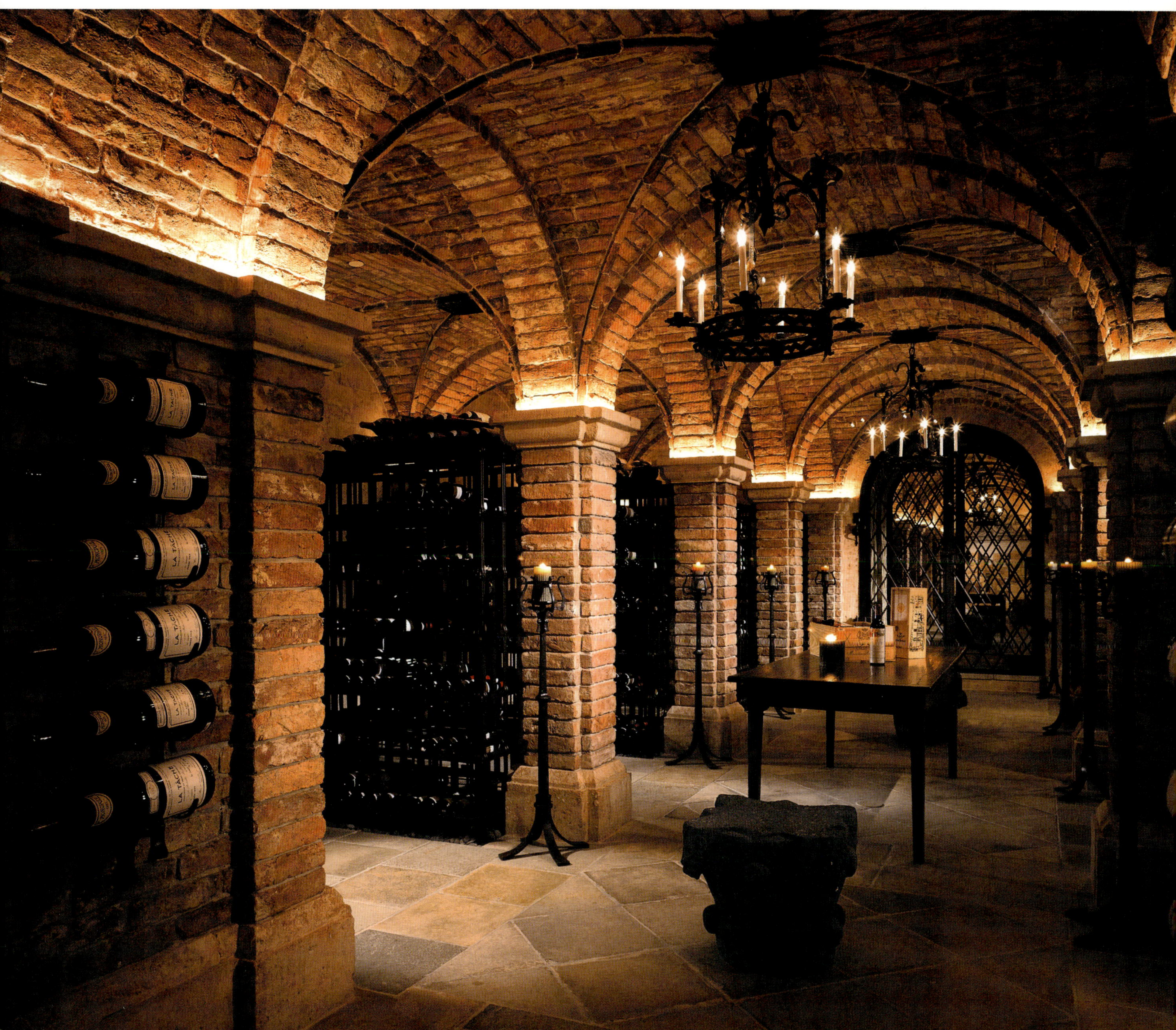

Fig. 14. The wine cellar at Koch's Palm Beach home

Are you willing to trade up, as it were?

I have traded up. I recently bought a new Russell, a wonderful, colorful painting of two Mounties in their bright red uniforms arresting whiskey smugglers going into Canada (p. 128). Charlie Russell portrays himself as one of the whiskey smugglers. It reveals color, humor, the life in the West, and the history of the West. I sold some lesser paintings to buy that one. After a while your tastes alter, and you may get tired of something and want a change. Opportunities to buy some greater works occasionally come along.

Your collection is very eclectic, but do you notice any kind of common thread?

Yes, some people have pointed out to me (and I've seen it later, although I didn't consciously plan it) that I like things in which there's a very luminous or airy quality, a quality of light. You see this in the marine paintings, you see it in some of the cowboy and Indian paintings, and, of course, you see it in the Impressionists.

I think in addition to the ways in which many of your artworks reflect aspects of your personality and represent power or pleasure—or inversely recall a difficult moment in your life—it seems that you've put together something that has tremendous importance for you, but that also provides an ideal environment for your family.

That's right. Many of my artworks are family oriented. A painting I'd love to have is Van Gogh's *The First Steps* (after Jean-François Millet), of the farmer and the mother teaching the child to walk. That's magnificent. In my painting by Homer of the kids in a rowboat, the unity of the family and their affection for one another come through. The Picasso of the two kids drawing together has a similar feel (p. 84). And my sculpture by Hans Arp is a friendly, loving figure (p. 69); my daughter just loves to grab it and hug it. She's getting a little old and tired of it now, and someone's cleaned her finger prints off it. I used to say, leave the fingerprints on, because it's a reflection of how it related to her—of how loved it is.

Do your children talk to you about the art, about their surroundings, at all?

A little bit. I used to take them around and ask which painting they liked the best. It varies with the boys and the girls. They all like the Boilly faces (p. 49) because they're so crazy; the boys like the cowboys and Indians; the girls like the more peaceful pictures. They actually like the Gabriele Münter because that's of a little girl (p. 75). They like the Degas ballet dancers, too.

What's their response to the sculptures?

The boys like the Remington bronzes; the girls like the Arp. They all love the Robert Indiana *Love* sculpture (p. 96) because they can climb all over it, and they love "Roseanne" and climb all over the Botero family sculpture out front. They enjoy climbing and sitting piggyback on the daddy. There was an independent movie called *David and Lisa* in the 1960s about some kids in a mental institution. They were taken to an art gallery, and there was a statue of a naked woman lying down almost like an Aristide Maillol, and one girl crawled up into her lap and put her arm around the sculpture. It's such a beautiful, touching moment that shows how much that poor little girl really wanted a mother.

You're a frequent lender to exhibitions. So your collection, although it lives in your home, gets known in a variety of different ways. Is it important for you to have people benefit from seeing the works of art?

I rarely lend an individual piece now unless it's for a project like the recent Modigliani exhibition, and I want to see how the painting that I have fits in with the artist's entire history. Generally what I've done in the past is to lend a good portion of my collection to various museums. In addition, I have schoolchildren come to see the collection in my Palm Beach house.

When I talk to the students about my art, I tell them what I've told you—that when I look at a painting I have a certain emotional reaction to it, and generally if it's pleasant and makes me feel good for a long period of time, then I want the painting in my collection. Like most people, I want to feel good rather than unhappy. I want to share that experience with others.

How many people would you say come through your collection every year—strangers, that is, people who otherwise wouldn't have access to it?

We probably have about five hundred kids come through each year. Five local schools are invited to tour. Also, I've hosted fundraising parties here for different charities; I've probably had several hundred people come through for each party. We've held as many as five charity parties in one year, though I'm cutting that back now. I'm still going to invite the kids to come through because they seem to enjoy the experience the most, particularly the underprivileged kids. The rich kids sometimes walk through and say, "My dad's got a better Picasso than you."

Do you have a sense of what you'd like your legacy to be, what you'd like people to think about the collection you've assembled?

I think the art collection reflects, to me anyway, a lot of what life's all about. I know it's about family, it's about love, it's about peace and contentment, it's about striving, it's about accomplishment, and it's about hard times and overcoming them. We all experience those things, in varying degrees. I've been lucky enough and fortunate enough to be able to accomplish some good things; I've experienced many losses but still had money to be able to assemble an art collection that reflects what I value in life and what I've accomplished in life.

In a way, my art collection is a little bit of a fantasy world. If you look at all the nudes, I'm sure that's a man's fantasy—the ideal woman. But every person has a fantasy. I've had a fantasy of being a cowboy, for instance, and I've been one—well, for a tiny little bit of time. I had a fantasy about being a skipper and I've been one. And a gunfighter, but thank God I'm not one!

What I've assembled has been purely selfish, but I like to share it with people who appreciate and enjoy it. It's like having a good wine with dinner: You want to share it with someone who really values the quality, taste, beauty and the love the vintner had for making the wine. You don't want to share it with a bozo who says, "Nah, give me a scotch and soda instead," or someone who wants to dump ice in the white wine because it's not cold enough. Many people don't appreciate it and that's fine. They have their taste, I have mine. I enjoy sharing the collection with people who take pleasure in it; it gives me gratification, because we all like to have our tastes reaffirmed.

A dealer once said to me, "You've got a great collection here, but you should get rid of this Chagall." Some people come through my house in Palm Beach and tell me I ought to turn it into a museum. I've thought about that, about how each museum has its own purpose that's a function of the people who run it and the audience that visits it. I've read about all the problems that the Barnes Collection has been going through, and I don't want to create that.

I don't know what I'll do with the collection. Museums have been after me for particular pieces, of course, because this or that fits in with their collection. I think about the artwork I've acquired over my lifetime, and I wonder, what do I really want to do with my assets in the future? What institutions do I want to help, and how do I want to help my kids? I look at the collection and think, this is something I've created and enjoyed, it's time for my kids to enjoy and create their own thing. Why should I saddle them with my tastes? They can have the thrill that I did doing my own thing; everybody has to find his or her own way in life.

If one of your children really loved a piece, though, do you think you'd let him or her have it?

I went through that with my brothers: after twenty years of litigation and agony we finally came to an economic understanding that made us all marginally happy. We've reached the point where we've made peace, and that's wonderful. During the settlement discussions we were dealing with large sums of money but the biggest thing we argued about was who was going to get what painting out of my father's collection. The most valuable painting he had in there was worth peanuts compared to what we were talking about. It wasn't the money, it was the emotional stake; for example, which brother was going to get the portrait of my dad.

Finally, I said, "I've got my own collection, just let me copy the paintings that I want of my father's, and let me have one or two others." We reached an agreement, but it took a long time and a lot of haggling. I don't want to do that to my kids. I don't want them to have any reason whatsoever to fight. That's much more important to me than the so-called integrity of the collection. The integrity of the collection is what I gave it, it's my taste, and it's irrelevant to most other people. I'm much more interested in having my children being my legacy than this art collection being my monument.

You say your kids are your greatest works of art.

Yes, because they're alive. They change every moment from being absolute hellions to being the most beautiful things you can imagine. They continually bring a lot of joy and happiness to my life.

Your collection is sort of a family as well.

Yes, it is.

Something very beautiful but also very disturbing about art is that you feel it's going to go on forever, but you won't go on forever, so it makes you value life even more. Do you feel that?

Well, I used to feel that way completely, until I had my children. I look at my children and think I can go on for a long period of time through them. I'm now interested in what happens beyond my death. I used to think I didn't care what happened to me after I died. I would think, I'm going into nothingness, the world be damned. I want my children to enjoy life. I want them to enjoy the things I've enjoyed, or to find fine things they'll enjoy as much as I have. If I can teach them passion, that will be wonderful.

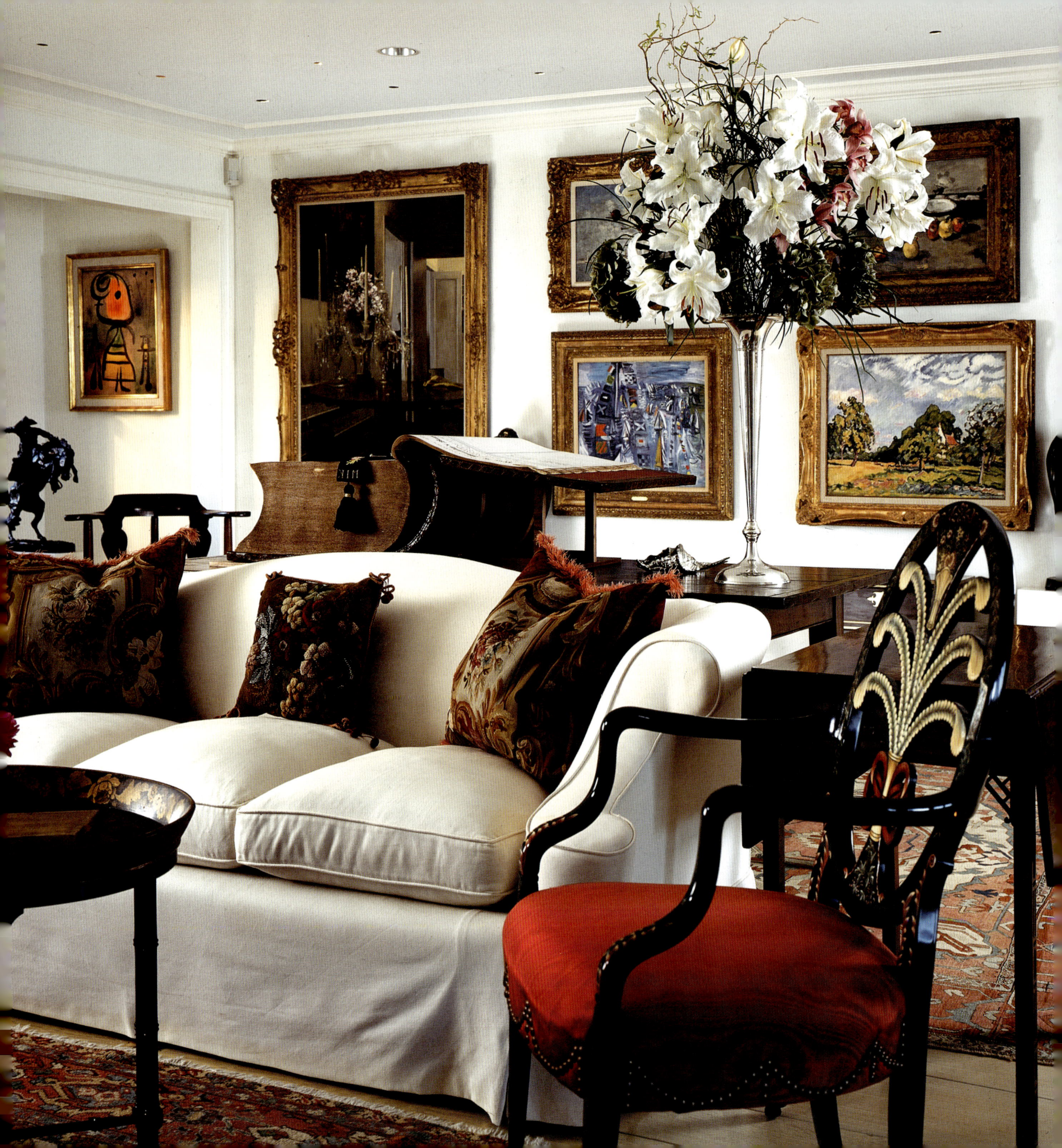

IMPRESSIONISM AND ITS AFFINITIES

*****

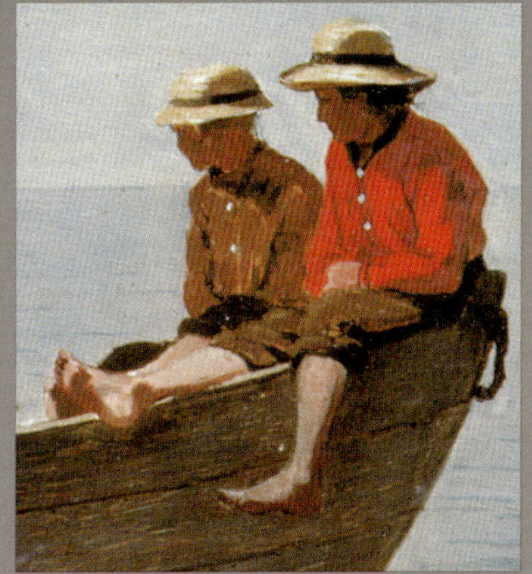

Fig. 15. The living room at
Osterville, Cape Cod

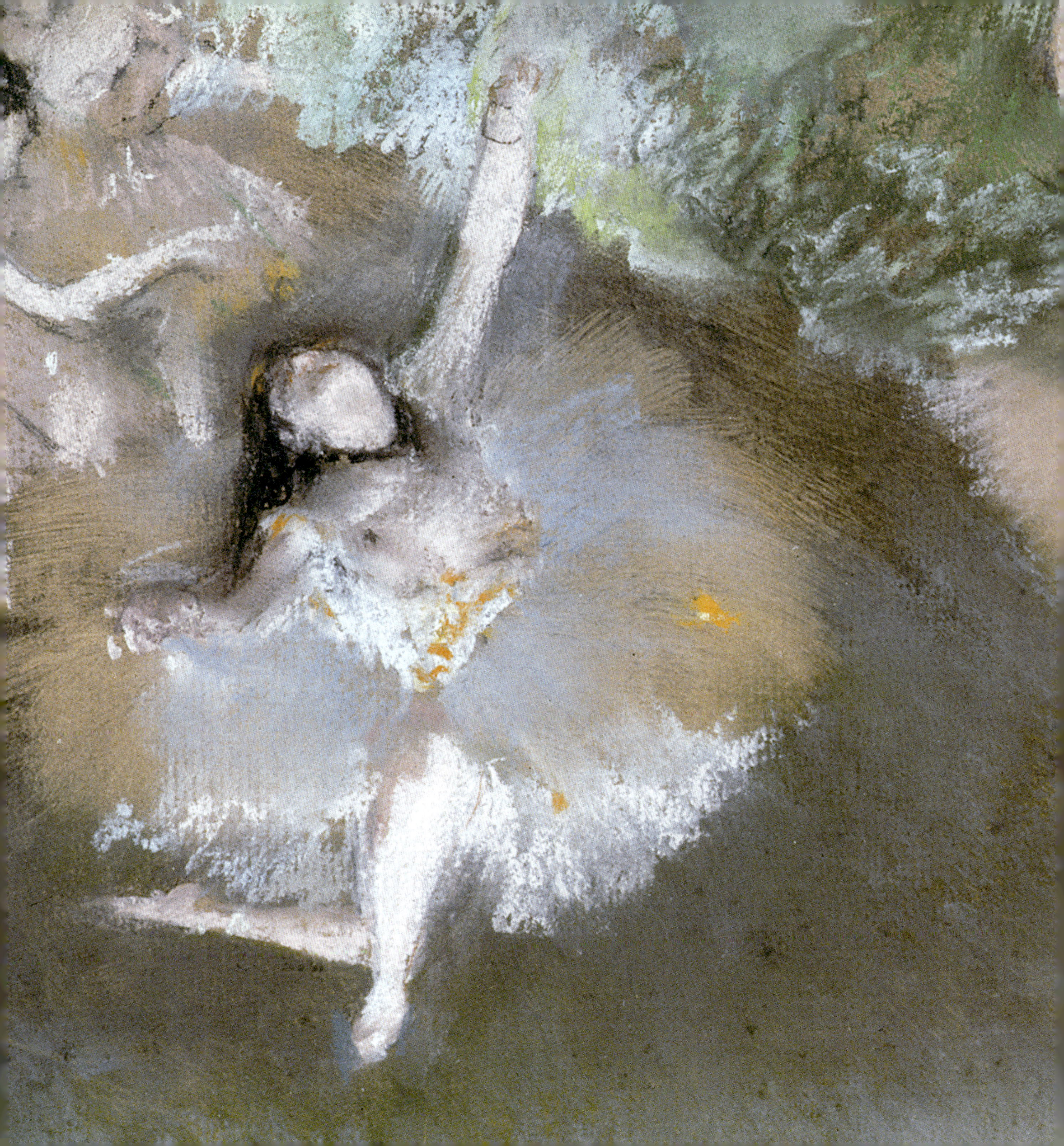

IMPRESSIONISM AND ITS AFFINITIES

* * * * * * *

During his college years at MIT, Bill Koch went for a weekend to New York City, where his girlfriend at the time introduced him to the collections of the Museum of Modern Art. There, before Monet's *Water Lilies* triptych—a painting from the 1920s, measuring some thirty feet across—he felt the intense power that a work of art could have to influence his emotions. Monet's painting inspired peacefulness and calm in him. From that time to the present, he has been interested in nineteenth-century painting, both European and American.

The Koch Collection includes several late-eighteenth- and early-nineteenth-century paintings, including an exquisite display of flowers and fruit by the Dutch master Jan van Os (p. 48) and the witty *Thirty-five Expressive Heads* by the French genre painter Louis-Léopold Boilly (p. 49). But the nineteenth-century collection is dominated by an important group of paintings and sculpture by the Impressionists, notably a fine group of canvases by Monet.

The earliest of these, *Windmills in Holland* (p. 43), shows a sailboat on a canal that recedes into the distance, flanked by houses and windmills. The picture dates from Monet's first visit to the Netherlands, where he spent part of the summer of 1871 after a nine-month exile in London during the Franco-Prussian War. *Windmills in Holland* shows the techniques that Monet had evolved in the late 1860s to render the effects of light and climate on the appearance of the landscape. Reflections of buildings in the canal at right are indicated by short rectangular strokes of gray and green, while smooth patches of pale gray represent the surface of the water lightly rippled by the wind. The overcast sky above is painted in feathery strokes of gray and mauve on a pale ground.

The Impressionists' use of a shorthand, staccato application of paint to suggest motion is seen in two more works from the Koch Collection that were painted during the early years of the movement. Pierre-Auguste Renoir's *Ice-Skating in the Bois de Boulogne* (p. 50) dates from the beginning of 1868, when unusually cold temperatures allowed for skating all over France. Renoir later said that he had "never been able to stand the cold" and considered snow "a blight on the face of nature."[1] Here, however, it seems he relished the opportunity to abandon his usual bright palette of colors for an almost grisaille tonality. Patches of black and nearly pure white stand out against soft grays and ochers, relieved only by the occasional dash of red, blue, or brownish-green. The Parisians flocking to skate or to observe the skating on the frozen ponds are conveyed with seemingly haphazard dots and dashes of paint—a technique that Renoir would use in the summer months of 1868, painting with Monet on the banks of the Seine.

Louis-Eugène Boudin used a similar brushstroke technique in his *Camaret, Fishing Boats Anchored in the Port* (p. 51). Boudin was Monet's first champion—they met in 1858, when Monet was still in his teens. Boudin recommended to the younger artist that he paint out-of-doors, to observe nature firsthand. His own methods involved not only painting directly from the motif, but making countless studies of the transient effects of weather and light, particularly through pastel studies of clouds over the sea. In this view of the Breton port of Camaret, painted in 1873, Boudin captured the movement of low clouds over the water, reinforcing that movement through the tiny detail of the French tricolor flag flying on the rigging of the ship at right. At Monet's invitation, the artist showed two paintings in 1874—including another view of Camaret—in the first exhibition of the painters who would become known as the Impressionists.[2]

Also present in that show was Paul Cézanne, a native of Aix-en-Provence who had arrived in Paris in 1861 to study art and attempt to find recognition for his paintings in the official Salon exhibitions. By 1872 he had settled in the town of Auvers-sur-Oise, some forty miles north of the capital, where he could be near his friend and mentor Camille Pissarro. *Cup, Glass, and Fruit* (p. 53) is one of many still lifes he painted in the early 1870s, and despite its relatively small size—just over twenty inches wide—it is among the most monumental. This force is achieved by Cézanne's extreme simplification of the pictorial space of the composition: bands of color denote the mottled top of a table or chest, a dark brown dado, and a figured blue-gray wallpaper bordered in green and white. Against this simplified structure the artist set out two man-made objects—a thick-walled wineglass and a large ceramic cup—and six apples, painted in lively tones of yellow, orange, and red. Light, coming from the left, flickers over the spherical forms of apples and within the bodies of glass and cup; deep shadows lock the forms in place against the geometric background.

By contrast, the light in Edgar Degas's *Ballet Dancers* (p. 54), of about 1879, lifts the figures away from the ground, as they leap into the air above the stage of the Paris Opera. The source of illumination—gas jets at the edge of the stage itself, outside the picture window—makes the legs and arms of the dancers glow, while their faces are cast into relative shadow. Degas's technique emphasizes this contrast of shadow and light: the pastel color is applied over a black-and-white ground, consisting of the second pulling from one of Degas's inky monotypes. Traces of the monotype texture are clearly visible in the background at left and right.

Degas was among the most inventive and experimental of all the Impressionists, working in virtually every medium. Beginning as early as the 1860s, and continuing until after 1900, he made small-scale sculpture, treating the themes that he had already explored in paintings, pastels, and prints. (Only one of his statuettes was ever exhibited during his lifetime; after Degas's death, his heirs commissioned a bronze edition of many of the original models, which the artist had executed in wax or clay.) Dancers and racehorses were among his favorite subjects (see p. 55). He studied them in movement—capturing, for instance, the tension of a dancer's musculature as she holds an arabesque—or at rest, as in the elegant racehorse shown on page 55, which has more in common with the reliefs of ancient Greece (see p. 19) than with the bucking broncos of Frederic Remington's contemporaneous bronzes (see pp. 114–16).

It happens that the Koch Collection includes two paintings by artists who became close friends of Degas in Paris: Alfred Stevens and Giuseppe de Nittis. Stevens, born in Belgium in 1823, about a decade before Degas, had settled in Paris and had become a close friend of Degas's mentor Edouard Manet. Like Manet and Degas, Stevens flirted with gritty Realism early in his career but was equally attracted to subject matter drawn from the daily life of fashionable French men and women. His *Coquette* (p. 56) plays on the theme of human vanity in showing a young woman looking at her image in a mirror; but Stevens seems to have used the subject as a pretext for displaying the cascading auburn hair of his stylish sitter.

Like Manet, Stevens never exhibited with the Impressionists. De Nittis, who was of a younger generation still, was invited to participate in the first of the Impressionist exhibitions. He had initially come to Paris in 1867 and settled there the next year. The Koch Collection canvas, *In the Woods of Portici* (p. 59), probably dates from a few years before his arrival in France. It shows the artist's keen interest in the behavior of light in the landscape, as sunshine, filtered through a screen of trees, casts long, slanting shadows on the sandy terrace. The simplification of forms into patches of color, touched with light and shadow, hints at de Nittis's admiration for the Florentine painters known as the Macchiaioli, while the raking perspective foreshadows the scenes of Paris boulevards that he would paint under Degas's influence a decade or more later.

The use of simply applied patches of color, barely modeled, that characterizes de Nittis's Italian view could be seen, in various forms, in the work of painters throughout Europe in the 1860s. In France one variation on this method led to the development of the type of brushwork commonly associated with Impressionism, but artists in northern and eastern Europe, as well as in the south, were experimenting with similar techniques at the same time. Parallel developments took place in the work of American artists, usually as a result of some contact with European art. Winslow Homer, for example, who began painting in oils shortly before the end of the Civil War, would have known examples of French Barbizon painting from exhibitions in Boston and New York. But after his 1866–67 visit to France, he seems to have adopted some elements of the new manner. In the Koch Collection's *Three Boys in a Dory* (p. 57), painted in Gloucester, Massachusetts, in 1873, Homer contrasted areas of subtly modulated shadow with bold bits of bright color: the vivid red of a boy's shirt, the gleaming yellow of sunlight on a straw hat.

From the 1850s on, but particularly in the decades after the Civil War, more and more American artists traveled to

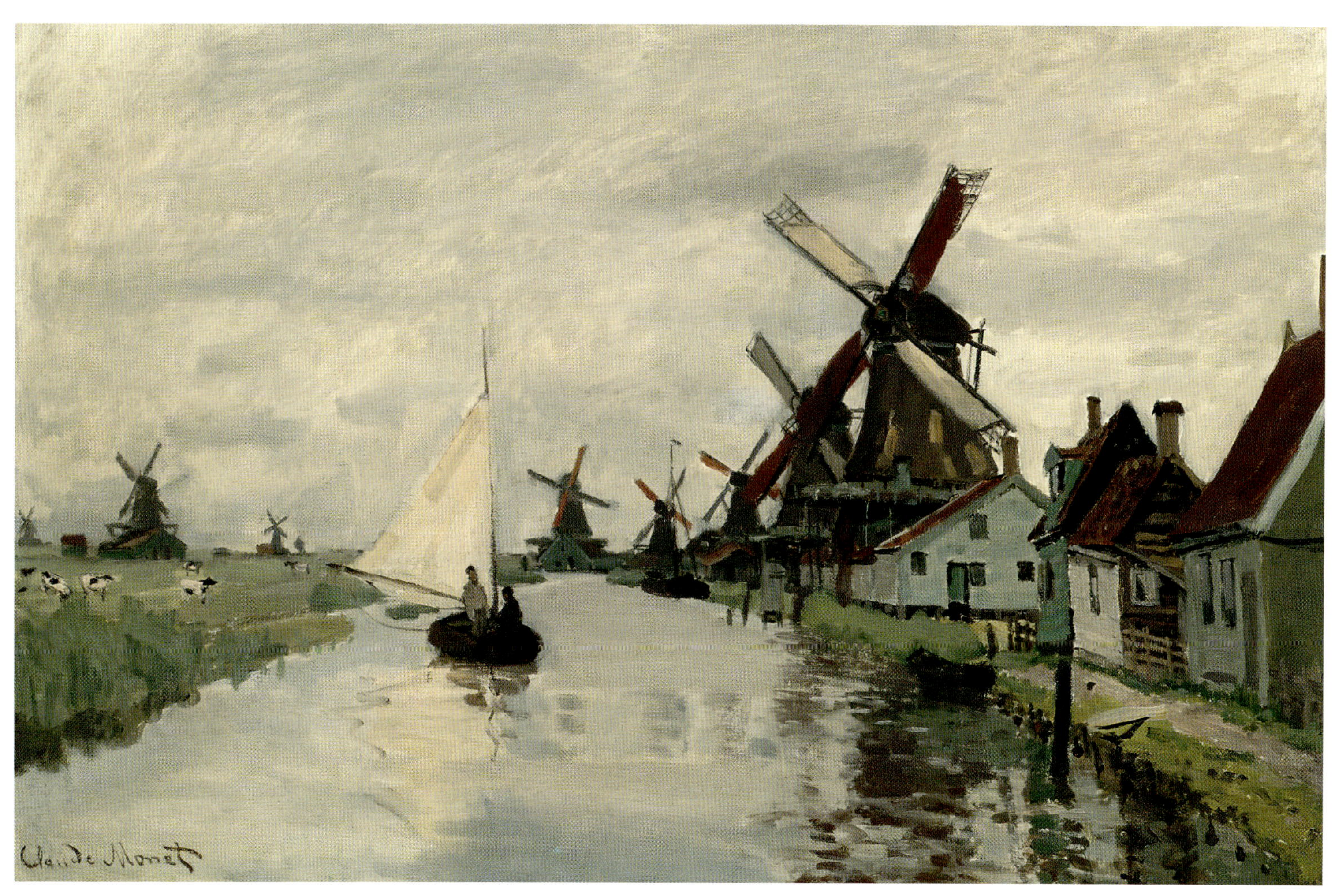

CLAUDE MONET

French, 1840–1926
Windmills in Holland, 1871
Oil on canvas
19 x 29 in.

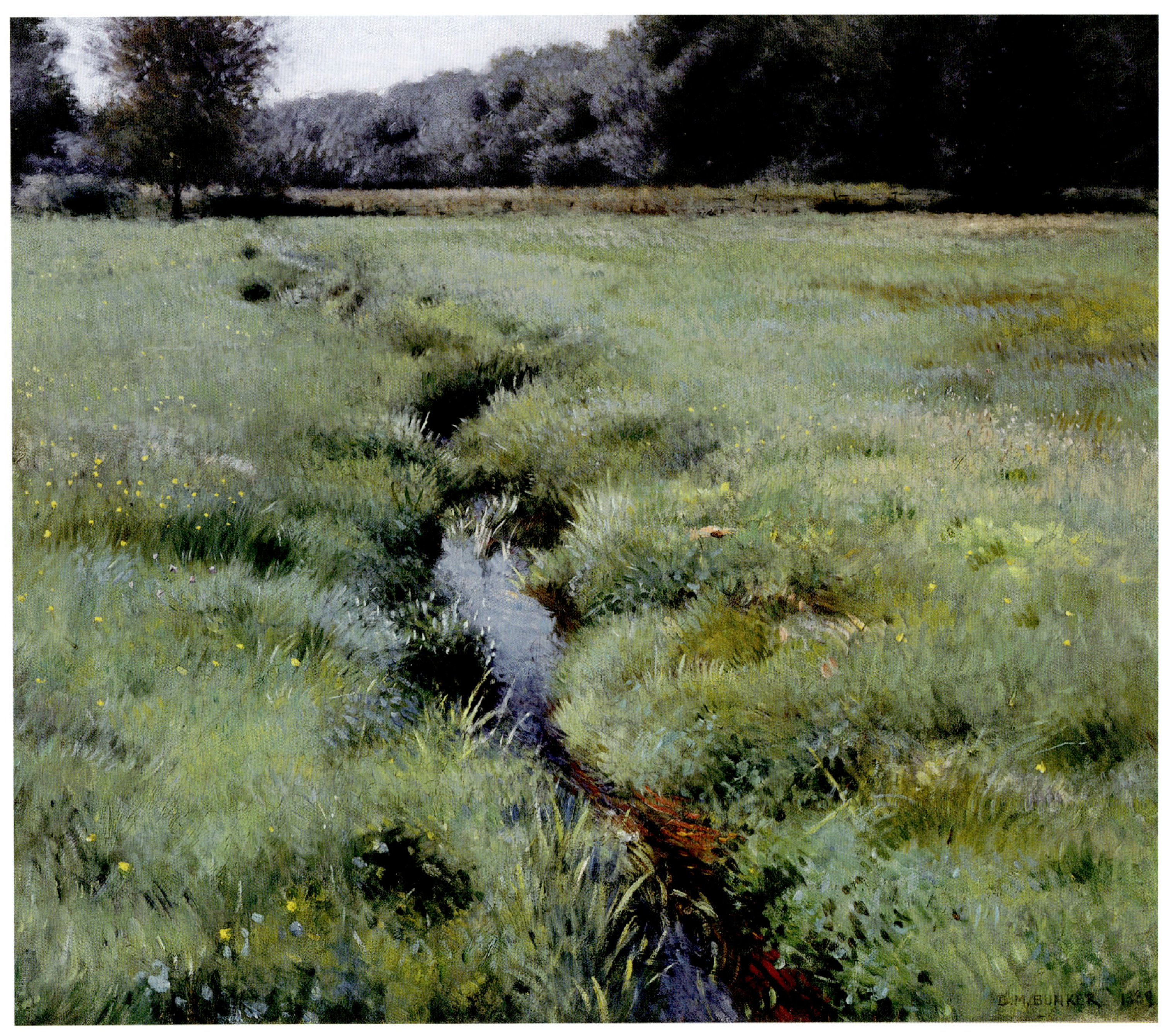

DENNIS MILLER BUNKER

American, 1861–1890
The Brook: Medfield, 1889
Oil on canvas
25 x 30 in.

Europe for formal training—in Paris, above all—and to study the works of the Old Masters in the original, in museums and private collections. James Abbott McNeill Whistler had arrived in Paris in the late 1850s, and John Singer Sargent, born in Florence, had entered a fashionable Parisian studio in the mid-1870s. Their influence was strong on the career of William Merritt Chase, who followed in Sargent's footsteps to Venice and to Spain. There, like Sargent—and Manet before him—he was impressed by the work of the seventeenth-century Spanish painter Diego Velázquez. Perhaps because of a shared admiration of Venetian and Spanish painting, Chase's portrait of about 1896 of his wife in a mantilla (p. 58), a study in blacks accented with touches of red in a rose and a fan, recalls the portraits and genre pictures that the precocious Sargent had painted in the early 1880s.

By the late 1880s, modern French paintings were well known in America, particularly in New York and Boston, where dealers had begun to show the works of Monet and his contemporaries. Dennis Miller Bunker may have seen Monet's works in either city in 1886 or 1887, and his friend Sargent, with whom he spent time in England in the summer of 1888, was a great friend and partisan of the French painter. On his return to Boston in autumn 1888 and, above all, in the summer of 1889, Bunker revealed his interest in, and mastery of, the Impressionist idiom in such works as *The Brook: Medfield* (p. 44).

The view of a field of flowers bounded by shady trees is reminiscent of many of Monet's most successful compositions of the 1880s. But it is memory of an important place—in this case the meadow surrounding a house he once owned in Dover, Massachusetts—that drew Bill Koch to Bunker's *The Brook: Medfield*, which he purchased in 2000. A similar principle had guided Koch in his first really important acquisition some twenty years before, the first of his paintings by Monet—*Field of Oats and Poppies* (p. 60). Completed in the summer of 1890, this painting is regarded by art historians as a magnificent example of Monet's use of extreme, yet subtle, juxtapositions of hue, value, and tone—brilliant orange-red set against deep emerald green; passages of deep blue shadow countered by startling zones of bright yellow sunlight. To Koch, the opinion of historians is much less important than the fact that the painting makes him remember a place that was important in his life: the meadow in Kansas where he and his brothers would picnic with their father when they were young.

That sense of memory and reverie inspired by a place or a motif, as evoked by a painting, accords perfectly with Monet's intentions, at least as they have been interpreted for more than a century. Monet's series of Grainstacks, exhibited in 1891, and his Poplars, first shown in 1892, explore the ways in which a subject can be transformed by the artist's changing point of view and by the shift in light over the course of a day or through a season. In the views he painted of Rouen Cathedral, shown in 1895, Monet reduced the number of variables, allowing the time of day to be the most important factor in the effect produced by his depiction of a Gothic facade. Critics often comment on the poetic qualities of Monet's series paintings and on the artist's ability to evoke, rather than to transcribe, the motif for the viewer.

A group of paintings that Monet began in the summer of 1896, working from the north bank of the Seine, facing toward the rising sun, is perhaps the most reductive and controlled of all his series to that date. Sitting in a boat, moored in the same place morning after morning in the summers of 1896 and 1897, Monet created a score of canvases in which a large mass of foliage at left and a smaller mass at right are reflected in the surface of the river. Some of the compositions are horizontal, as in a painting in the Museum of Fine Arts dated to 1896 (fig. 17), in which Monet placed the line of the river low on the canvas. Others, such as the 1897 painting given to the Museum in 1911 (fig. 16) or another, dated 1896, in the Koch Collection (p. 47), are essentially square. In these, the horizon line bisects the canvas at or slightly above the center. Within this group of three paintings, a remarkable variety of effects is produced, depending on conditions of light and atmosphere. In the first, the green mass of willows at left detaches itself from the soft blue background; in the second, subtle changes in tonality suggest spatial and atmospheric depth; while in the third, the Koch Collection canvas, the deep blue-green mass of the foliage is remarkably united in tone and in hue, and contrasts sharply with the pale yellow glow of the morning sky. Despite their formal differences, each painting in the series perfectly evokes the

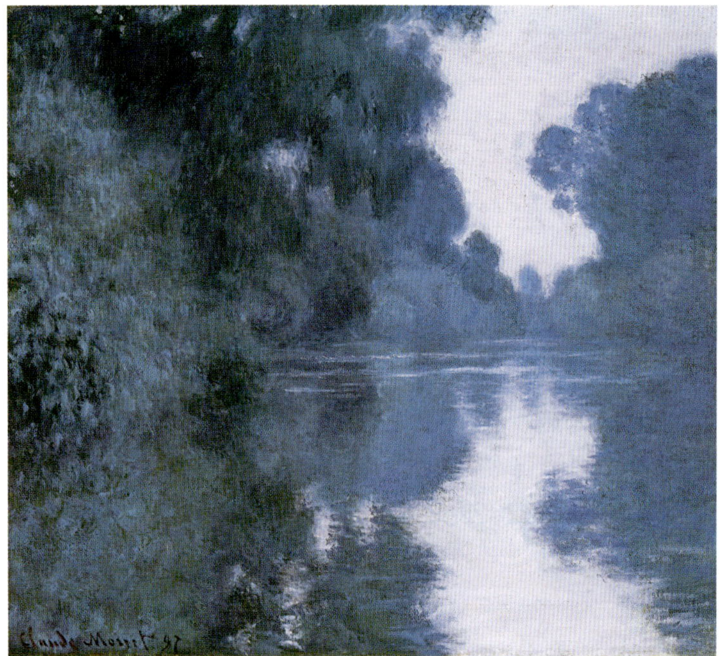

Fig. 16. Claude Monet (French, 1840–1926), *Morning on the Seine, near Giverny,* 1897, oil on canvas, 32 x 36½ in., Museum of Fine Arts, Boston, Gift of Mrs. W. Scott Fitz, 1911, 11.1261

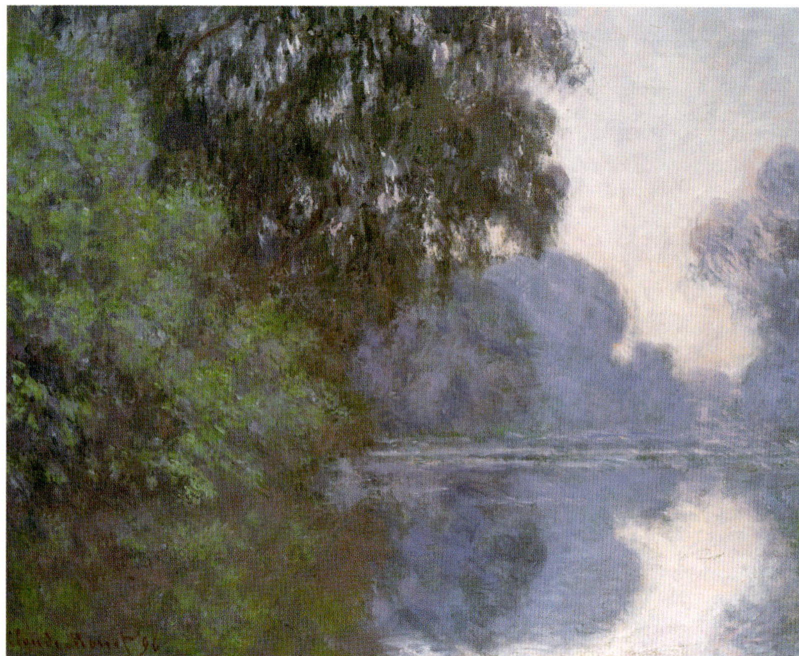

Fig. 17. Claude Monet (French, 1840–1926), *Morning on the Seine, near Giverny,* 1896, oil on canvas, 29 x 36⅝ in., Museum of Fine Arts, Boston, Juliana Cheney Edwards Collection, 1939, 39.655

peaceful moment of dawn on the river; as a group their power only grows.

Between 1903 and 1908 Monet turned his attention to another motif, equally concerned with reflection—in both the physical and psychological sense. He concentrated on the surface of the water-lily pond that he had constructed in the garden near his home and studio at Giverny, where the water reflected the vertical lines of trees against sky, interrupted by horizontal islands of leaves and flowers. In six summers Monet produced more than seventy canvases depicting the pond, including the Koch Collection *Water Lilies* (p. 61), which probably dates from the end of this extended campaign, in 1908.

In 1909 Monet exhibited forty-eight of his "water landscapes" at the Galerie Durand-Ruel. Reviewing the exhibition, one critic cautioned his readers that "M. Claude Monet is interested in pleasing only himself. His exertions are directed at recording the multifaceted differences of the pleasures he experiences during the course of the day as he works in one single place: such are the apparently selfish goals of his art, and it suits him to subordinate everything to this end." But the importance of any one of Monet's themes, he went on, "lies in its potential for increasing the number of sensations aroused in the viewer and enriching their quality."[3] Koch would say, and we would agree with him, that the potential of Monet's paintings to arouse sensations is unlikely to be exhausted in our time. They first inspired Koch nearly half a century ago, and they continue to do so now.

— GEORGE T. M. SHACKELFORD

1. See Charles S. Moffett et al., *Impressionists in Winter: Effets de Neige* (Washington, D.C.: The Phillips Collection, 1998), 132.

2. Ruth Berson et al., *The New Painting: Impressionism 1874–1886* (San Francisco: Fine Arts Museums of San Francisco, 1996), II:3.

3. Roger Marx, "Les 'Nynmphéas' de M. Claude Monet," *Gazette des Beaux-Arts,* June 1909, trans. in *Monet: A Retrospective,* ed. Charles F. Stuckey (New York: Hugh Lauter Levin Associates, 1985), 255.

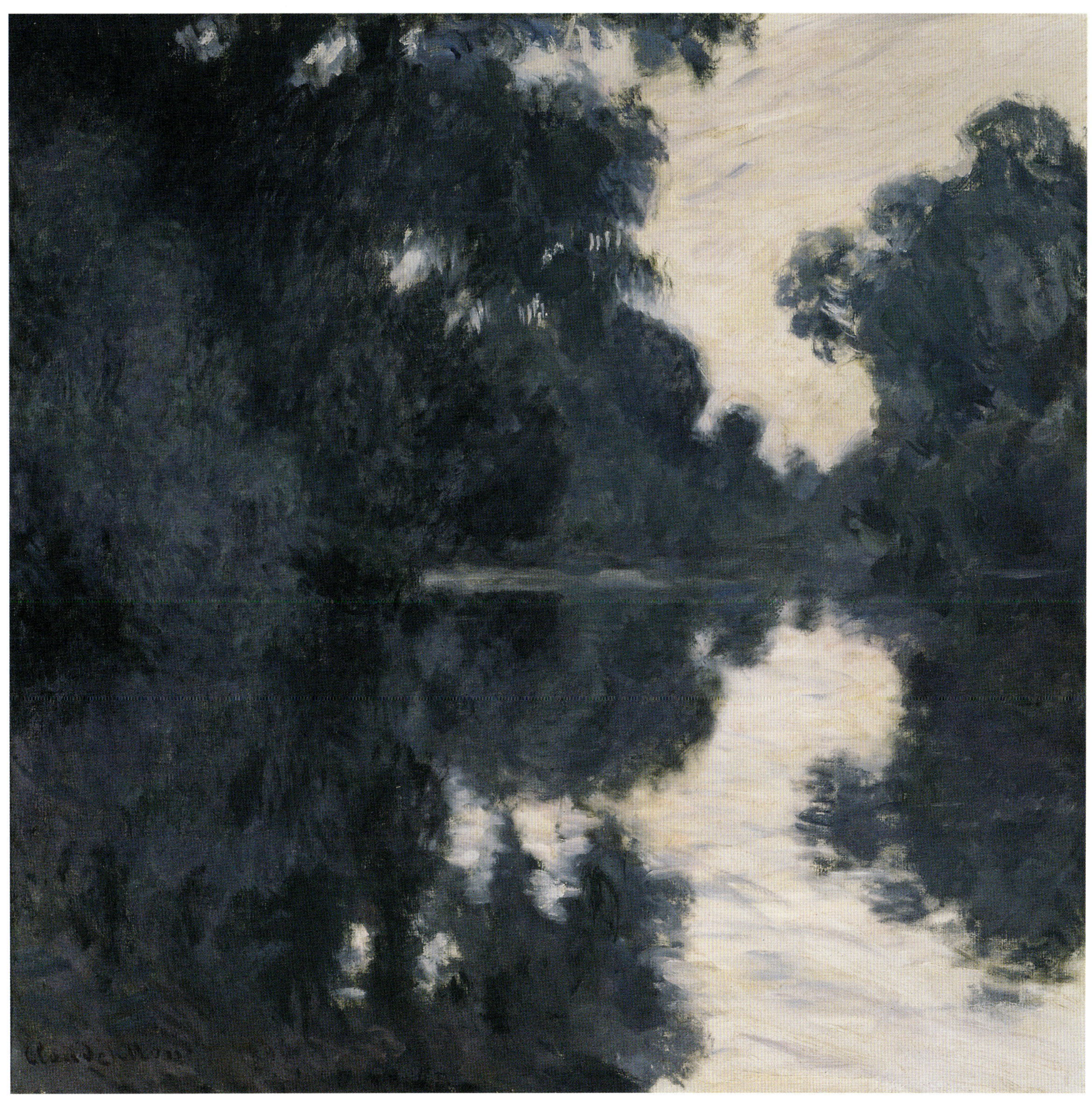

CLAUDE MONET

French, 1840–1926
Morning on the Seine, 1896
Oil on canvas
35⅜ x 36½ in.

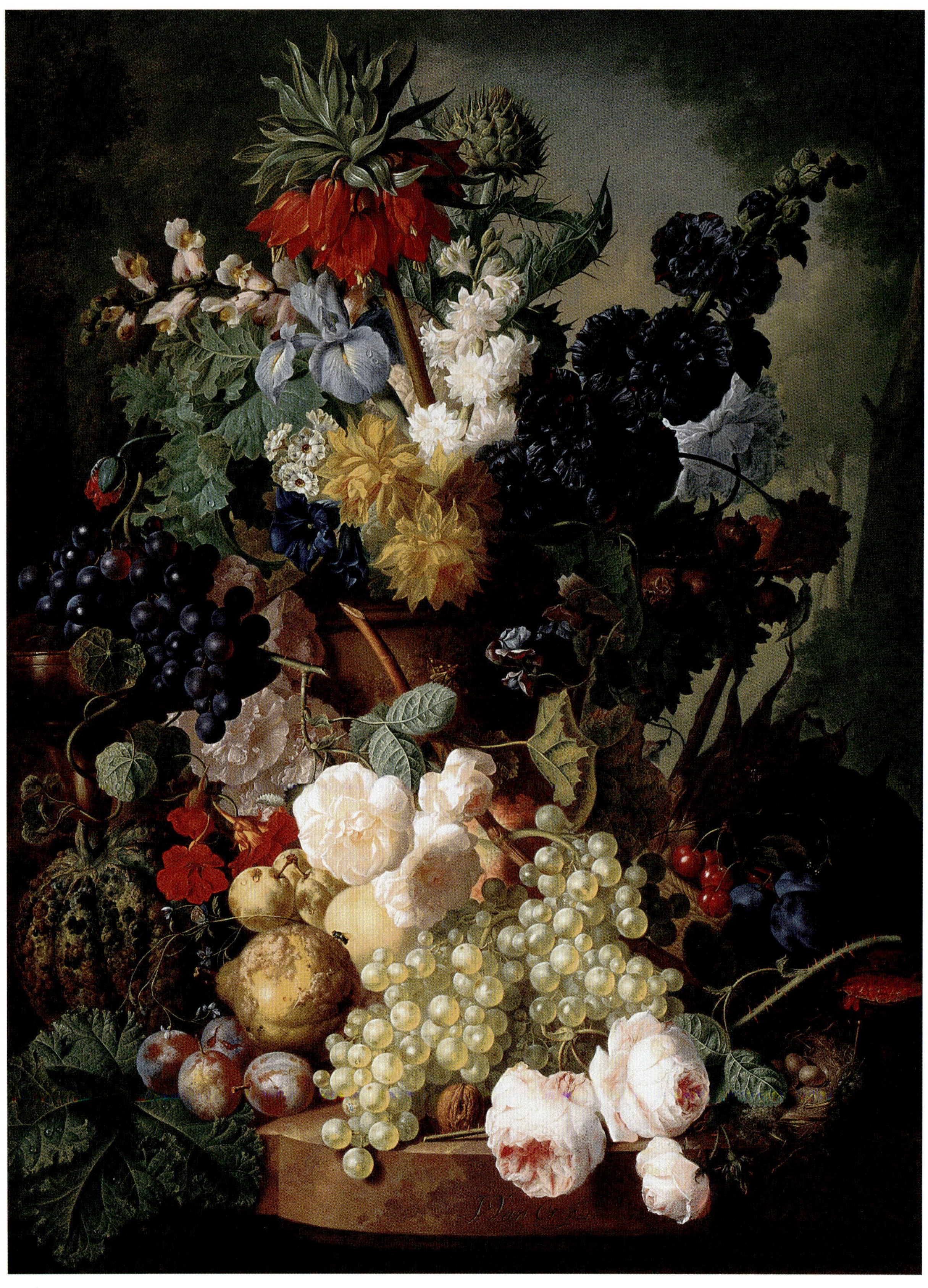

JAN VAN OS

Dutch, 1744–1808
Still Life of Flowers and Fruit,
late 18th century
Oil on panel
34¼ x 27⅛ in.

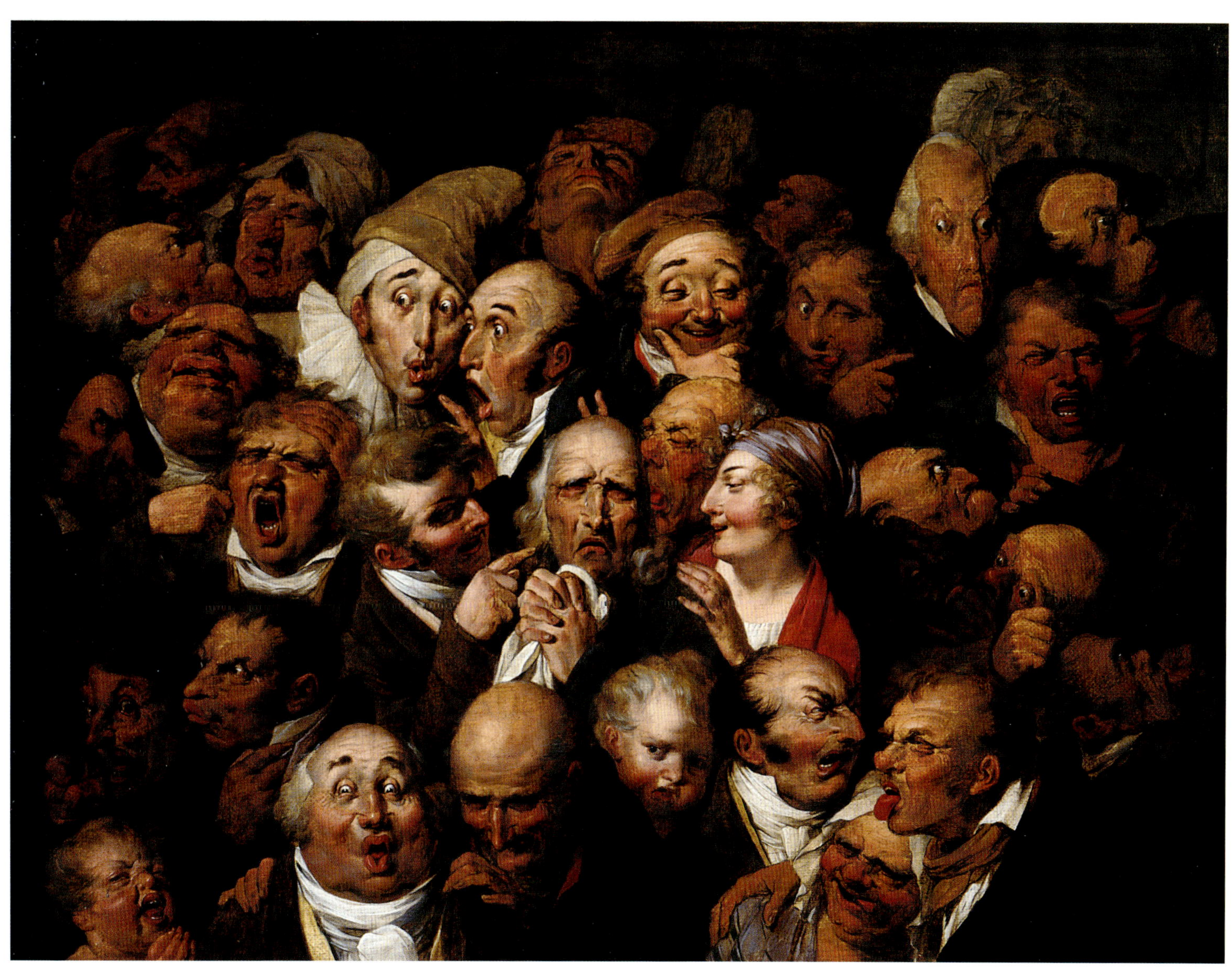

LOUIS-LÉOPOLD BOILLY

French, 1761–1845
Thirty-five Expressive Heads,
about 1823–28
Oil on board
16⅜ x 21¾ in.

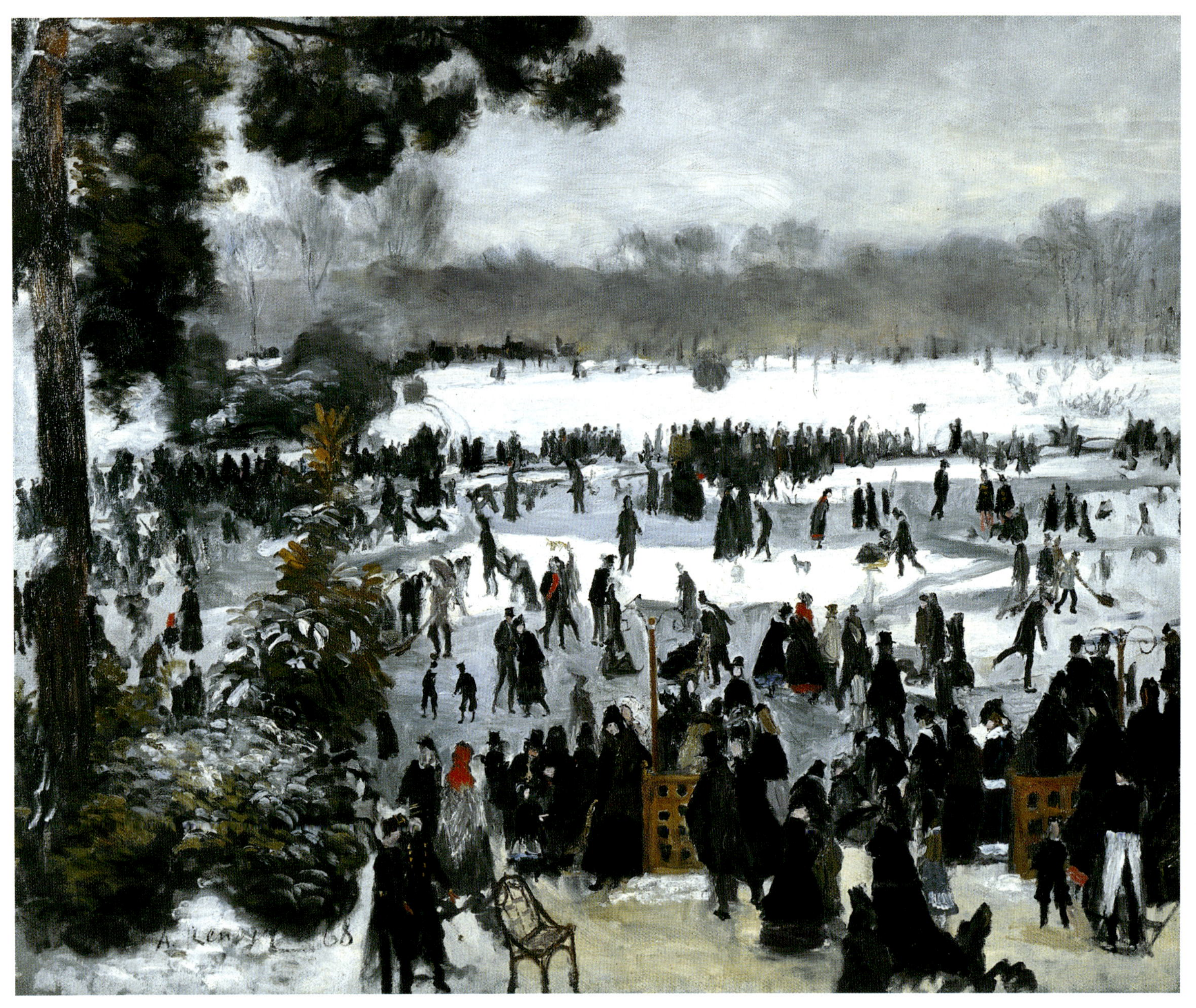

PIERRE-AUGUSTE RENOIR

French, 1841–1919
Ice-Skating in the Bois de Boulogne,
1868
Oil on canvas
28⅜ x 35⅜ in.

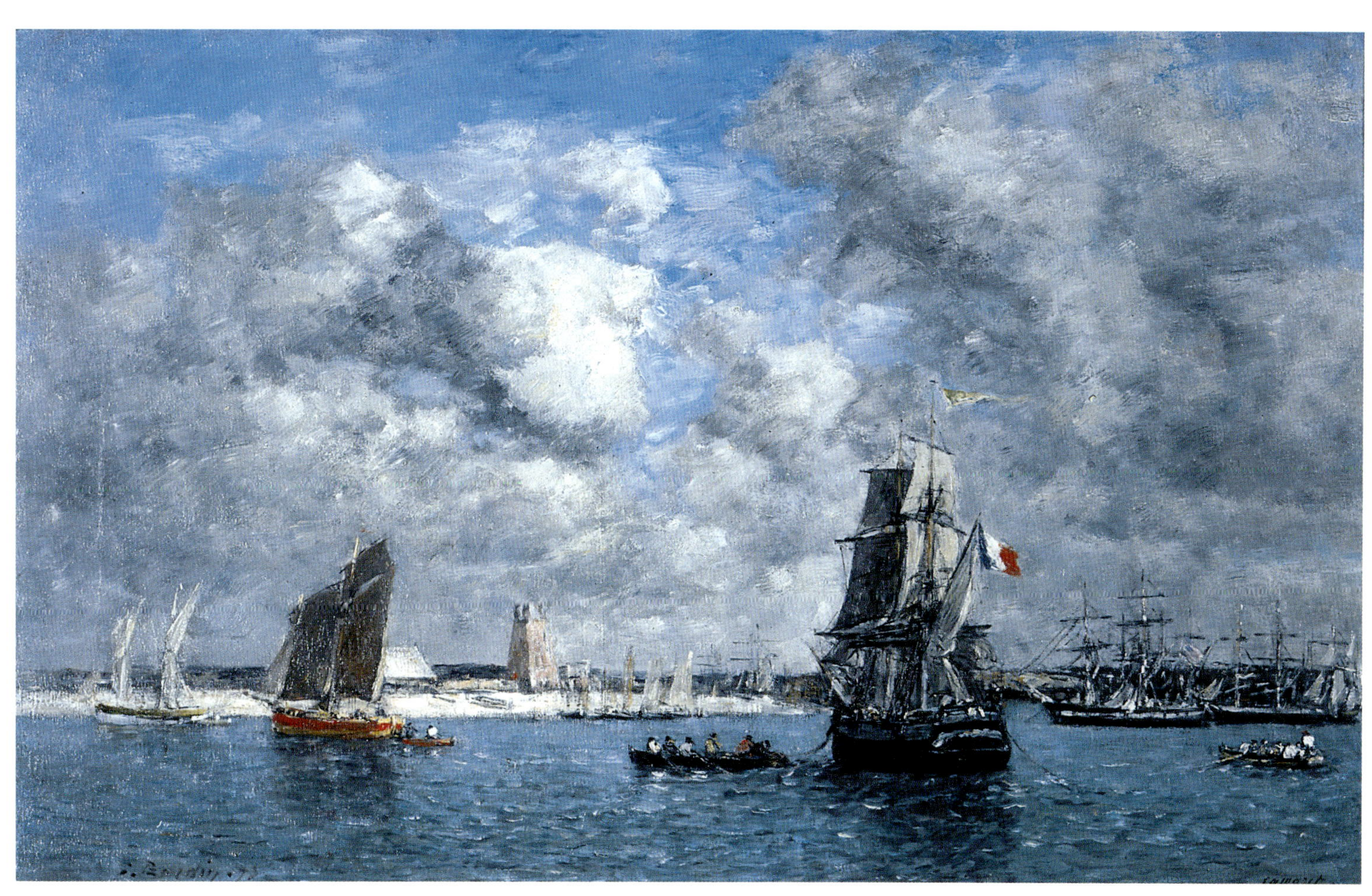

LOUIS-EUGÈNE BOUDIN

French, 1824–1898
Camaret, Fishing Boats Anchored in the Port, 1873
Oil on canvas
15¾ x 25¾ in.

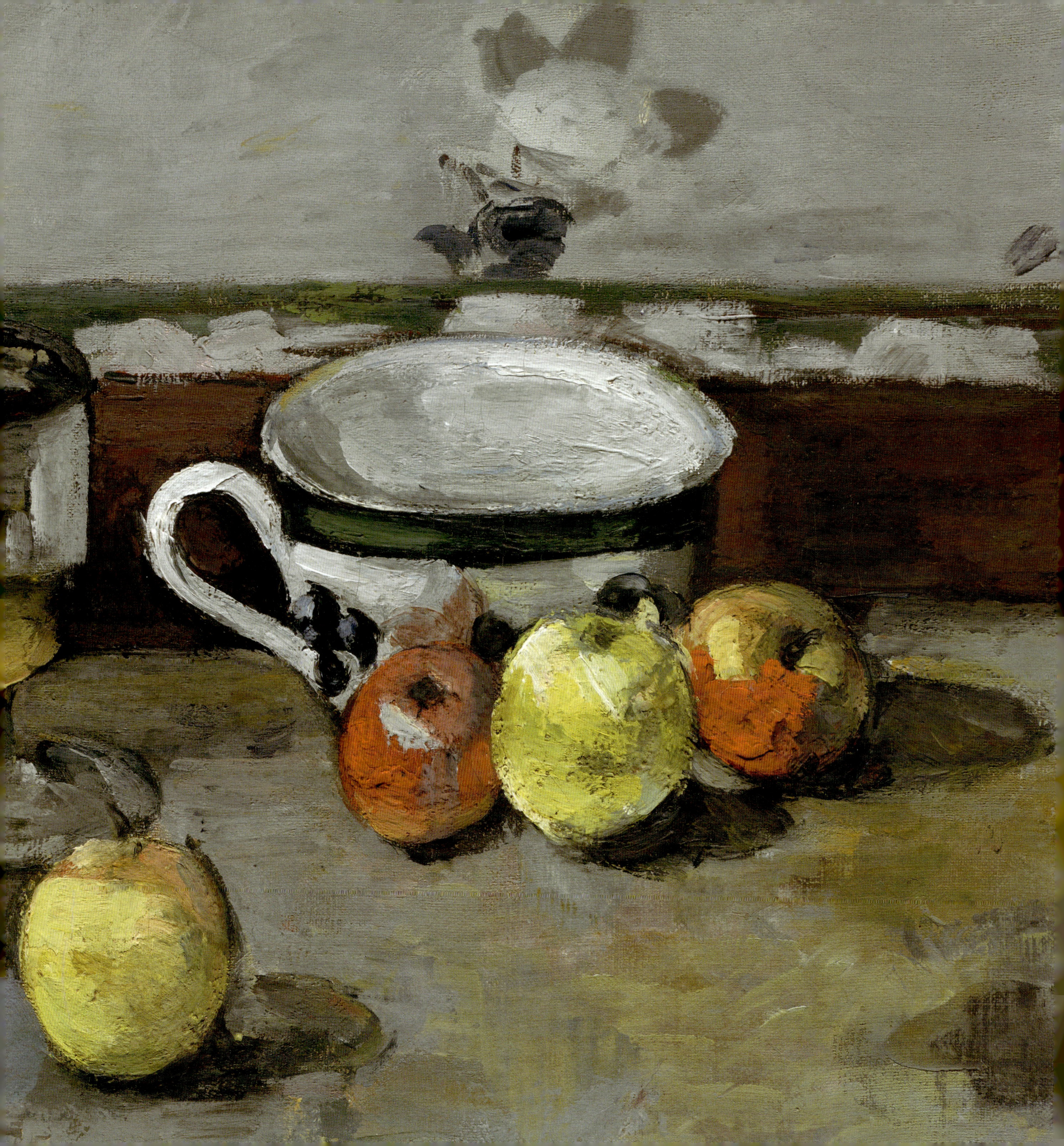

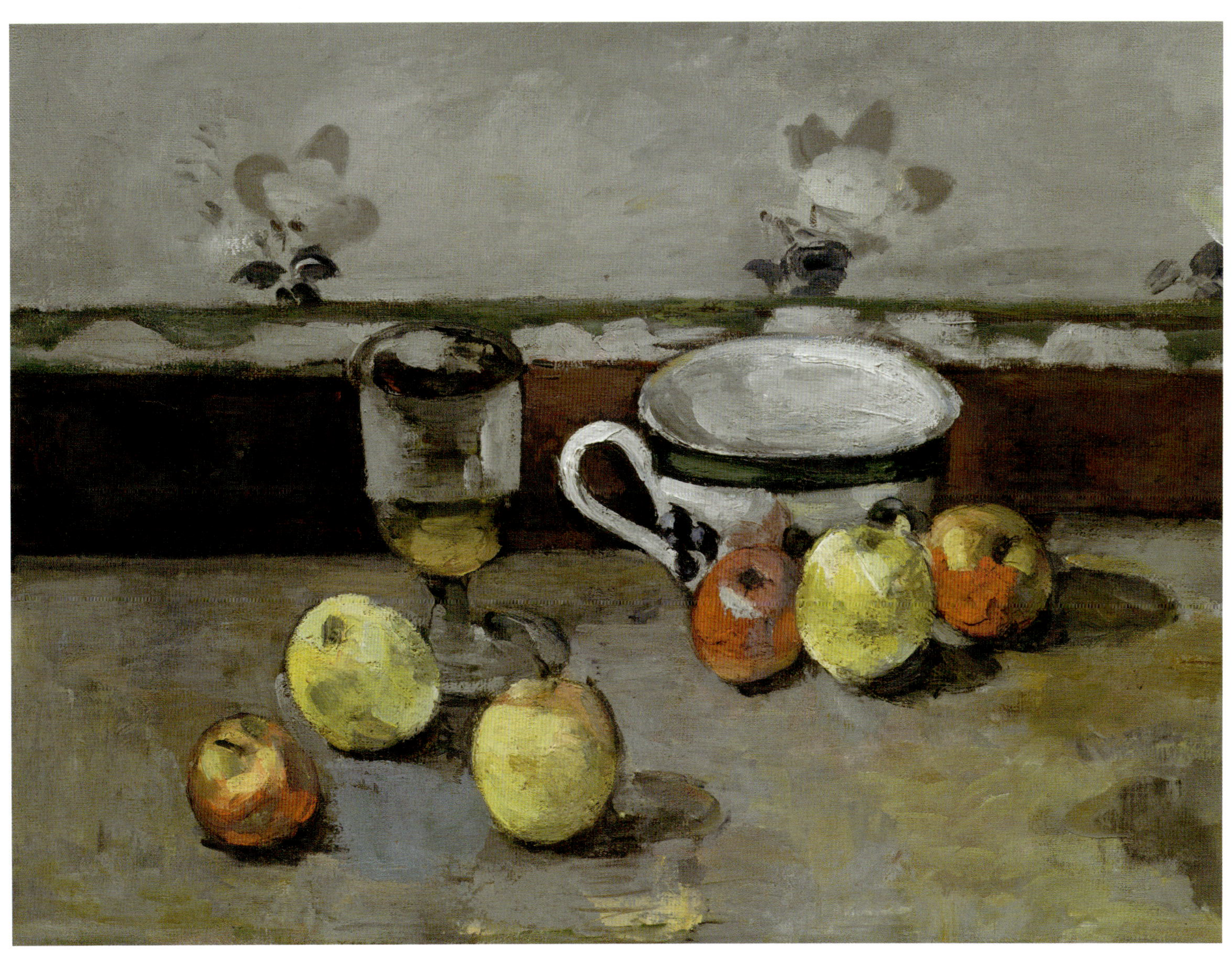

PAUL CÉZANNE

French, 1839–1906
Cup, Glass, and Fruit,
about 1873–77
Oil on canvas
16¼ x 21½ in.

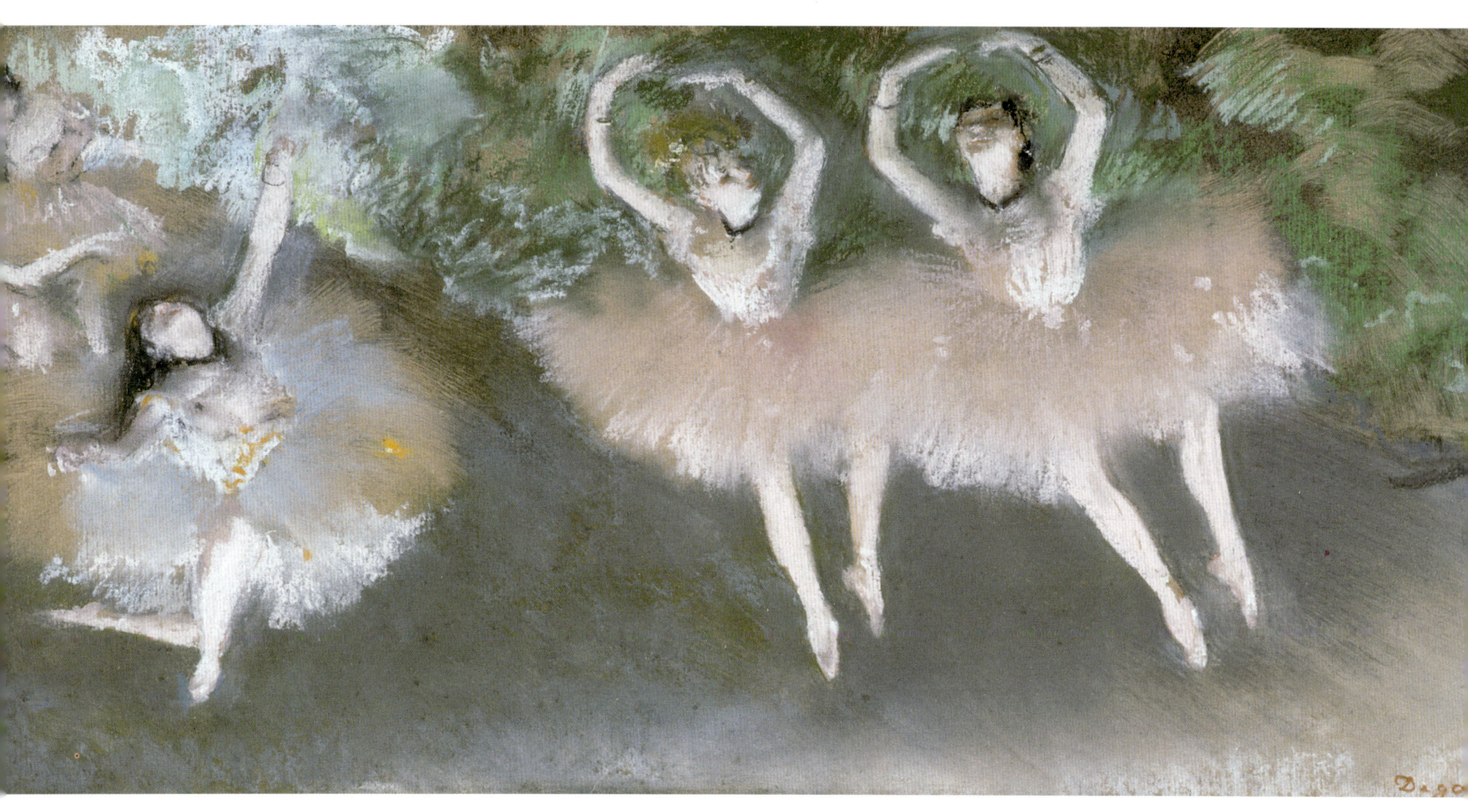

EDGAR DEGAS

French, 1834–1917
Ballet Dancers, about 1879
Pastel over monotype on paper
8 x 16 in.

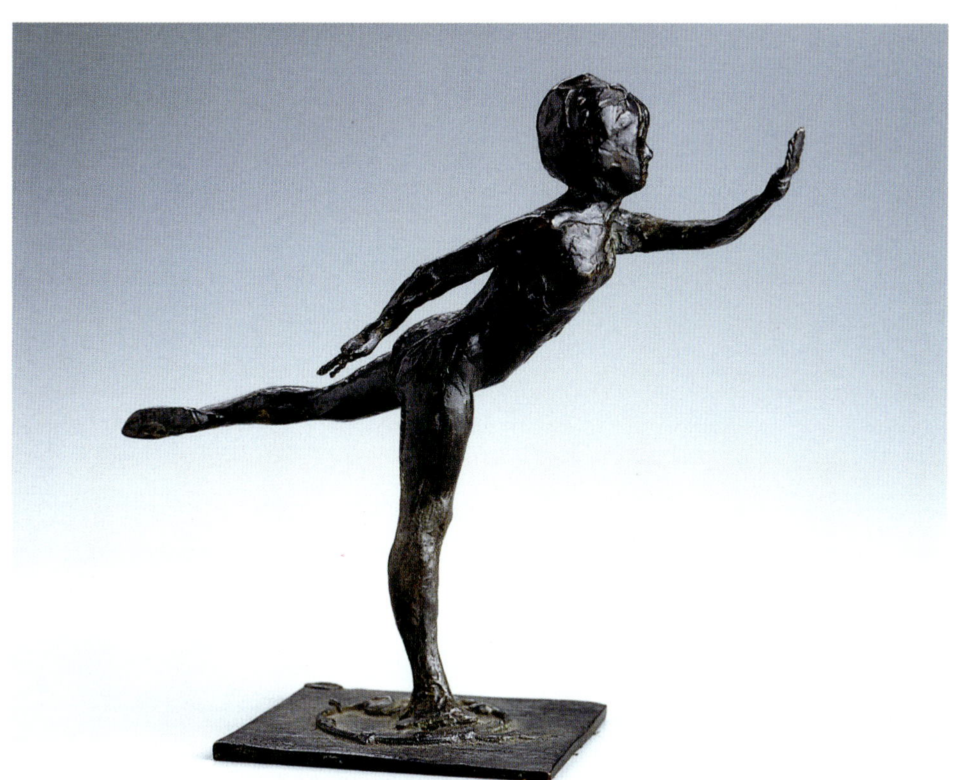

EDGAR DEGAS

French, 1834–1917
Open Arabesque on Right Leg,
modeled about 1882–95, cast after 1919
Bronze with brown patina
H. 8¼ in., w. 4 in., d. 9½ in.

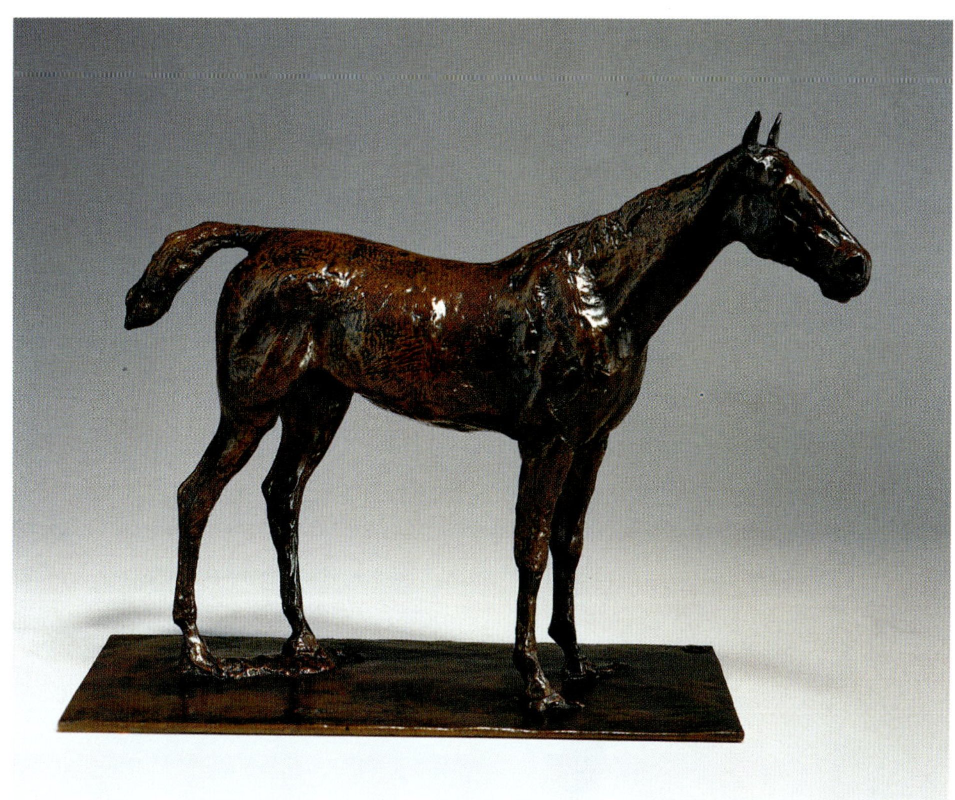

EDGAR DEGAS

French, 1834–1917
Standing Horse, modeled about
1865–81, cast after 1919
Bronze with brown patina
H. 11⅜ in., w. 7 in., d. 15¾ in.

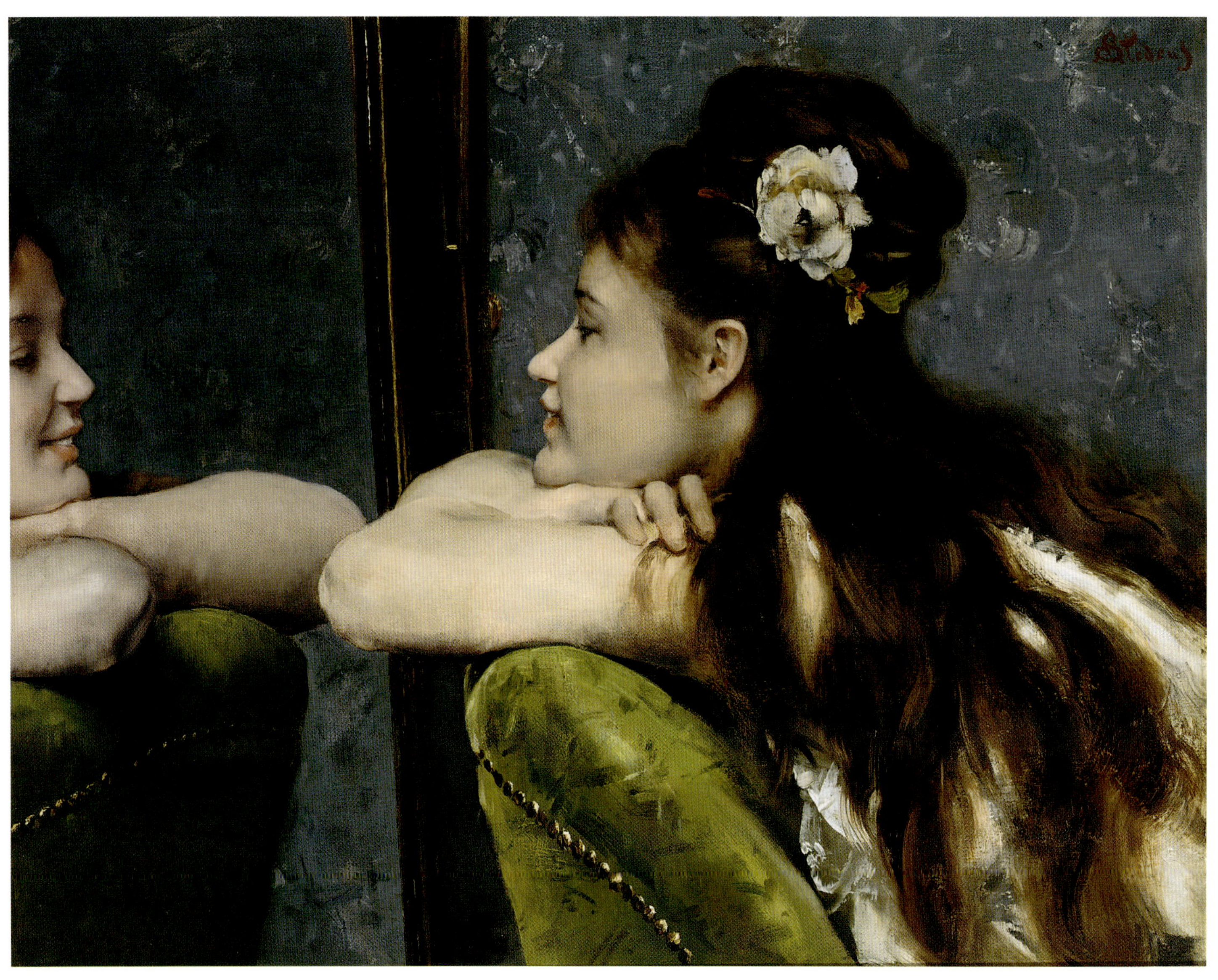

ALFRED STEVENS

Belgian, worked in France,
1823–1906
The Coquette, early 1870s
Oil on canvas
22⅛ x 28½ in.

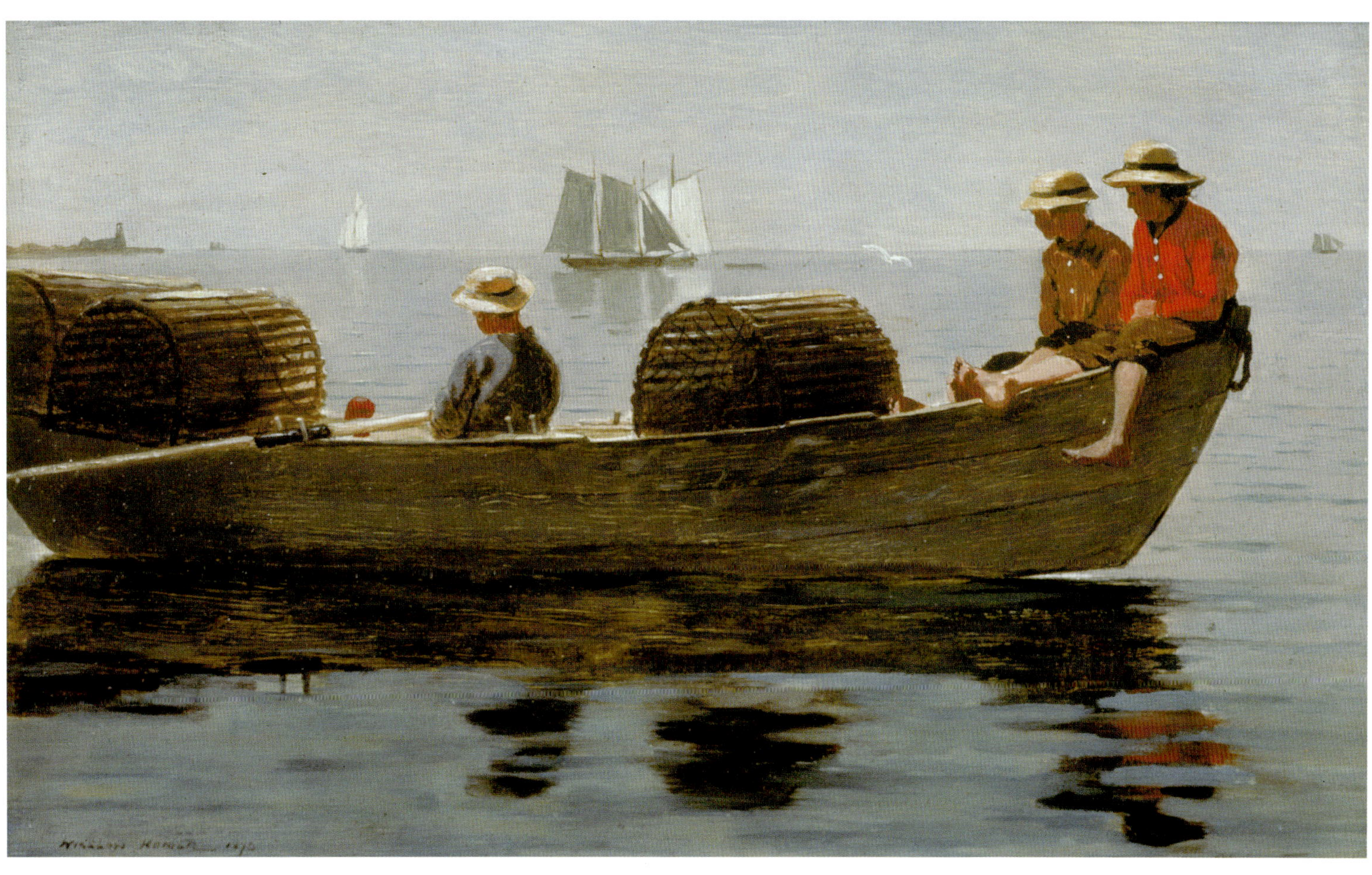

WINSLOW HOMER

American, 1836–1910
Three Boys in a Dory, 1873
Oil on panel
5⅞ x 10 in.

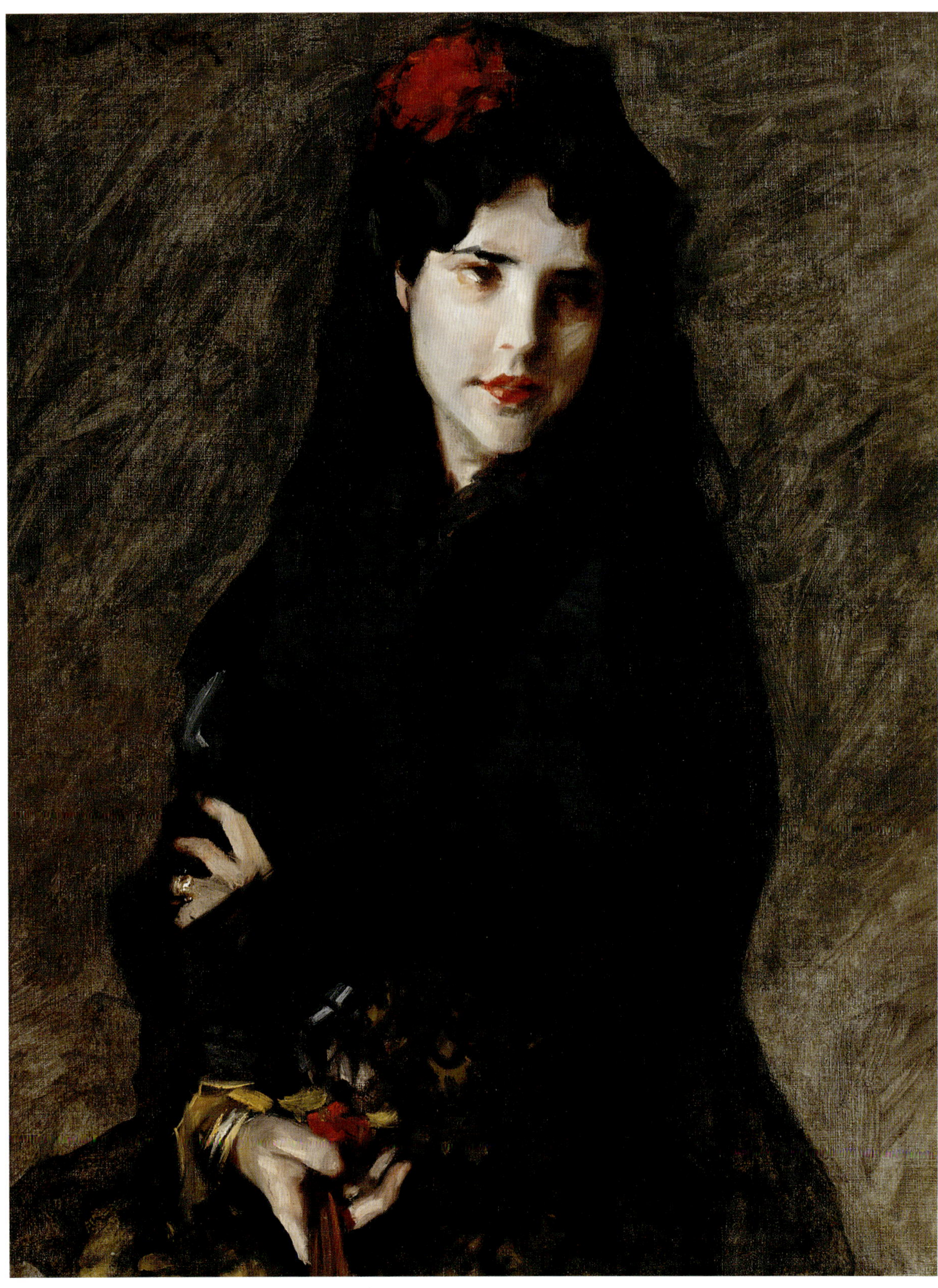

WILLIAM MERRITT CHASE

American, 1849–1916
Mrs. Chase in Spanish Costume,
about 1896
Oil on canvas
32 x 25 in.

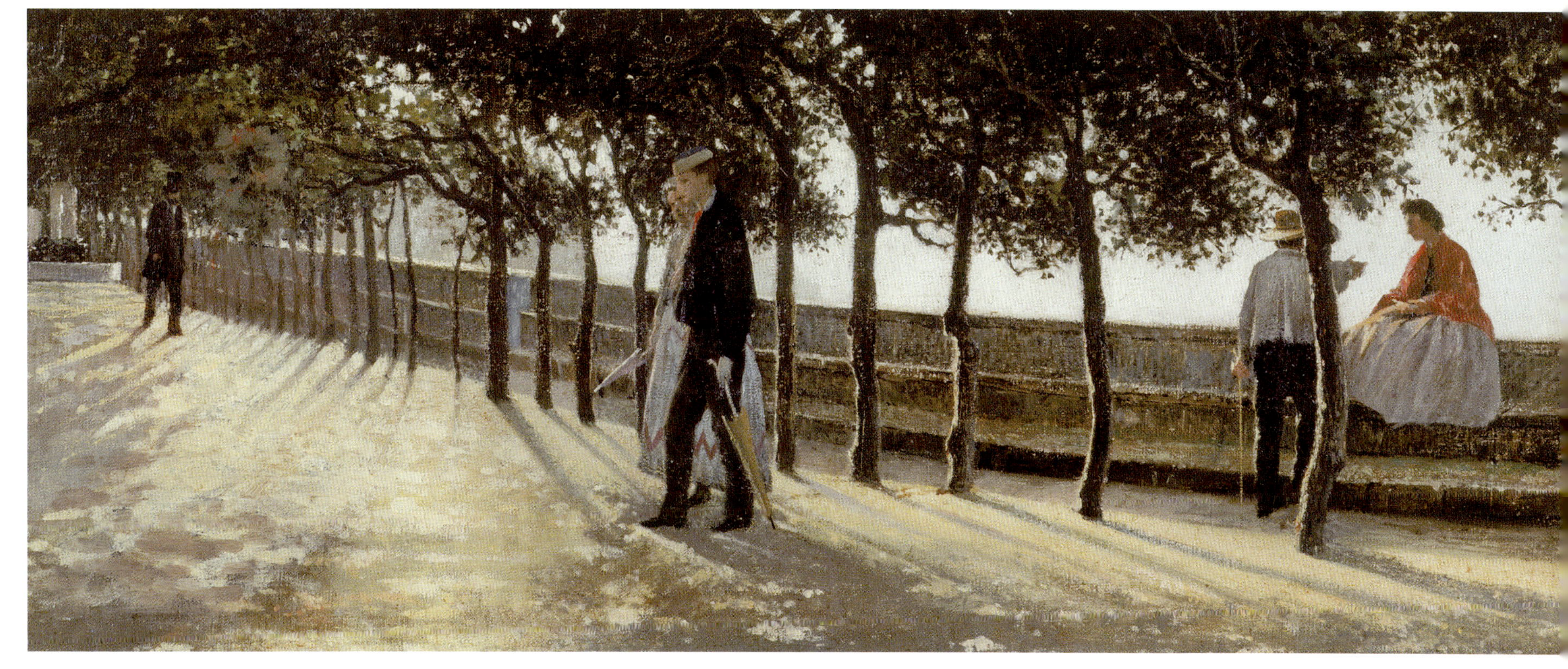

GIUSEPPE DE NITTIS

Italian, worked in France,
1846–1884
In the Woods of Portici, about 1865
Oil on canvas
8¾ x 21 in.

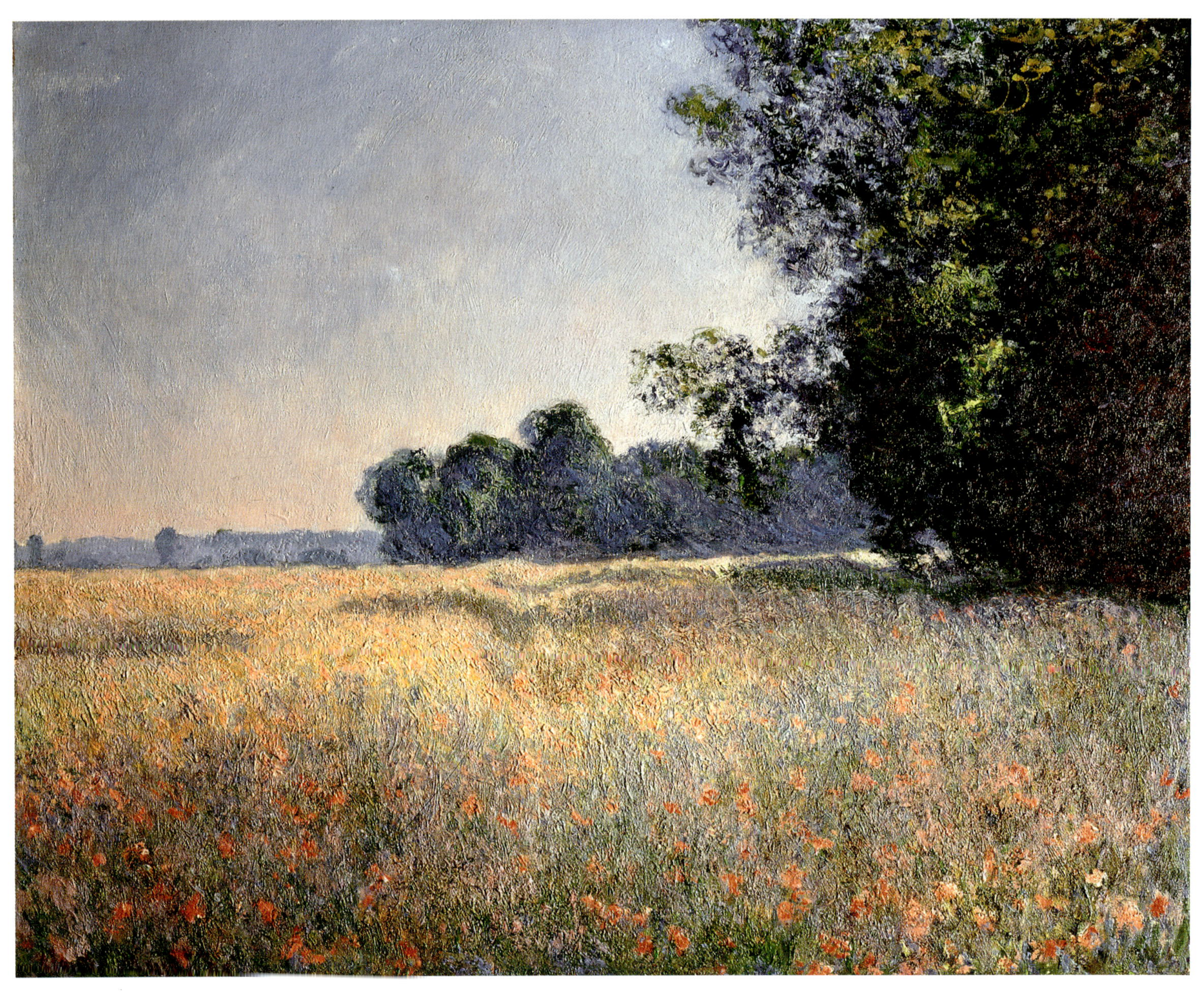

CLAUDE MONET

French, 1840–1926
Field of Oats and Poppies, 1890
Oil on canvas
28¾ x 36¼ in.

CLAUDE MONET

French, 1840–1926
Water Lilies, about 1908
Oil on canvas
39⅜ x 32 in.

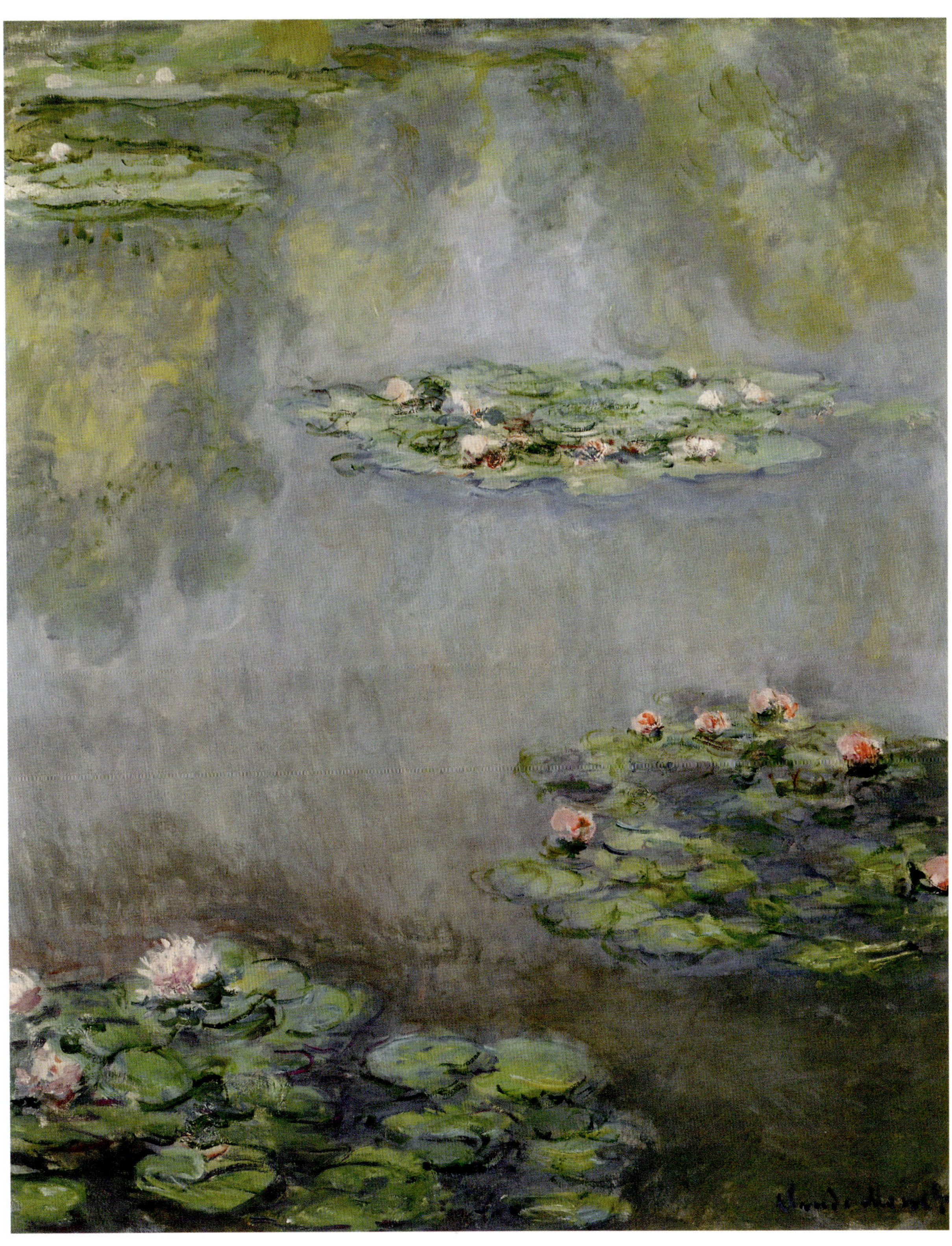

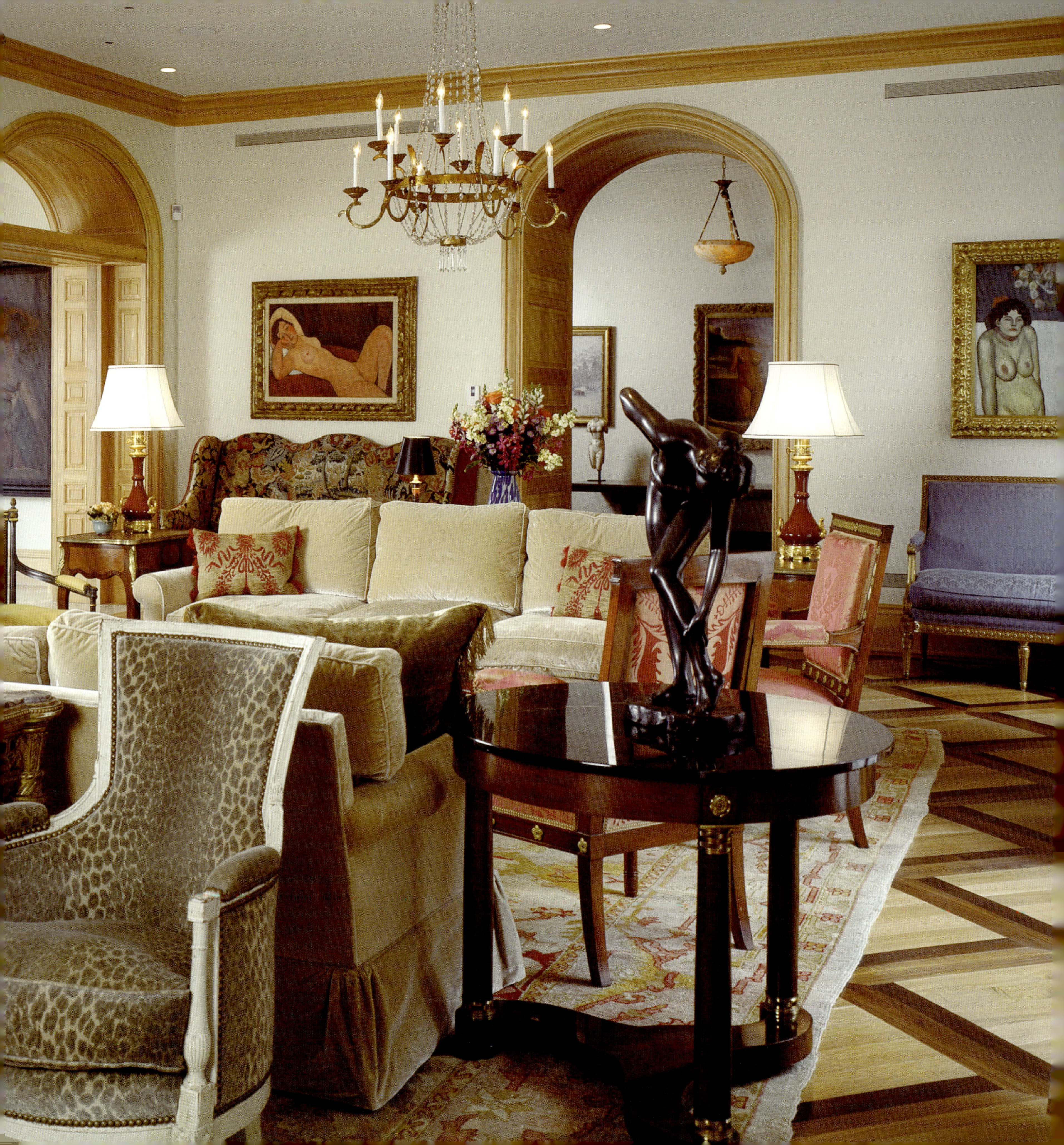

MODERN AND CONTEMPORARY ART

*****

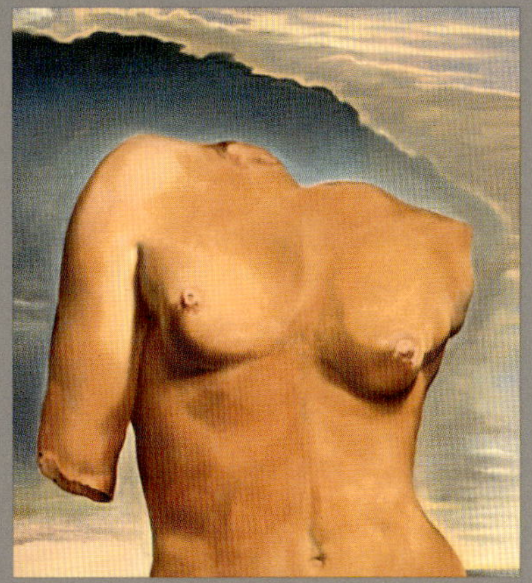

Fig. 18. The living room in Koch's
Palm Beach home

FERNANDO BOTERO

Colombian, born in 1932
Woman Smoking a Cigarette, 1987
Bronze with dark brown patina
H. 75 in., w. 49½ in., d. 135 in.

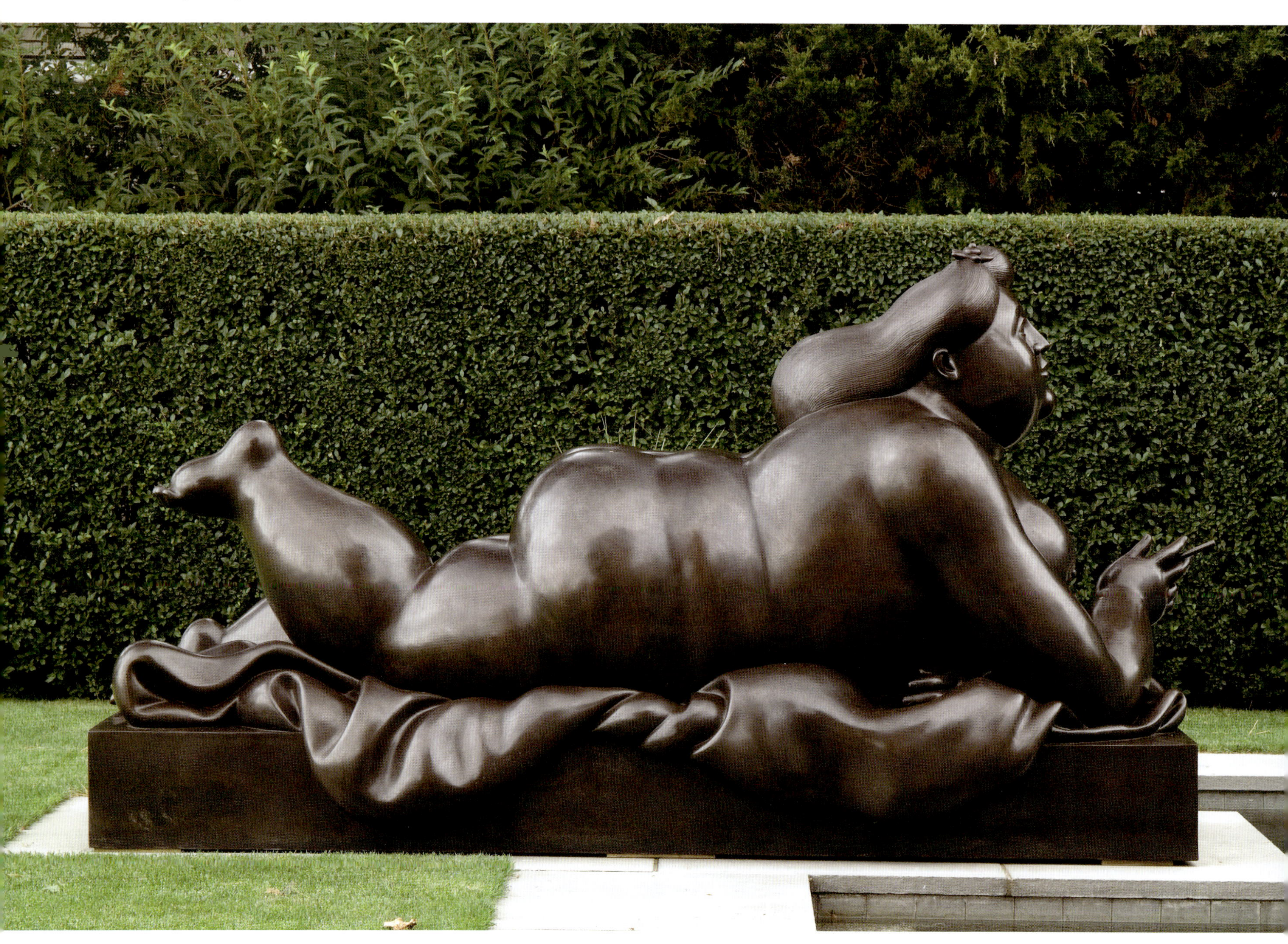

MODERN AND CONTEMPORARY ART

* * * * * * *

The Koch Collection of twentieth-century art is, like the collection as a whole, remarkably diverse, even eclectic. In addition to paintings by such universally recognized figures as Pablo Picasso and Henri Matisse, Koch has collected intriguing works by Tom Wesselmann, the Pop master of the female nude, and Altoon Sultan, a photorealist painter of the rural landscape. But these seemingly diverse paintings turn out to have a logic within the collector's sensibility. Wesselmann's *Seascape #20* (p. 94) is a contemporary continuation of a group of female nudes from the first half of the twentieth century, just as Sultan's *Farmyard, Cambridge, New York* (p. 95) fits into a selection of rural landscapes that includes works by Thomas Hart Benton (pp. 10 and 11) and Grant Wood (p. 12).

The central grouping of images of the female nude is anchored, chronologically, by Picasso's *Night Club Singer* (p. 67), a masterwork from the beginning of the artist's so-called Blue Period. The subject of the painting—is she a singer or a prostitute, or both?—stares grimly or smugly at the viewer, her shoulders hunched, her breasts hanging heavily above her swelling belly. Pushed to the side of the canvas, she sits isolated against the simple background of white and blue. She wears a red bow or flower in her hair (much like the one in William Merritt Chase's portrait of his wife, p. 58) and a coral-orange spotted or jeweled choker around her neck; her scarlet lips and dark pink nipples echo these colors, as do the red stockings of a dancing figure on the wall above her. It's unclear whether this figure is an element in the decor in which the model sits—perhaps a stylish reference to one of the many posters of dancers that were printed at the time (and which Picasso certainly knew)—or, in the manner of a Symbolist portrait by Odilon Redon, a projection of the sitter's imagination.

Picasso's glum vision of a woman on the fringes of society echoed his own increasing marginalization. Although still a young man, in the wake of a successful first Parisian exhibition, he was keenly aware of the difficult position of the artist in society; his subjects, in every medium, reflected that pessimism. In *Carmelina* (fig. 19), one of the Museum of Fine Arts' best-known twentieth-century paintings, Picasso's contemporary Matisse turned to a similar subject. His female nude, begun only two years after Picasso completed the *Night Club Singer*, differs from Picasso's despondent mood, eliciting instead a forceful confrontation between model and audience. The viewer in Matisse's painting is synonymous with the painter—whose image can be discerned in a mirror at left.

On the reverse of the *Night Club Singer* is another painting, only recently discovered in the process of restoration (p. 67). Painted when Picasso was just nineteen, at lightning speed and perhaps under the influence of alcohol, it is a satirical portrait of his friend and dealer, the Catalan Pedro Manach. It depicts Manach's head, with a turban, on a female body with two necklaces; the figure is dancing and urinating at the same time. It was to be a birthday present—the inscription translates "A souvenir to Manach on his Saint's Day"—and probably reflects Picasso's affection for his friend, as well as his resentment of Manach's exploitation of him as his dealer. Later, Picasso reused the canvas for the depiction of the naked singer.

The dark cynicism of Picasso's *Night Club Singer* and the disquieting defiance of Matisse's *Carmelina* contrast with the aims of two sculptors who were working at the same time: Aristide Maillol and Wilhelm Lehmbruck. Although Maillol is known today as a sculptor, his earliest work is pictorial. He was a member of the Nabis group—with Pierre Bonnard, Maurice Denis, and Edouard Vuillard—and, like them, was strongly influenced by Japanese art and by the stylized paintings of the post-Impressionist master Paul Gauguin. Maillol's *Bather with Raised Arms* (p. 78) of 1900 is among the artist's first large-scale sculptures, an amalgam of Gauguin's Tahitian nudes and ancient Greek statuary. Pure, static, and almost emotionless, the woman raises her hands to her shoulders in a self-referential gesture that Maillol sometimes transformed and heightened by the addition of a garland of flowers between the model's fingers. She is presented without context, yet her form seems to suggest an architectural purpose. In fact, Maillol once said that what

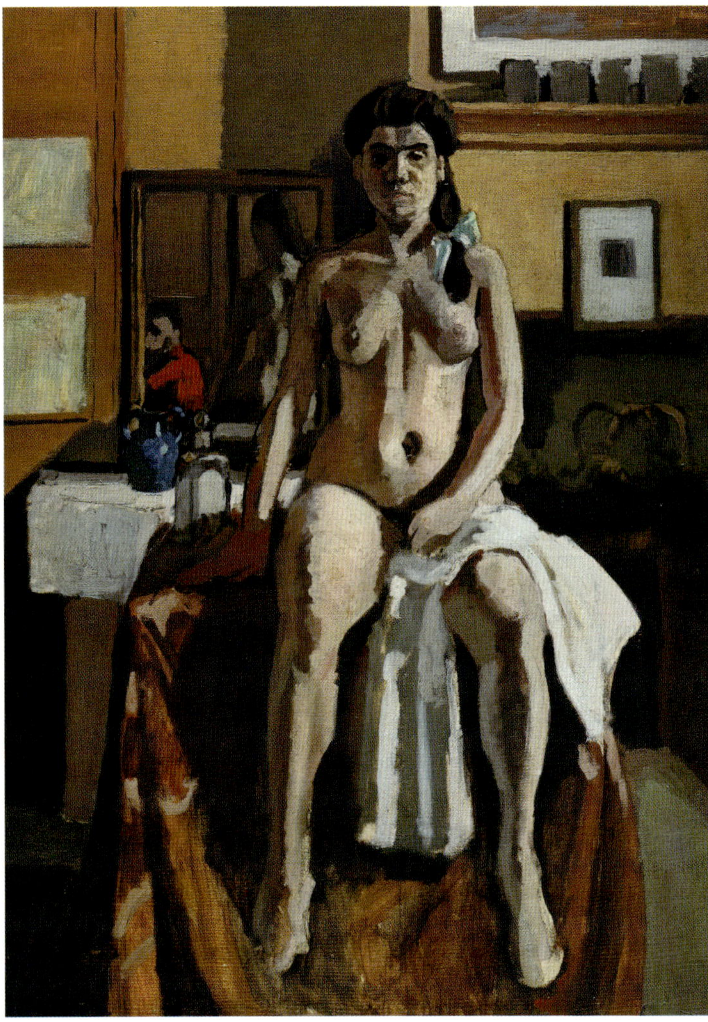

Fig. 19. Henri Matisse (French, 1869–1954), *Carmelina*, 1903, oil on canvas, 32 x 23¼ in., Museum of Fine Arts, Boston, Tompkins Collection, 1932, RES.32.14, © 2005 Succession H. Matisse, Paris / Artists Rights Society (ARS), New York

he was "striving for [was] architecture and volume. Sculpture," in his view, was "architecture, . . . the equilibrium of the masses, . . . composition with taste."[1]

Lehmbruck, one of the most important sculptors of the German Expressionist movement, began his career in Düsseldorf, studying at the Academy there. *Bathing Woman* (p. 74), his first major work, modeled about 1902, treads a fine line between natural gesture in the manner of Degas's bathers and a seductive elegance—the figure is at once ungainly and graceful, straining to reach down to her ankle and yet twisting her body into a pose of coy vulnerability. A bronze cast of the composition was acquired by the Düsseldorf Academy in 1905, giving impetus to the sculptor's continuing exploration of the nude figure, which eventually led to the highly stylized and attenuated—almost mannerist—statues of nude men and women that marked Lehmbruck's work from 1910 until his suicide in 1919.

Stylization and attenuation characterize the work of Amedeo Modigliani, an Italian painter and sculptor who settled in Paris in 1906. Among his most important works of 1910 to 1920 is a series of drawings and carvings of upright female nudes or caryatids that, like Maillol's *Bather with Raised Arms*, seem destined to serve some architectural purpose. Modigliani's *Reclining Nude* (p. 76) of 1917, by contrast, is horizontal and frankly seductive, displaying her glowing body with languorous directness. Like Matisse's *Carmelina*, she meets the gaze of the painter and the viewer, but hers is not a challenging expression; instead, she seems completely relaxed. The painter emphasizes the model's elongated torso by massing her arms in a circle around her head at upper left, and by bending her knee to raise her leg into a balancing form at the lower right. Modigliani displayed her body against a background of glowing red, drawing an erotic connection between her eyes, lips, breasts, and genitals. When he first showed his series of thirty nudes in 1917, the exhibition was forced to close by the Paris police, who found that his frank display of flesh and body hair was an affront to public mores.[2]

Little more than a decade later, at the end of the 1920s, Matisse painted *Young Woman Made-up in Oriental Style* (p. 77), part of a series of odalisques—seated or reclining nudes in exotic middle-eastern costume—that he had begun early in the decade. Leaving Paris in 1917 to settle in Nice, on the French Riviera, Matisse had sought there the color and light of the south, and over the succeeding decade, he studied the female nude in a variety of poses, often displaying the figure against elaborately patterned draperies or carpets. In 1928 Matisse relocated his studio to a large, bright space on the fourth floor of his apartment building, and his work became both more luminous and simpler.[3] In this painting, for example, the nude and the Moroccan-style chair on which she sits are freely sketched in pink, with touches of black applied as accents—notably on the starlike "tattoos" on the woman's face and chest. The model is shown against the pure white ground of the canvas, with only patches of yellow, pink, and green to hint at the decor of the studio.

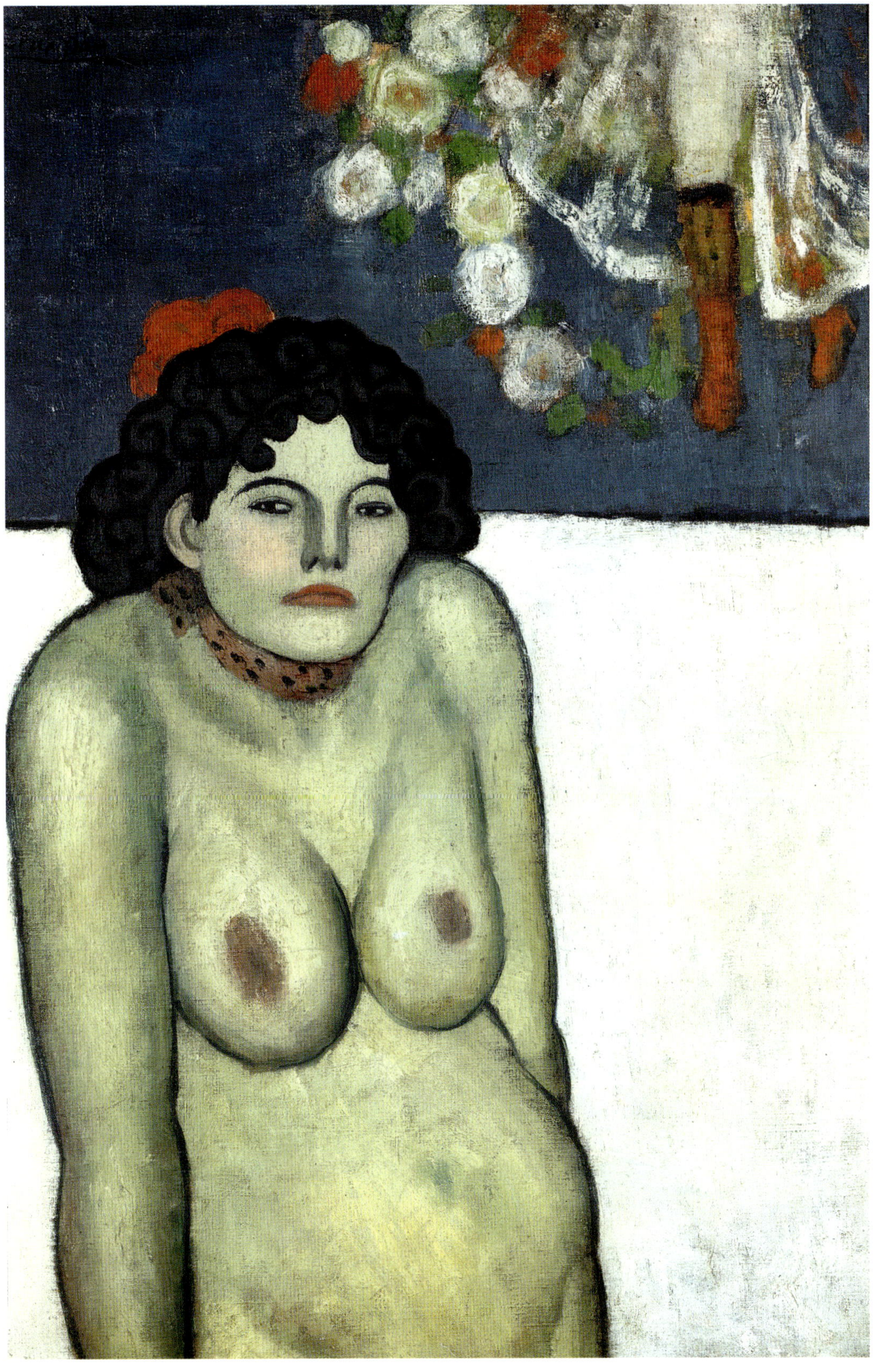

PABLO PICASSO

Spanish, worked in France,
1881–1973
Night Club Singer, 1901
Oil on canvas
31⅞ x 21¾ in.
© 2005 Estate of Pablo Picasso / Artists Rights Society (ARS), New York

Below:
Reverse of *Night Club Singer*
© 2005 Estate of Pablo Picasso / Artists Rights Society (ARS), New York

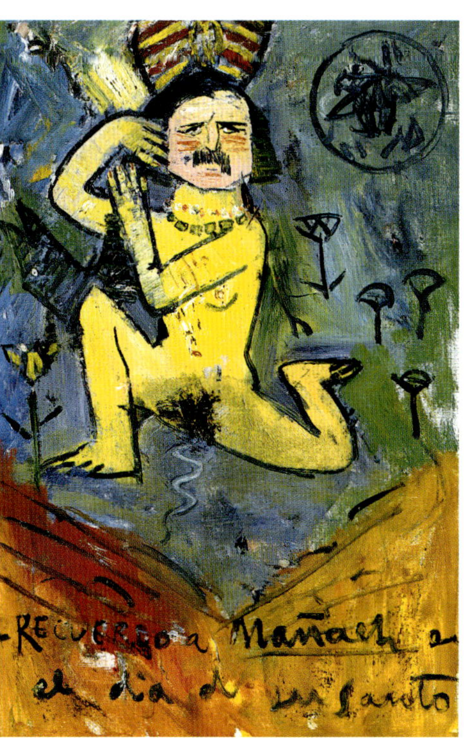

This simplified execution, which gives Matisse's painting a great sense of intimacy and immediacy, is paralleled in other works in the Koch Collection. Kees van Dongen's *Reclining Nude* of 1935–40 (p. 80) is a mature work by the Rotterdam native who had come to Paris at the end of the nineteeenth century. With Matisse, Van Dongen had explored the intense color and bravura brushstrokes of Fauvism in the early years of the century; the sketchlike application of paint here recalls his earlier experiments. Matisse was also a formative influence on a younger artist, the American Milton Avery, whose early paintings, with subtly modulated colors, gave way, in the years after World War II, to highly simplified compositions in a few, pure colors, sometimes separated by thin contours of black. The painter's *White Chemise* of 1961 (p. 81) juxtaposes the model in her slip with a background of luminous red and purple, worthy of Avery's young friend Mark Rothko.

Two enigmatic paintings in the Koch Collection depict female nudes against vast stretches of water, felicitously reflecting the waterside settings of Koch's homes in Palm Beach and Osterville. The earlier of these is by René Magritte, the Belgian Surrealist, celebrated for his unexpected arrangements of people and objects in disquieting spaces or settings. Magritte's 1941 *The Clearing* (p. 83) shows three versions of the same woman facing away from the viewer, toward a distant horizon; blue curtains frame the scene at left and right, but whether they are draperies at a window or door, or theatrical curtains, is left to the viewer's imagination. The figures gesture mysteriously: one holds her hands before her as a singer might at the end of a performance; another raises both arms, her left hand supporting a dove; the third holds in her raised right hand a single rose. The figures at the left, who are draped to the hip, recall ancient images of Venus—the famous Venus de Milo, most notably—and the three, as a group, must surely make reference to the three Graces of ancient legend.

Similarly, Salvador Dalí's *Rhinocerontic Gooseflesh* (p. 82), an oil of 1956, refers to the birth of Venus. Dalí, born in the Catalan province of Spain but active in Paris from the late 1920s, was obsessed with the world of dreams and fantasy. The poet-theorist of Surrealism, André Breton, said, "It is perhaps with Dalí that for the first time the windows of the mind are opened fully wide."[4] In the Koch Collection's painting, a headless, armless torso floats above a form that combines elements of shell and wave, against a background

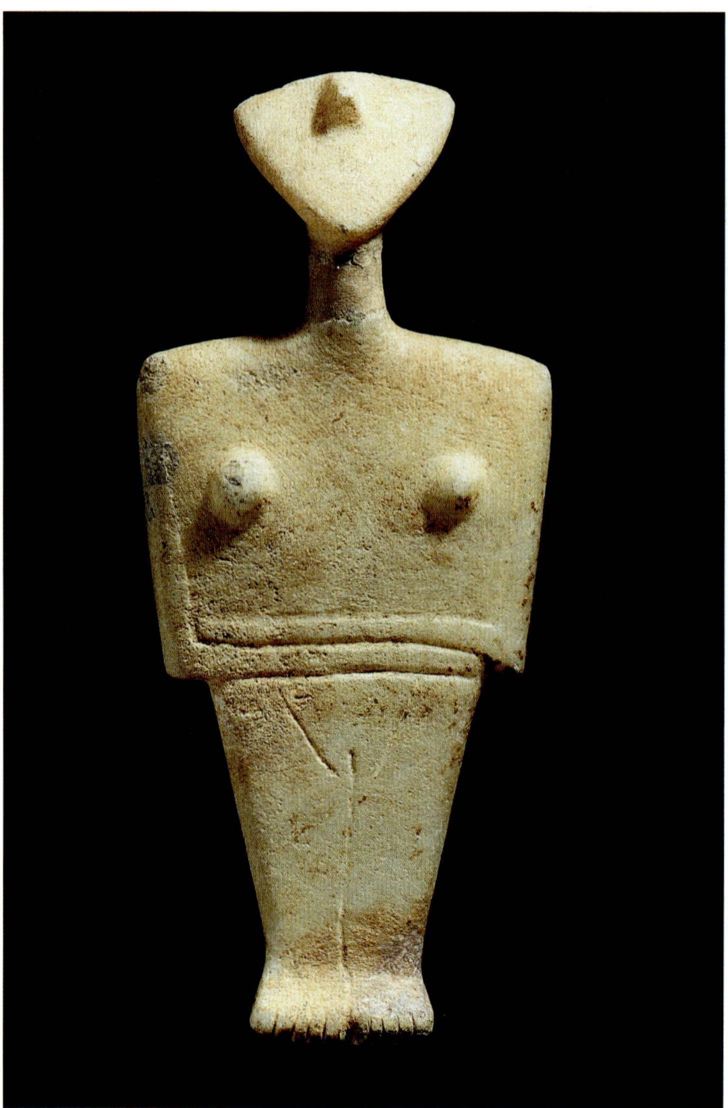

Fig. 20. *Female figure (idol)*, from the Cyclades, Bronze Age, about 2300–2000 B.C., h. 7⅞ in., Museum of Fine Arts, Boston, Gift of Mr. and Mrs. J. J. Klejman, 1961, 61.1089

HANS (JEAN) ARP

German, worked in France and Switzerland, 1886–1966
Mythical Figure, 1950
Polished bronze
H. 45 in., w. 14½ in., d. 13½ in.

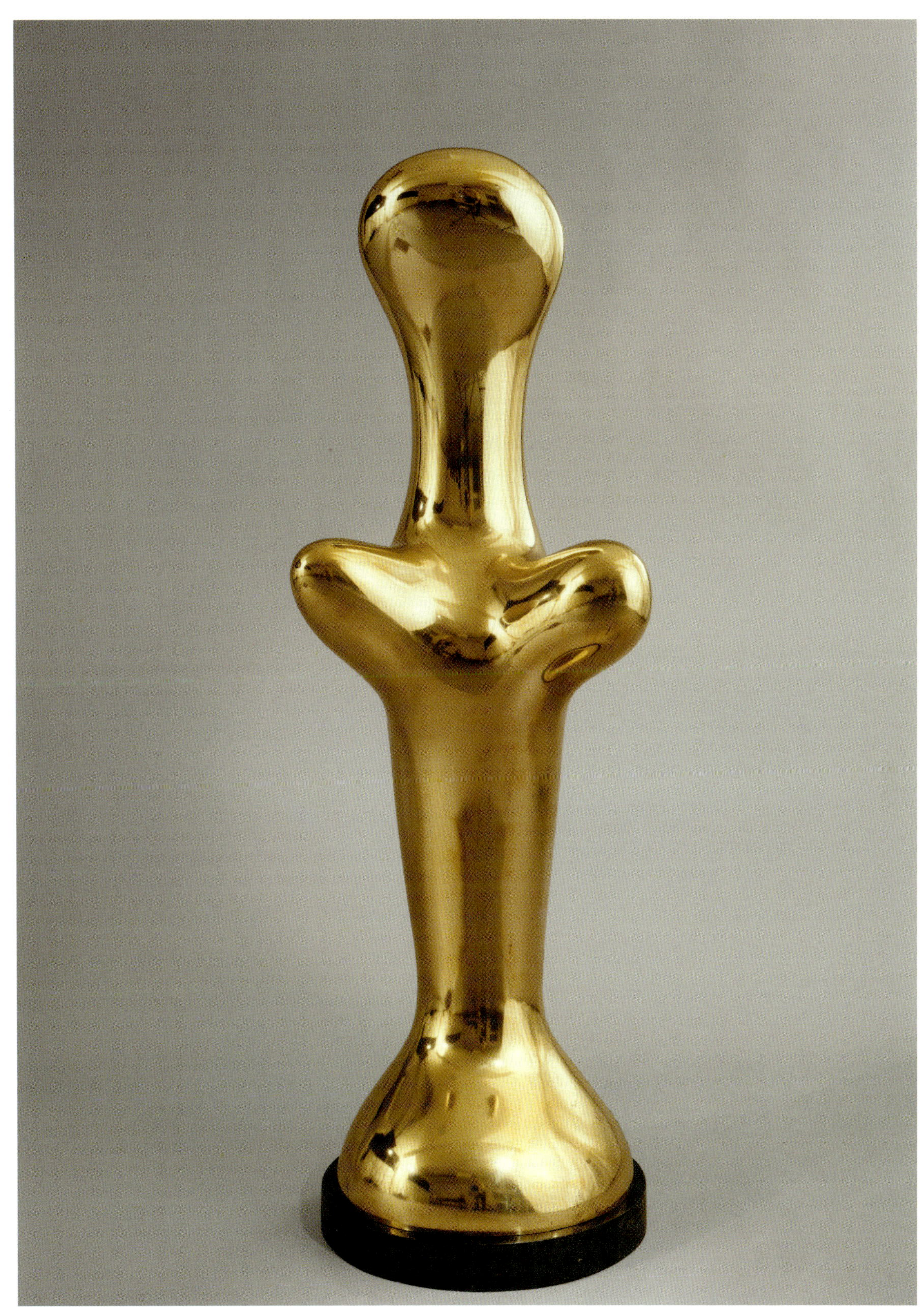

of sea and clouds that seem to caress the form of the body. Like Pygmalion, Magritte and Dalí brought ancient sculpture to life; a Roman marble torso of Aphrodite (p. 82), from the first or second century, is displayed in Koch's home beside Dalí's painting.

Something of the qualities of archaic sculpture can be discerned in Hans Arp's *Mythical Figure*, of 1950 (p. 69). Arp was involved with the Dada and Surrealist movements in his early years, but by 1950 was best known for "biomorphic" sculpture in wood, stone, or metal. His painted cut-out reliefs and sculpture in the round suggest plant or animal forms without precise reference, although the titles he gave to his works sometimes hint at their connection to ancient subject matter. Made of bronze so highly polished that it looks as if it were cast in gold, *Mythical Figure*—nearly four feet tall—seems to rise up, arms lifted, head held high. The sculpture, for all its biomorphic modernity, has the timeless simplicity of Bronze Age carvings from the Cyclades, such as an idol in the Museum's collection (fig. 20); like these figures, it is totemic, perfect, inscrutable. But for some viewers, it has an inviting side: in spite of the hardness of its bronze surface and its polished perfection, it is a favorite work of Koch's daughter, who as a toddler would rush to embrace it several times a day. Her proud father never told her not to touch.

That spirit of play, of unspoiled pleasure and joy in works of art, can be seen in another group of works in Koch's twentieth-century collection. Although the subject of the German painter Gabriele Münter's 1909 *Child with Doll* (p. 75) seems poised between contemplation and melancholy, the artist's admiration for folk art and technique—which she shared with her lover Wassily Kandinsky—reveals itself in simplified contours and colors, coinciding perfectly with the childlike theme. Similarly, when Picasso—a master then in his seventies—painted his son Claude and daughter Paloma playing (and drawing, perhaps) he adapted his style to his subject, drawing with the simplicity and innocence of his young children (p. 84). The Russian Expressionist Marc Chagall, in turn, celebrated the joys of life in his *Dancer in a Floral Dress*, a late work of about 1971 (p. 91).

Joan Miró had made the innocent simplicity of children's art part of his visual vocabulary in the 1920s, in Surrealist works of extreme sophistication, sometimes combining writing with strange animal- or plantlike forms floating in space, connected by webs of wiggling lines. As late as 1950, in such works as the Koch Collection's *Woman and Cat* (p. 92), he played on the language of the stick figures common in children's drawings, making a circular blob, a dot, and a dash stand in for head, eye, and mouth, a curve for arms, two strokes for legs. By 1973, however, he had seen his own language of lines and shapes transformed by a younger generation—specifically, by the young painters who rose to prominence in New York after World War II. Miró's *Bird Woman* of 1973 (p. 93), with its broad, calligraphic strokes of black, its isolated patches of primary color, and an emphatic pattern of drips at the lower right, looks back at his Surrealist images of the 1930s and reshapes his own iconography through the gestural language of postwar abstraction.

Nowhere is Koch's delight in play more present than in the group of bronzes he has collected by the sculptor Fernando Botero. Botero, born in Colombia in 1932, arrived at a signature style—characterized by "fattened" or "inflated" figures that balance sweetness with grotesqueness—in his New York paintings of the 1960s, which offer wry commentary on the history of art. Moving to Paris in the early 1970s, Botero took up sculpture, to which he applied the same stylistic idiosyncrasies, treating themes from daily life as well as ancient myth. The collection includes a portrait in oils of Koch's son Wyatt (p. 73), painted in 1995, as well as eleven bronzes by the artist. In Koch's garden, Botero's *Man with a Cane* and *Woman with an Umbrella*, both about 1977, are joined by a little girl and a dog, both sculpted in 1981, and a 1995 cat to make up an assembled family (p. 31). Botero's sculpture *Cat*, from 1984, stalks a *Little Bird*, from 1988 (p. 71). And by a fountain, the Colombian sculptor's *Woman Smoking a Cigarette*, made in 1987 (p. 64), provides a postmodern complement to the great nudes of the first decades of the twentieth century that Koch displays indoors—paintings by Picasso, Matisse, and Modigliani, and sculpture by Maillol.

—GEORGE T. M. SHACKELFORD

1. Aristide Maillol, in *Maillol: Sa vie, son oeuvre, ses idées*, by Judith Cladel (Paris: Editions Bernard Grasset, 1937), quoted in *French Art Treasures at the Hermitage: Splendid Masterpieces, New Discoveries*, by Albert Kostenevich (New York: Harry N. Abrams, 1999), 240.

2. Lisa N. Peters et al., *A Personal Gathering: Paintings and Sculptures from the Collection of William I. Koch* (Wichita, Kans.: Wichita Art Museum, 1996), 30.

3. See John Elderfield, *Henri Matisse: A Retrospective* (New York: Museum of Modern Art, 1992), 295.

4. Quoted in Fiona Bradley, "Salvador Dalí," *Grove Art Online*, Oxford University Press, accessed January 5, 2005, http://www.groveart.com.

FERNANDO BOTERO

Colombian, born in 1932
Cat, 1984
Bronze with red-brown patina
H. 41 in., w. 30 in., d. 134 in.
© Fernando Botero, courtesy,
Marlborough Gallery, New York

FERNANDO BOTERO

Colombian, born in 1932
Little Bird, 1988
Bronze with light brown patina
H. 15¾ in., w. 16½ in., d. 14½ in.
© Fernando Botero, courtesy,
Marlborough Gallery, New York

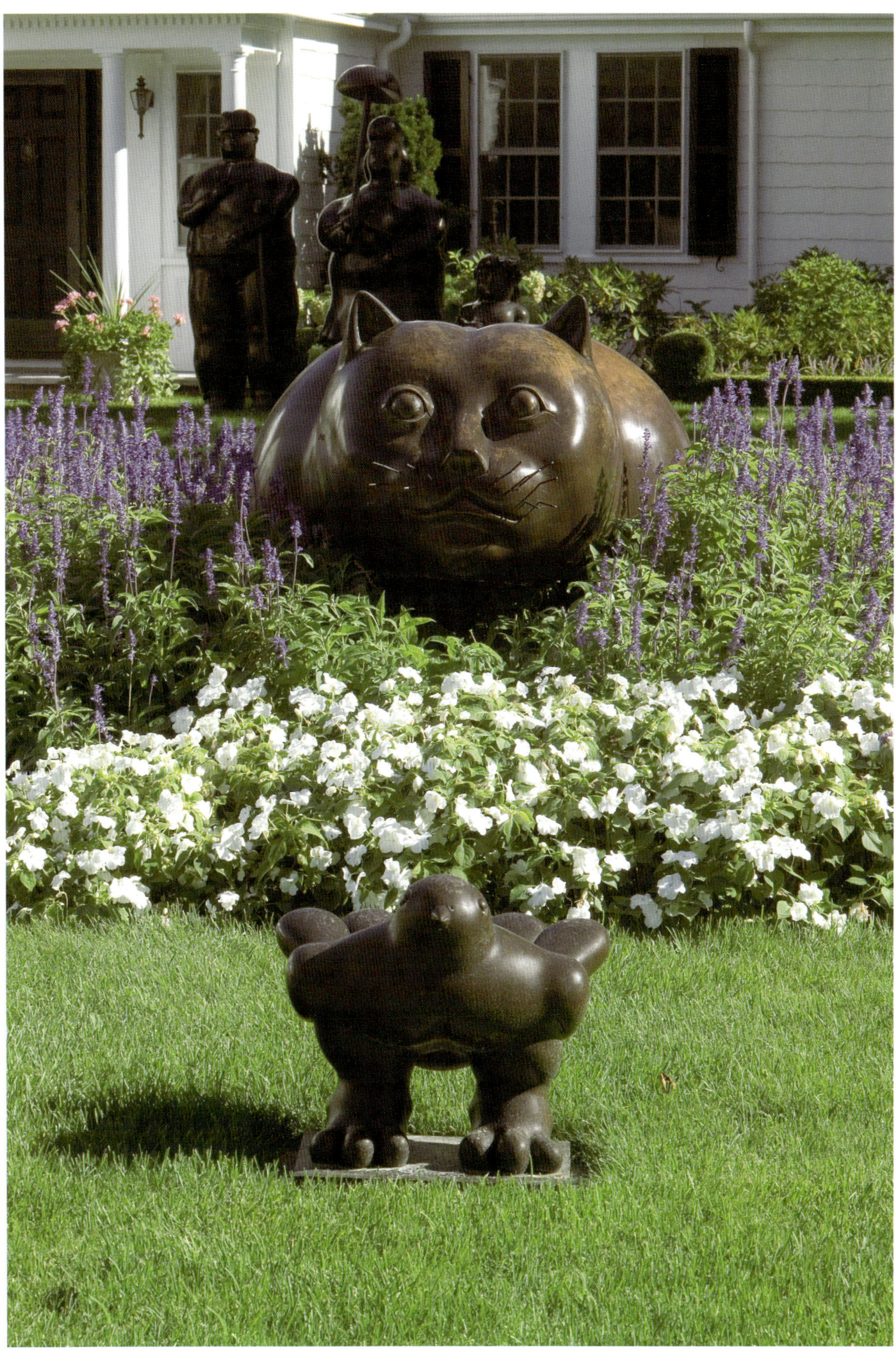

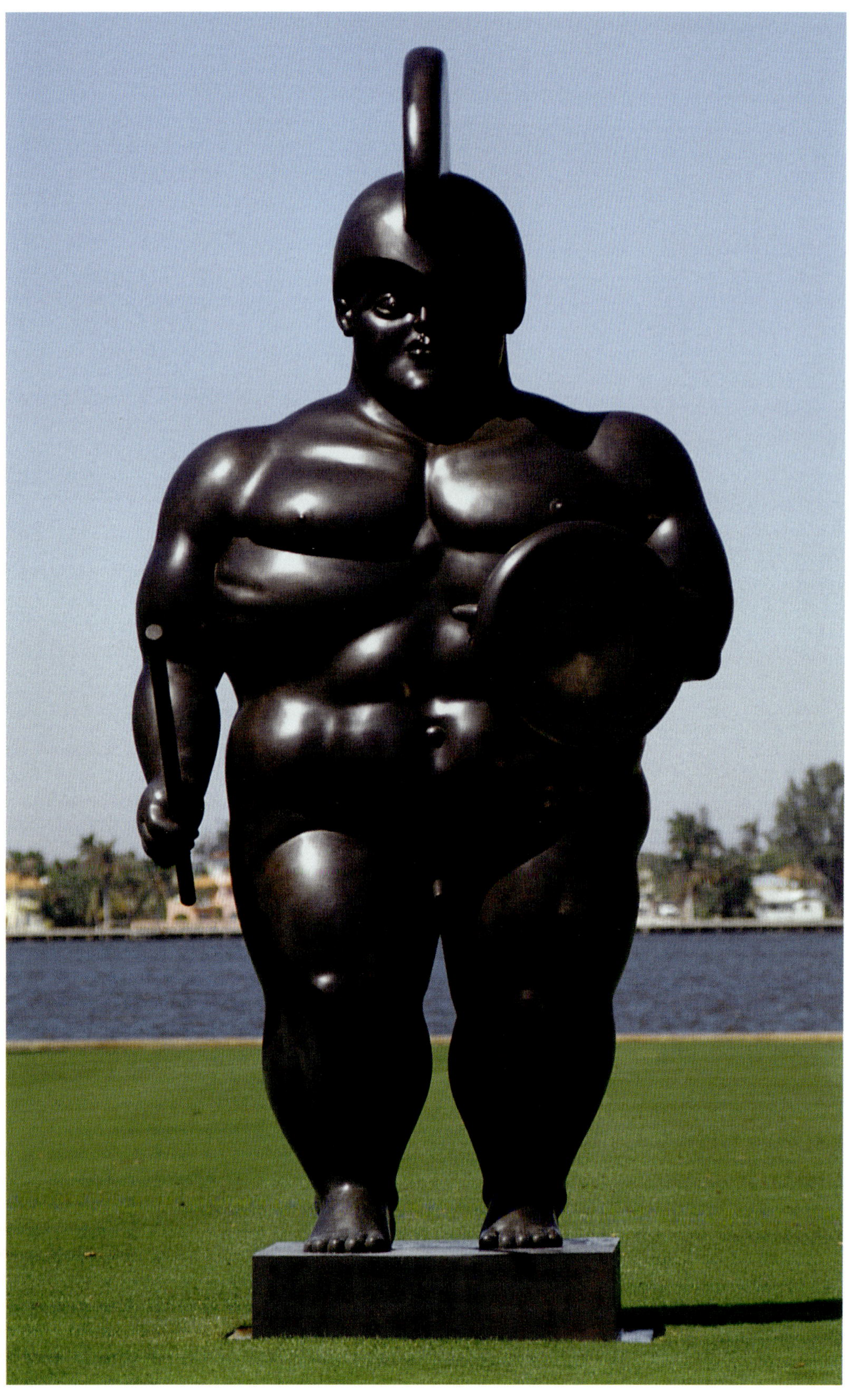

FERNANDO BOTERO

Colombian, born in 1932
Roman Soldier, 1986–89
Bronze with brown patina
H. 147 in., w. 111 in., d. 88⅝ in.
© Fernando Botero, courtesy,
Marlborough Gallery, New York

FERNANDO BOTERO

Colombian, born in 1932
Wyatt
Oil on canvas
53½ x 38½ in.
© Fernando Botero, courtesy,
Marlborough Gallery, New York

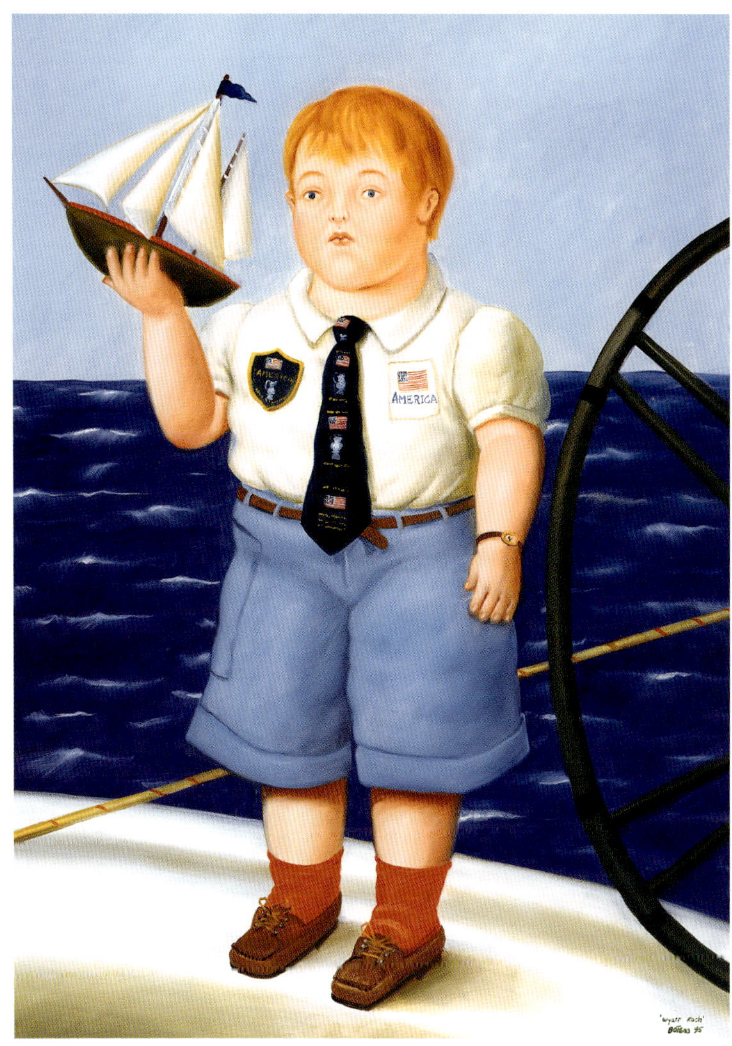

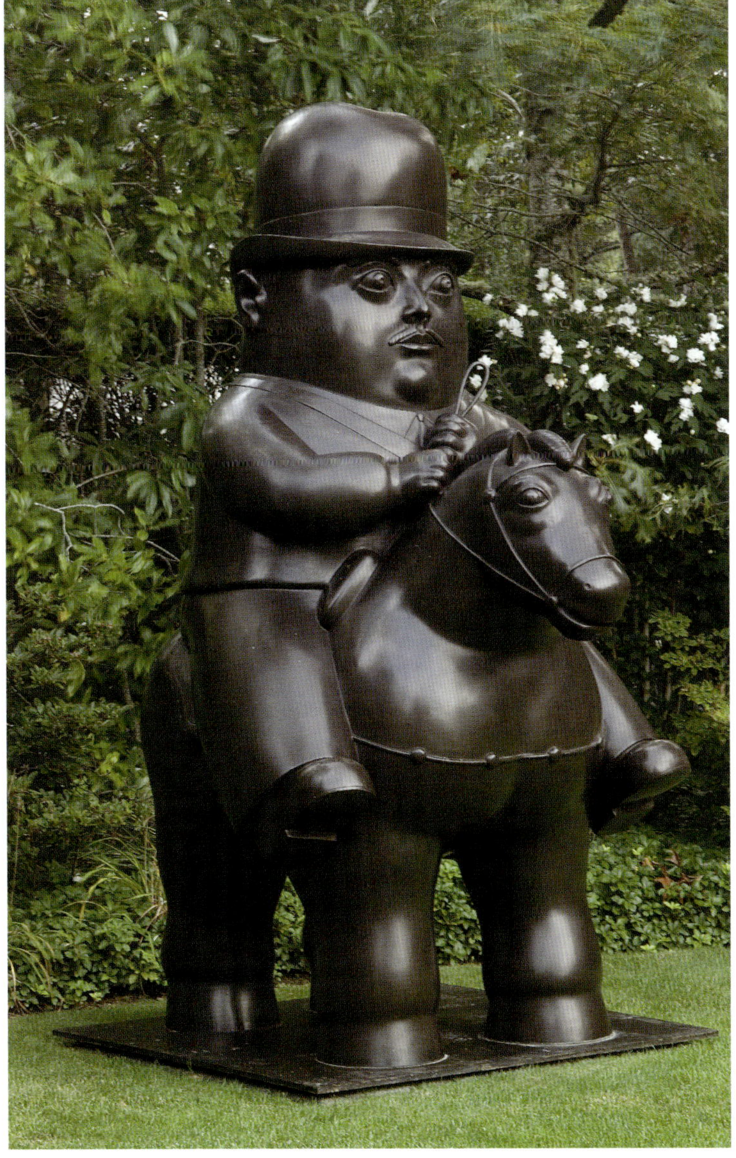

FERNANDO BOTERO

Colombian, born in 1932
Man on Horseback, 1986–89
Bronze with brown patina
H. 98½ in., w. 76 in., d. 58 in.
© Fernando Botero, courtesy,
Marlborough Gallery, New York

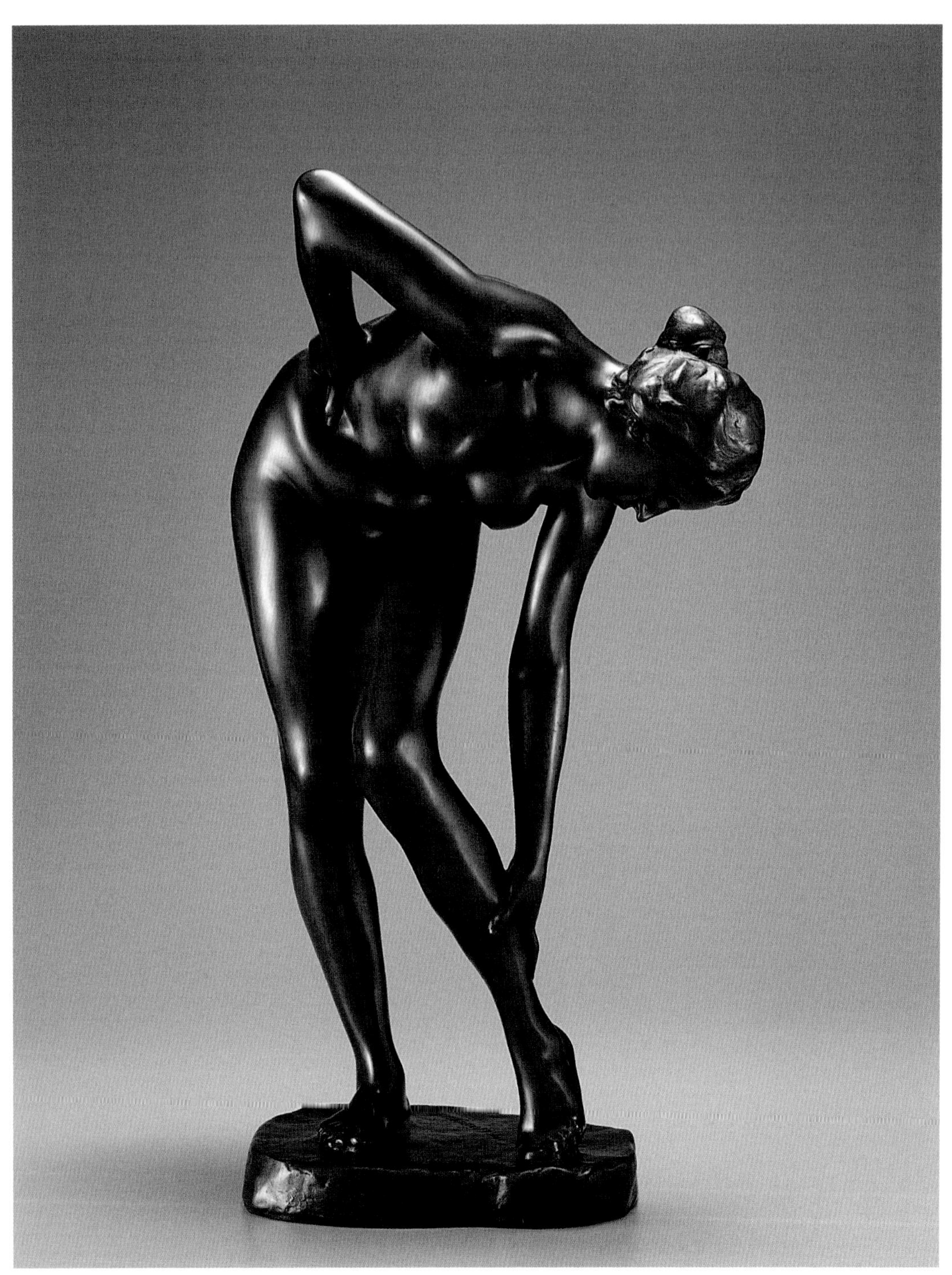

WILHELM LEHMBRUCK

German, 1881–1919
Bathing Woman, modeled about 1902, cast 1992
Bronze with dark brown patina
H. 25¼ in., w. 12 in., d. 8½ in.

GABRIELE MÜNTER

German, 1877–1962
Child with Doll, 1909
Oil on board
27⅜ x 19 in.

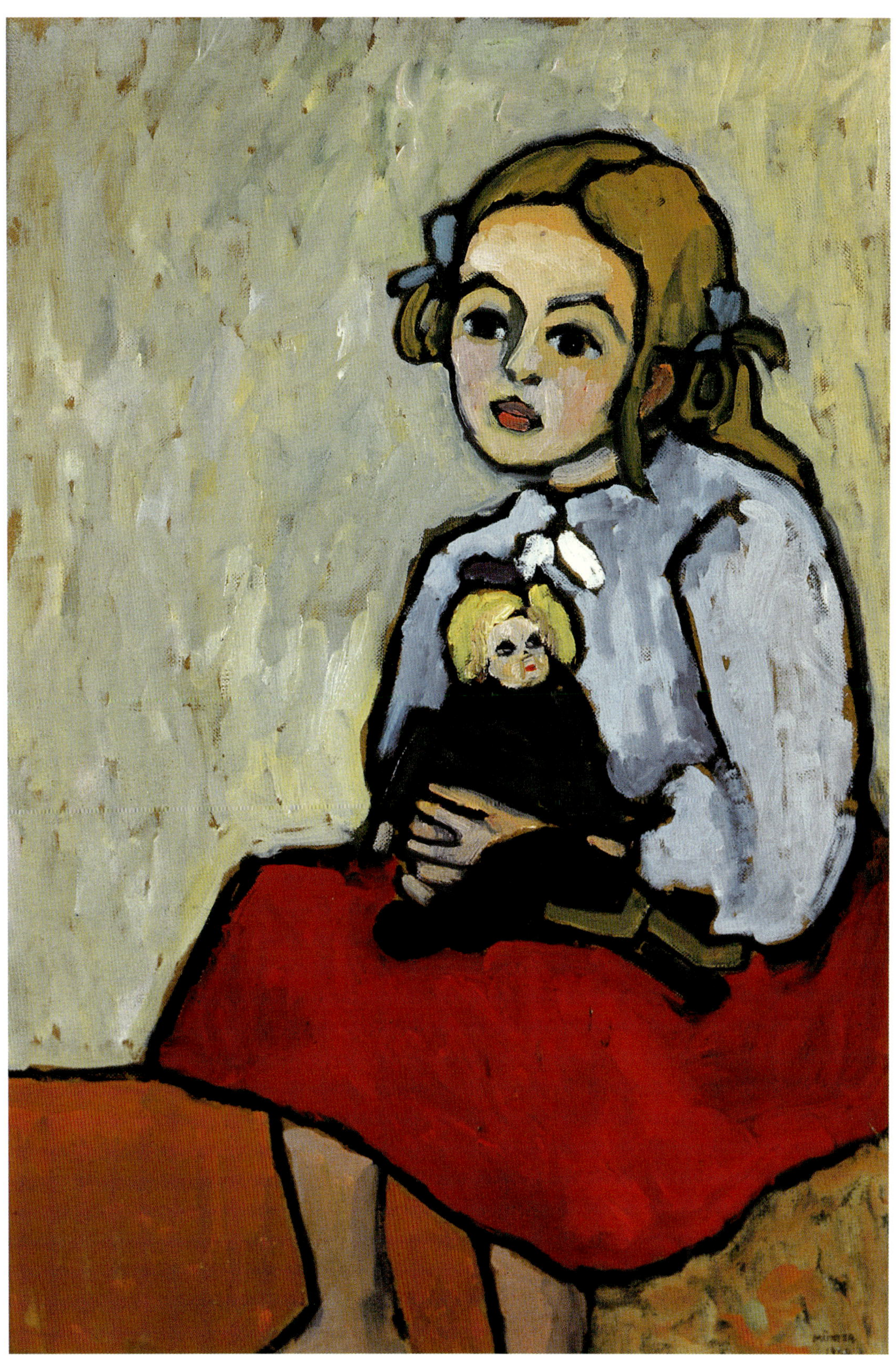

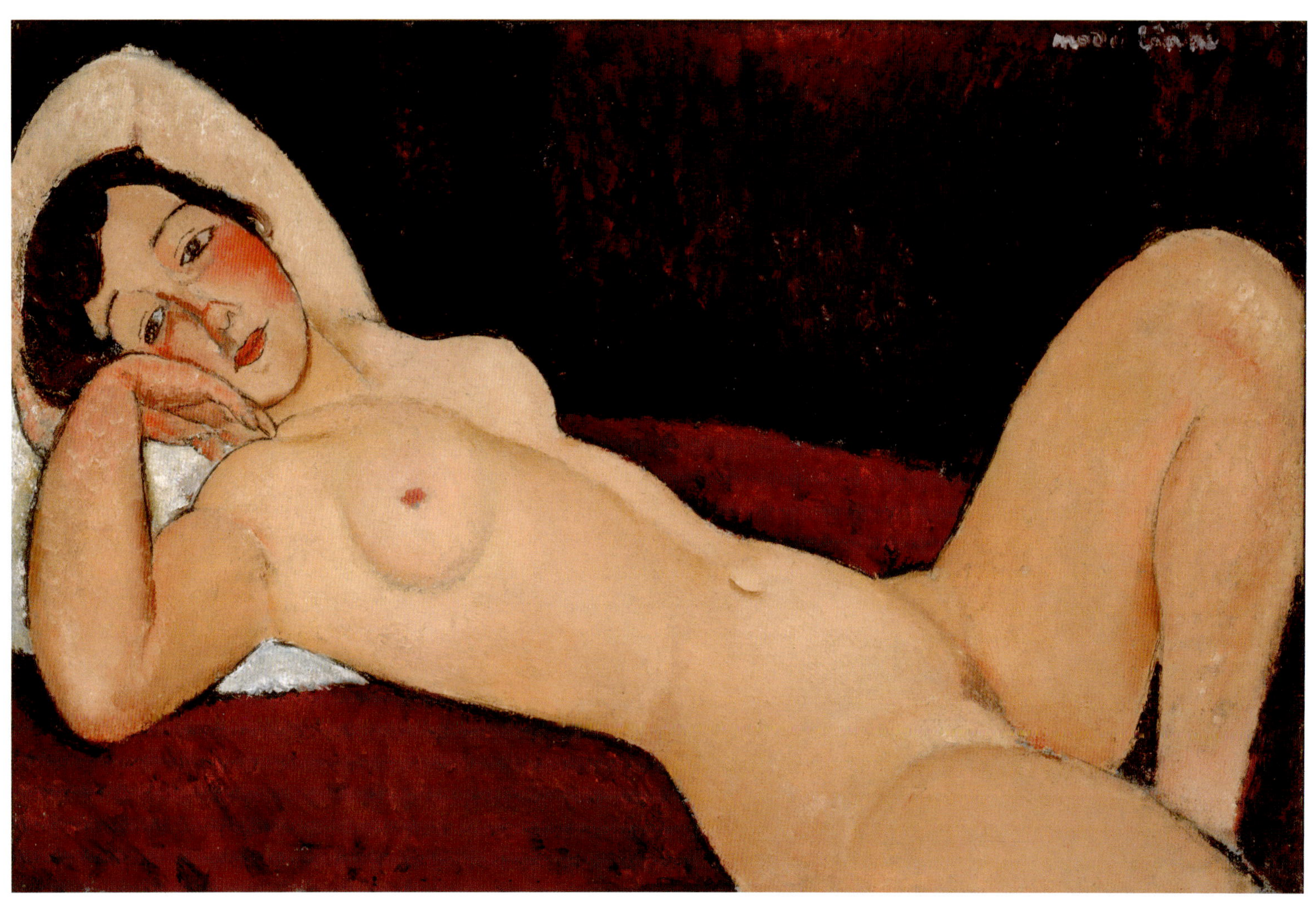

AMEDEO MODIGLIANI

Italian, 1884–1920
Reclining Nude, 1917
Oil on canvas
23½ x 36¼ in.

HENRI MATISSE

French, 1869–1954
Young Woman Made-up in Oriental Style, 1929
Oil on canvas
28⅝ x 23½ in.

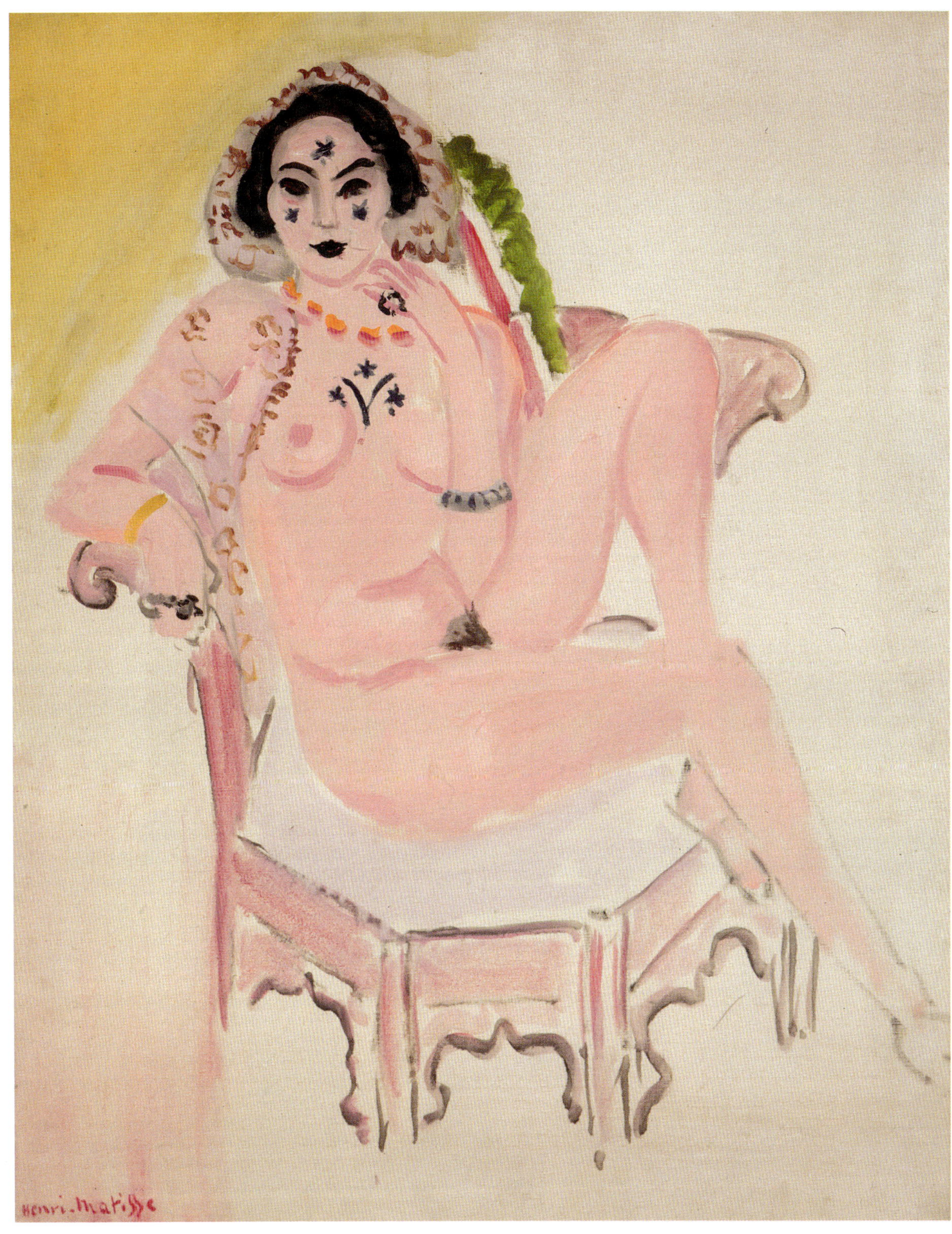

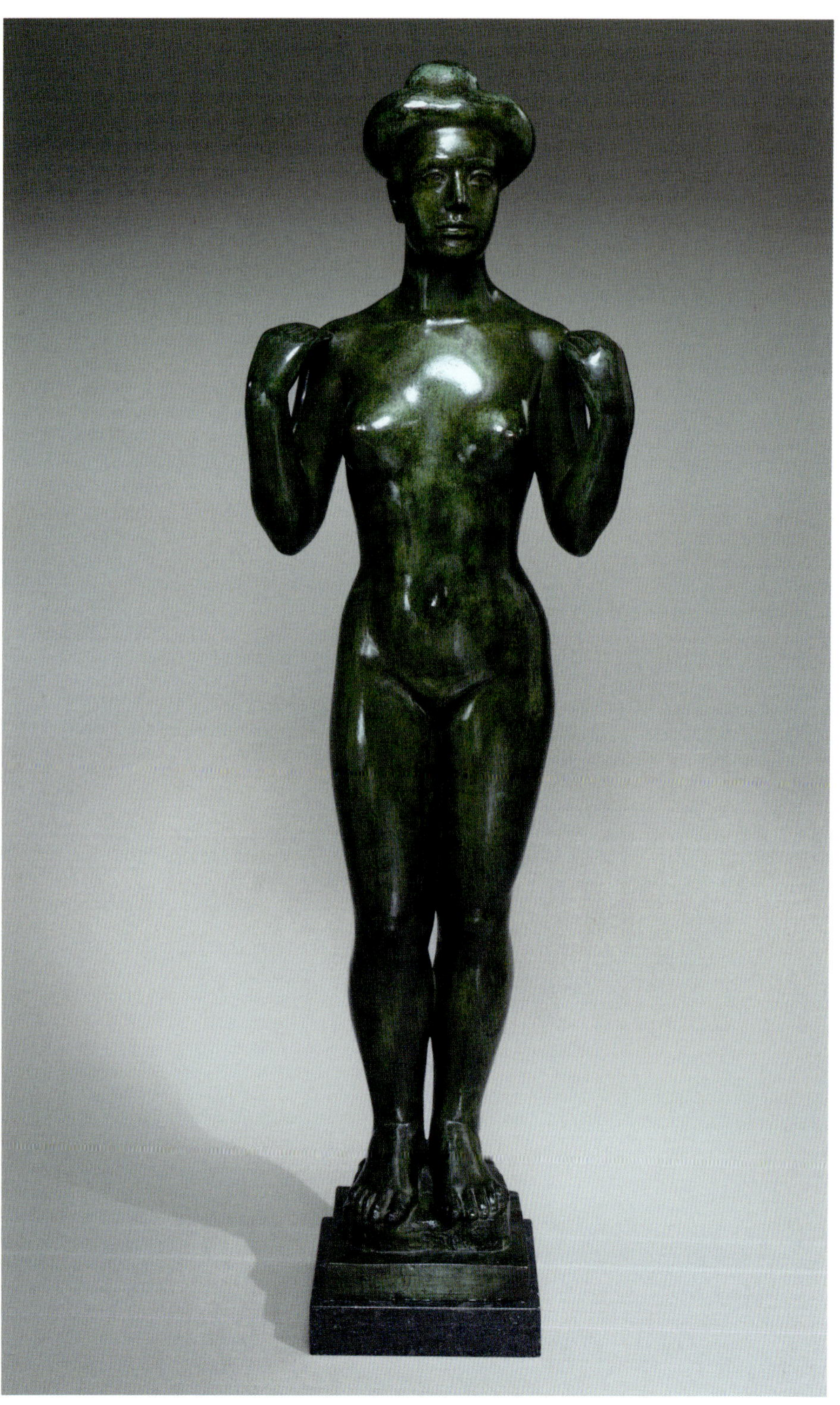

ARISTIDE MAILLOL

French, 1861–1944
Bather with Raised Arms, 1900
Bronze with green and brown patina
H. 49 in., w. 16 in., d. 7¼ in.

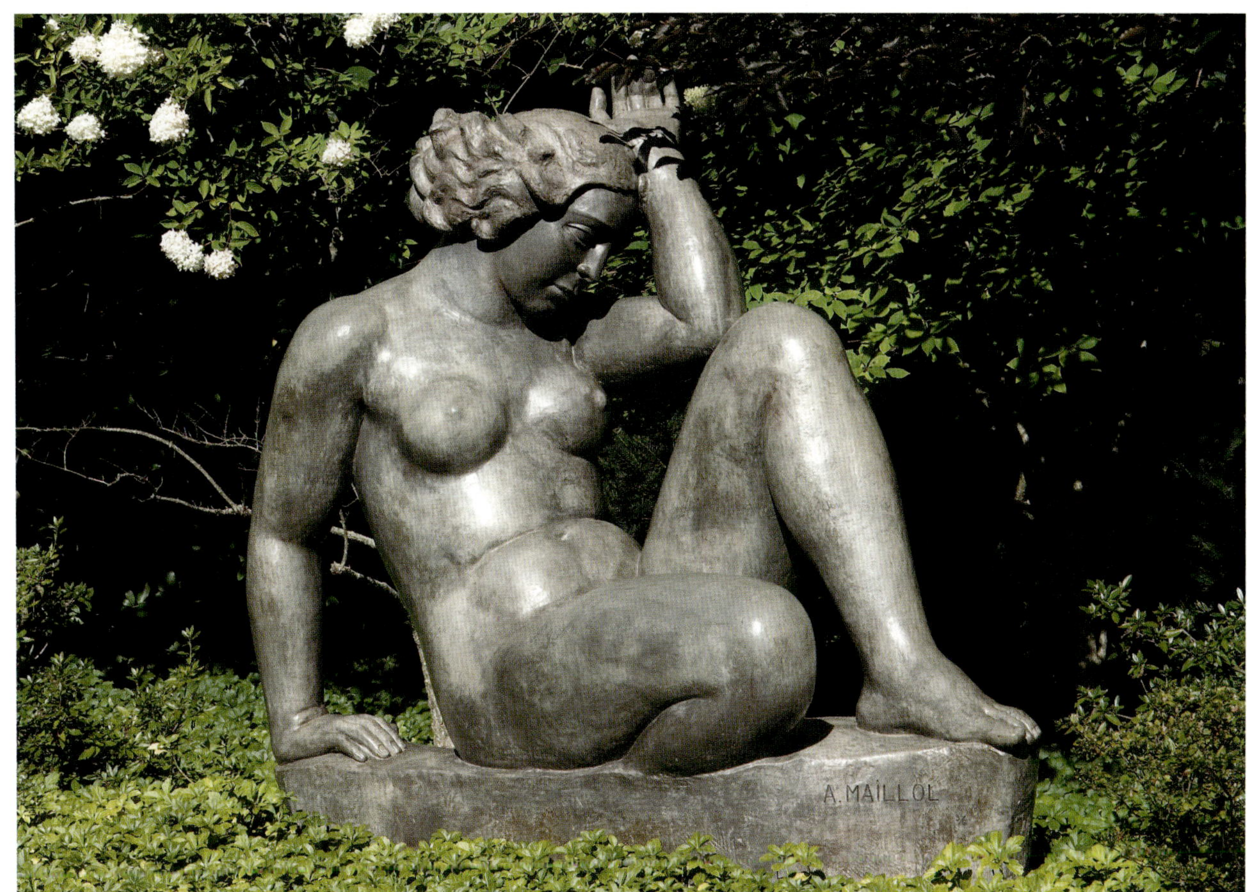

ARISTIDE MAILLOL

French, 1861–1944
The Mountain, about 1936–37
Lead
H. 67 in., w. 74 in., d. 36 in.

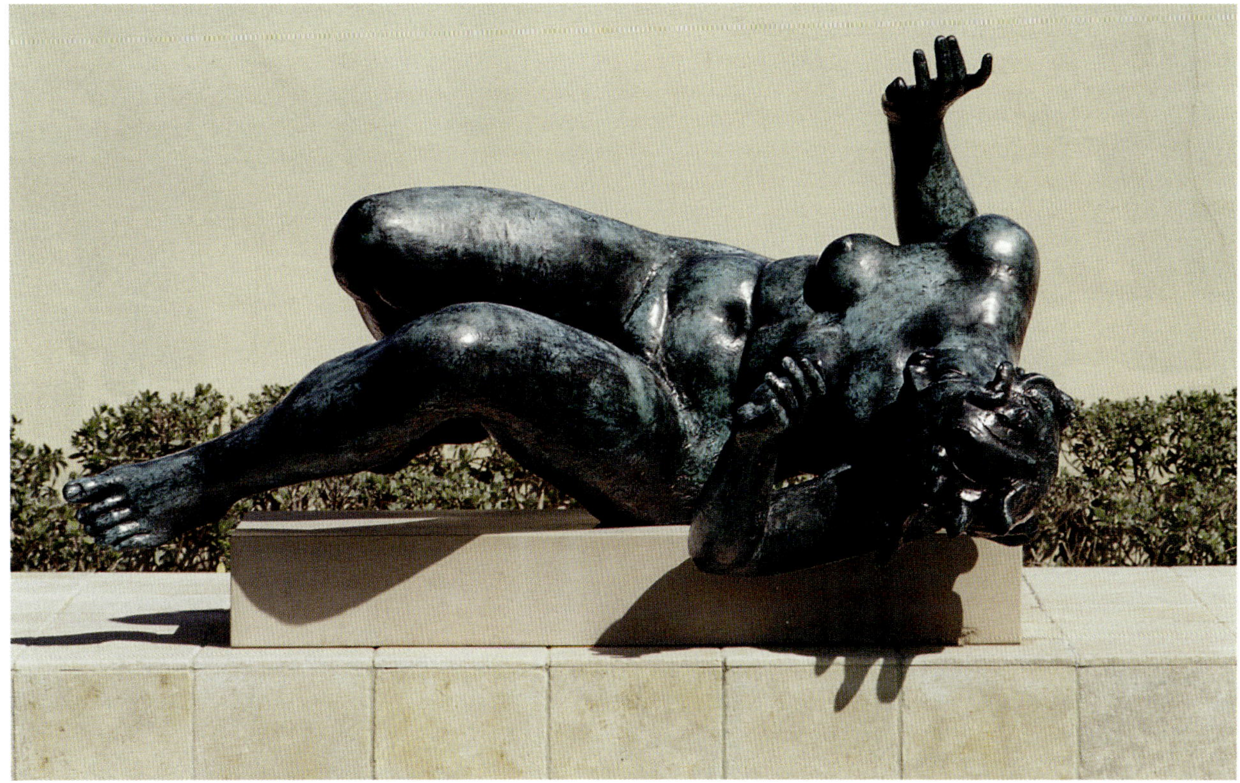

ARISTIDE MAILLOL

French, 1861–1944
The River, 1938–43
Bronze
H. 44 in., w. 96 in., d. 58 in.

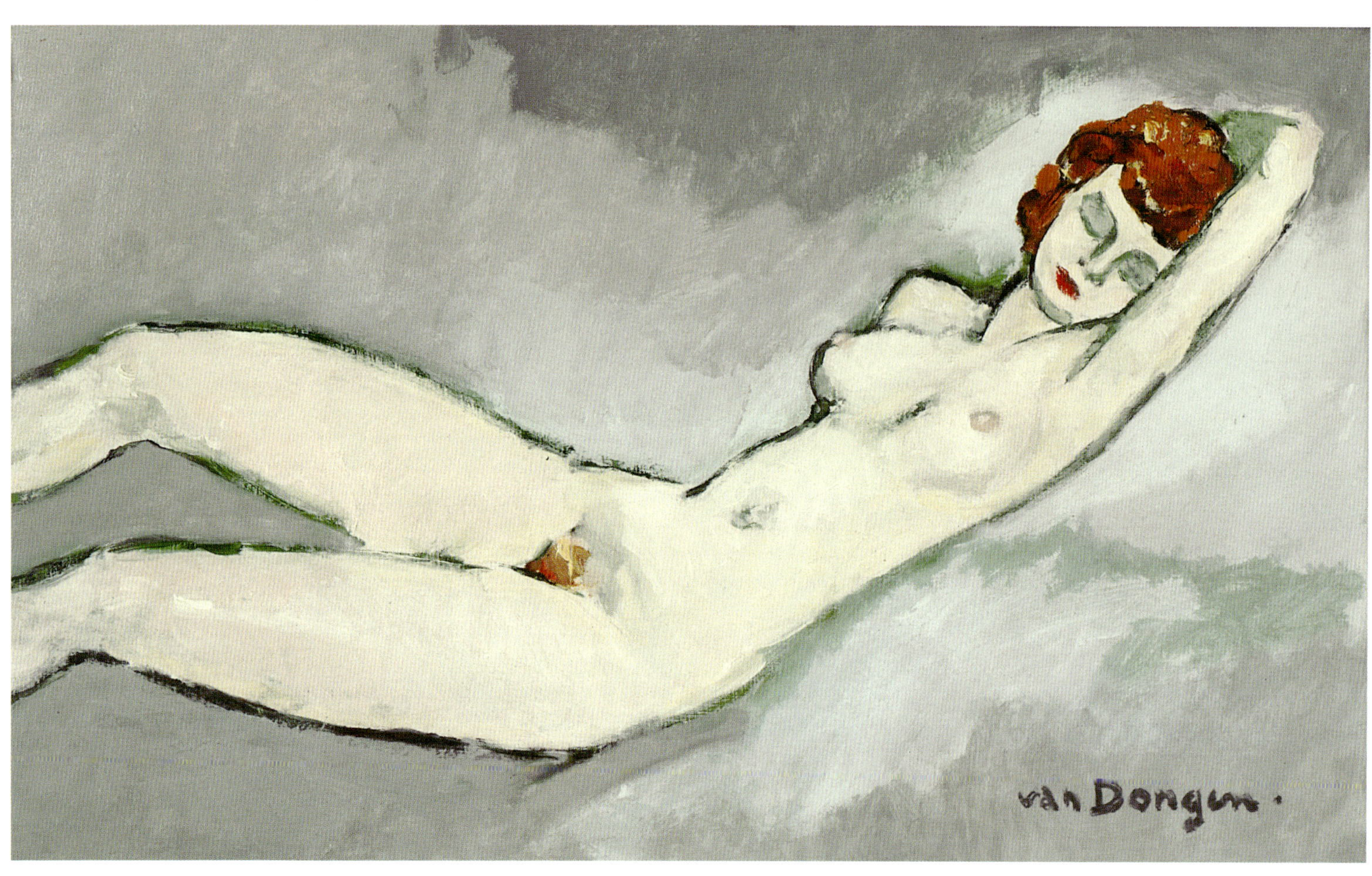

KEES VAN DONGEN

Dutch, 1877–1968
Reclining Nude, 1935–40
Oil on canvas
13 x 21¾ in.

MILTON CLARK AVERY

American, 1885–1965
White Chemise, 1961
Oil on canvas
40 x 30 in.

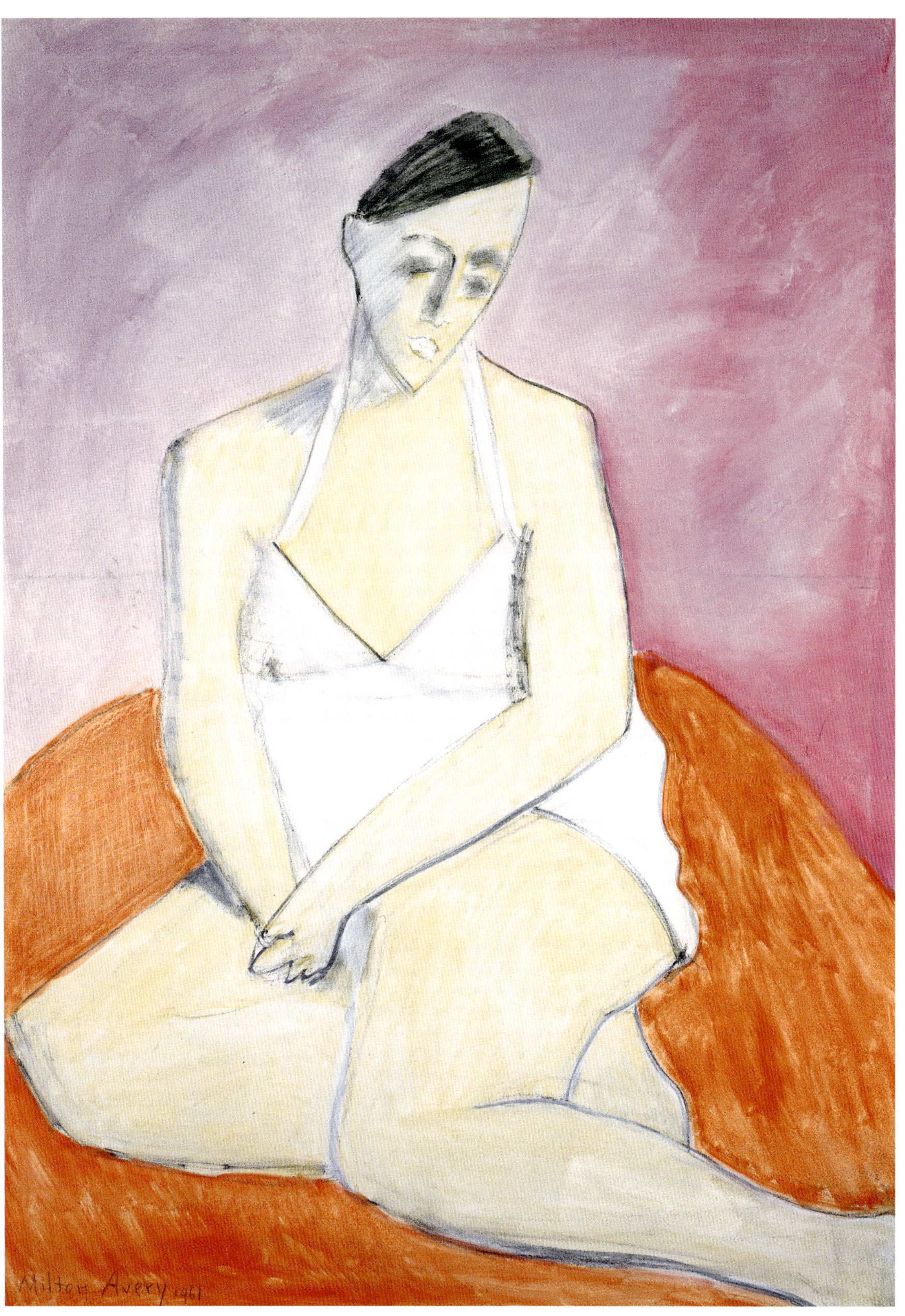

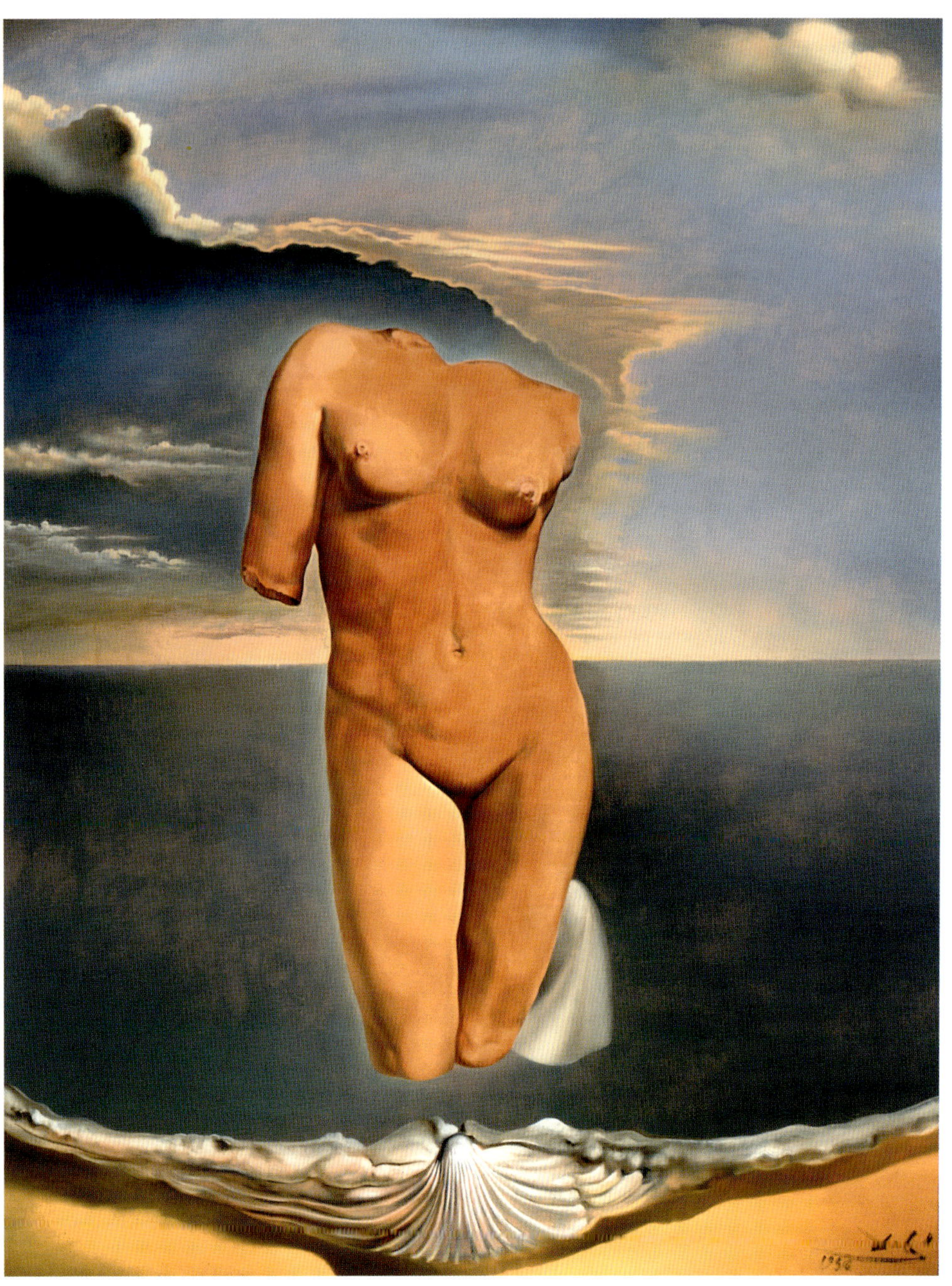

SALVADOR DALÍ

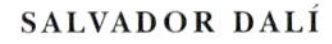

Spanish, 1904–1989
Rhinocerontic Gooseflesh, 1956
Oil on canvas
36⅛ x 27¾ in.

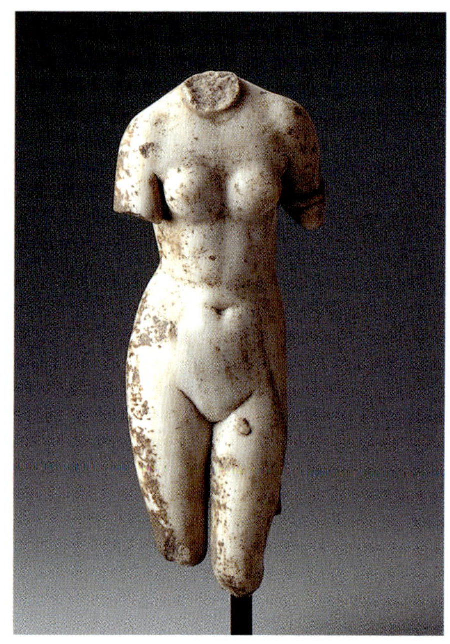

Roman, after a Greek original
Torso of Aphrodite, 1st–2nd century A.D.
Marble
H. 19¼ in., w. 5½ in., d. 4½ in.

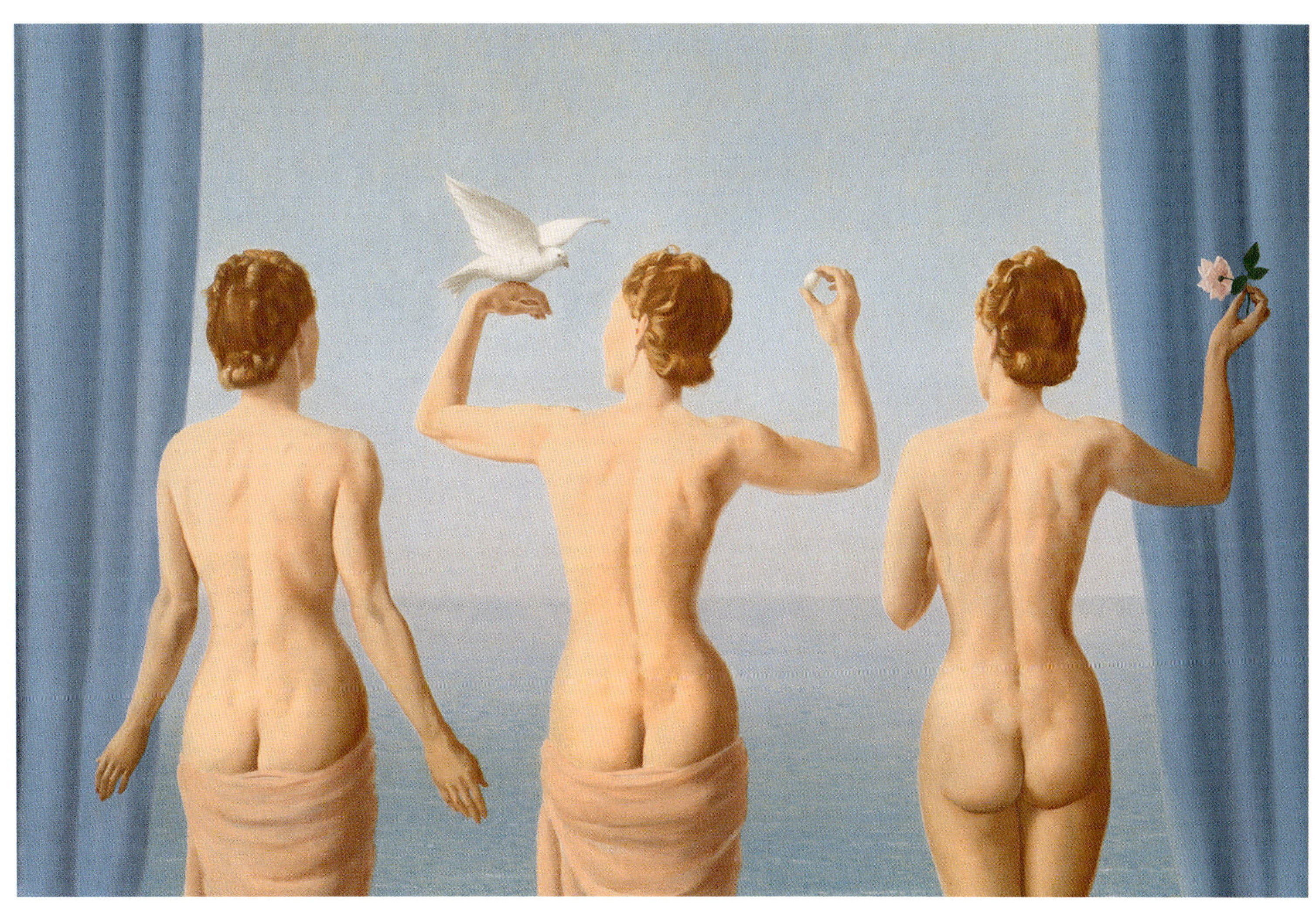

RENÉ MAGRITTE

Belgian, 1898–1967
The Clearing, 1941
Oil on canvas
25¾ x 39½ in.

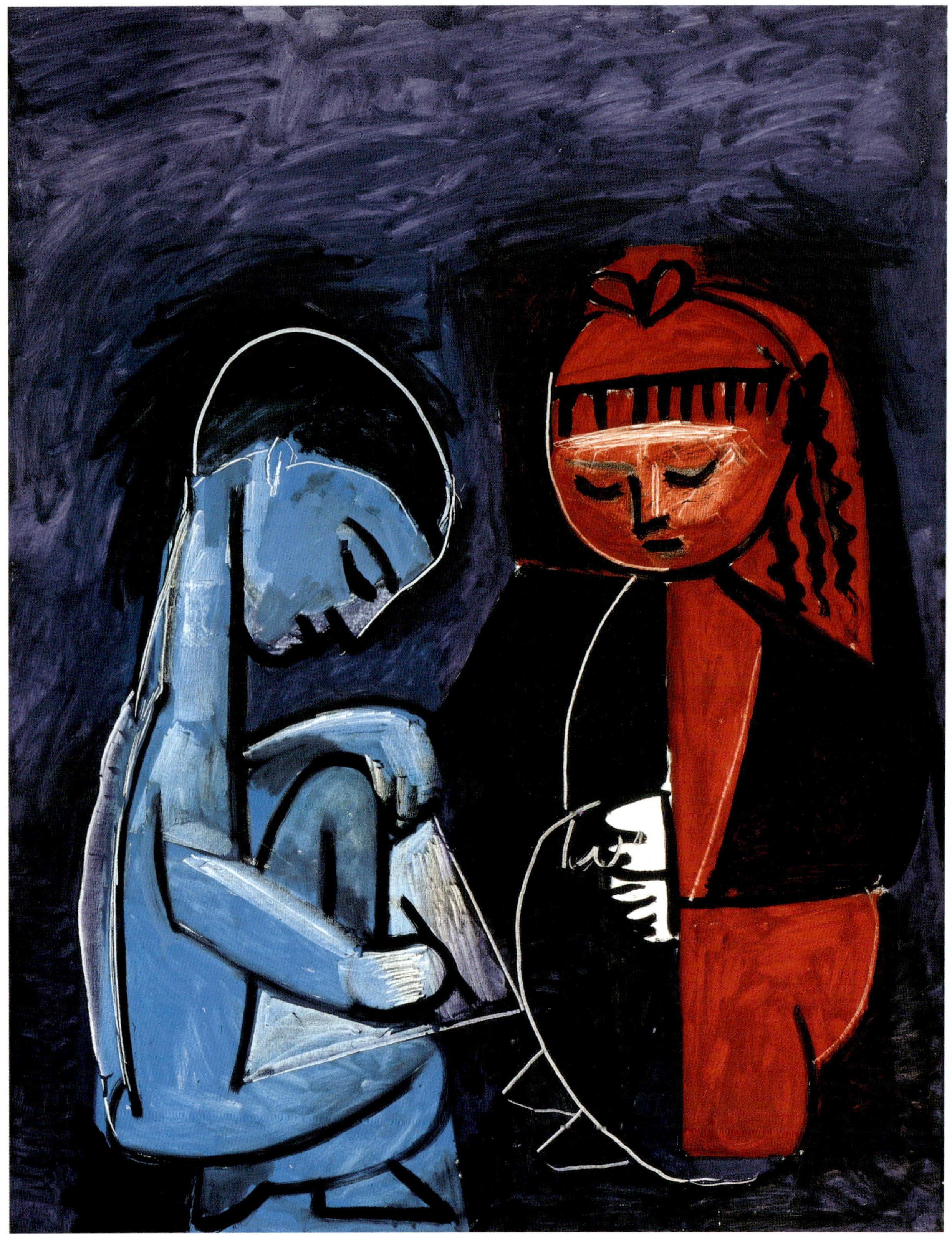

PABLO PICASSO

Spanish, worked in France,
1881–1973
Two Children, 1954
Oil on canvas
36¼ x 28¾ in.

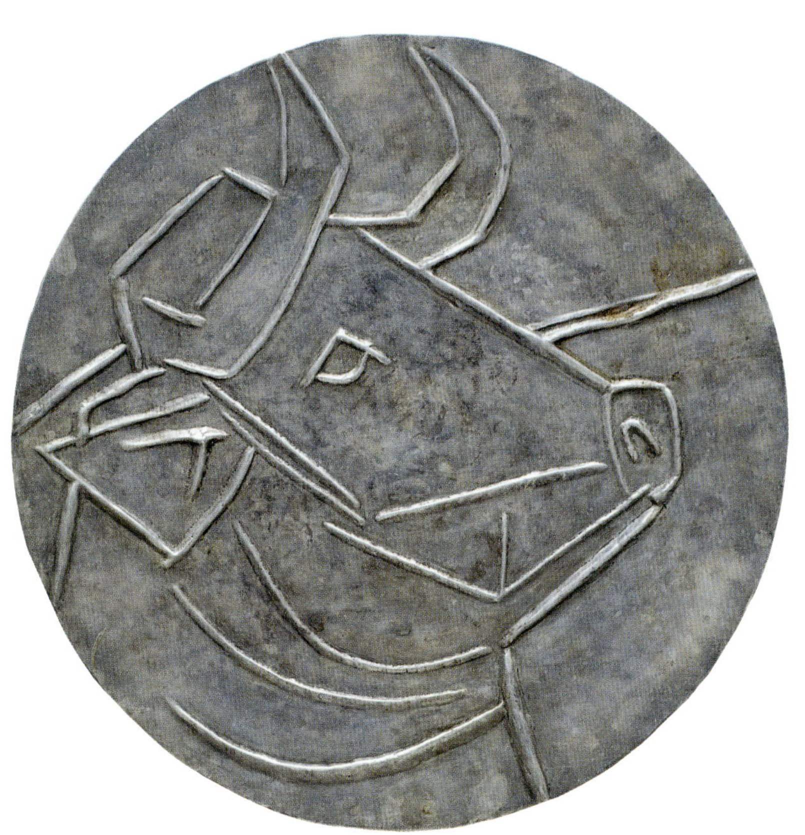

PABLO PICASSO

Spanish, worked in France, 1881–1973
Head of a Bull in Profile, 1956
Cast bronze and silver plate
Diam. 16³⁄₁₆ in.

PABLO PICASSO

Spanish, worked in France, 1881–1973
Satyr, 1951
Painted plaster relief
H. 7⅞ in., w. 3 in., d. 1¾ in.

PABLO PICASSO

Spanish, worked in France, 1881–1973
The Drinkers under the Bower, 1957
Glazed ceramic tiles
24 x 24 in.

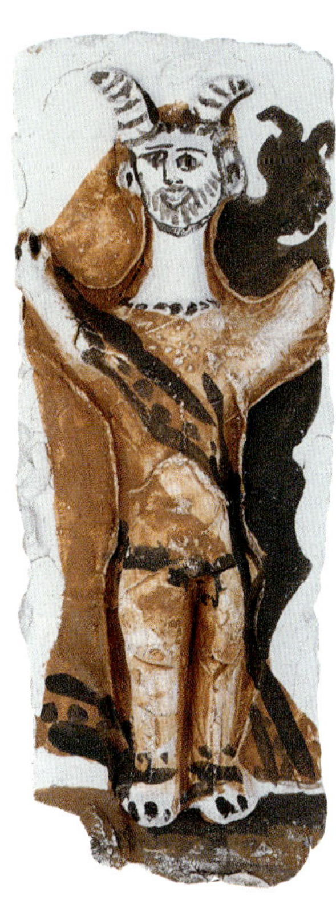

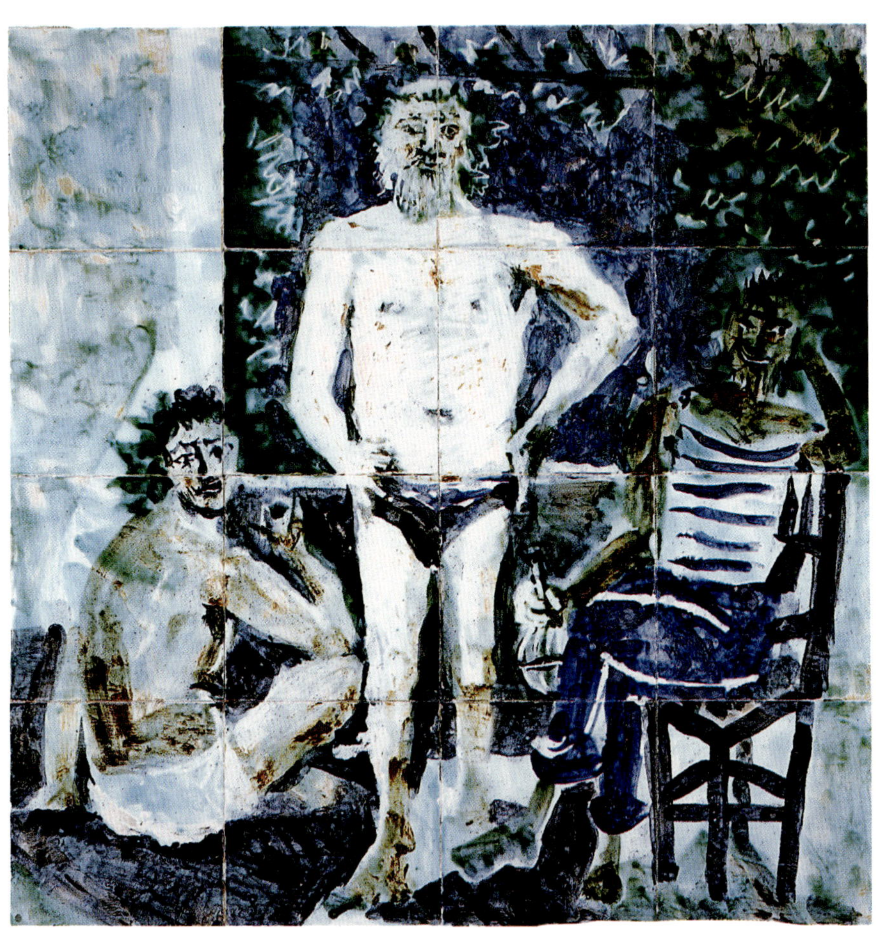

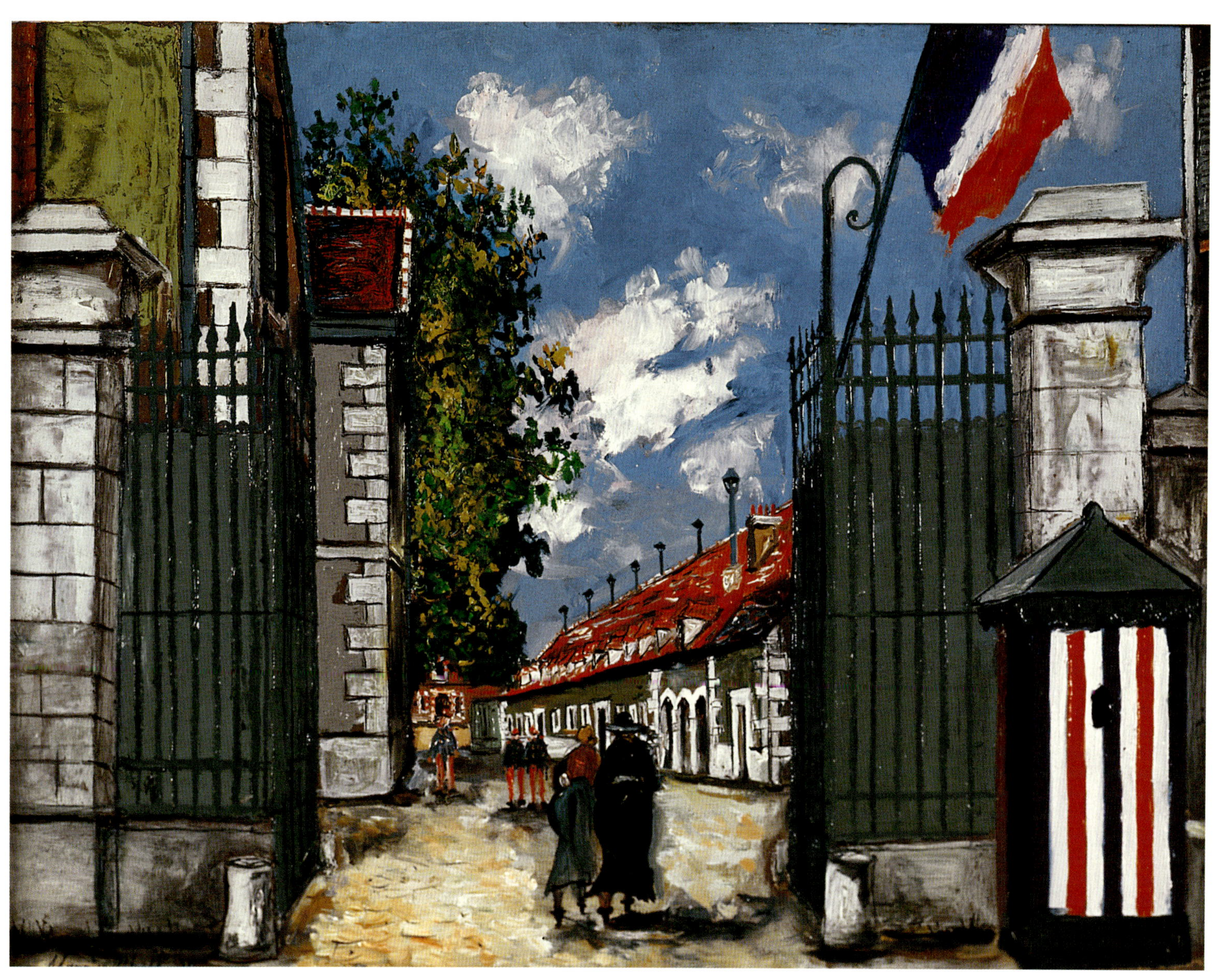

MAURICE UTRILLO

French, 1883–1955
Barracks at Limoge, Upper Vienne, 1922
Oil, pen, and black ink on board
12 x 15½ in.

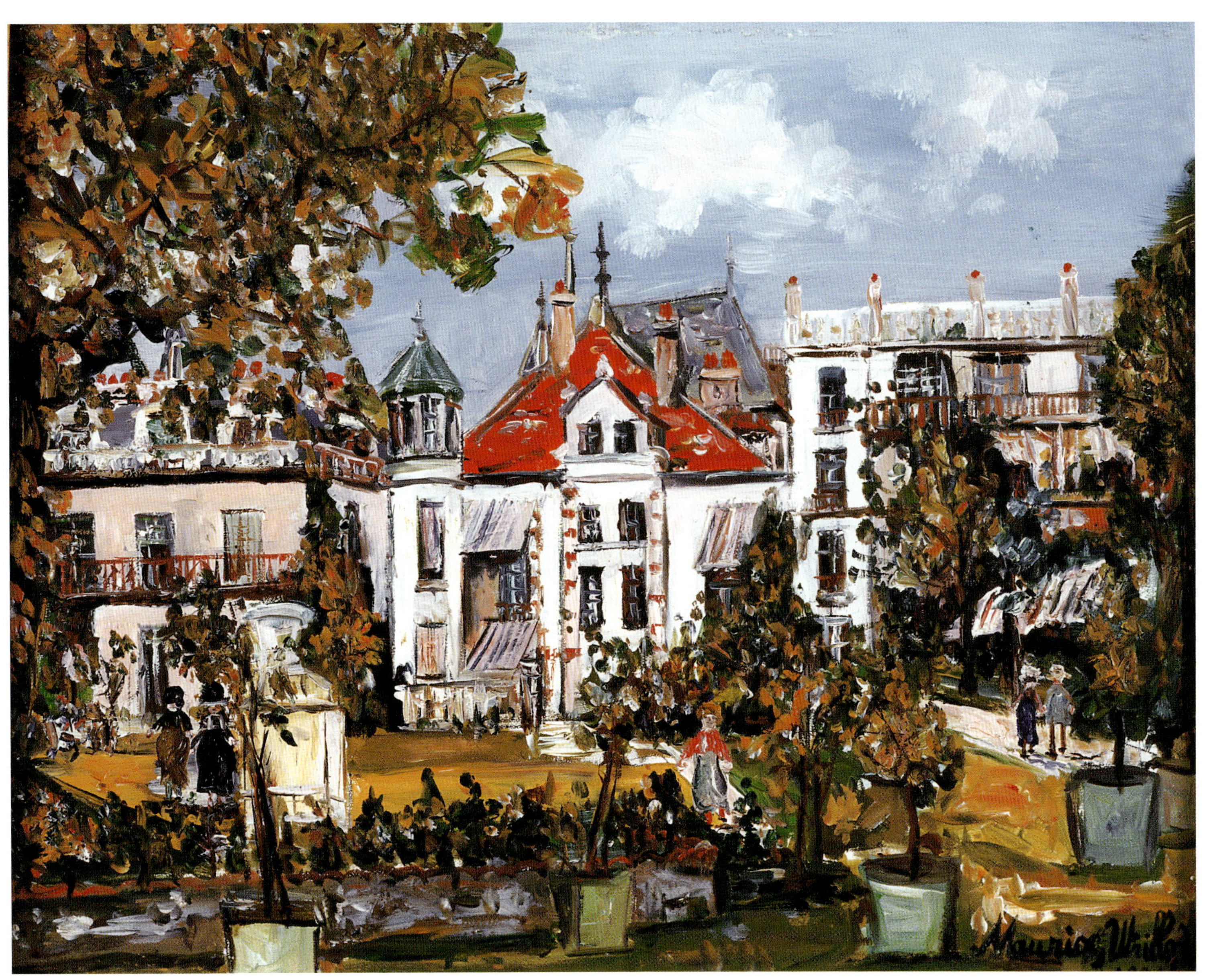

MAURICE UTRILLO

French, 1883–1955
The Sévigné Pavillion, Vichy, 1934
Oil on panel
13 x 16¼ in.

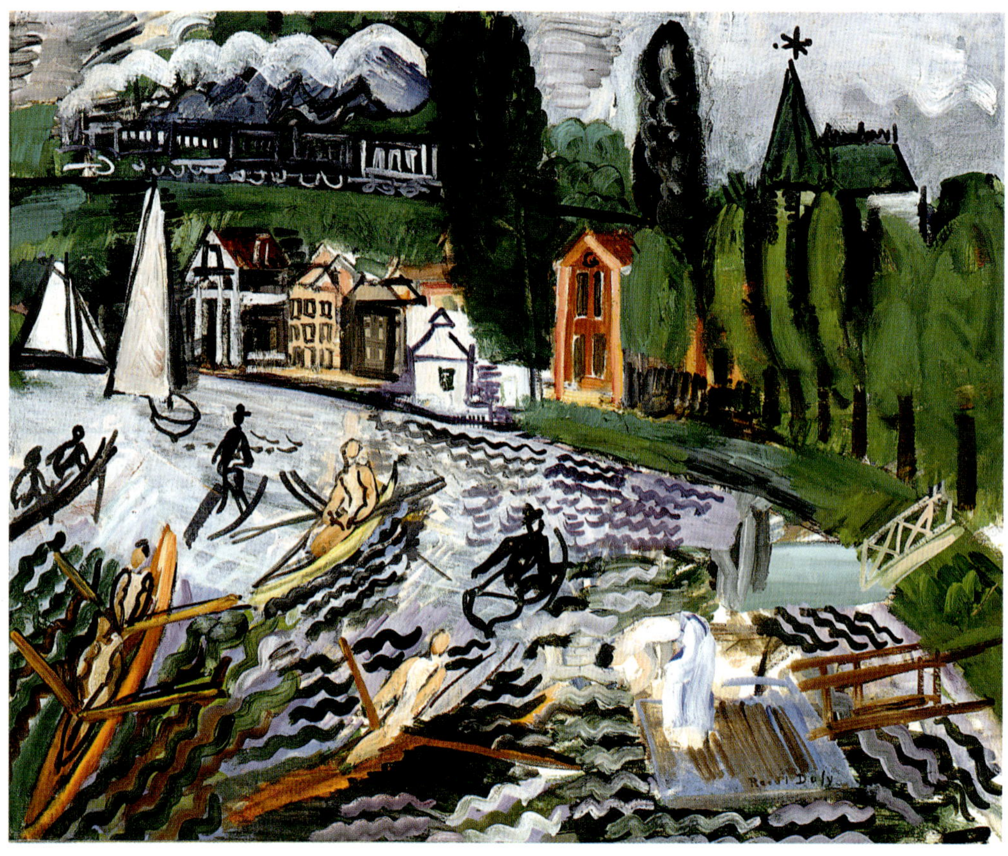

RAOUL DUFY

French, 1877–1953
Rowing on the Marne, 1923
Oil on canvas
24 x 29 in.

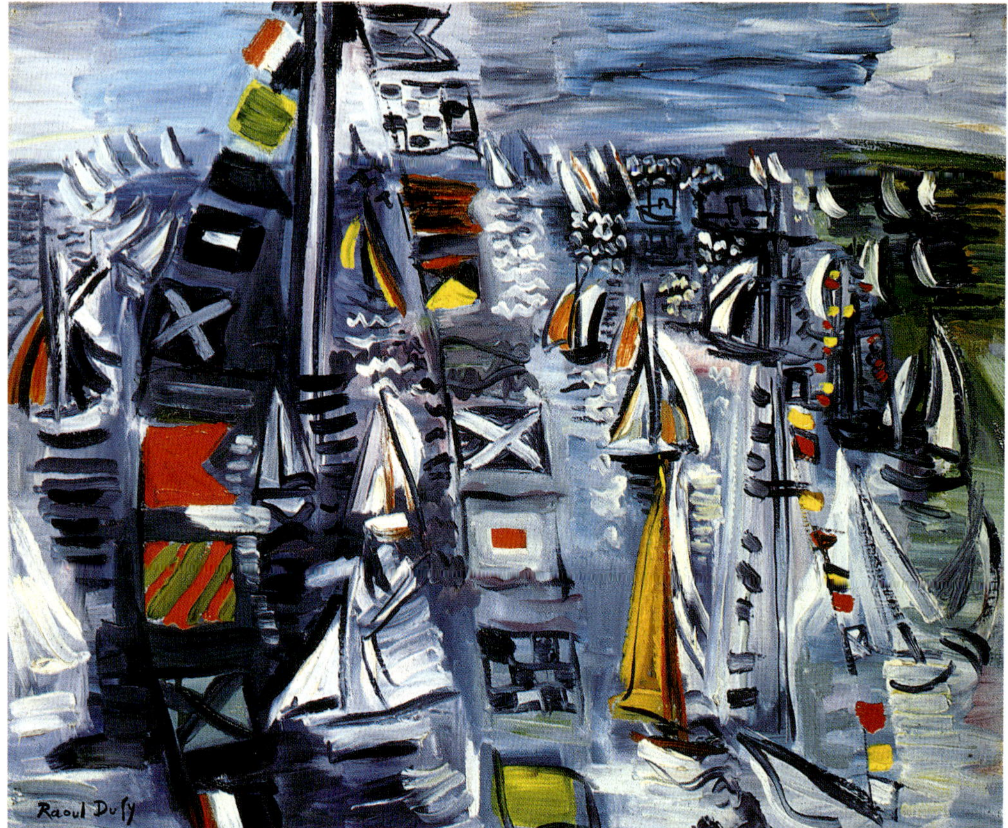

RAOUL DUFY

French, 1877–1953
Regatta at Cowes, about 1930–34
Oil on canvas
19⅞ x 24¼ in.

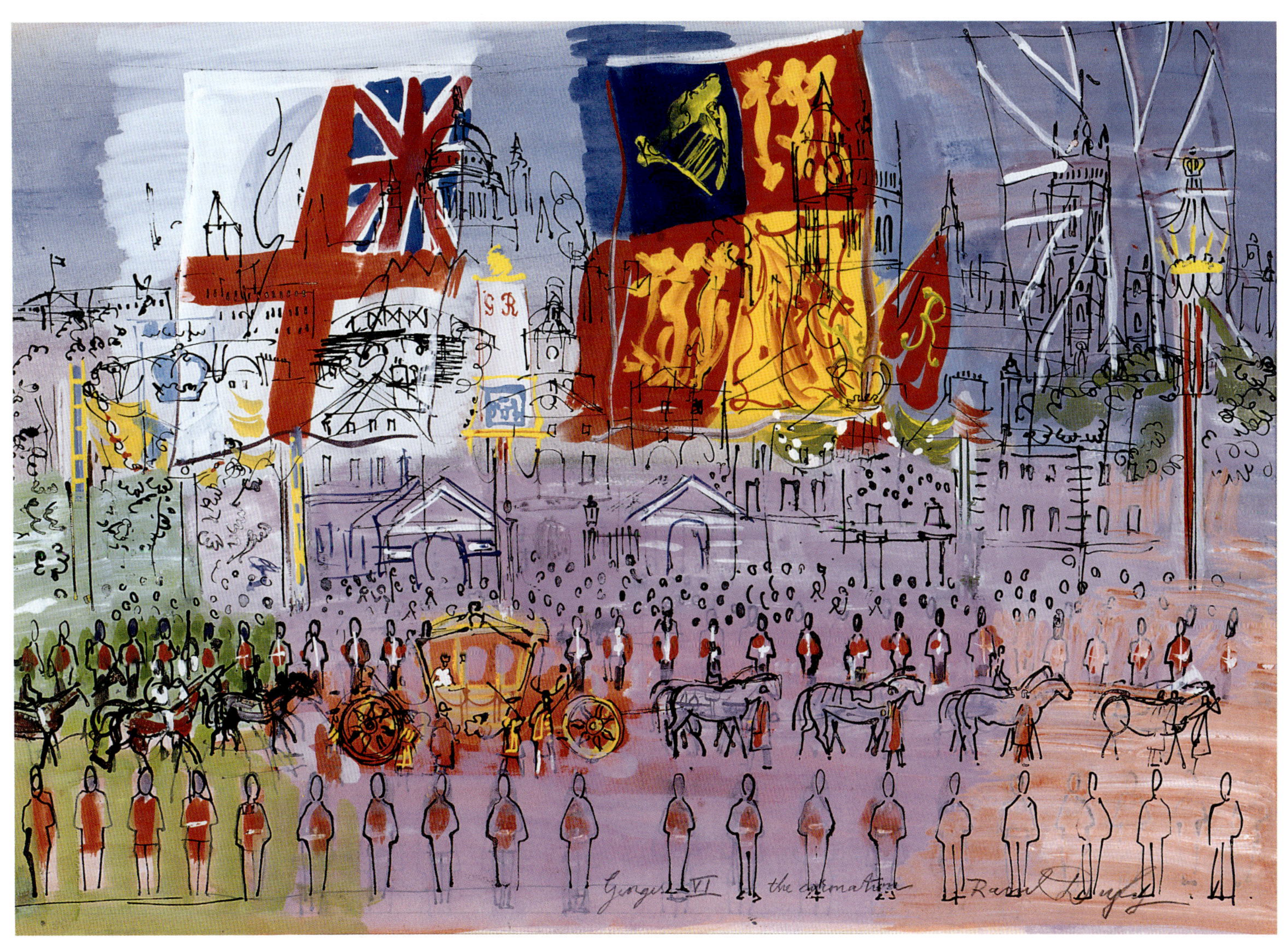

RAOUL DUFY

French, 1877–1953
The Coronation of George VI, 1937
Gouache and India ink on paper
17⅞ x 25½ in.

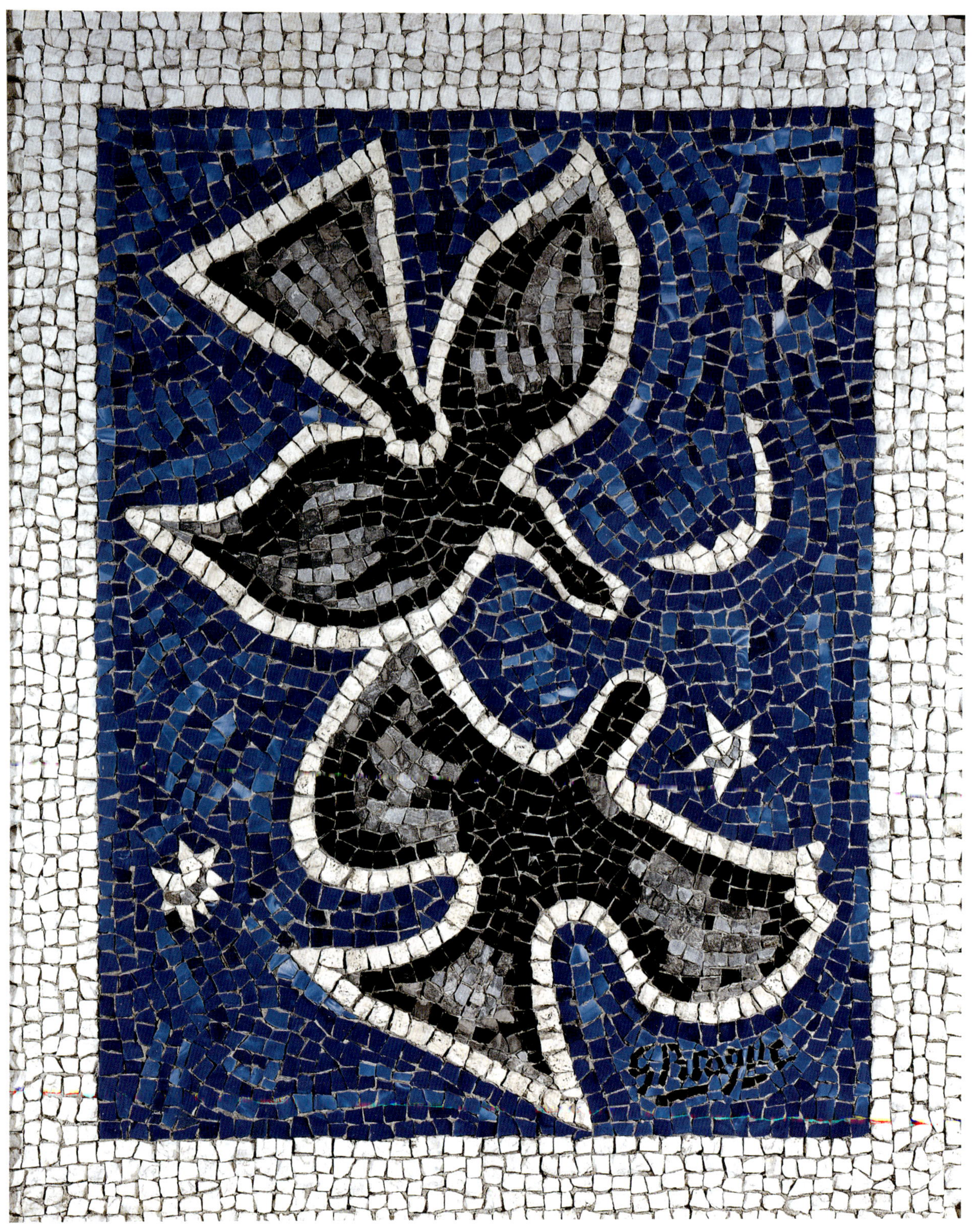

GEORGES BRAQUE

French, 1882–1963
Birds, about 1950
Cement, stone tile, and glass tile
H. 57 in., w. 47 in., d. 3 in.

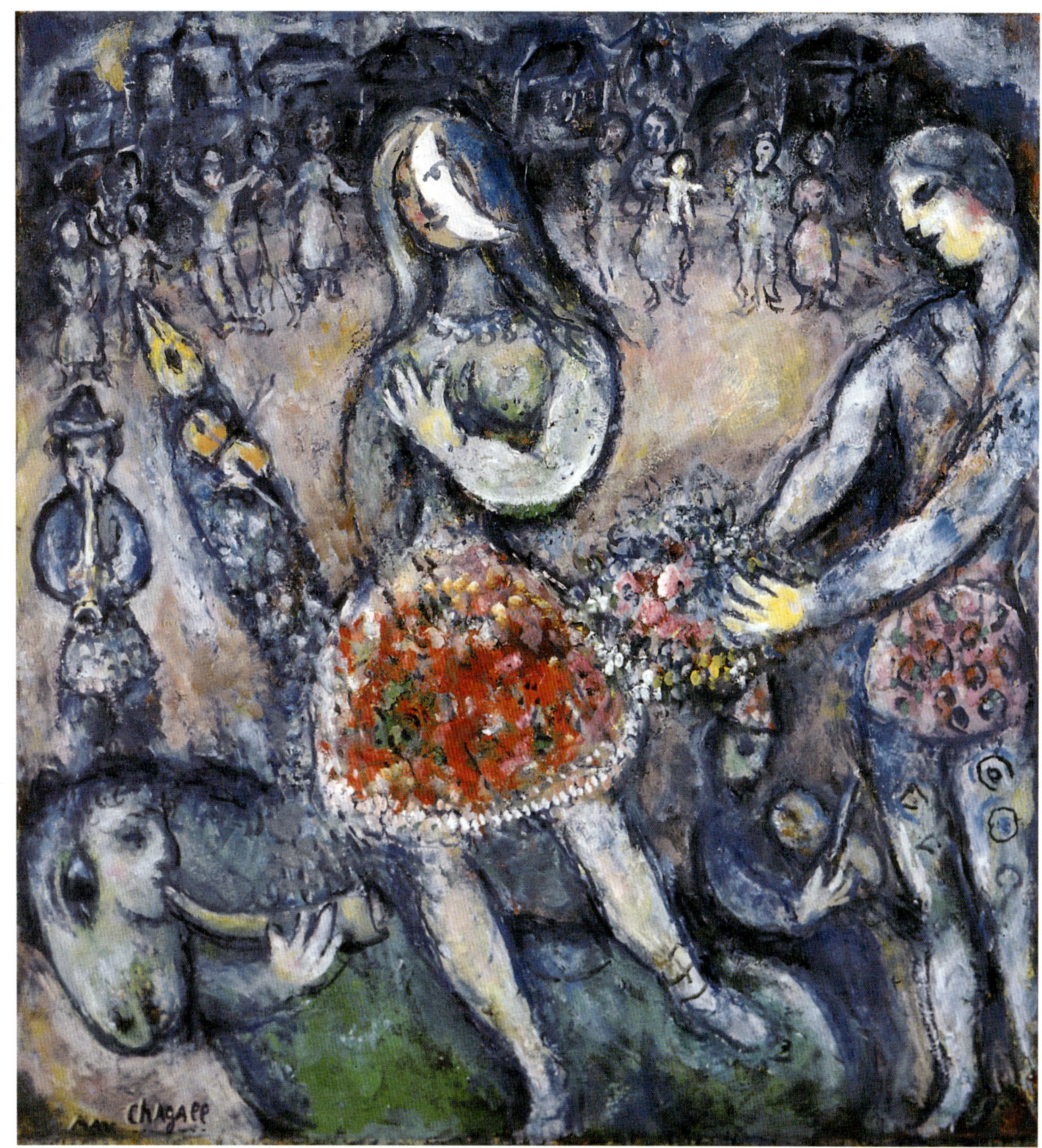

MARC CHAGALL

Russian, worked in France, 1887–1985
Dancer in a Floral Dress, about 1971
Oil on panel
20⅞ x 19¾ in.

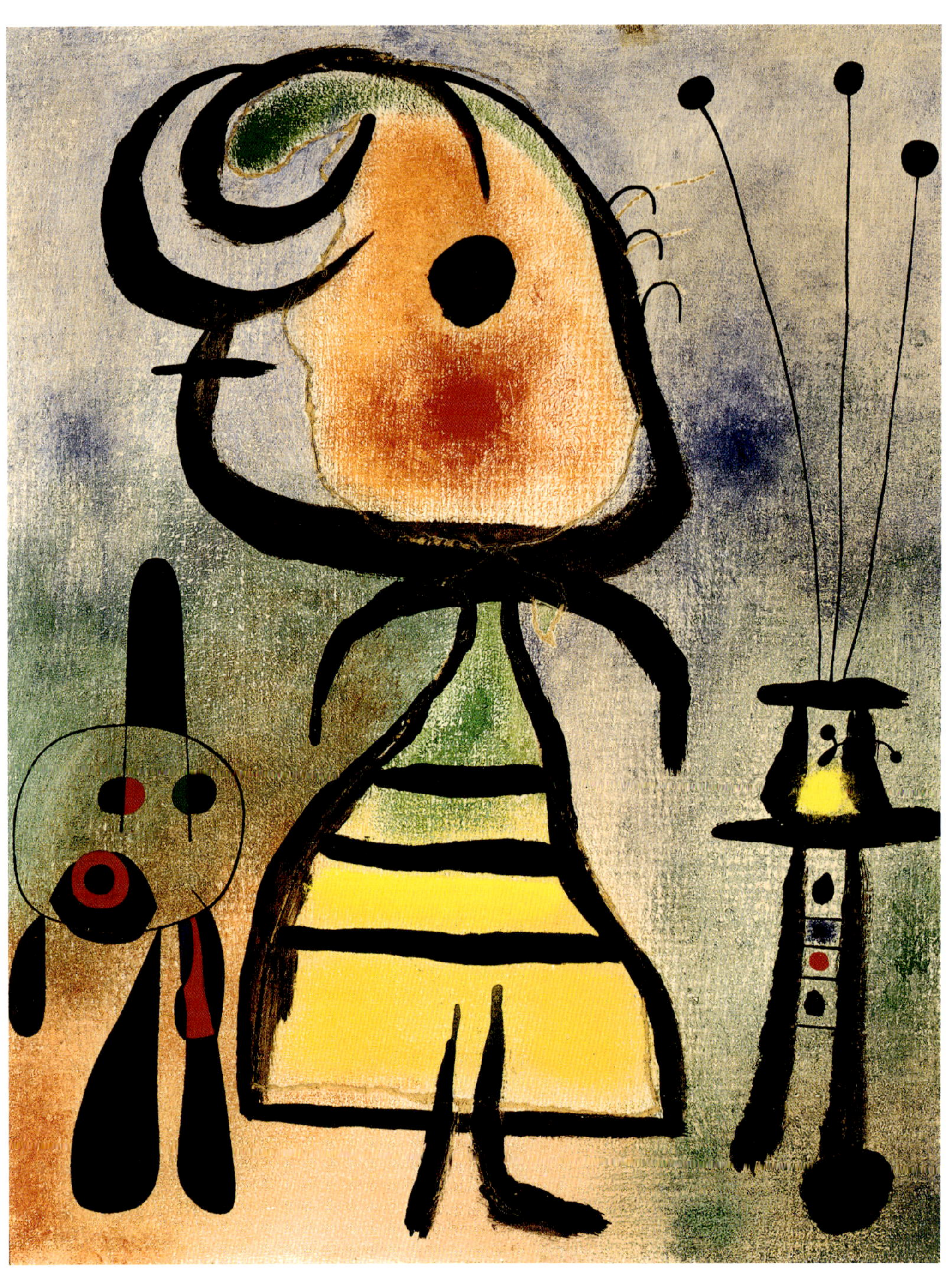

JOAN MIRÓ

Spanish, worked in France,
1893–1983
Woman and Cat, 1950
Oil on board
23⅞ x 19½ in.

Opposite:
JOAN MIRÓ

Spanish, worked in France,
1893–1983
Bird Woman, 1973
Oil on canvas
79 x 79 in.

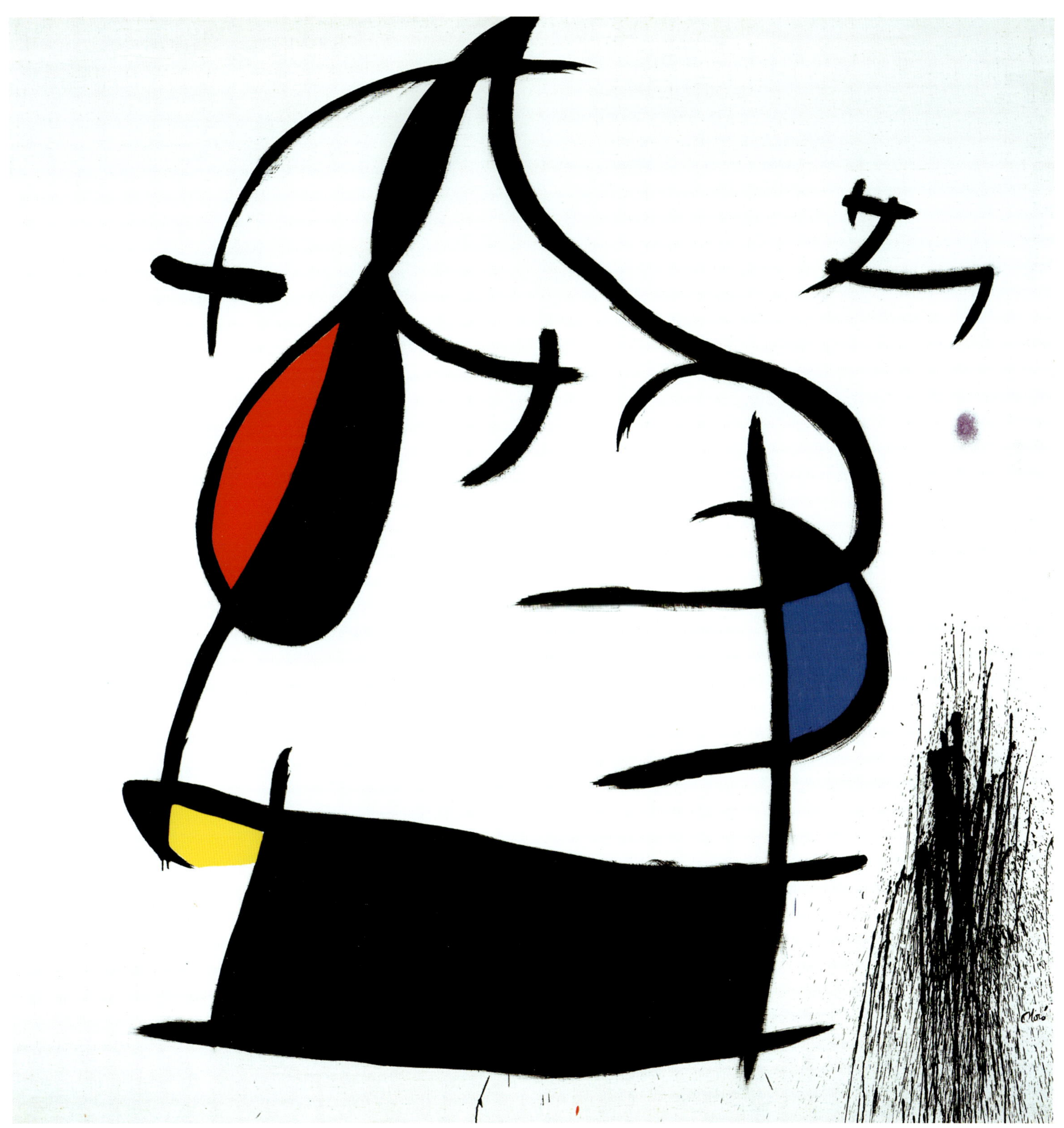

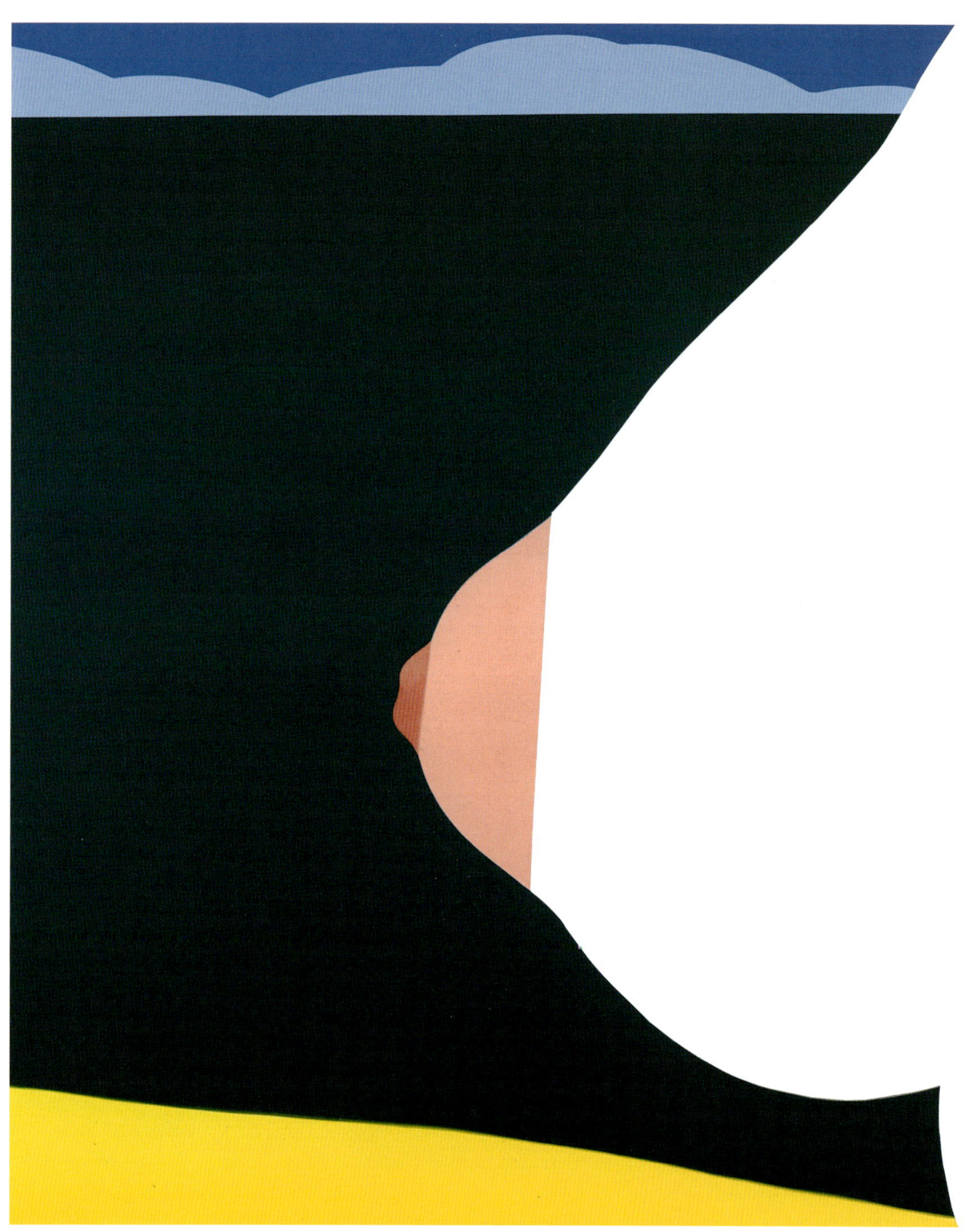

TOM WESSELMANN

American, 1931–2004
Seascape #20, 1967
Acrylic polymer emulsion, gesso, and oil on canvas
72¼ x 60¼ in.

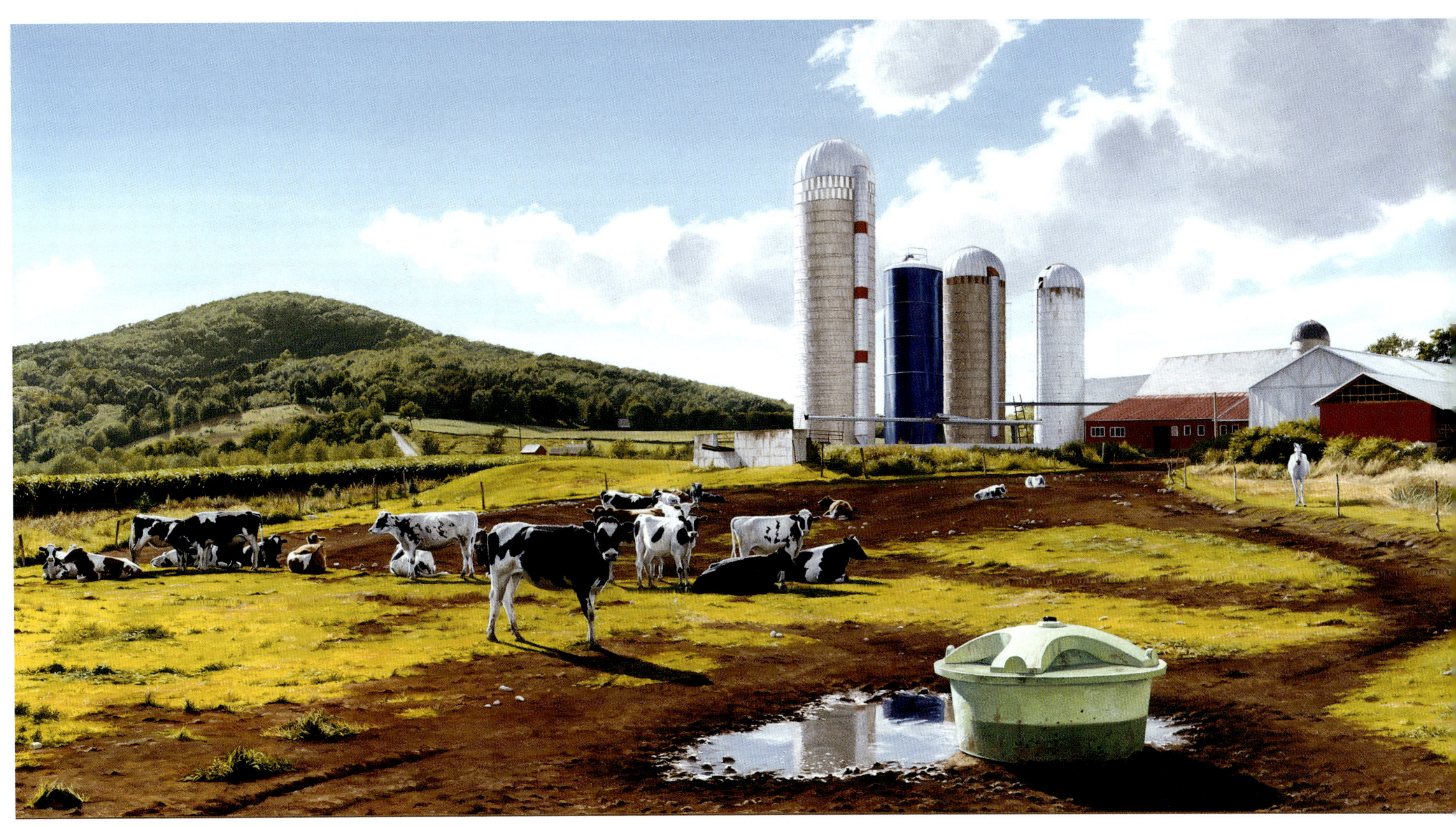

ALTOON SULTAN

American, born 1948
Farmyard, Cambridge, New York, 1987
Oil on canvas
38 x 74 in.

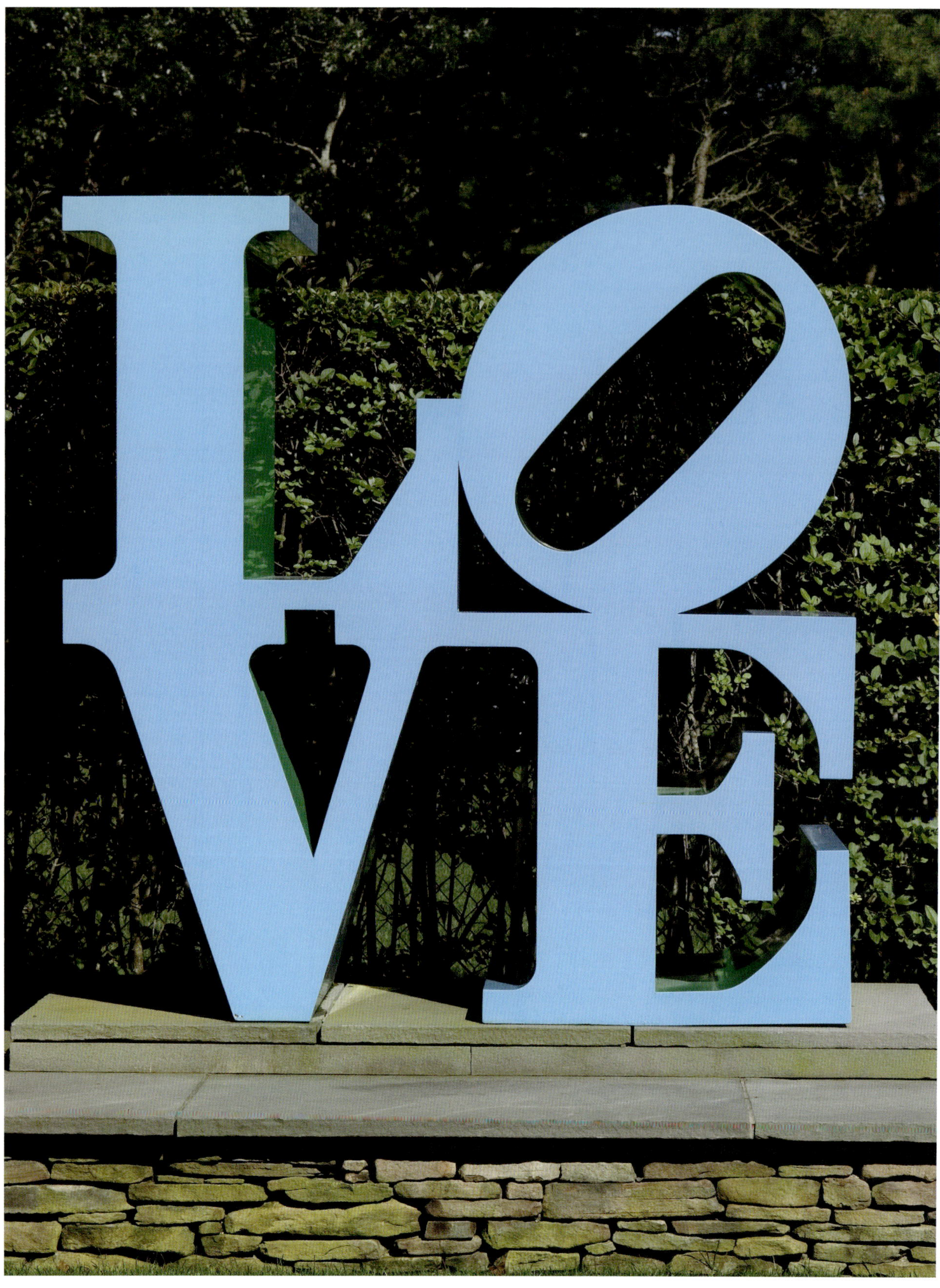

ROBERT INDIANA

American, born 1928
Love, 1995
Painted aluminum
H. 72 in., w. 72 in., d. 36 in.

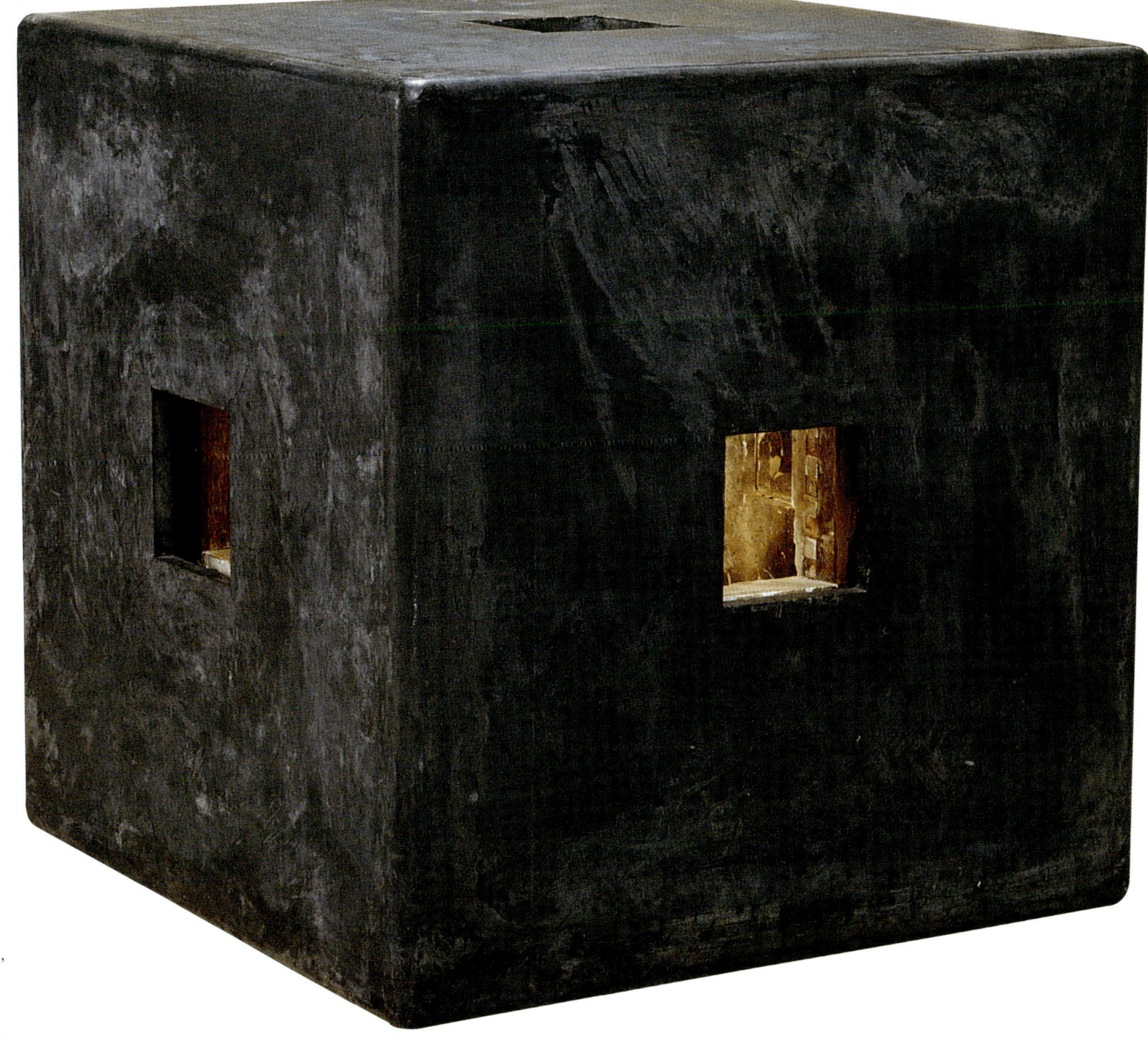

JACKIE WINSOR
American (born in Canada), born 1941
Exploded Piece, 1980–82
Concrete, plaster, and wood
34½ x 34½ in.

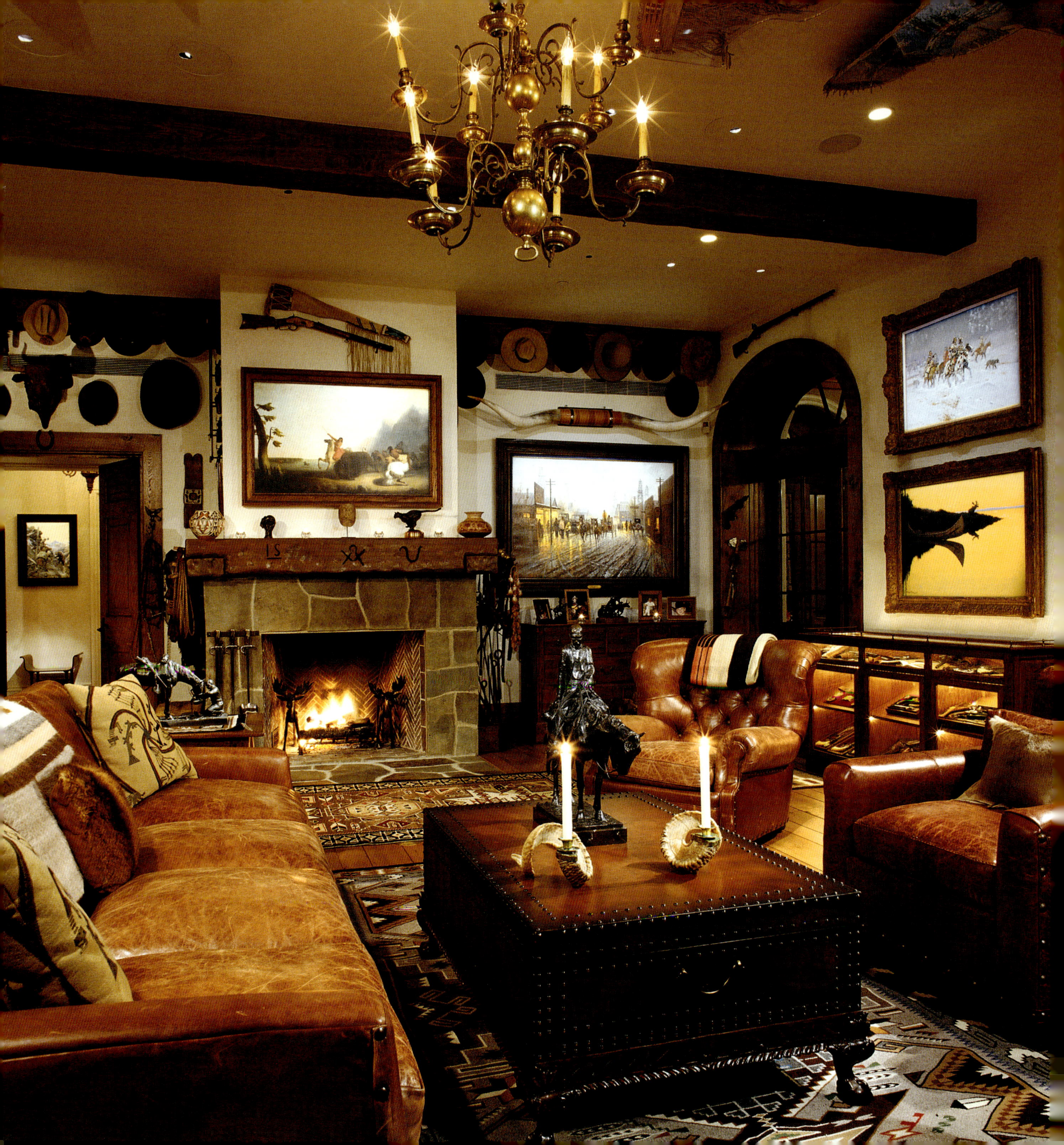

AMERICAN WEST

*****

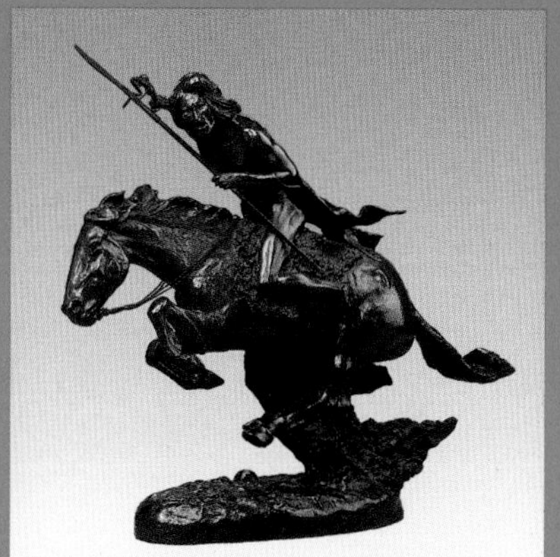

Fig. 21. Koch's Western Room
in Palm Beach

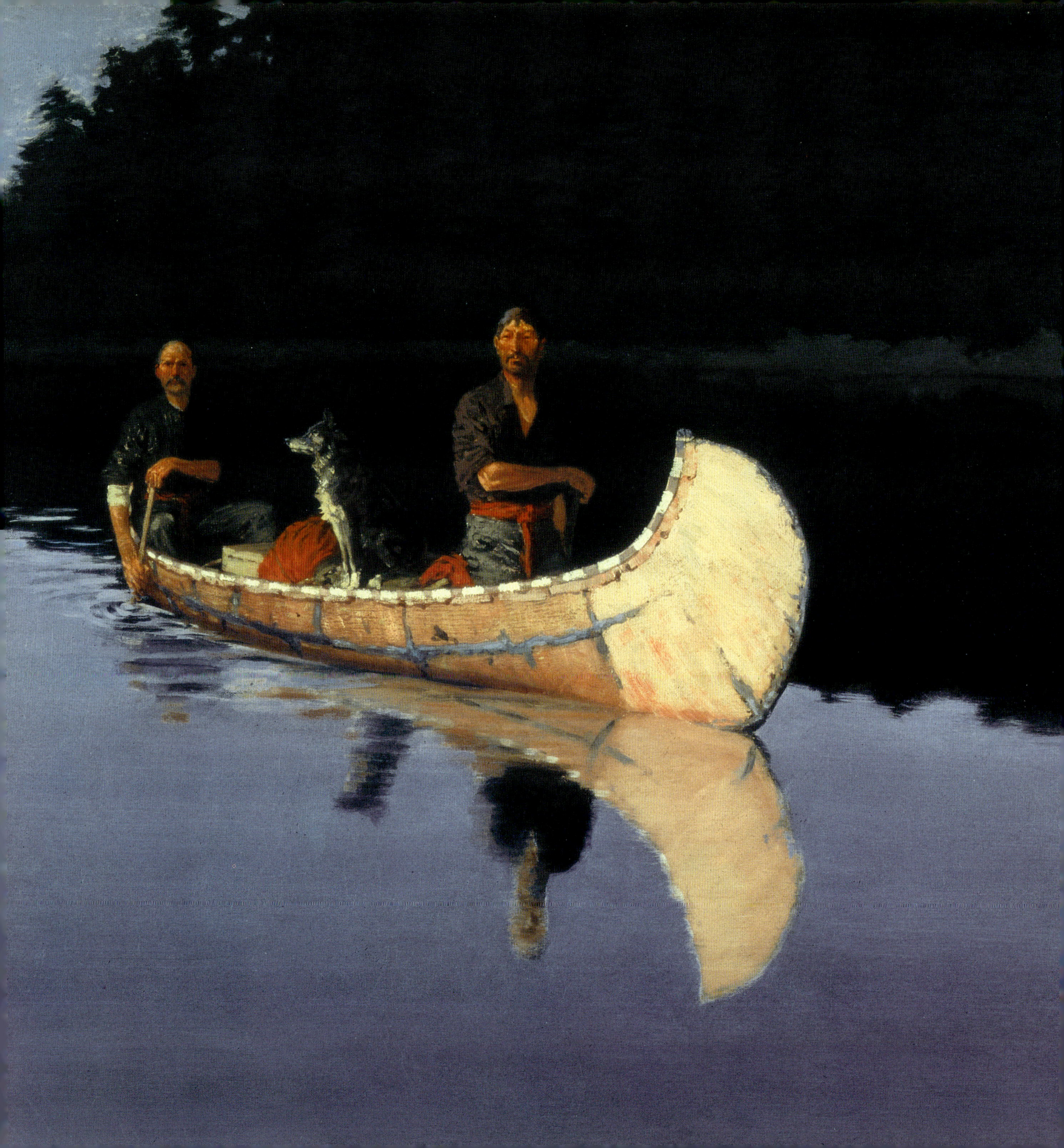

IMAGES OF THE AMERICAN WEST

* * * * * * *

Crossing the threshold of Bill Koch's Western Room in his Palm Beach home, one is transported to another place and time. Paintings and sculptures by Frederic Remington and Charles Russell line the walls; firearms, holsters, sabers, and spurs are arranged like precious talismans of the Old West; and overhead, Native American robes and beaded costumes create a sense of intimacy like that found inside a teepee. In his youth, Koch spent summers on his father's ranches, where he was expected to work hard from sunup to sundown for the going wage of five dollars a day. There, he experienced firsthand the beauty of the western landscape and the great American myths of cowboys and Indians. At sixteen, he earned right of passage as a full-fledged cowboy. His exhilaration at coming of age is reflected in his admiration for Phillip Goodwin's *A Pause on the Journey* (p. 112), a painting Koch fondly refers to as "the Marlboro Man." Goodwin's portrayal of the independent, gun-slinging, cigarette-smoking, quintessential western cowboy always hung at Koch's father's ranch house and now occupies pride of place in the Western Room.

Images of the American West embody our nation's most dearly held beliefs, aspirations, and contradictions. From the earliest scenes of North America by sixteenth-century artist-explorers Jacques Le Moyne and Joyne White, Native Americans became the predominant symbol of the New World. The first major western expedition by Lewis and Clark in 1804 led the way for generations of American artists and photographers to capture the spectacular vast open spaces, indigenous peoples, and wildlife that inhabited the frontier. In 1820 John James Audubon sought to document the natural history of the region by creating the comprehensive record *Birds of North America*, eventually published as 435 elephant folios in 1838. Following in the footsteps of painter Charles Bird King, George Catlin created more than five hundred Native American portraits for his Indian Gallery in 1837. The portraits were widely disseminated as copies and well-known illustrations, and Catlin eventually traveled with his Indian Gallery and Wild West Show to England, Holland, and France, where the critic Charles Baudelaire praised his likenesses for their rendition of "the proud and free character and noble expression of these good people."

Catlin's generation of western artists is vividly represented in the Koch Collection by Alfred Jacob Miller's dramatic scene of Native Americans engaged in a bison hunt (p. 102). Miller, the son of a Baltimore grocer, studied portraiture with the American painter Thomas Sully and pursued a career as a history painter abroad, where he learned all he could by copying Old Masters on view at the Louvre. *The Buffalo Hunt* recalls many of the dramatic lion hunts on horseback portrayed by the seventeenth-century Flemish painter Peter Paul Rubens, as well as romantic scenes of the early nineteenth century by the French painters Eugène Delacroix and Theodore Géricault. After Miller's return to America, the Scotsman William Drummond Stewart invited him to join a hunting trip out West in 1837. Stewart commissioned the artist to create large-scale paintings commemorating their adventures for his Scottish castle, and, despite Miller's dismay at having to catch his own horse each morning by running "a considerable distance in moccasins," he produced some of the most memorable early-nineteenth-century western scenes based on the expedition.

Working from watercolors sketched on the trail to facilitate the rapid pace of Stewart's hunting party, Miller later completed large oils like *The Buffalo Hunt* in his studio. Rather than drawn strictly from life, Miller's romantic scene is conjured from his mind's eye and suspends the battle for all time. A bison faces off against Indians on horseback, their death struggle evoking late-eighteenth-century notions of the sublime and awe before powerful forces of nature. Eschewing the scientific accuracy of his contemporaries Catlin and Karl Bodmer, Miller portrayed a generalized landscape with a distant view of the plains and a large rocky precipice in the foreground. The drama

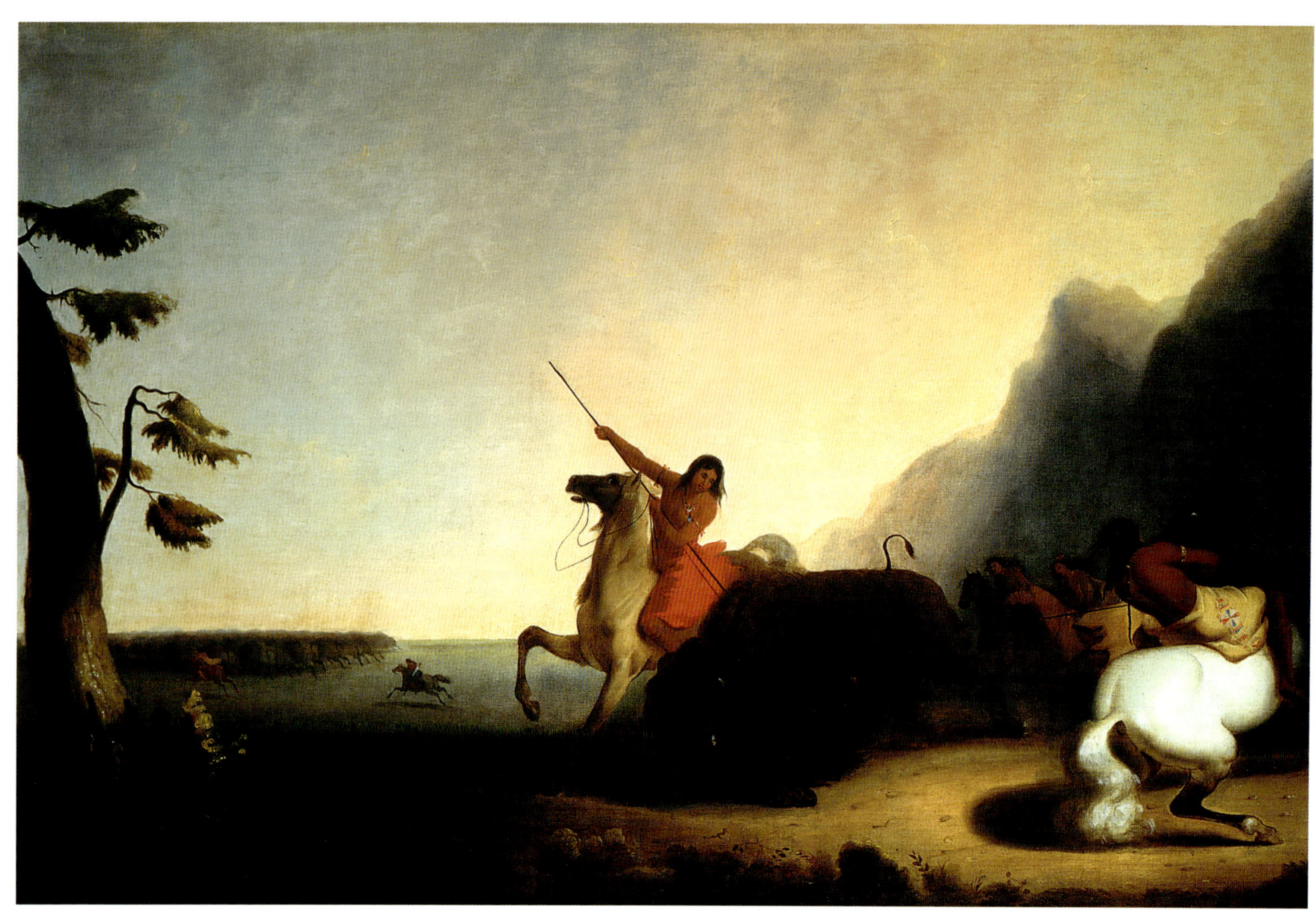

ALFRED JACOB MILLER

American, 1810–1874
The Buffalo Hunt, 1850
Oil on canvas
30¼ x 50⅛ in.

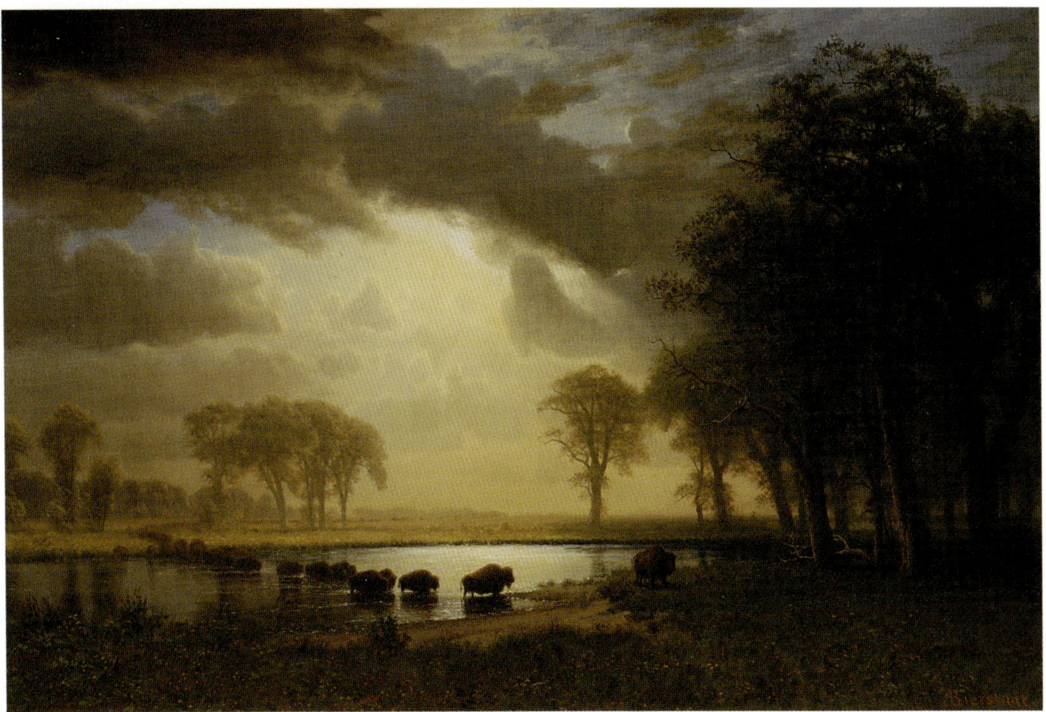

Fig. 22. Albert Bierstadt (American, born in Germany, 1830–1902), *The Buffalo Trail*, about 1867, oil on canvas, 31⅞ x 48 in., Museum of Fine Arts, Boston, Gift of Martha C. Karolik for the M. and M. Karolik Collection of American Paintings, 1815–1865, 47.1268

unfolds with only the slightest hint of bloodshed at a comfortable distance from the viewer that tempers the undercurrent of terror. Angles formed by the Indian's spear and the massive silhouette of the kneeling bison anchor the composition in a way that suggests Miller's debt to Old Master painting. By the mid-nineteenth century, paintings like *The Buffalo Hunt* ultimately fixed in common memory a potent and enduring image of the western frontier that would rapidly disappear by the 1870s.

Several generations of artists followed the trail of Catlin and Miller, including the painters Albert Bierstadt, Charles Deas, Seth Eastman, and Thomas Moran, and the photographers William Bell, William H. Jackson, Timothy Sullivan, and Carleton Watkins. Among them, Bierstadt's scenes based on his trips to the Rocky Mountains beginning in 1859 cultivated a demand for images of the West as the New Eden. Like Miller, Bierstadt executed small-scale oil sketches in the field that would later inspire mammoth canvases he sold for record prices. His panoramic pictures, often teeming with bison roaming freely across the plains (fig. 22), set the stage for Remington and Russell to capitalize on the public's nostalgia for images of the West before Indians and the herds of game they hunted were threatened with extinction.

By the late nineteenth century, Remington and Russell were the artists most widely associated with the American West. Frequently compared, the merits of their respective styles were vigorously debated during their lifetimes. One scholar sized them up as follows: "Russell was a cowboy who loved to paint, while Remington was a painter who loved cowboys."[1] Although Remington traveled more widely throughout the West, Russell called the West home. Both artists' scenes feature prominently in the most prestigious twentieth-century collections of western art, including that of Bill Koch.

Collections of Remington and Russell's work initially emerged on the East Coast between the world wars, when the Colonial Revival period witnessed a keen sense of patriotism fomented by waves of foreign immigrants reaching our shores. Renewed interest in American culture kindled among connoisseurs a desire to acquire both American paintings and decorative arts—particularly those embodying the Anglo-American past and the American West. Dr. Philip G. Cole, based in Tarrytown, New York, not far from

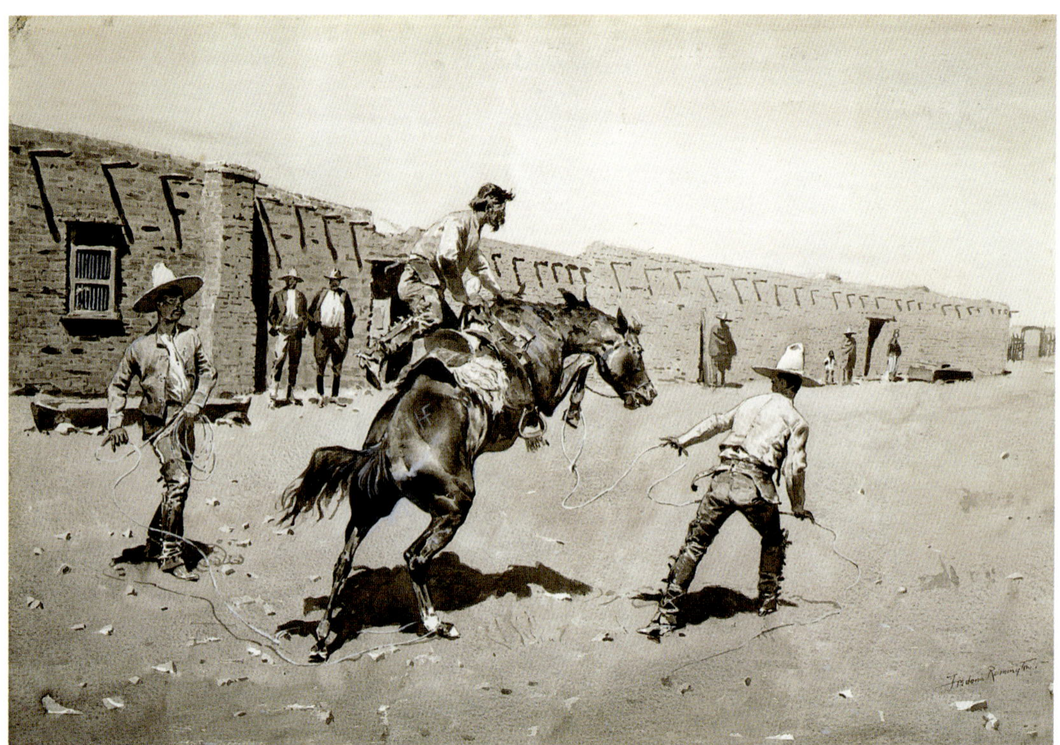

Fig. 23. Frederic Remington (American, 1861–1909), *Mexican Vaqueros Breaking a Bronc'*, pen and India ink wash with opaque white highlights, 25¼ x 38½ in., Museum of Fine Arts, Boston, Bequest of John T. Spaulding, 48.874

Remington's studio in New Rochelle, assembled an important representation of both artists that would later form the core holdings of the Thomas Gilcrease Collection in Tulsa, Oklahoma, an institution Bill Koch visited. Following Remington's lead of embellishing his studio with various western props used in his paintings, early collectors of western art tended to display works by Remington and Russell in specially decorated western rooms featuring cowboy gear, hunting trophies, and Indian artifacts. Malcolm S. MacKay incorporated such a room into his home in Tenafly, New Jersey, and Russell's friend, the entertainer Will Rogers, did the same in his sprawling ranch house in the Pacific Palisades, in California.[2] Will Hogg of Houston, Texas, distinguished himself as the first collector to assemble a comprehensive selection of Remington's work in oil and bronze. Hogg's passion for western art inspired other collectors to follow, and a posse of prominent businessmen from the Southwest who were united by their shared appreciation of western expansiveness went on to found their own eponymous institutions featuring Remington and Russell.[3]

As had many American artists before him, including Fitz Henry Lane and Winslow Homer, Remington spent his early career creating black-and-white illustrations for magazines such as *Harper's Weekly* and *Collier's Magazine* (fig. 23). His first big break occurred in 1887, when *Century Magazine* commissioned him to illustrate Theodore Roosevelt's articles based on the president's adventures out West, an artistic campaign that branded Remington as a western artist. By 1890 his popular illustrations made him one of the best-known artists in the United States, and in 1903 *Collier's* established an exclusive contract to reproduce his paintings in color, further disseminating Remington's vision of the West. Writing from the White House in 1907, President Roosevelt praised the artist: "I regard Frederic Remington as one of the Americans who has done real work for this country. . . . He is, of course, one of the most typical American artists we have ever had, and he portrayed a most characteristic yet vanishing type of American life."[4] In 1910 the Remington biographer Owen Wister wrote a feature-length article in *Collier's* declaring that "Remington is not merely an artist; he is a national treasure."[5] The cover illustration, which pictured Remington in his studio, reproduces some of the most famous works by the artist. Of those, three entered the influential collection of Will Hogg and three are included in the Koch Collection.[6]

Three of the Remington oils in the Koch Collection date from 1905, when the artist was poised to take on the challenges of painting nocturnes. Inspired by the emergence of nocturnal scenes in paintings by James Abbott McNeill Whistler (fig. 24) and contemporaneous photographs by Edward Steichen, Remington was keen to change the course of his career as an illustrator. While visiting Ingelneuk, an island he had purchased in the 1890s on Canada's St. Lawrence River, he frequently spent evenings floating adrift and sketching by moonlight. He discovered that nocturnes posed the intrinsic difficulty of rendering colors seen in the absence of daylight, and he initially lamented that he had been working too long in black and white to capture the distinctive qualities of lunar light.[7] Nonetheless, he ultimately became adept at rendering nocturnes in his inimitable western style. New York critics responded to the 1909 exhibition of his moonlight pictures with high praise: "It must be extremely trying for those commentators on picture art who always insisted this distinguished artist was 'only an illustrator' and decried his ability to paint, to visit such an exhibition as the present one. For by this time, they must be impressed with the fact that Remington's work is at once splendid in its technique, epic in its imaginative qualities, and historically important."[8]

Central to the two canoeing pictures in Koch's collection, *Evening on a Canadian Lake* (p. 106) and *Coming to the Call* (p. 107), is a series of contradictions: daytime and

Fig. 24. James Abbott McNeill Whistler (American, worked in England, 1834–1903), *Nocturne in Blue and Silver: The Lagoon, Venice,* 1879–80, oil on canvas, 19¾ x 25¾ in., Museum of Fine Arts, Boston, Emily L. Ainsley Fund, 42.302

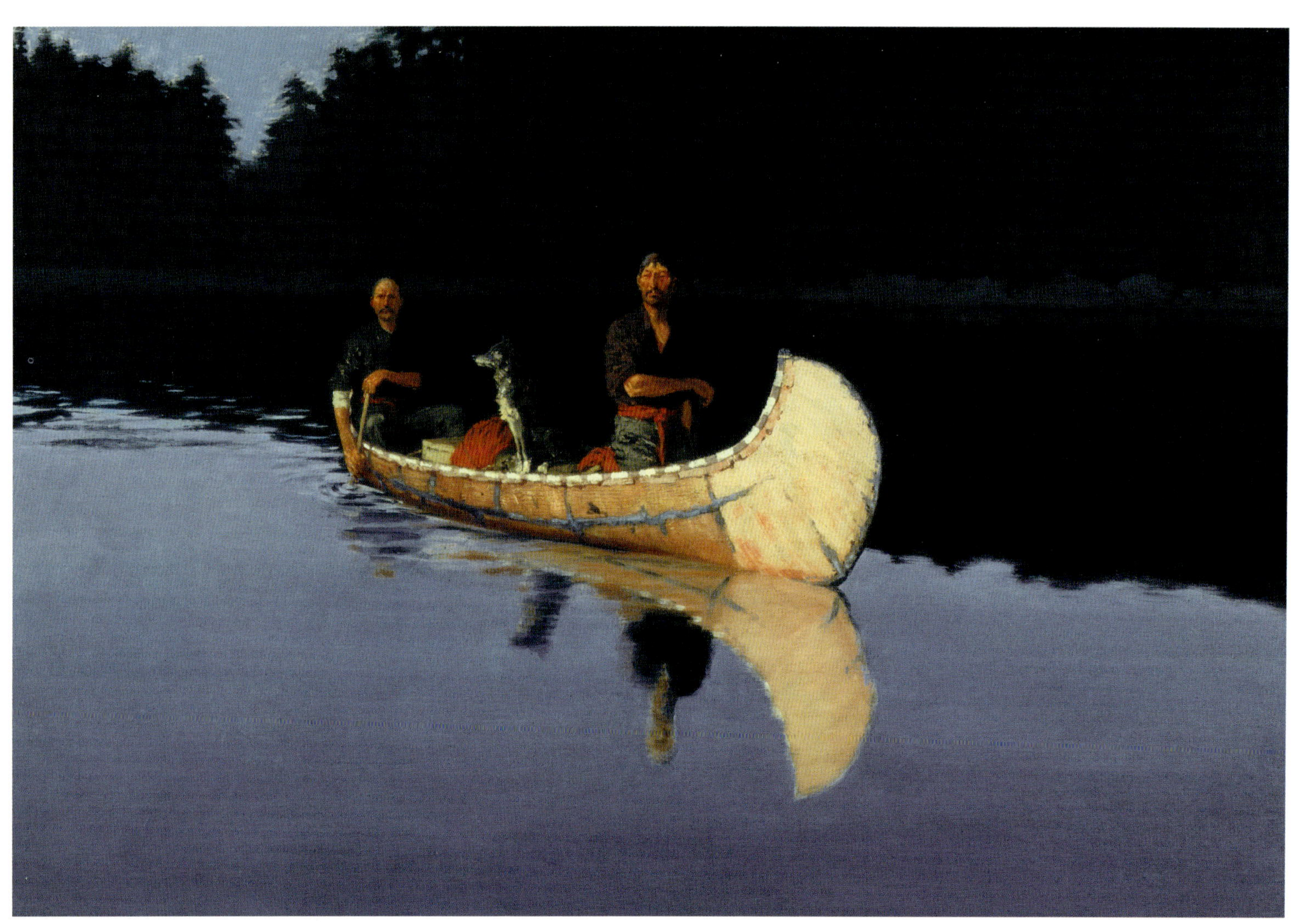

FREDERIC REMINGTON

American, 1861–1909
Evening on a Canadian Lake, 1905
Oil on canvas
27¼ x 40⅛ in.

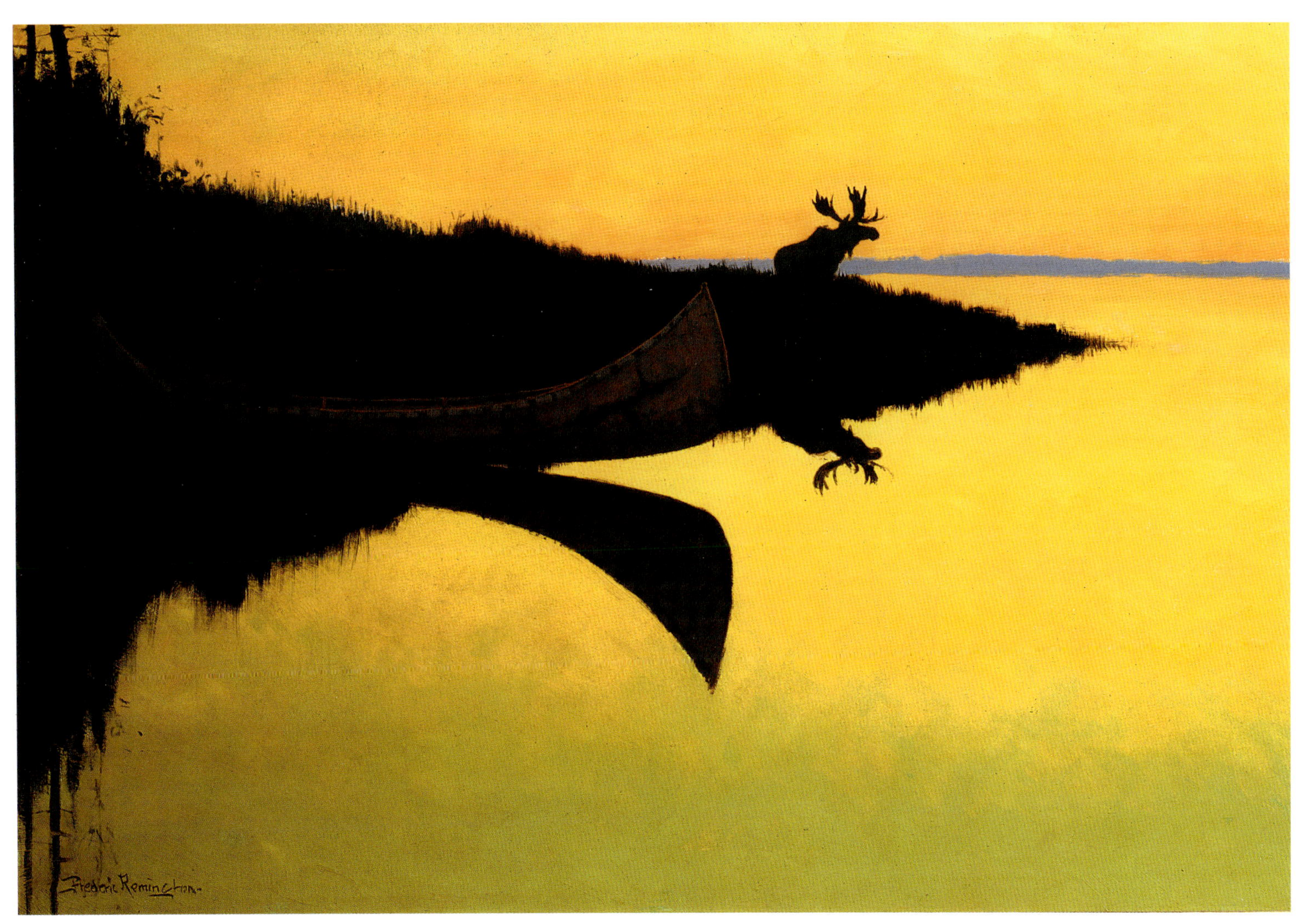

FREDERIC REMINGTON

American, 1861–1909
Coming to the Call, 1905
Oil on canvas
27⅛ x 40⅛ in.

nighttime; the hunter and the hunted; peace and apprehension in the face of death. Both images suggest Remington's admiration for late-nineteenth-century American painting, particularly George Caleb Bingham's scenes of fur traders descending the Missouri River and John Frederick Kensett's luminous seascapes. *Evening on a Canadian Lake* recasts the calm and carefully constructed genre scenes of Bingham in a far more dramatic light derived from Remington's experiences in the wilderness surrounding the St. Lawrence River. The birch-bark canoe, Remington's own, juts into the viewer's space, demarcating the watery seam between darkness and light, as the husky dog pricks up his ears as though sensing imminent danger.

In *Coming to the Call*, Remington made dramatic use of the reflections against a brilliant yellow evening sky to obscure a hunter crouching in the canoe shrouded in the darkness at the water's edge. The strong emphasis upon the horizon and the sweep of the bank that is whittled down to a fine point recall mirror images in Kensett's seascapes. One of Remington's most abstract compositions, it is also one of the most subtle in its rendering of the hunter hidden in the shadows. The calm of the scene belies the ear-splitting gunshot about to erupt and the impending death of the moose, which stands with a majestic rack silhouetted against the evening sky.

The boldness and simplicity of Remington's *An Argument with the Town Marshal* (p. 109), also a nocturne, contribute to its enduring quality as the quintessential image of a western shoot-out. Exploding gunfire and the piercing brightness of stars overhead illuminate the scene. Front and center, a cowboy and his horse stand poised for battle. They tensely embody the larger-than-life attributes of the West: virility, bravery, and independence in the face of overwhelming odds. Chestnut browns depicting horse and rider emerge rigidly against the roughly scumbled foreground, which is rendered in haunting gray-green tones sparked by the moon. After Remington's death in 1909, scenes like this one became etched in the popular memory of American moviegoers when filmmaker John Ford based some of his greatest western gunfights on the artist's unforgettable and masterfully corralled compositions.

Remington was an accomplished sculptor as well as a painter, and his virtuosity in rendering horses is clearly evident in his bronzes. He produced twenty-four sculptures of western subjects, and the Koch Collection includes five of the best-known works. The bronzes are carefully arranged along the windows in the Western Room to strike a remarkable balance of subject and form. The horse of *The Bronco Buster* (p. 114), the first bronze by the artist and an extraordinary accomplishment produced only one year after he began working with the medium, rears up on its hind legs as the cowboy steadies himself with an outstretched arm. In *Mountain Man* (p. 114), the ruggedly outfitted rider leans back and braces himself against the rear quarters of his mount, as the horse stretches its neck and forelegs fully forward in a struggle to secure footing on the steep slope. Remington was meticulous in his study of equestrian anatomy and constructed his New Rochelle studio so that a horse and rider could be brought in to pose. His special attention to cavalry scenes in which officers typically brandish their firearms while riding at breakneck speed is dramatically displayed in the juxtaposition of a bronze sculpture of a trooper and his mount modeled 1908, *Trooper of the Plains* (p. 116), with the full-blown oil painting of the same subject from about 1891–1902, *The Trooper* (p. 118). Nearby is a small bronze study of the officer's head, *The Sergeant* (p. 116), from about 1904. Remington's various renditions of the trooper are further brought to life by Koch's recent acquisition of firearms, tack, and accoutrements used to outfit a cavalry officer at the turn of the century (p. 119).

Contrasting the bronzes of white men are two of Remington's well-known sculptures of Indians. The artist's first portrayal of an Indian in bronze, *The Scalp* (p. 115), represents a forceful gesture of raising an arm directly overhead, a pose echoed by the horse, which fully extends its foreleg. Initially copyrighted as *The Triumph*, the sculpture expresses the pride of the conqueror with the figure's bold gesture, and betrays Remington's attitude about the savage nature of the Native American. Nearby, a bronze entitled *The Cheyenne* (p. 115) represents an Indian and his mount moving at top speed. Revealing his awareness of Eadweard Muybridge's strobe photography that documented the galloping horse with all four hooves coiled under its belly, Remington depicted the Indian warrior bending forward toward the horse's center of gravity at an angle echoed by the diagonal of the spear and the tail of the whip. The Cheyenne and his horse seem to spring from the earth yet appear otherworldly as they fly above the land. Koch's selec-

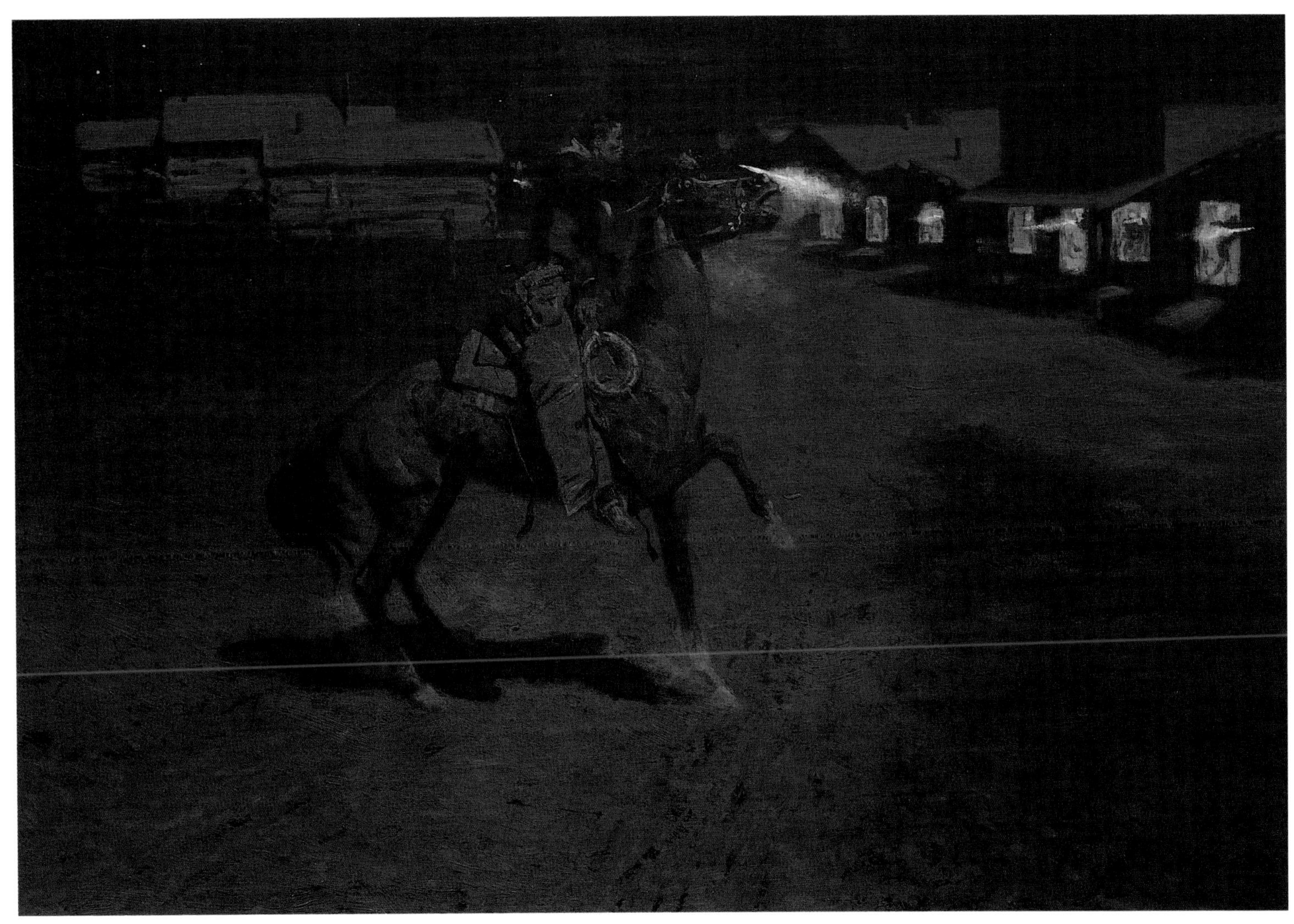

FREDERIC REMINGTON

American, 1861–1909
An Argument with the Town Marshal, about 1905
Oil on canvas
27 x 40 in.

tion of Remington bronzes represents a masterful display of poise and precariousness, further amplified by viewing all of them in concert with the artist's paintings.

Remington profited handsomely by his association with the West, yet he remained firmly entrenched in the New York art world throughout his life. Never comfortable in the East, Charles Russell epitomized the quintessential cowboy artist as free spirit. After running away from home to make his way in the rugged Montana territory, he eventually settled into work as a "nighthawk" rustling horses, to leave him time during the day for drawing and painting. A colorful personality and born storyteller, Russell fell into western life with ease, enjoying a good tale, a strong drink, and the company of fellow cowboys, ranchers, Indians, and animals alike. It is hardly surprising that his first commission was to create a western scene to hang over a bar, an opportunity he seized though he had no canvas at hand and had to make do with a smooth pine slab and house paint.

Russell worked as a cowboy until 1893, building his reputation as an artist along the way. Largely self-taught, he copied from nature and emulated the western artists he admired. His early compositions, from the 1890s, relied heavily upon Remington's illustrations culled from popular magazines. He was a prolific draftsman and often decorated his letters with diminutive watercolor drawings that resemble manuscript illuminations. One of the watercolors in the Koch Collection, *A Disputed Trail* (p. 123), exemplifies Russell's ease with the medium and portrays the perils of frontier life. Recalling Arthur Tait's 1859 painting *A Tight Fix*, which depicts a northern trapper facing a looming black bear and was widely reproduced as a popular Currier and Ives lithograph, Russell's work shows a similarly dire predicament out West. In 1911 Russell exhibited the watercolor at the Calgary Stampede in Alberta, Canada, where he may have been inspired to paint the colorful and amusing oil *Whiskey Smugglers Caught with the Goods* (p. 128). Russell included himself among the guilty bootleggers, who stand sullenly under the watchful eyes of two Canadian Mounties. His humor catches the viewer's eye in a visual pun: the Mountie on horseback points his gun at the smugglers, while the other officer points at the unlawful barrel of whiskey.

Following the successful appearance of his work at major international and national expositions in St. Louis and Seattle, Russell mounted his first one-man show of oils, watercolors, and bronzes in New York City in 1911, when nearly a page of the *New York Times* extolled the virtues of the "cowboy artist."[9] By July of that year, he received the prestigious commission to paint scenes of Lewis and Clark's expedition for the U.S. Capitol. Over time, Russell would rival Remington in popularity, and his engaging personality would be immortalized in many of the routines of Will Rogers, who first met the artist during one of his early trips to New York City, when Rogers was an unknown cowboy entertainer.

The core of Koch's collection of Russells portrays Native Americans, for whom the artist expressed a special affinity. While he was growing up in Missouri, Russell had ample opportunity to study the paintings of Native Americans by the German artist Carl Ferdinand Wimar, who settled in St. Louis in 1843 and painted Indian scenes and portraits in the surrounding territories.[10] One of Wimar's paintings at the St. Louis Art Museum, *The Captive Charger*, likely inspired Russell's characteristic arrangement of Native Americans clustered together either on horseback or standing on the ground at the center of the composition. Wimar also depicted Native Americans studying the enemy from above or riding across the plains, two motifs that feature prominently in Russell's *Trail of the White Man* or *Wagon's Dust Cloud* (p. 124) and *The Whoop-up Trail* (p. 126).

Russell's spiritual side emerges in two of the most brilliant paintings in Koch's western collection, *The Sun Worshipers* (p. 125) and *Trail of the White Man*. In a letter from May 1911, Russell described what he was after in *The Sun Worshipers*:

> All Plains Indians I think prayed to the sun and were much more devout than their Christian white brothers. This painting represents the advance of a hunting party. The old man is asking the sun for success in the buffalo run. The sun is in the sun river or as the Indians call it the Medicine River Valley in Montana. In the background the sun river buttes. In old times this was one of the favorite hunting grounds of the Blackfoot.[11]

The central Indian, highlighted by his white appaloosa horse, gestures with arms extended, as he raises his gaze and his torso toward the light. His horse echoes the entreaty by lifting its head and closing its eyelids before the blinding sun. At the left, the Indian leaning on his spear points skyward in the guise of acolyte for this outdoor cathedral. Russell often signed his letters and paintings with a longhorn skull. In this composition, the skeletal remains suggest the desired outcome of the hunt ahead and the impending death of the old man worshiping the sun.

In *Trail of the White Man*, painted in the year before Russell died, the artist returned to his passion for painting full Indian regalia. In one of his letters, he likened the Native American costume to their natural environment: "Our red brother stole his fashion from animals and birds he knew. He saw the sage cock dance and spred [*sic*] his tail fethers that's where Mr Injun got his dance bussel he liked the war bonnet that the Canadian jay and the King Fisher wore so he made himself one."[12] Arranged on a promontory that affords a spectacular vista of the valley below are three Native Americans displaying all their finery. Set off by his white horse, the central figure resembles a bird with feathers streaming from his spear and crown. The robe covering the Indian at the right suggests a bear skin studded with a decorative border of claws, a potent symbol for Native Americans and for the famous Chief Sitting Bull.

Ensconced within lariats, branding irons, tomahawks, and beaded moccasins, Bill Koch's expansive collection of western art embodies the image of rugged American masculinity and independence, and evokes nostalgia for a way of life long past. Koch's deep love of the West, spurred on by his early experiences on his father's ranches, endures in these paintings and sculptures by our nation's greatest western artists.

—ELLIOT BOSTWICK DAVIS

1. Lonn Taylor, *The American Cowboy*, by Lonn Taylor and Ingrid Maar (Washington, D.C.: American Folklife Center, Library of Congress, 1983), 104, as quoted in *Remington, Russell, and the Language of Western Art*, by Peter H. Hassrick (Washington, D.C.: Trust for Museum Exhibitions, 2000), 146.

2. See Emily Neff, *Frederic Remington: The Hogg Brothers Collection at the Museum of Fine Arts*, Houston (Princeton, N.J.: Princeton University Press in association with the Museum of Fine Arts, Houston, 2000), 26–27. Figure 20 depicts MacKay's Western Room, about 1925–30. The Will Rogers State Historic Park in Pacific Palisades was built in the late 1920s and became a California state park after his wife, Betty, died in 1944.

3. Among them were Amon Carter, R. W. Norton, Sid Richardson, C. R. Smith, and Lutcher Stark. See Neff, *Frederic Remington*, 3.

4. Quoted in Neff, *Frederic Remington*, 28.

5. Quoted in Neff, *Frederic Remington*, 29.

6. For illustration of *Collier's Weekly*, January 8, 1910, see Neff, *Frederick Remington*, 29, fig. 23.

7. Nancy K. Anderson et al., *Frederic Remington: The Color of Night* (Washington, D.C.: National Gallery of Art, 2003), 12.

8. Anderson, *Color of Night*, 69.

9. Frederic G. Renner, *Charles M. Russell: Paintings, Drawings, and Sculpture in the Amon G. Carter Collection* (Austin: University of Texas Press, 1966), 11.

10. Brian Dieppe, *Looking at Russell* (Fort Worth: Amon Carter Museum, 1987), 55–57.

11. Peters et al., *Personal Gathering*, 134.

12. Harold McKracken, *The Charles M. Russell Book: The Life and Work of the Cowboy Artist* (New York: Doubleday, 1957), 130.

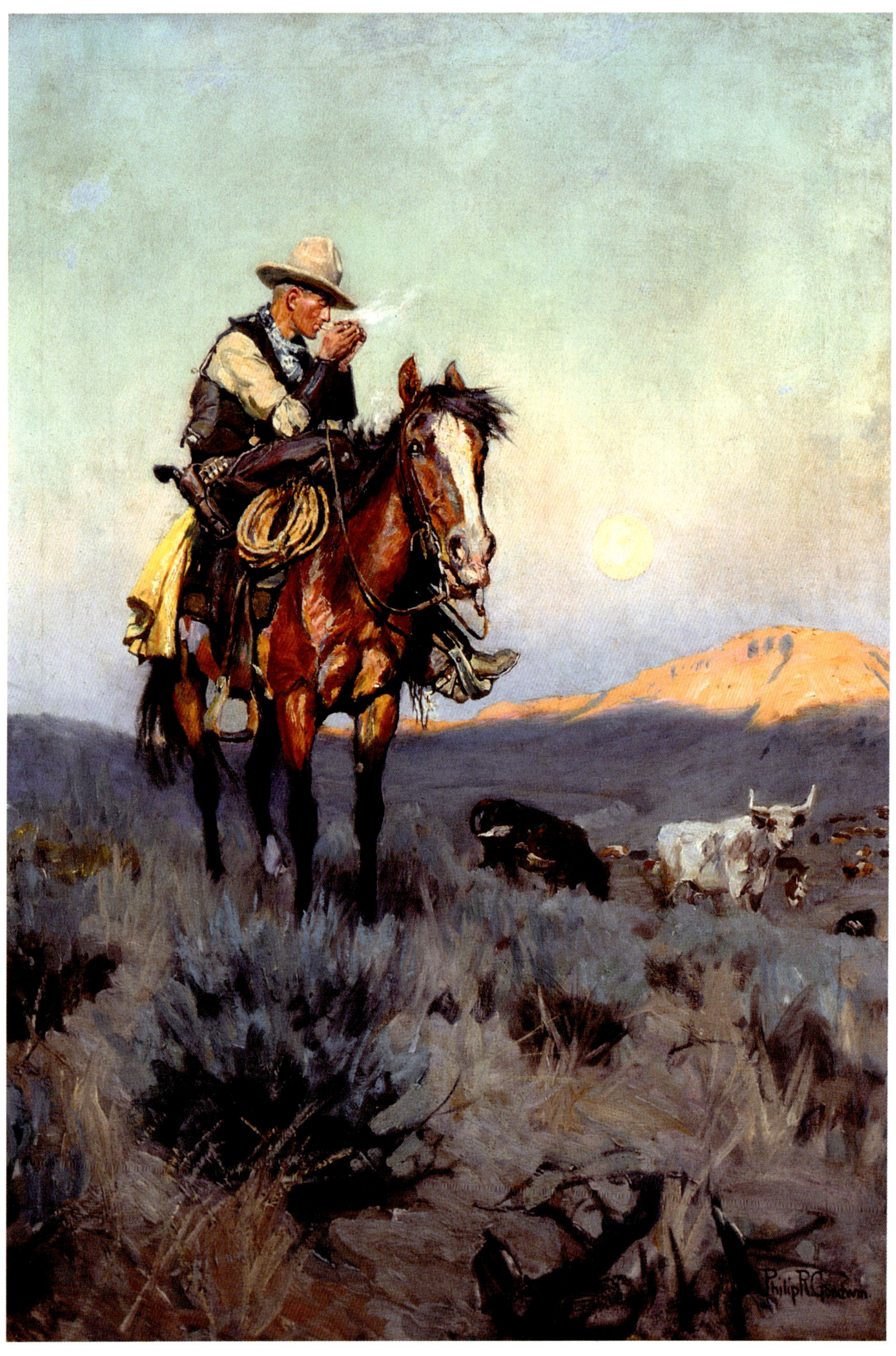

PHILLIP RUSSELL GOODWIN

American, 1882–1935
A Pause on the Journey
Oil on canvas
35½ x 25½ in.

Opposite:
Group of items used by a western cowboy, including braided horsehair halter, bit and reins, Damascus bowie-style knife with fringed leather scabbard, holster and cartridge belt, revolver, Stetson 5x beaver hat, leather lariat, pair of steel spurs, gold city marshal's badge, two gold Texas Ranger badges, nickel-plated handcuffs, and branding irons with two of the ranch brands of Bill Koch's father

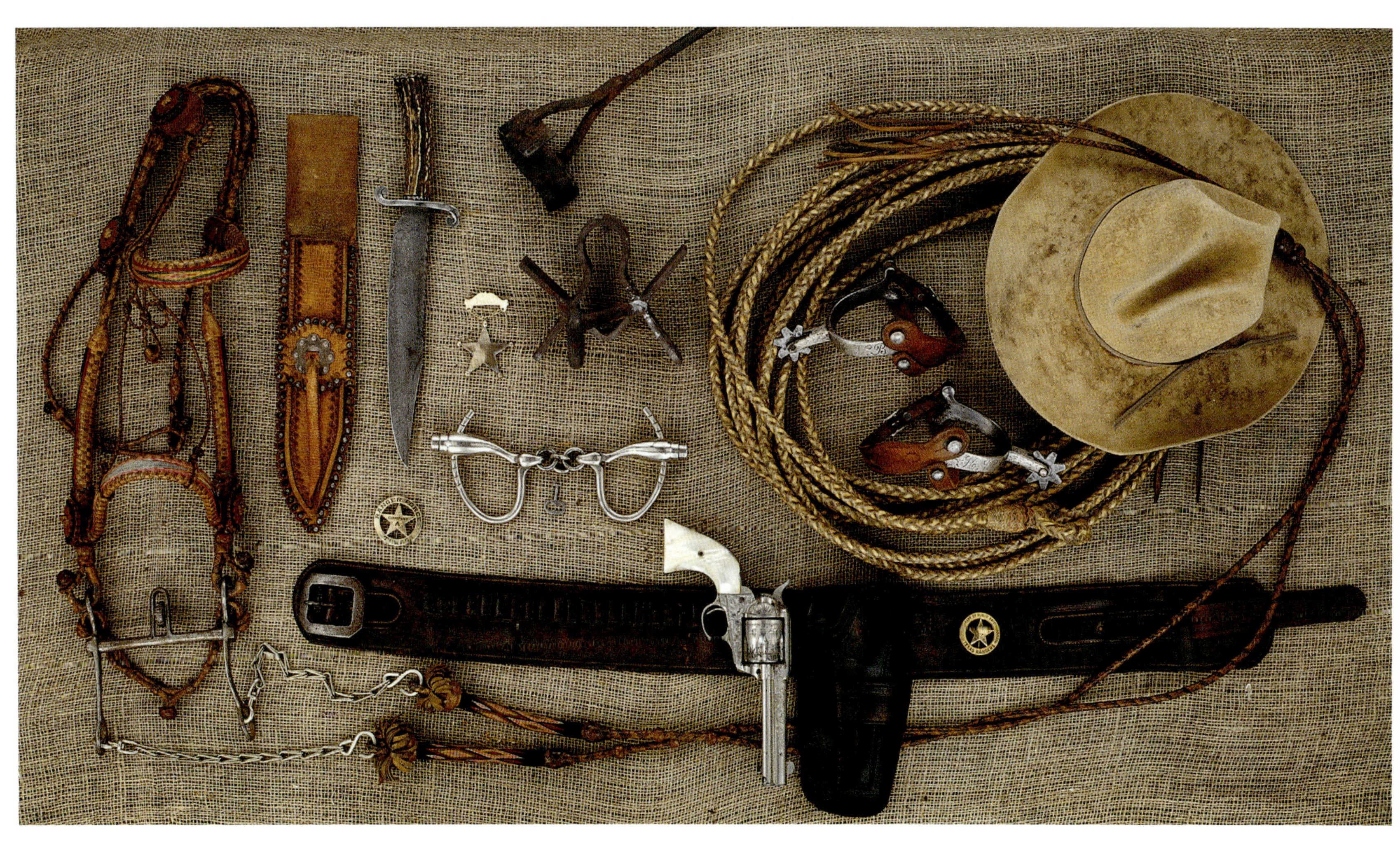

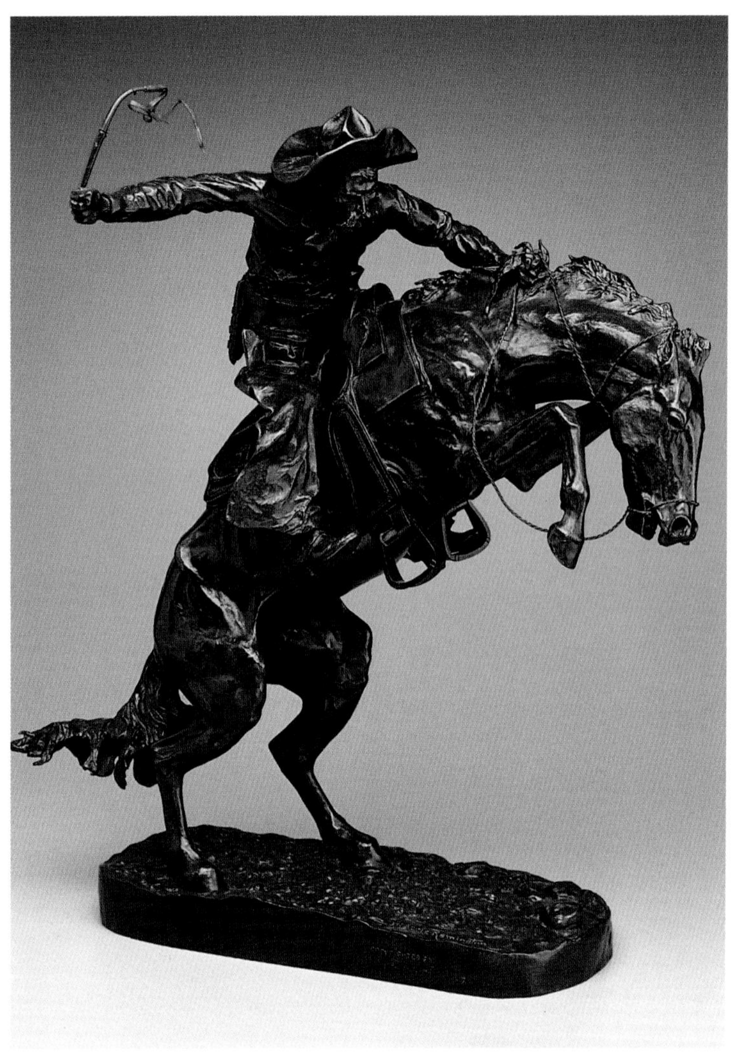

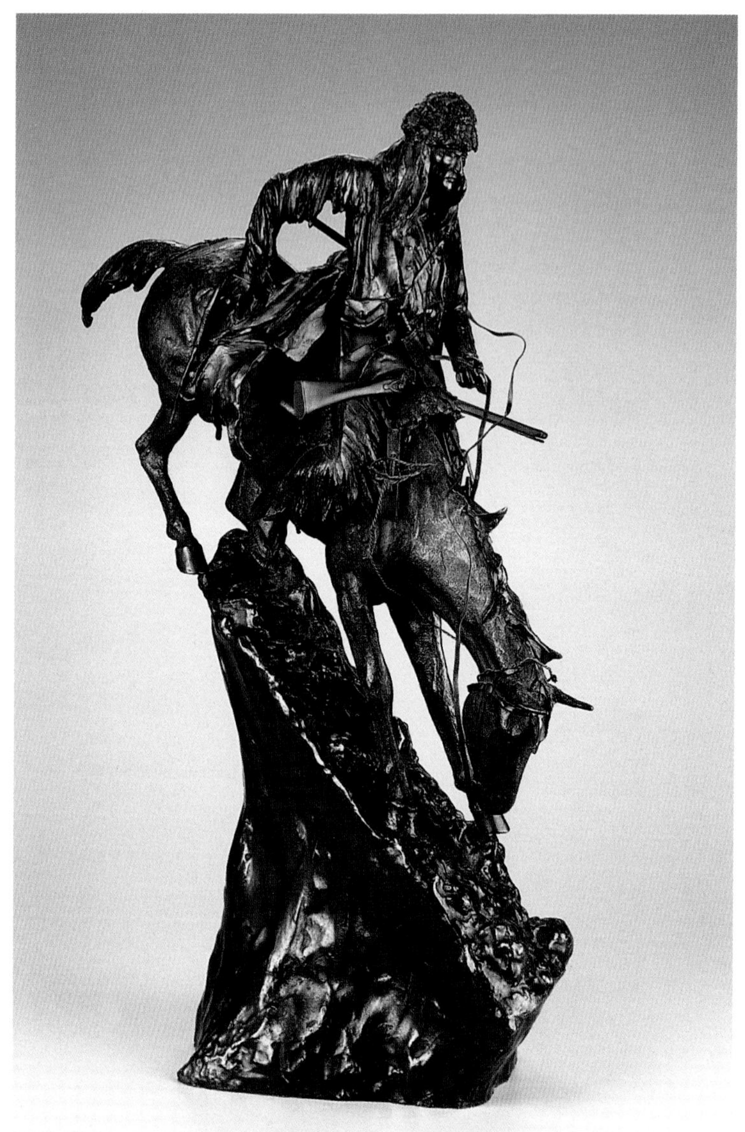

FREDERIC REMINGTON

American, 1861–1909
The Bronco Buster, modeled 1895,
cast 1898
Bronze with dark brown patina
H. 26¾ in., w. 12 in., d. 22 in.

FREDERIC REMINGTON

American, 1861–1909
Mountain Man, modeled 1903,
cast 1920
Bronze with dark brown patina
H. 28¾ in., w. 11 in., d. 16¼ in.

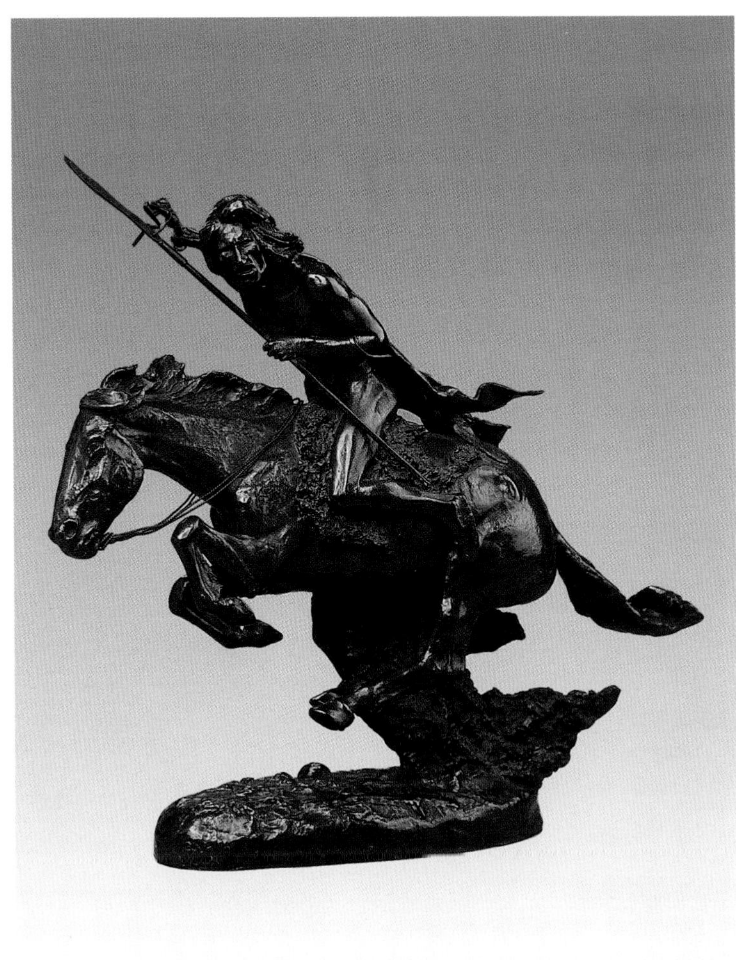

FREDERIC REMINGTON

American, 1861–1909
The Cheyenne, modeled 1901,
cast 1911
Bronze with dark brown patina
H. 21¼ in., w. 7 in., d. 23¾ in.

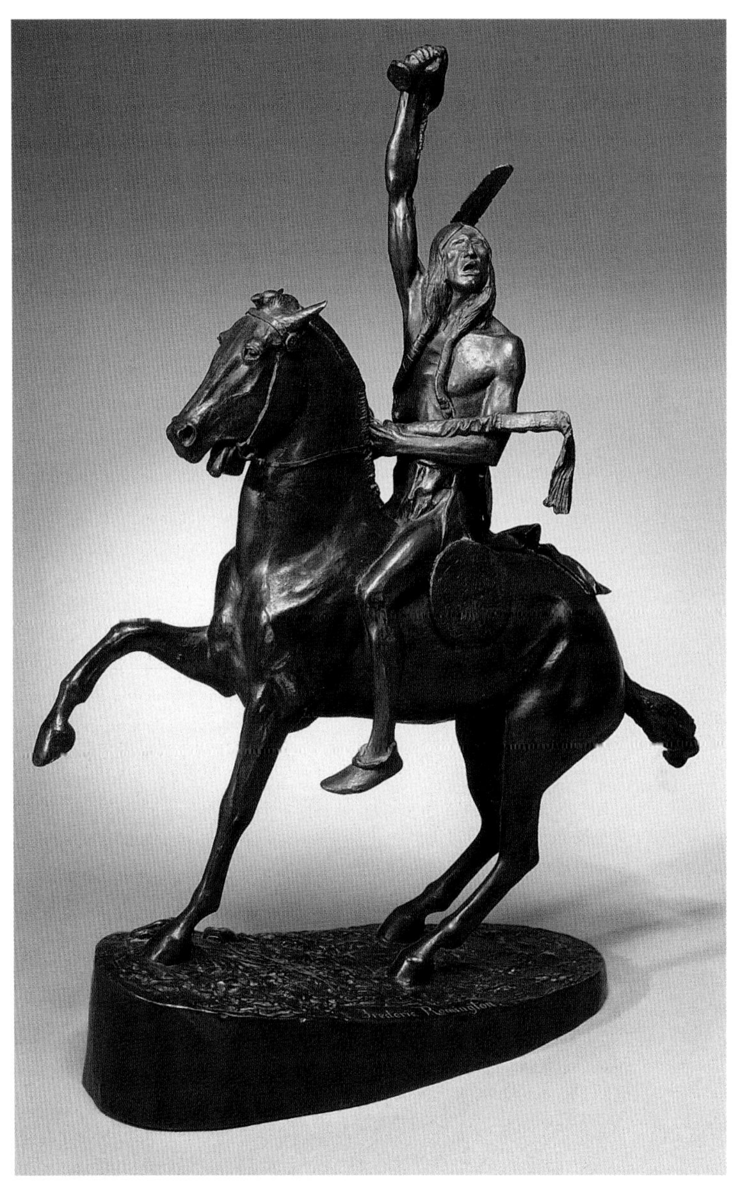

FREDERIC REMINGTON

American, 1861–1909
The Scalp, modeled and cast 1898
Bronze with dark brown patina
H. 26¼ in., w. 7¼ in., d. 21¼ in.

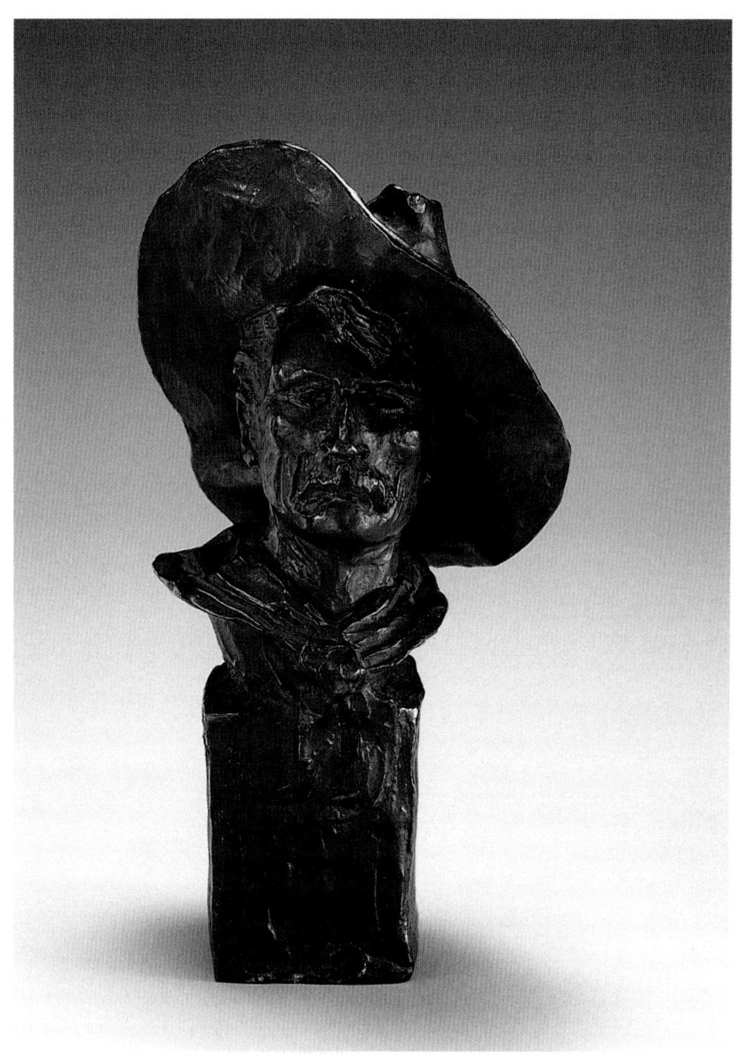

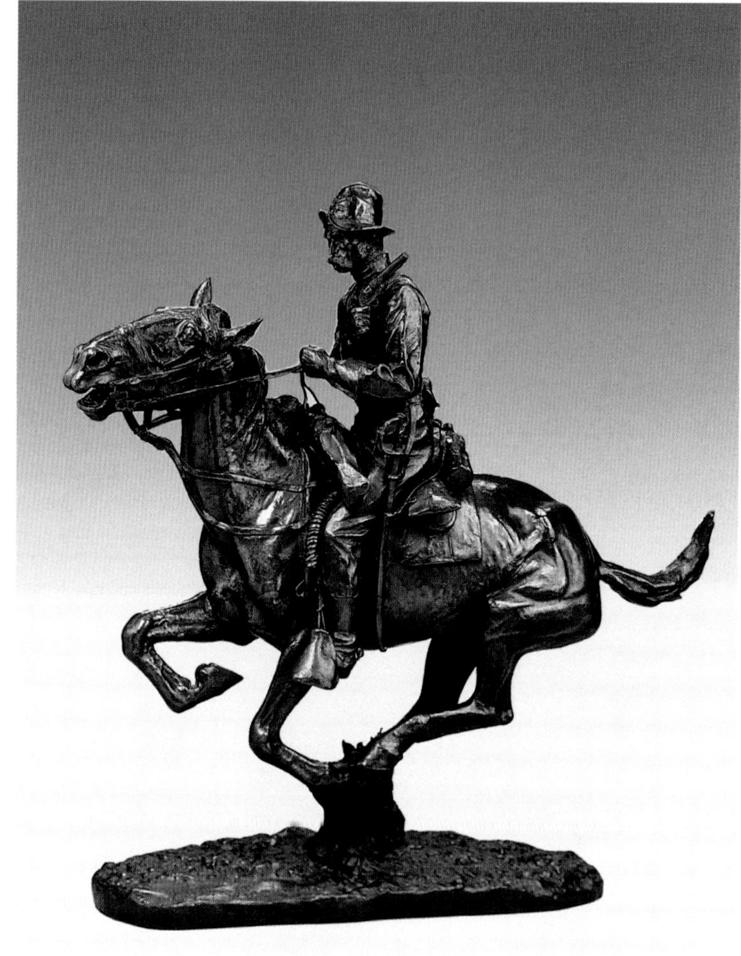

FREDERIC REMINGTON

American, 1861–1909
The Sergeant, about 1904
Bronze with dark brown patina
H. 10¼ in., w. 5½ in., d. 5 in.

FREDERIC REMINGTON

American, 1861–1909
Trooper of the Plains, modeled 1908,
cast 1909
Bronze with green and brown patina
H. 26¼ in., w. 8¾ in., d. 28¼ in.

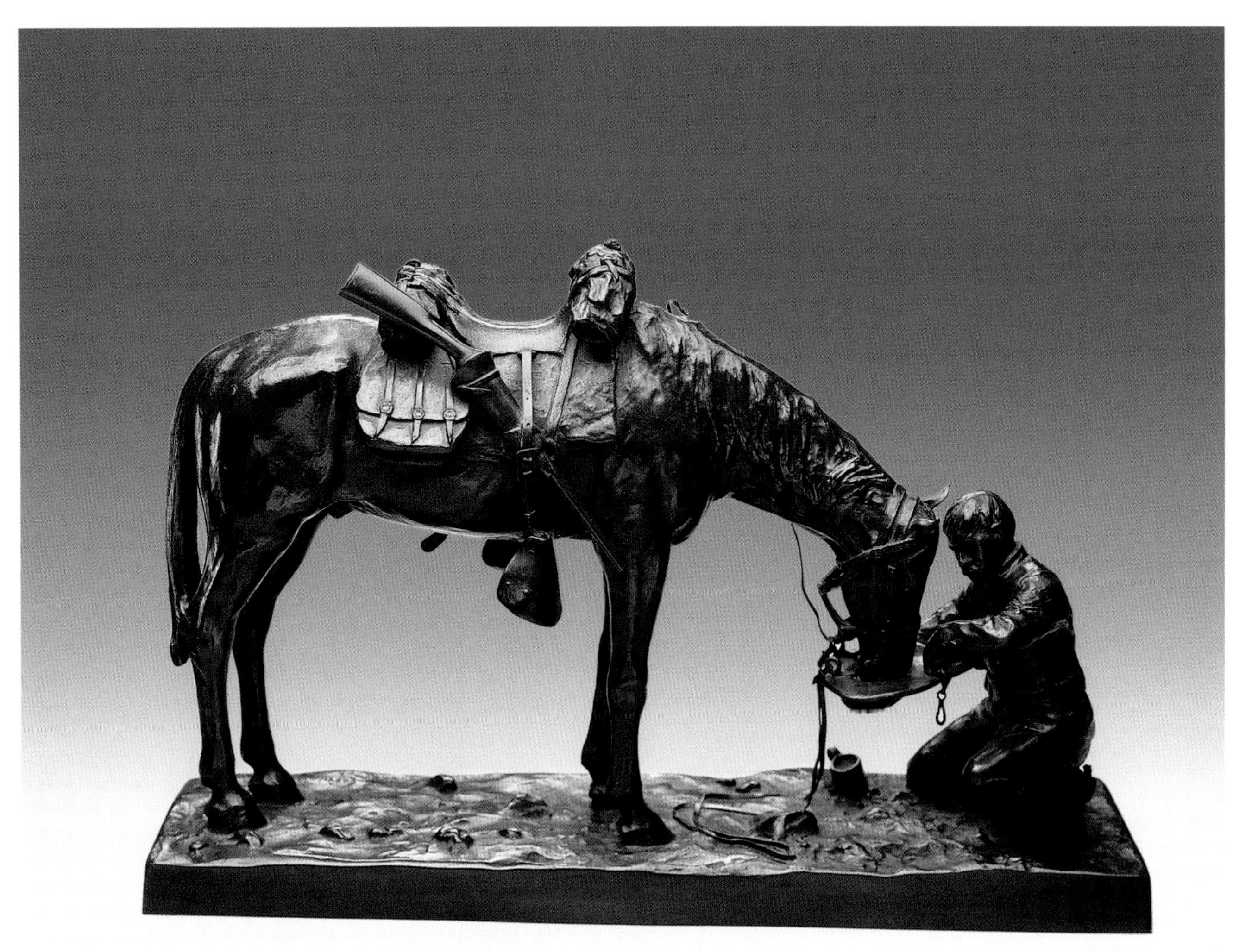

CHARLES SCHREYVOGEL

American, 1861–1912
The Last Drop, 1903
Bronze with dark brown patina
H. 11¾ in., w. 5¼ in., d. 18½ in.

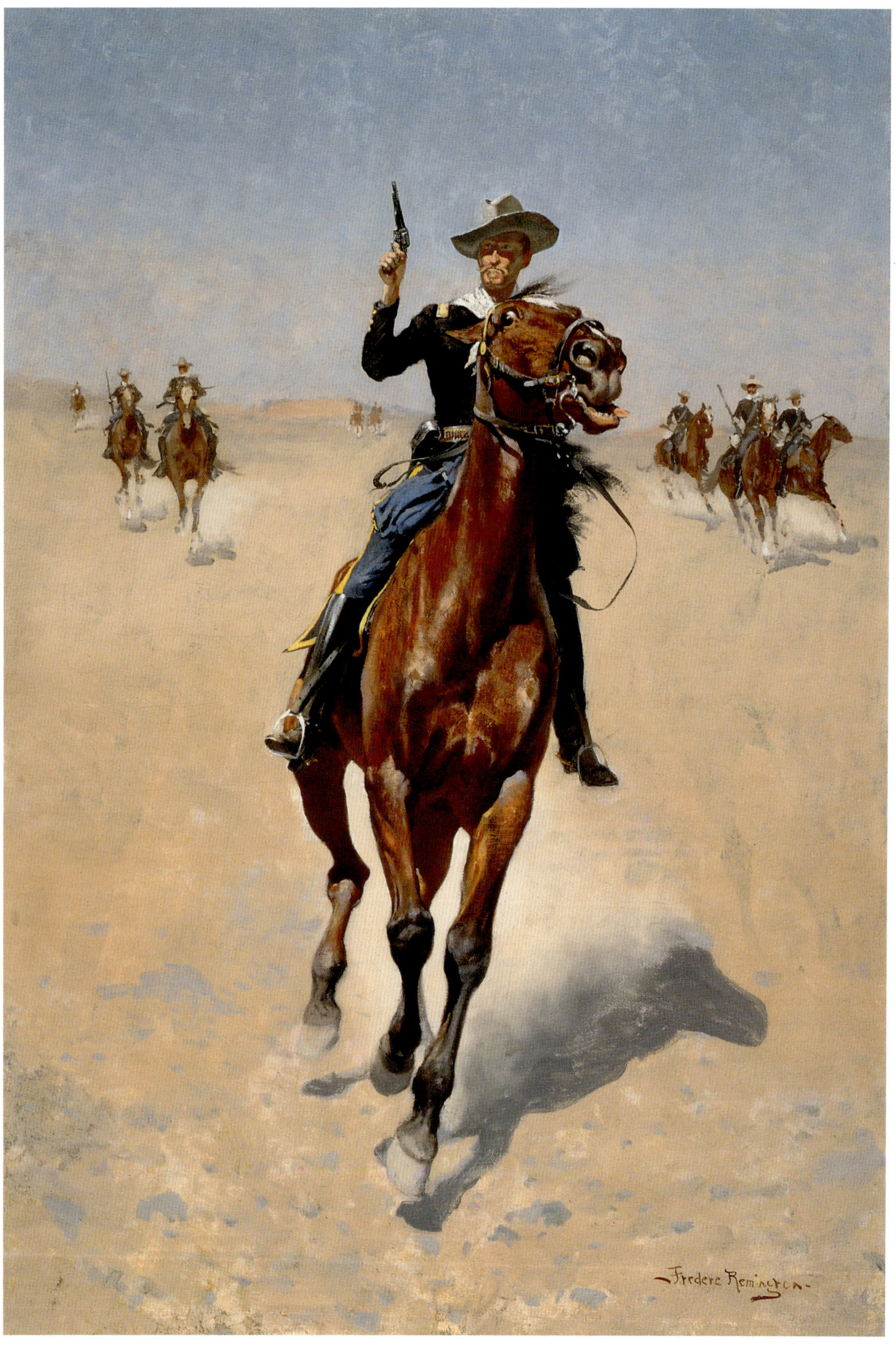

FREDERIC REMINGTON

American, 1861–1909
The Trooper, about 1891–1902
Oil on canvas
48¼ x 34 in.

Opposite:
Arms and accoutrements of U.S. Army cavalry troops, including Colt Model 1873 single-action army revolver no. 48139, U.S. Springfield Armory Model 1873 breechloading carbine, Model 1860 saber and Civil War–period C.S.A. sword with scabbard, cartridge belts, leather pouches, saddle bags, spurs, tin cup, officer's campaign hat and enlisted man's kepi, "Death to Traitors" Civil War–era knife with scabbard, and inert cartridges

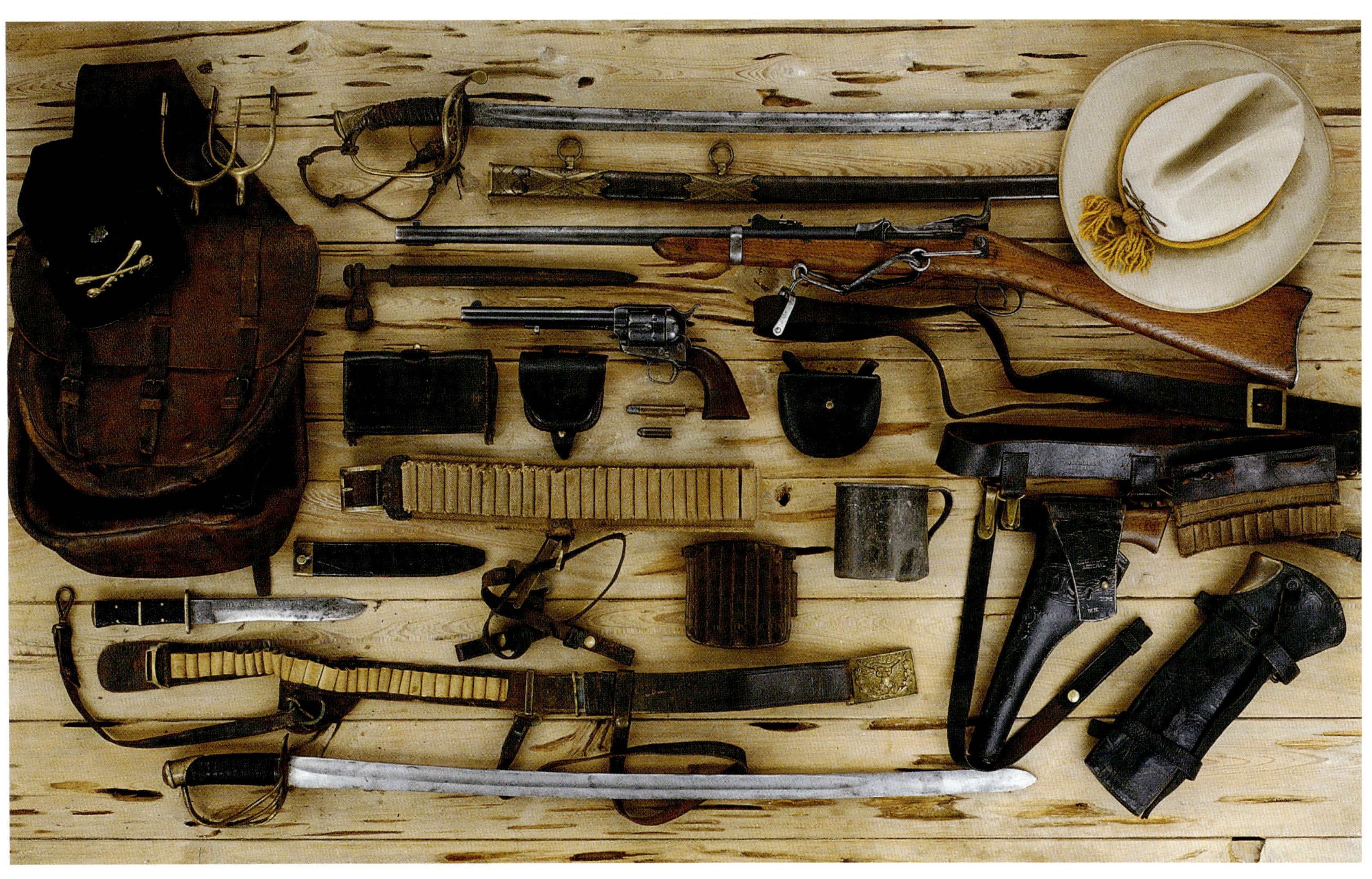

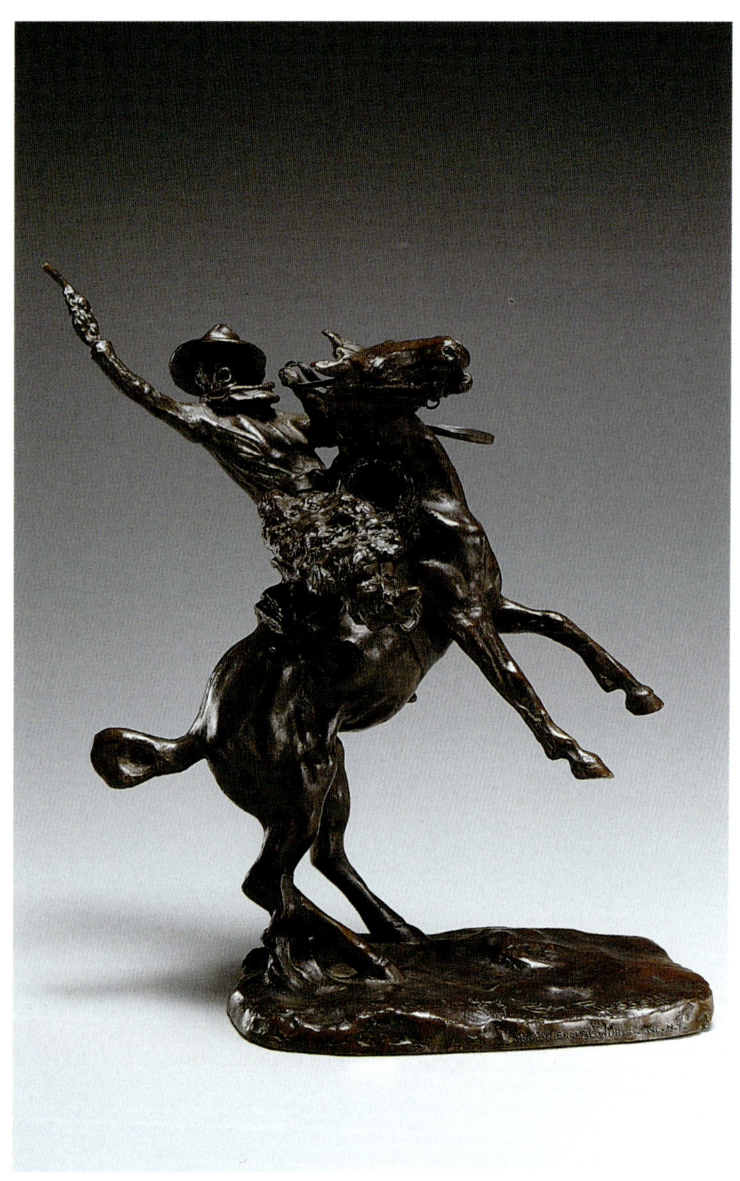

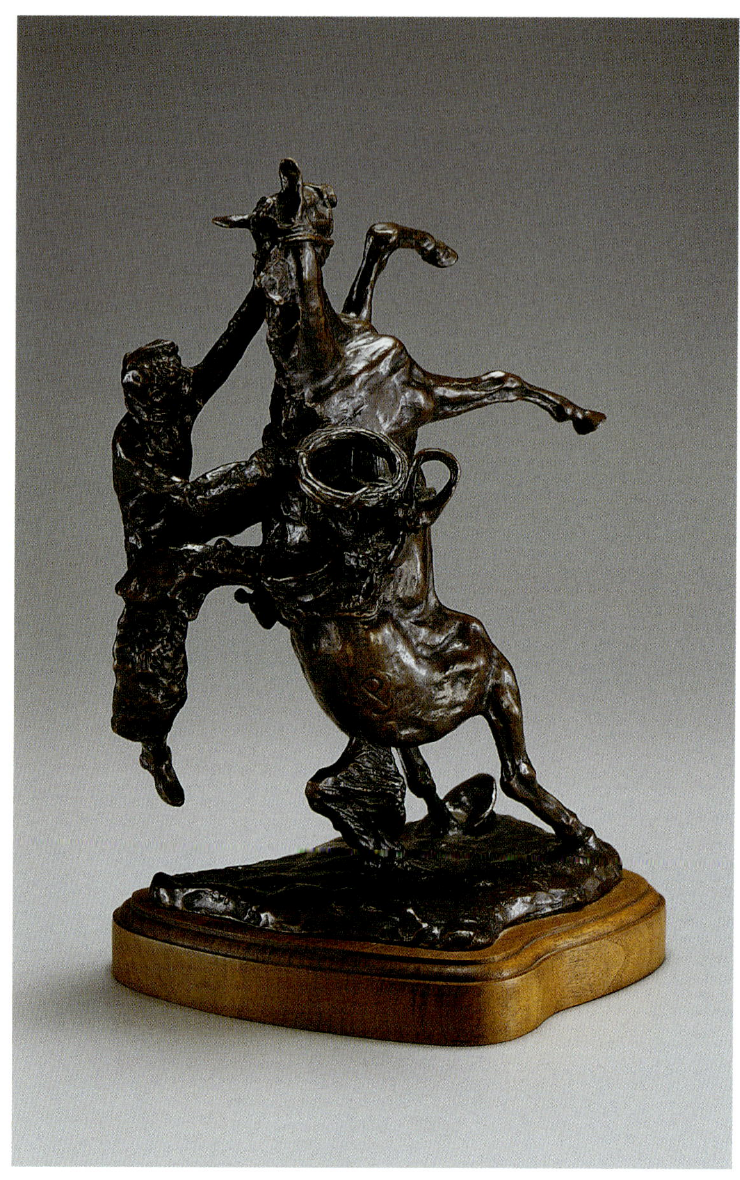

CHARLES MARION RUSSELL

American, 1864–1926
Smoking Up, modeled and cast 1904
Bronze
H. 11¾ in., w. 10½ in., d. 6½ in.

CHARLES MARION RUSSELL

American, 1864–1926
When the Best of Riders Quit, modeled 1921–22, cast about 1929–34
Bronze
H. 14 in., w. 11 in., d. 7¾ in.

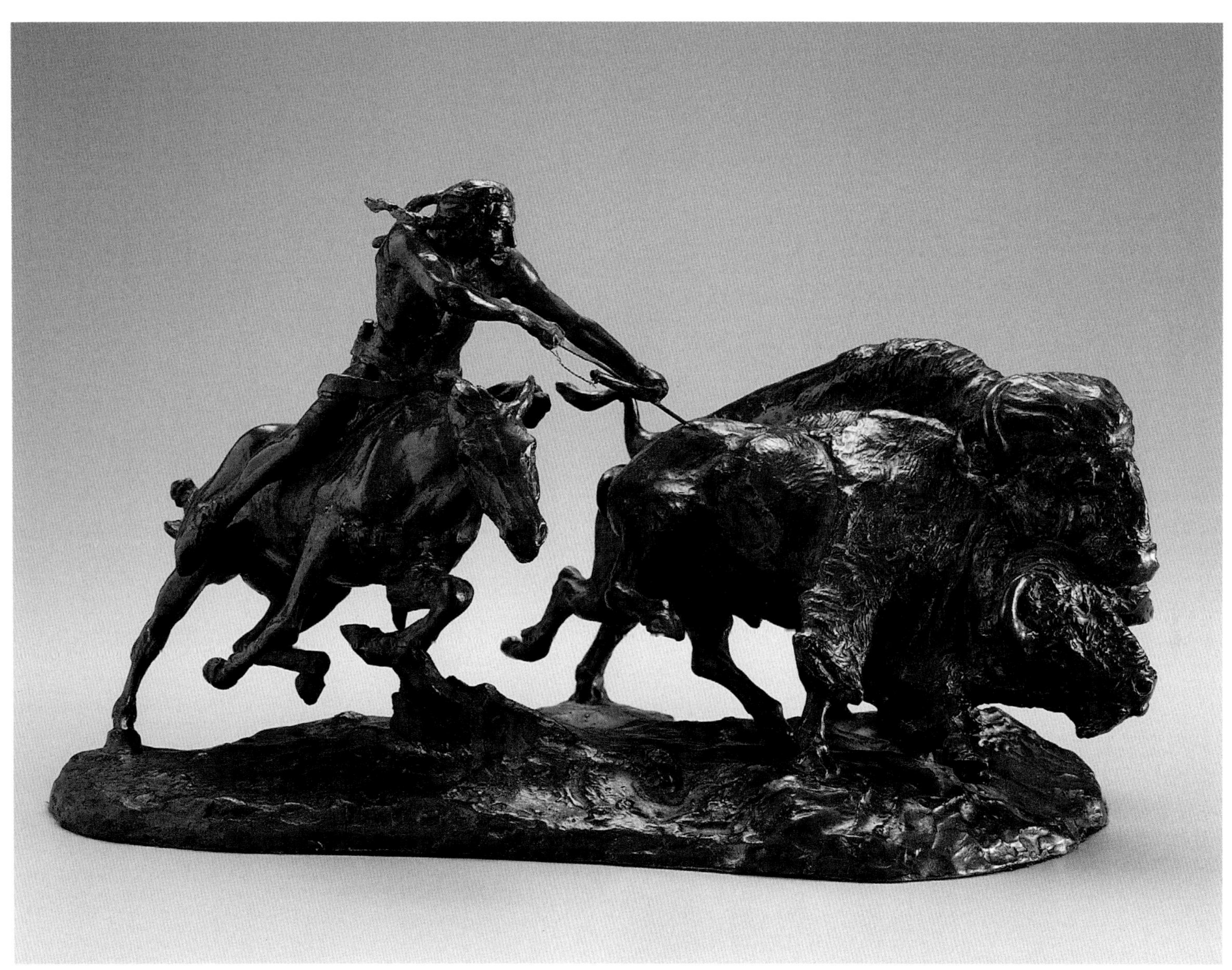

CHARLES MARION RUSSELL

American, 1864–1926
Buffalo Hunt, modeled 1905,
cast about 1925
Bronze with brown patina
H. 10¼ in., w. 17¾ in., d. 13 in.

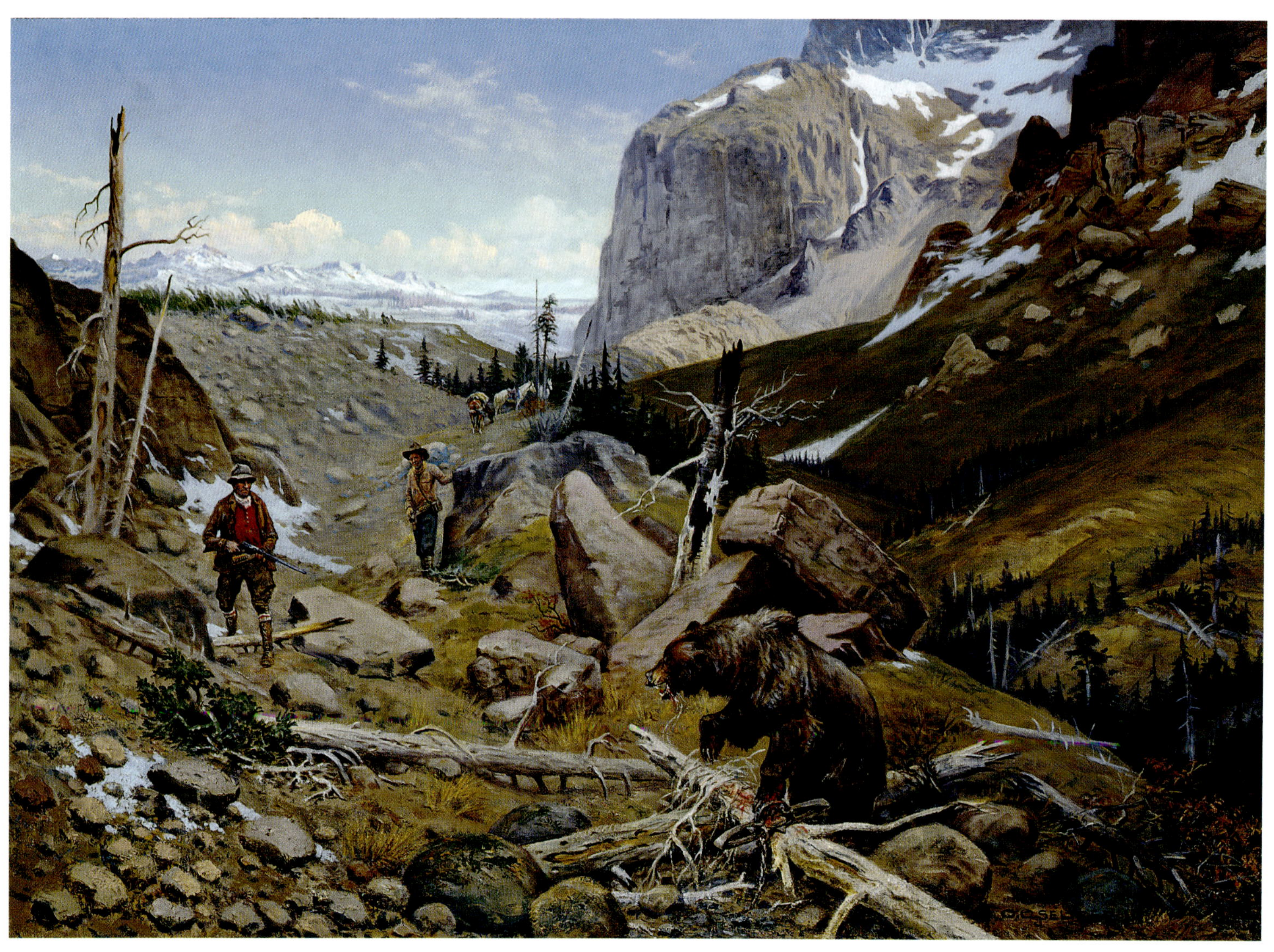

OLAF CARL SELTZER

American, 1877–1957
Cautious Encounter
Oil on canvas
28 x 40 in.

CHARLES MARION RUSSELL

American, 1864–1926
A Disputed Trail, 1908
Watercolor on paper
23¾ x 18 in.

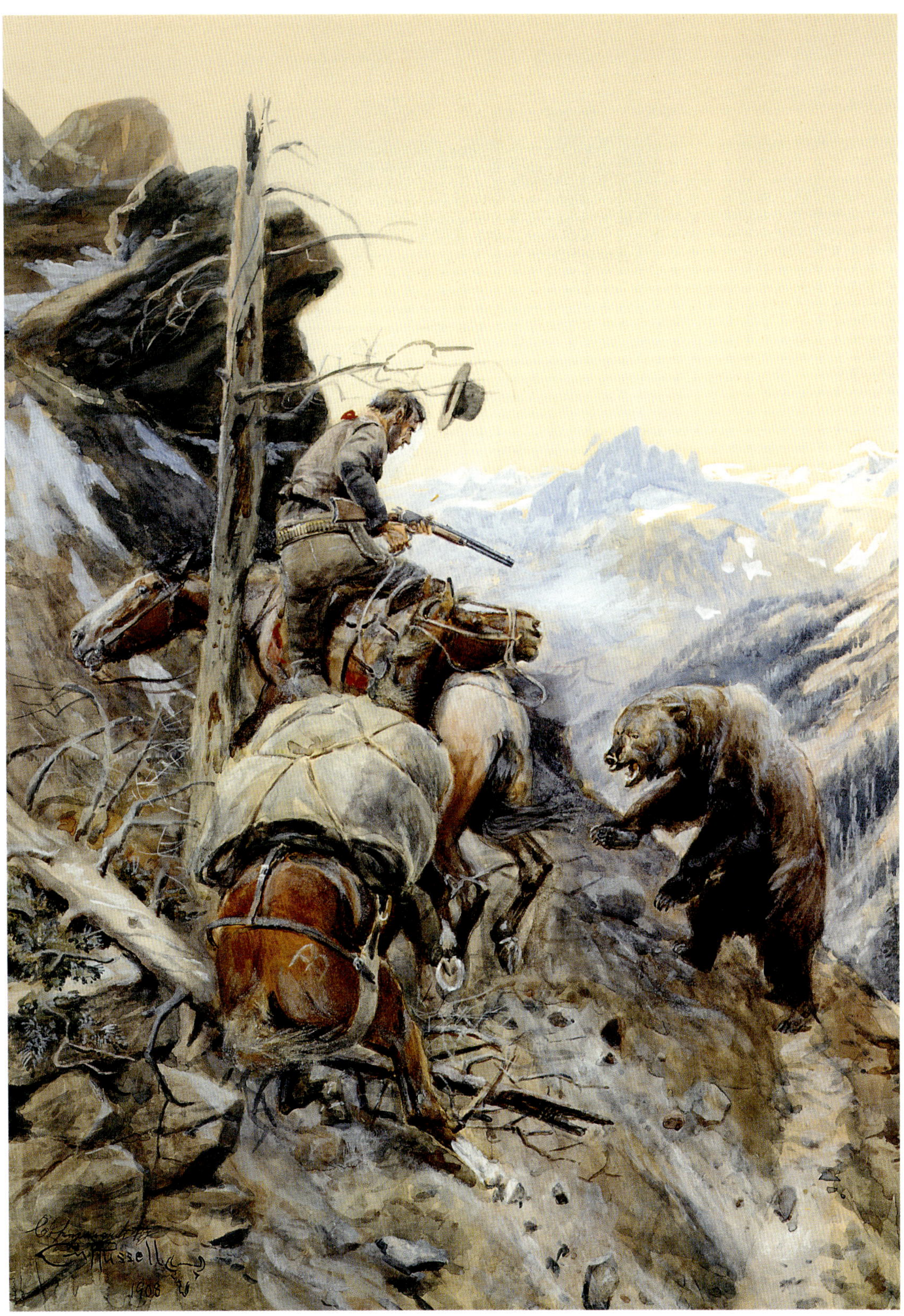

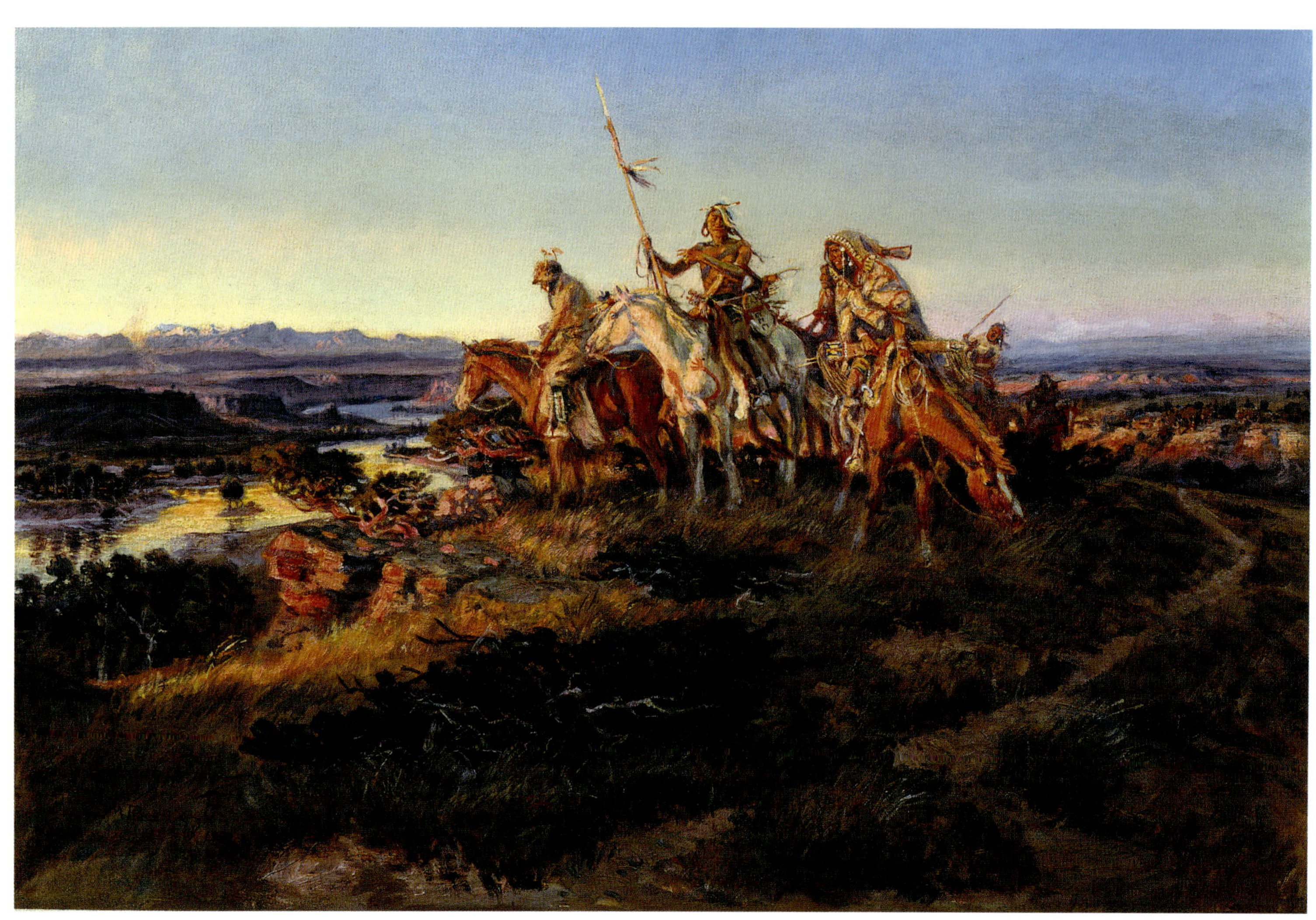

CHARLES MARION RUSSELL

American, 1864–1926
Trail of the White Man or
Wagon's Dust Cloud, 1925
Oil on canvas
24 x 36 in.

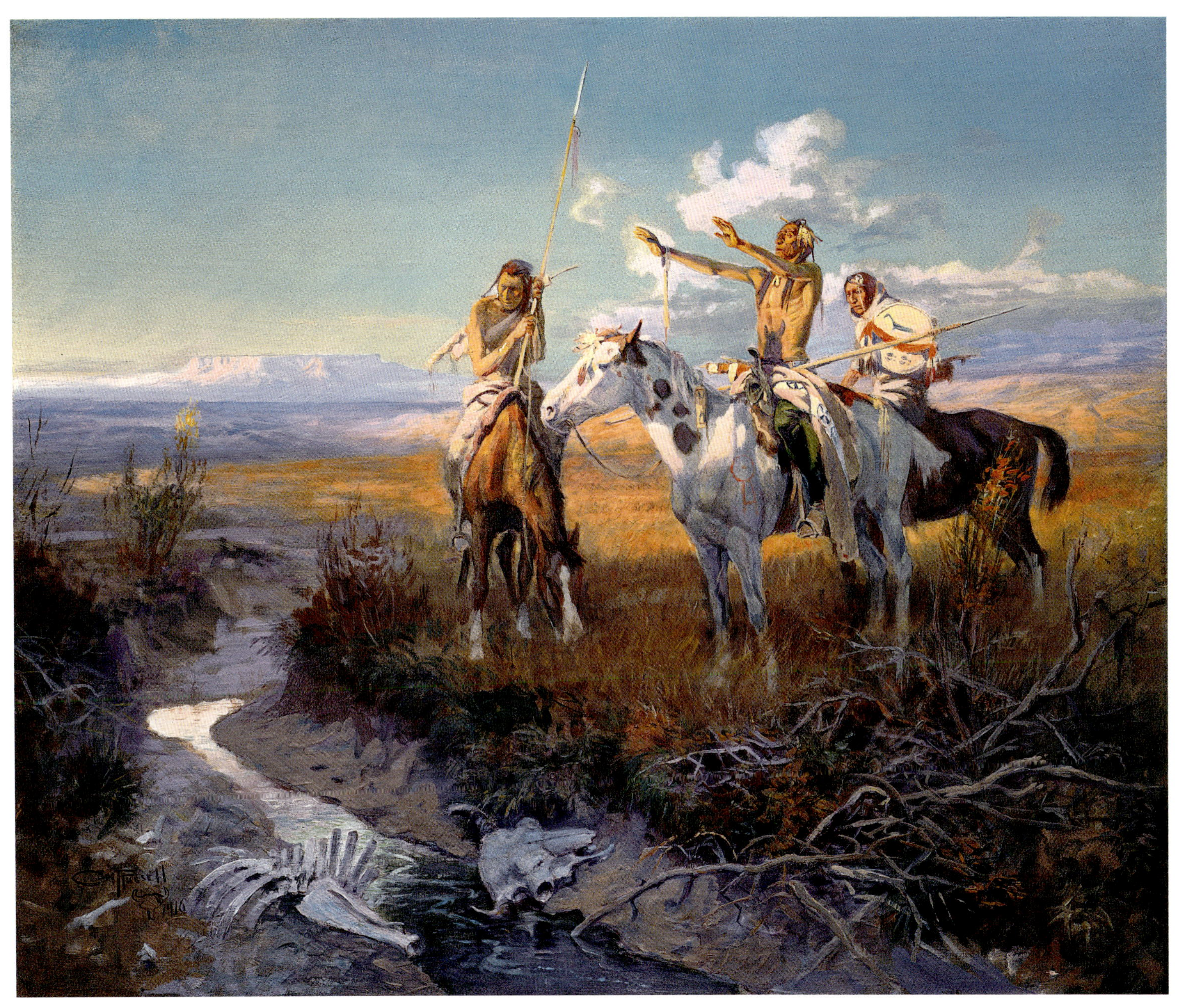

CHARLES MARION RUSSELL

American, 1864–1926
The Sun Worshipers, 1910
Oil on canvas
30¼ x 36¼ in.

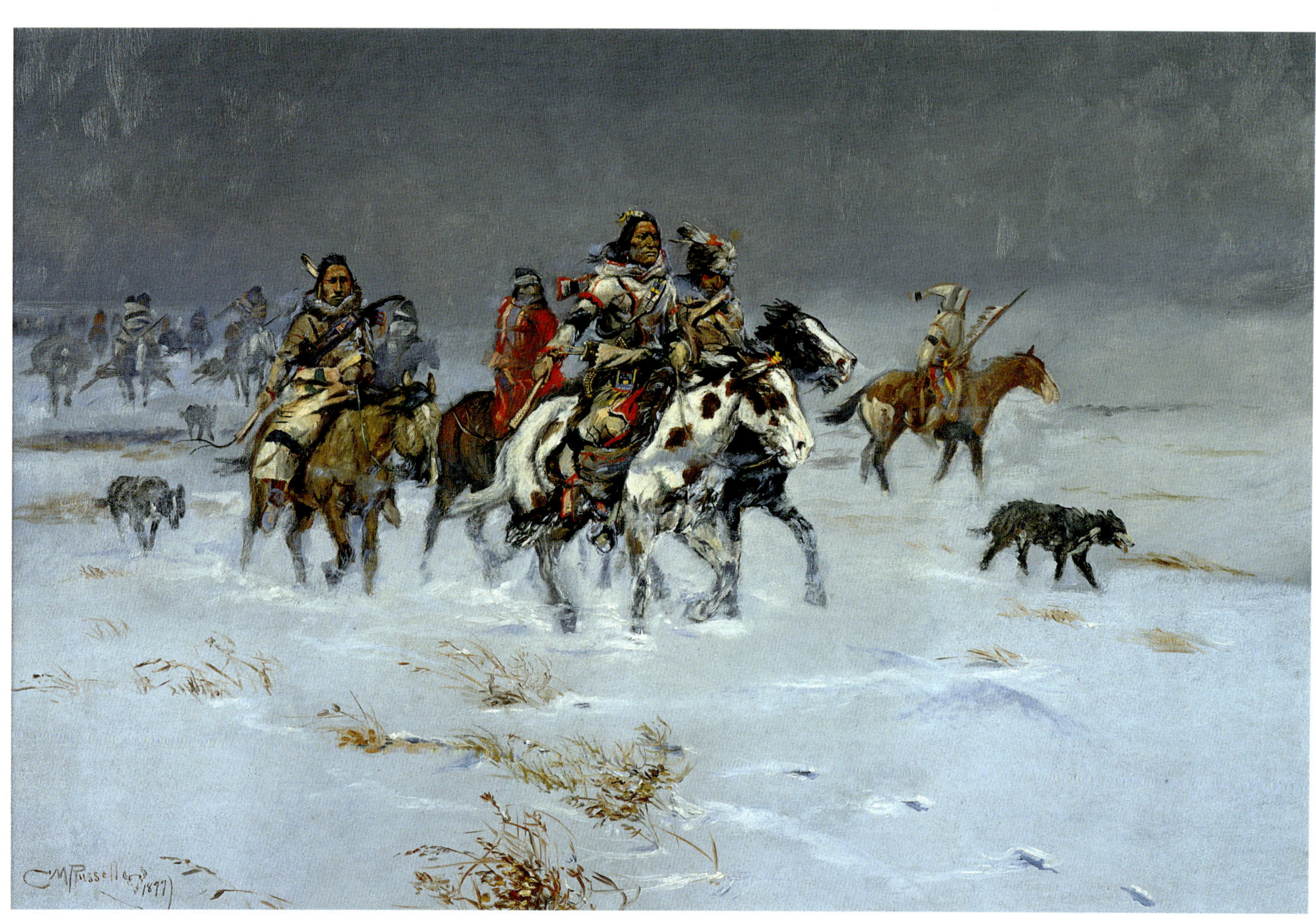

CHARLES MARION RUSSELL

American, 1864–1926
The Whoop-up Trail, 1899
Oil on canvas
24½ x 36½ in.

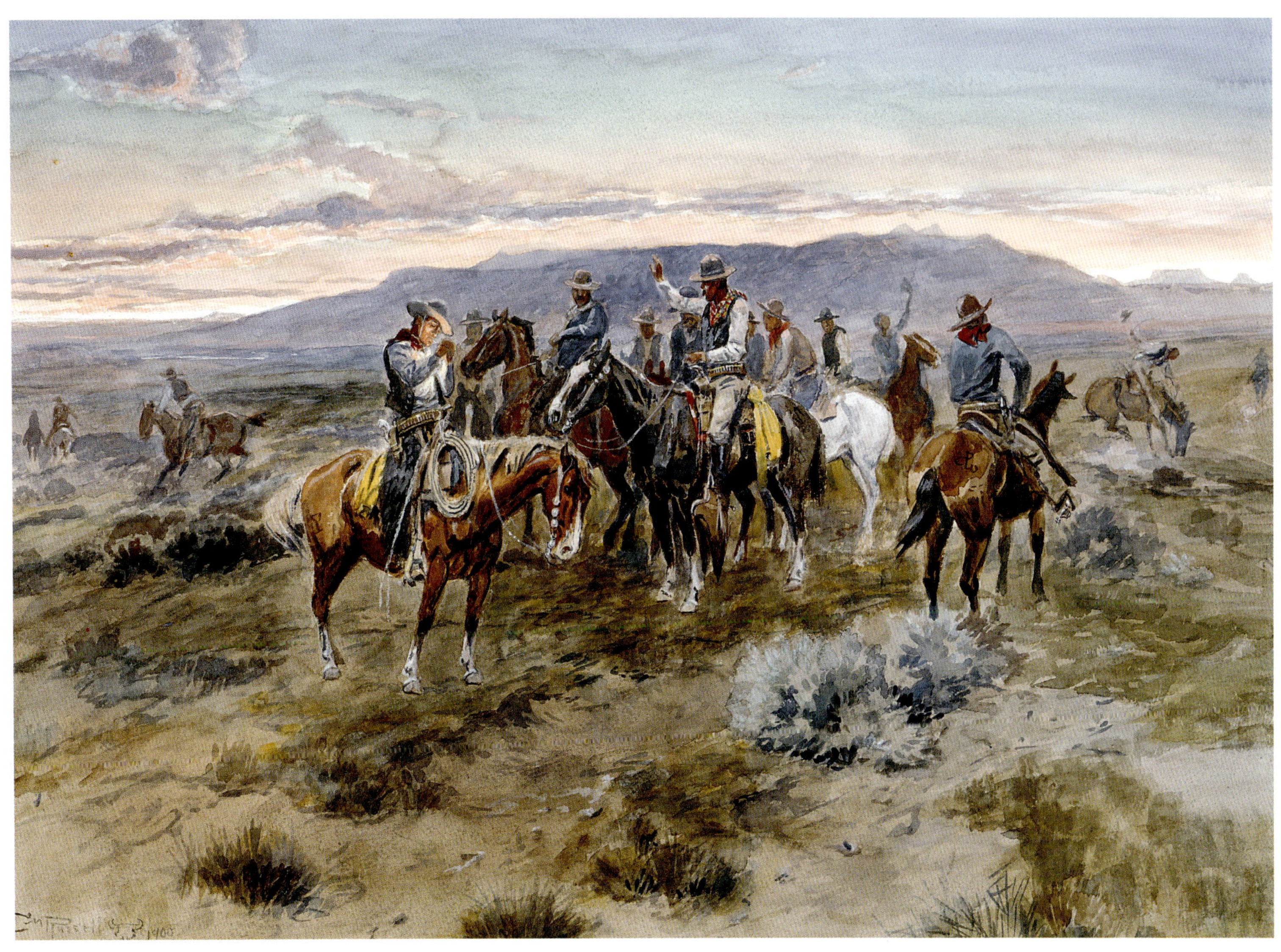

CHARLES MARION RUSSELL

American, 1864–1926
Scattering the Riders, 1900
Watercolor on paper
21 x 29 in.

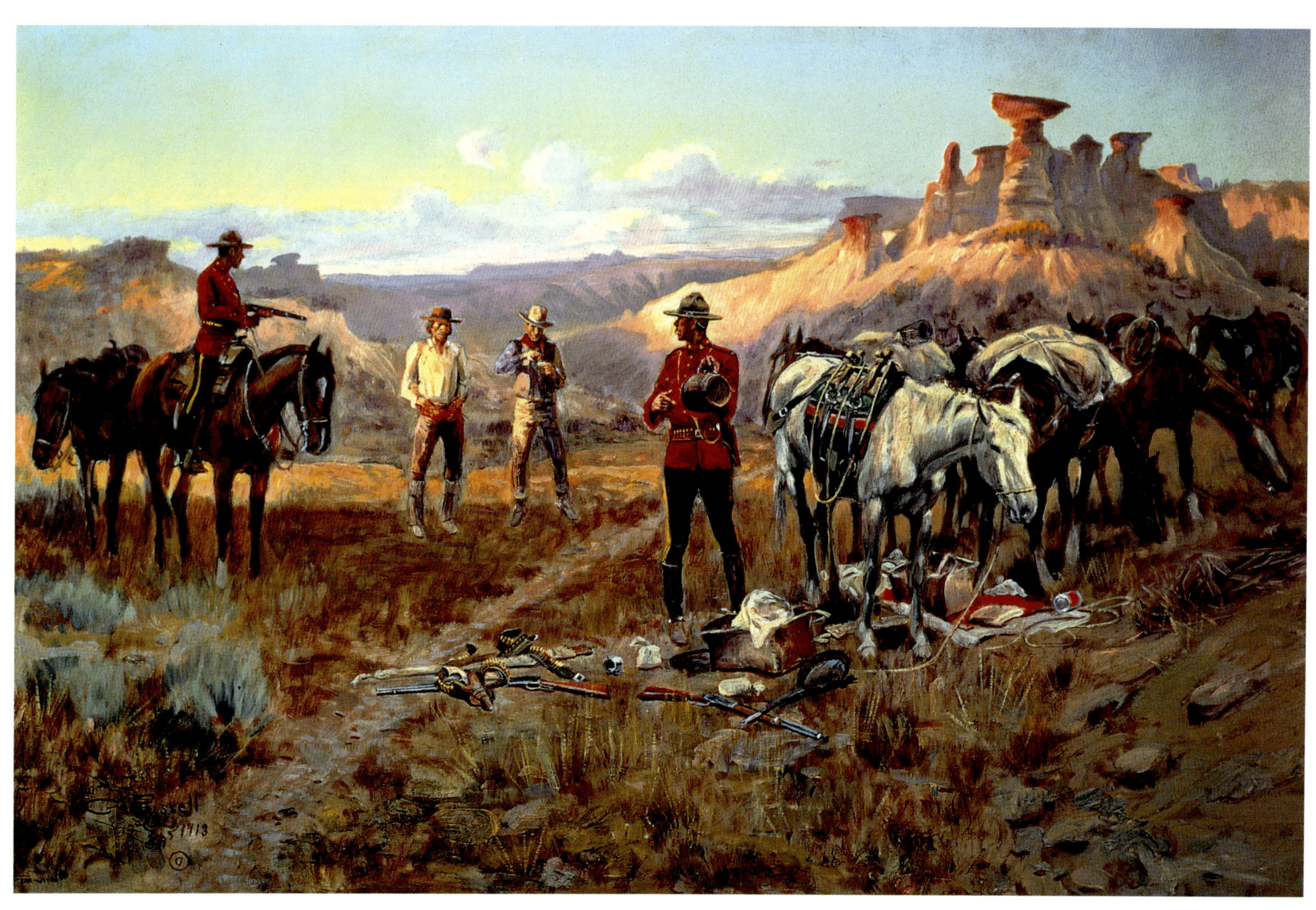

CHARLES MARION RUSSELL

American, 1864–1926
Whiskey Smugglers Caught with the Goods, 1913
Oil on canvas
24 x 36 in.

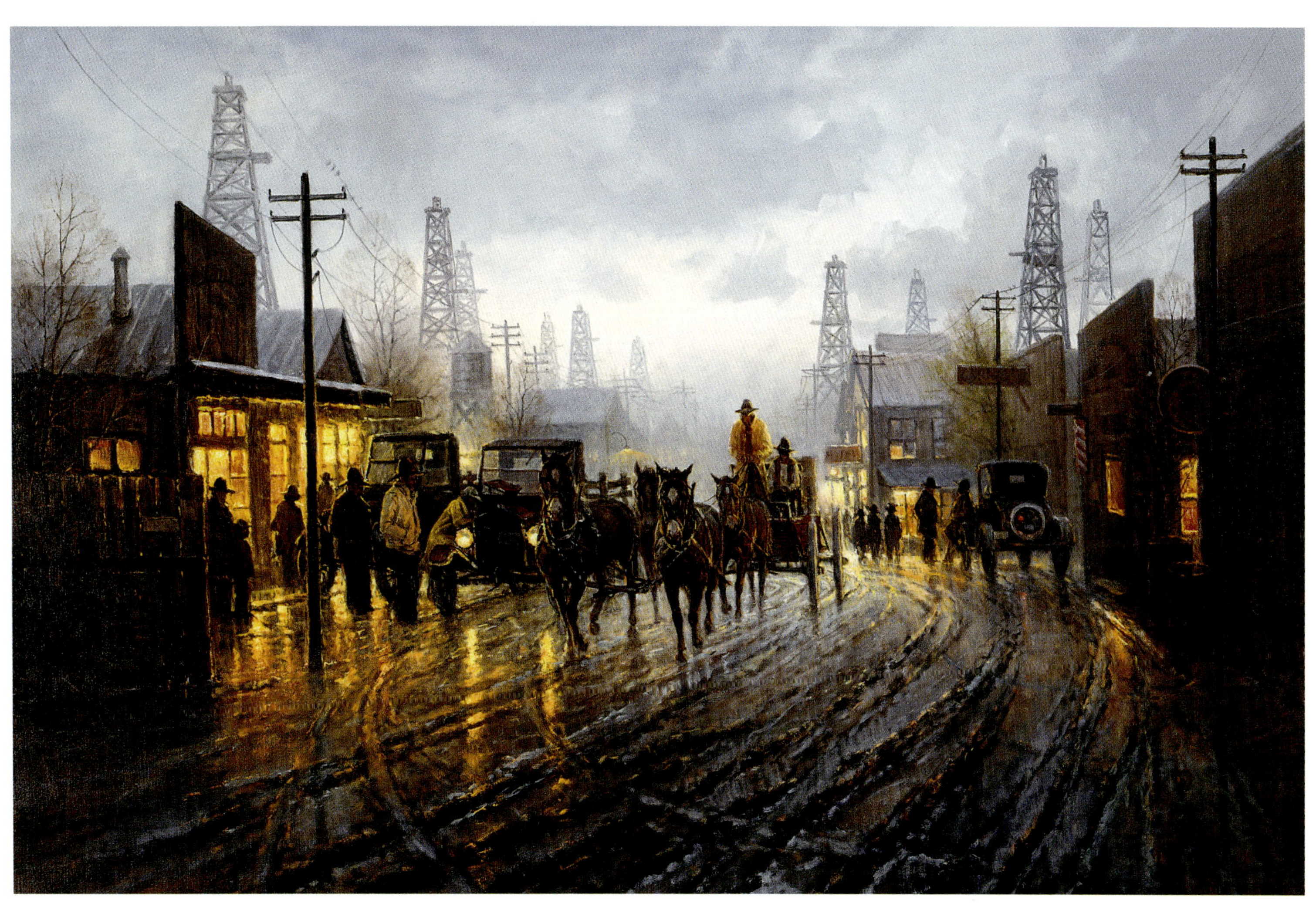

GERALD HARVEY

American, born 1933
Oil Patch, 1981
Oil on canvas
40 x 60 in.
© G. Harvey, 1981

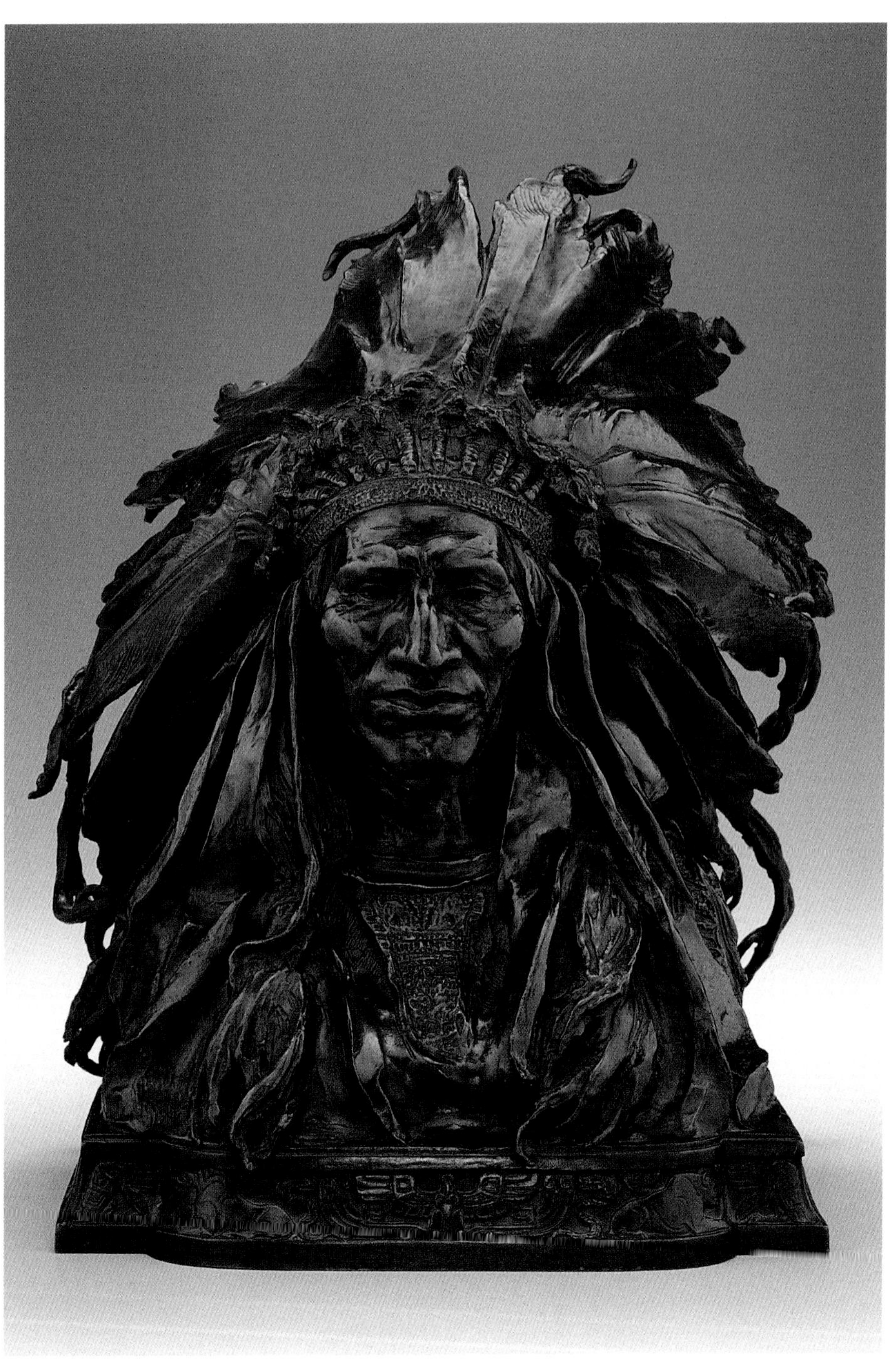

ADOLPH ALEXANDER WEINMAN

German, 1870–1952
Chief Blackbird, Ogalala Sioux,
modeled 1903, cast 1907
Bronze with dark brown patina
H. 18½ in., w. 14¼ in., d. 13 in.

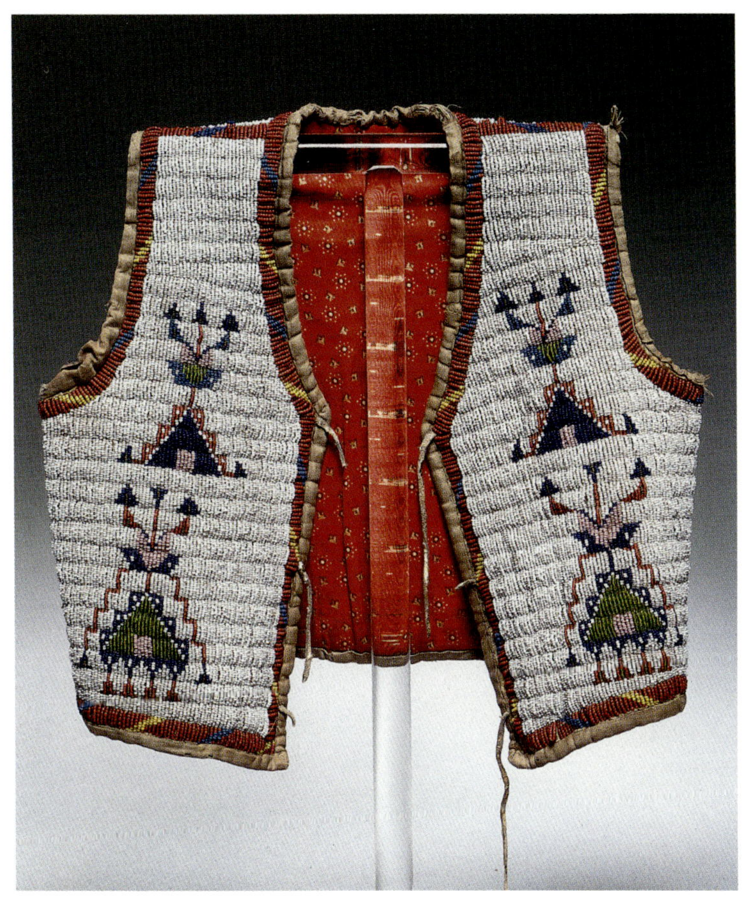

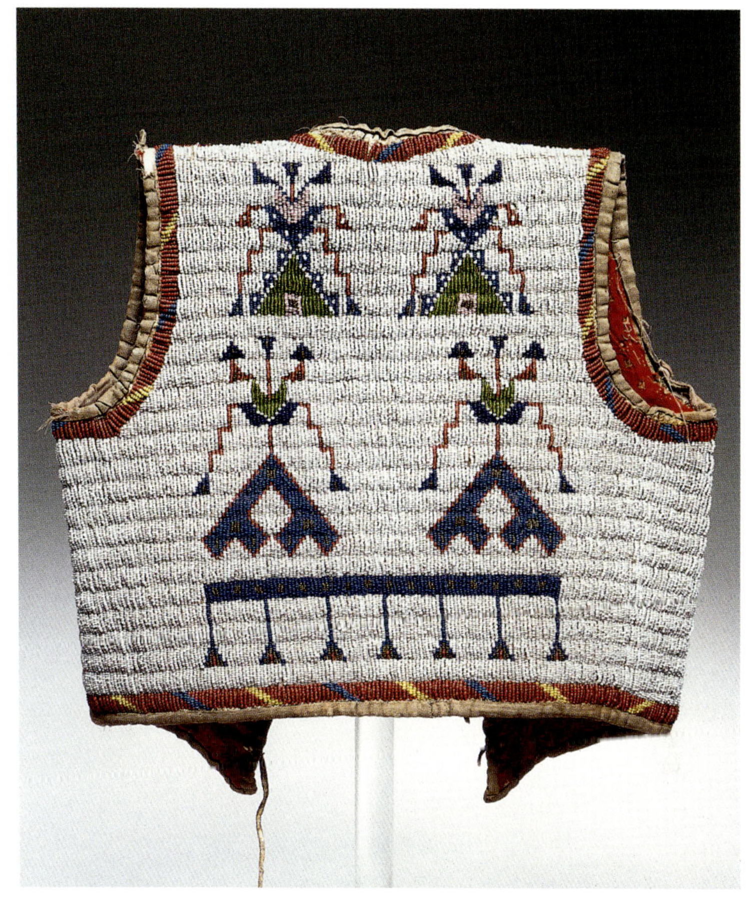

North American Indian
Child's vest
Cotton, cloth, hide, and beadwork
14½ x 14½ in.

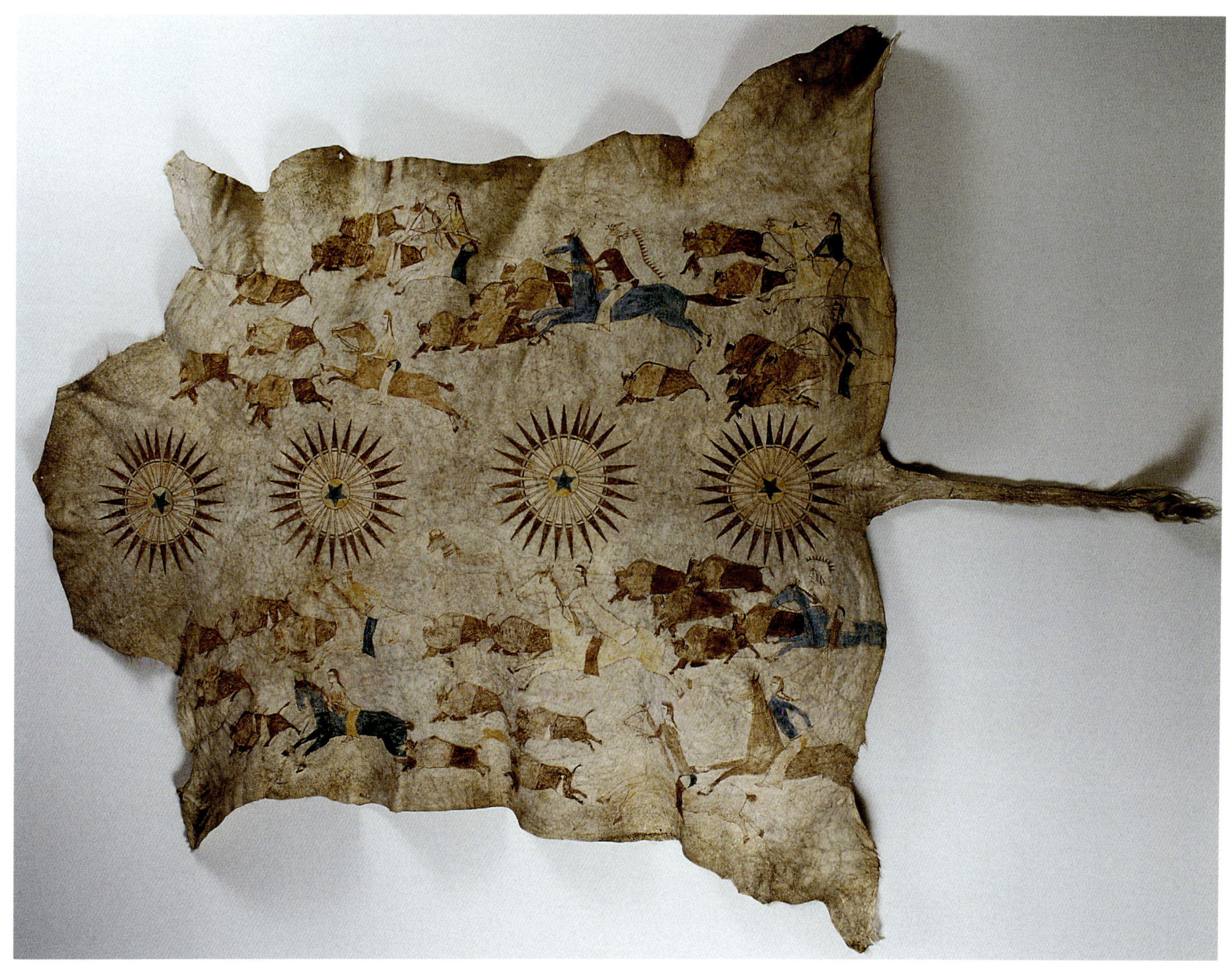

Hidatsa Indian
Pictorial robe
Painted buffalo hide
L. 96 in., w. 75 in.

Cheyenne Indian
Model tepee, about 1880
Hide, pigment, porcupine quills, and dewclaws
H. 29½ in.

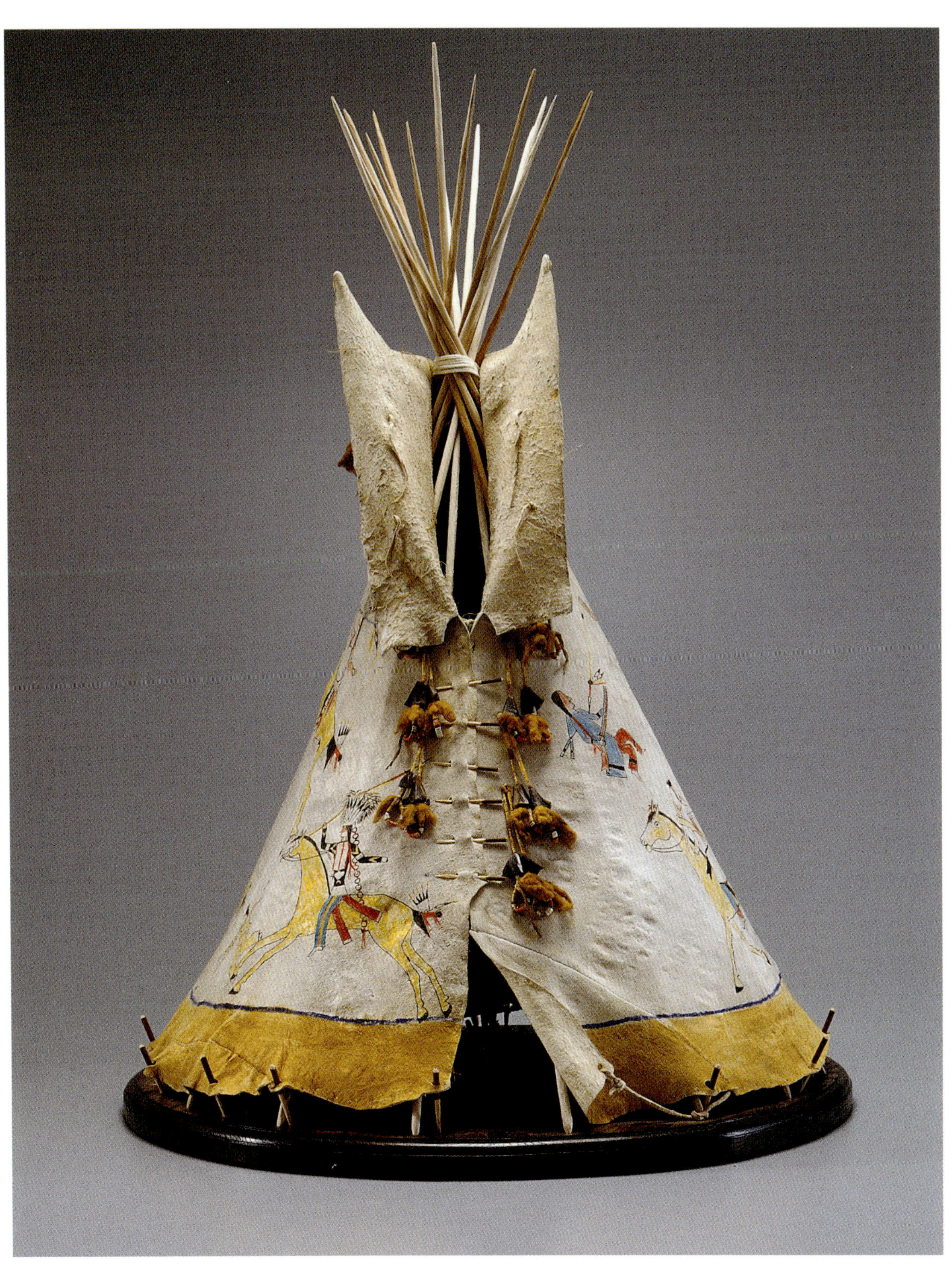

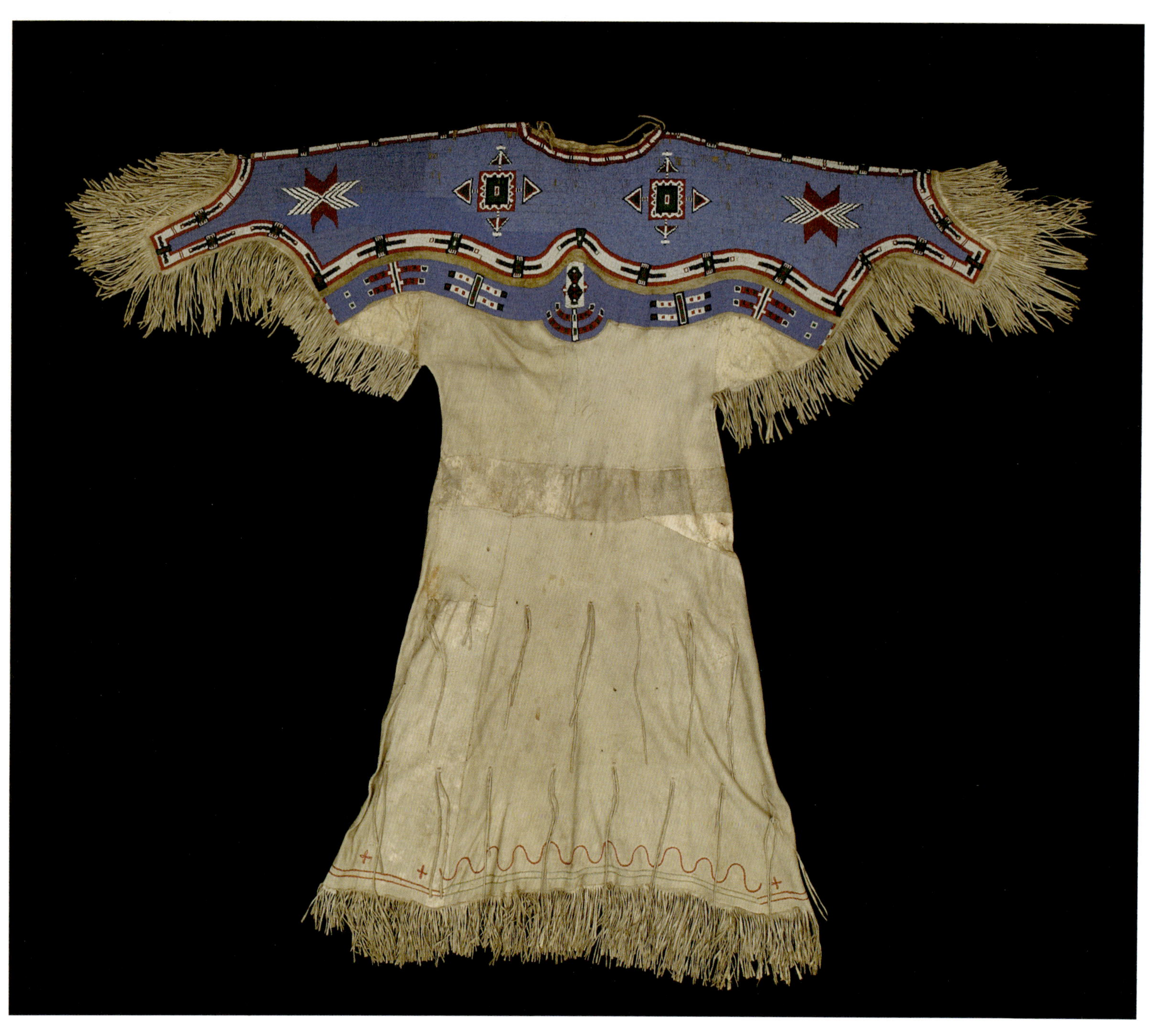

Sioux Indian
Beaded and fringed dress, about 1885
Hide and beads
H. 60 in., w. 52 in.

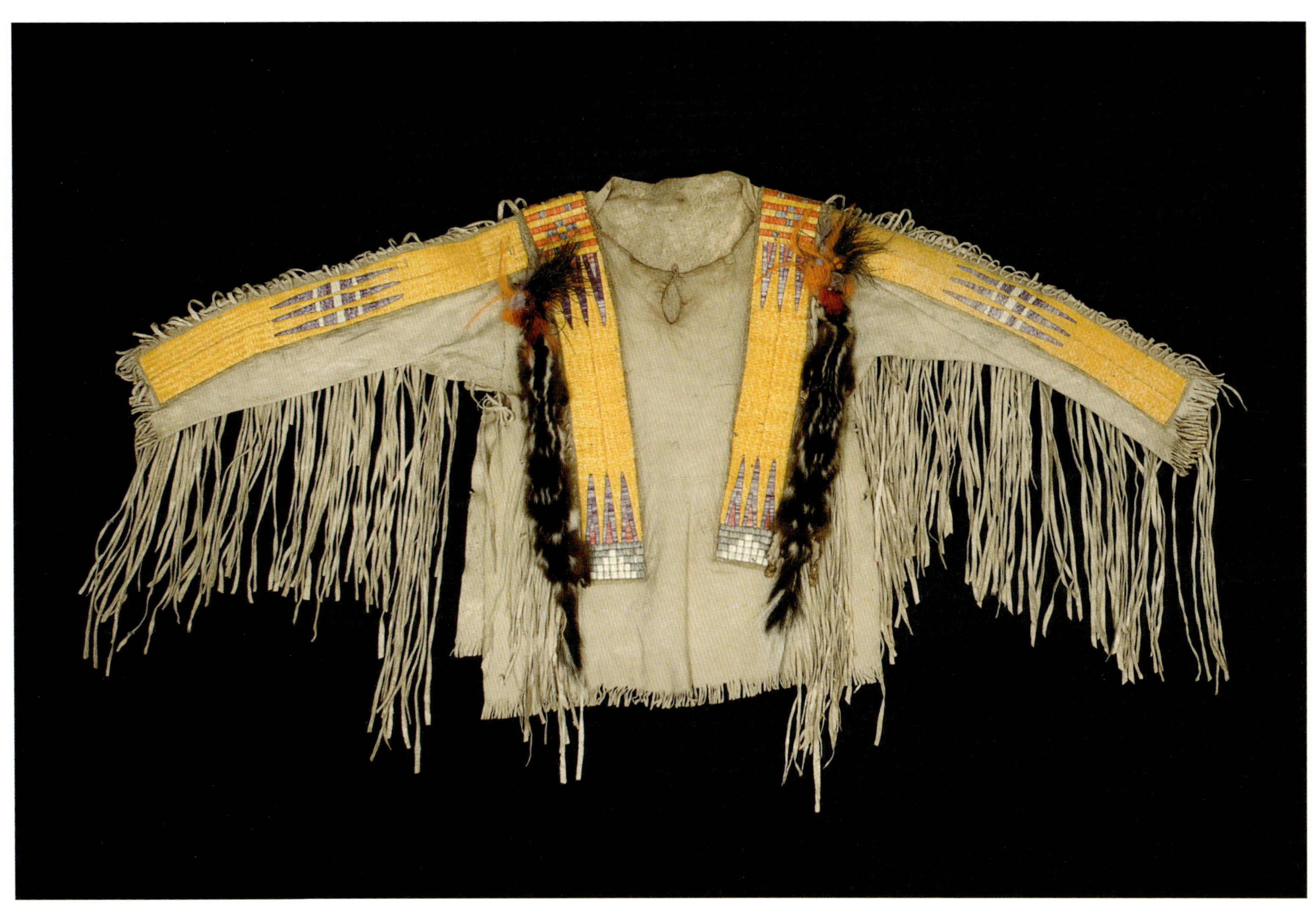

Hidatsa Indian
Quilled and fringed war shirt
Hide, dyed porcupine quills, animal pelts, and feathers
W. 59 in.

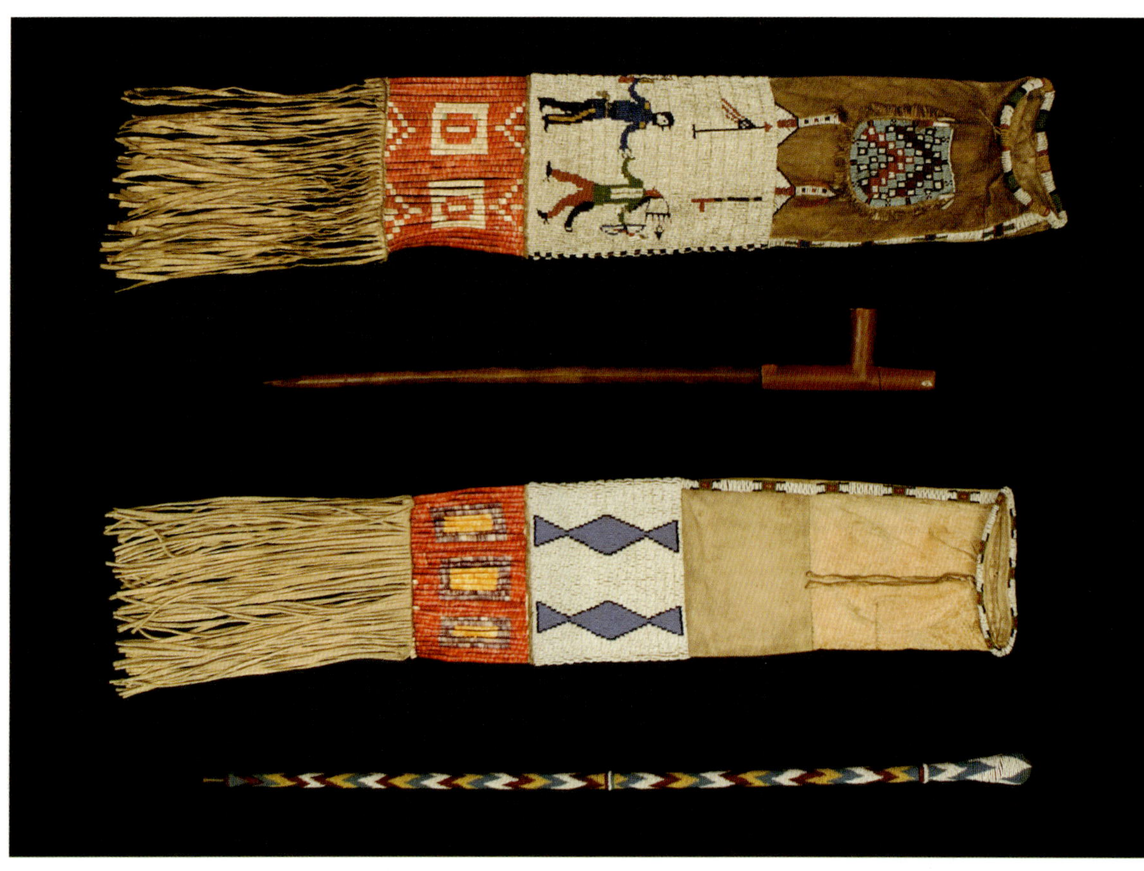

North American Indian
Tobacco bag, about 1880
Hide, beads, and reed
L. 36 in.

North American Indian
Pipe, about 1870
Catlinite and wood
L. 27 ¼ in.

Sioux Indian
Pictorial beaded and fringed tobacco bag
Hide and beads
L. 36 in.

Apache Indian
Beaded cane that belonged to Chief Geronimo
Beads and cartridge casing
L. 33 in.

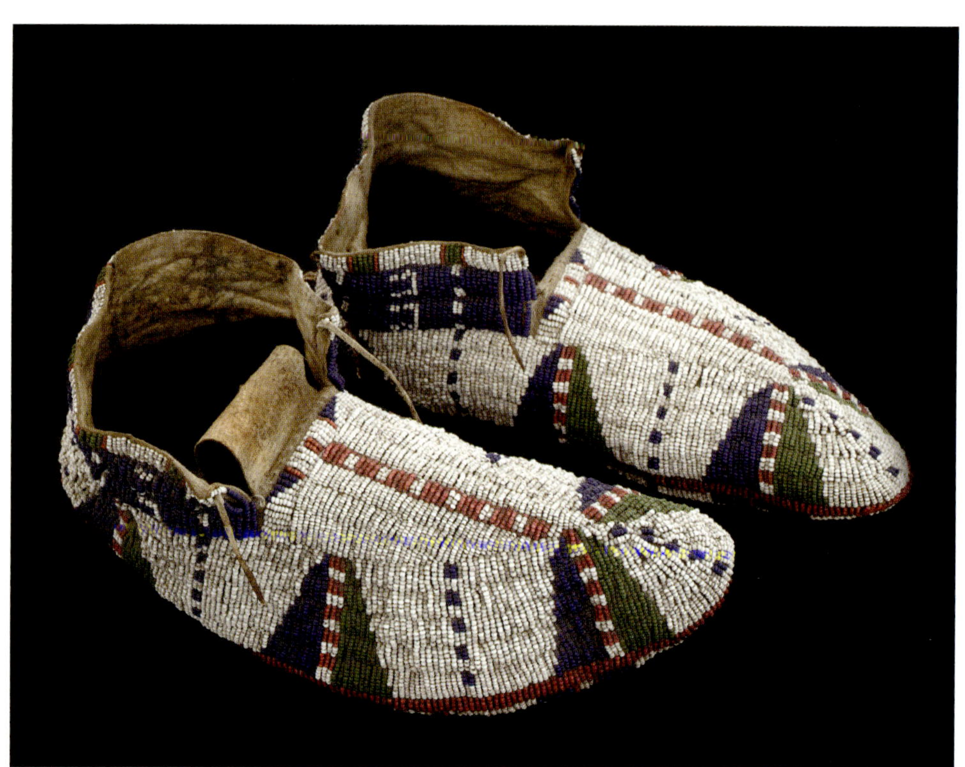

North American Indian
Pair of moccasins, about 1880
Hide and beads
L. 10½ in.

Custer-era Seventh Cavalry uniform and accoutrements that belonged to John Walsh, including a kepi, fedora, dress helmet, dress tunic, pants marked "United States Marines," Indian Wars–period belt buckle, sword belt, carbine sling, and carbine cartridge pouch marked "U.S. / WATERVILET / ARSENAL"

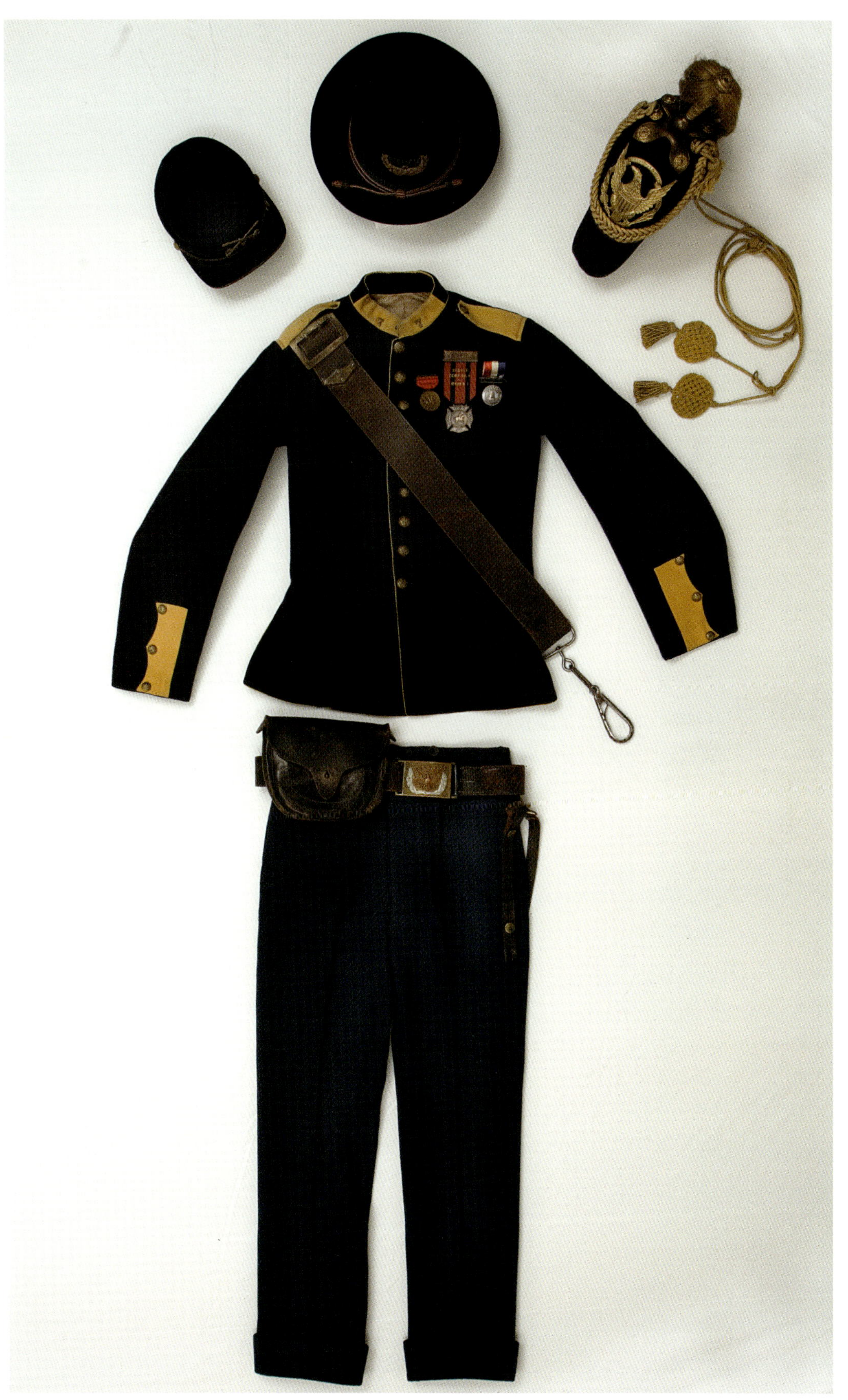

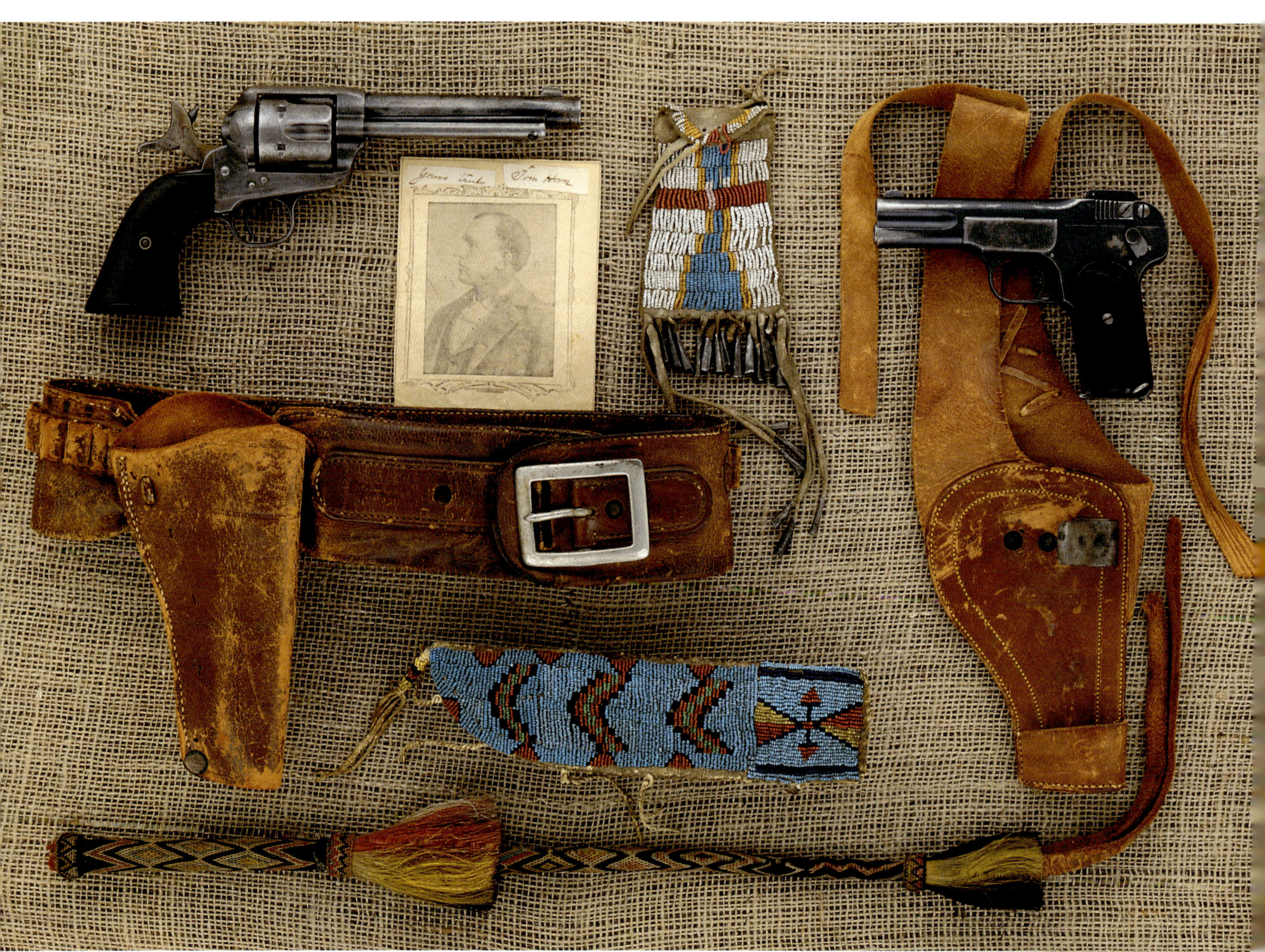
Tom Horn

WESTERN ARMS AND ACCOUTREMENTS

* * * * * * *

Of the many realms of collecting, that of firearms ranks among the most fascinating. Weapons are used in such diverse endeavors—hunting, warfare, personal protection, survival, presentations (including gifts of state), and shooting sports—that the serious collector must be a student of history, politics, psychology, mechanics, chemistry, art, and fashion. Beyond their utilitarian function, arms have been admired over the centuries for their intrinsic form and, often, their lavishly applied decoration. They embrace all the elements of the decorative arts. Further, they are symbols not only of independence and responsibility, but also of discernment, prestige, and position.

The tradition of fine American-made firearms was in evidence by 1750. A distinctive rifle, later known as the Kentucky, had evolved, frequently fitted with handsomely worked mountings, sometimes with silver inlays, engraved and carved with rococo scrolls, and embellished with patriotic and religious motifs. These rifles were utilitarian as well as elegant. Designed to hit targets at ranges up to two hundred yards, they were deadly accurate in the hands of hardy frontiersmen—and -women. Kentucky rifles often were built by master craftsmen whose skills equaled the finest cabinetmakers and metalsmiths. These arms have been termed America's first art form.

Gunmakers in the new nation had the distinct advantage of receiving government subsidies, since the defense industry was crucial to the survival of the United States. In the 1830s and 1840s the Industrial Revolution transformed production and introduced true interchangeability of parts, in what would become known as the American System of Manufacture. At the forefront were arms producers such as Samuel Colt, Simeon North, Eliphalet Remington, and the federal arsenals of Harpers Ferry, Virginia (now West Virginia), and Springfield, Massachusetts. Even with streamlined production, all relied heavily on master workmen of considerable hands-on talent, many of them emigrants from the United Kingdom, Germany, and Austria.

The collecting spirit, the iconic relationship between people and firearms, began even while their users were making history. William F. Cody ("Buffalo Bill") called his favorite hunting rifle "Lucretia Borgia." The artist George Catlin named his tried-and-true Paterson Colt revolving carbine "Sam Colt," for its inventor. And "Texas Jack" Omohundro, scout and showman, called his Plains rifle the "Widow." Innumerable diaries, letters, gunmakers' ledgers, and other documents—and thousands of surviving period photographs—attest to the importance of these artifacts. Often arms proved to be instruments of life insurance, whether or not they bore out the frontier verse about the Colt: "Be not afraid of any man, / no matter what his size, / Just call on me in time of need, / and I will equalize." Early collectors of firearms, often with Wild West associations, included Lt. Colonel George Armstrong Custer, General Nelson A. Miles, Captain Jack Crawford, Annie Oakley and her husband Frank Butler, and gunmakers Colonel Samuel Colt and Oliver F. Winchester.

The American legacy of arms collecting sprang from European roots, where every royal or imperial house included an armory, some dating from before the fifteenth century. These once-private armories often have become museums, and many have recognized the importance of including firearms representing the American West. Not a few Old World aristocrats mounted expeditions to the West during the nineteenth century; all collected arms, artifacts, and art, hunted extensively, and were early exponents of the wonders of the New World's frontier. The aristocratic interest in firearms coexisted with a love of painting, sculpture, decorative arts, antiquities, and architecture.

Bill Koch shares and perpetuates this tradition of collecting firearms alongside other objects and artworks. Few collectors pursue or appreciate these artifacts with more passion than Koch. He knows the stories of the brave and resourceful characters who depended on their marksmanship for their very lives. He has hunted in the West's mountains and plains, following the trails of the Indians, moun-

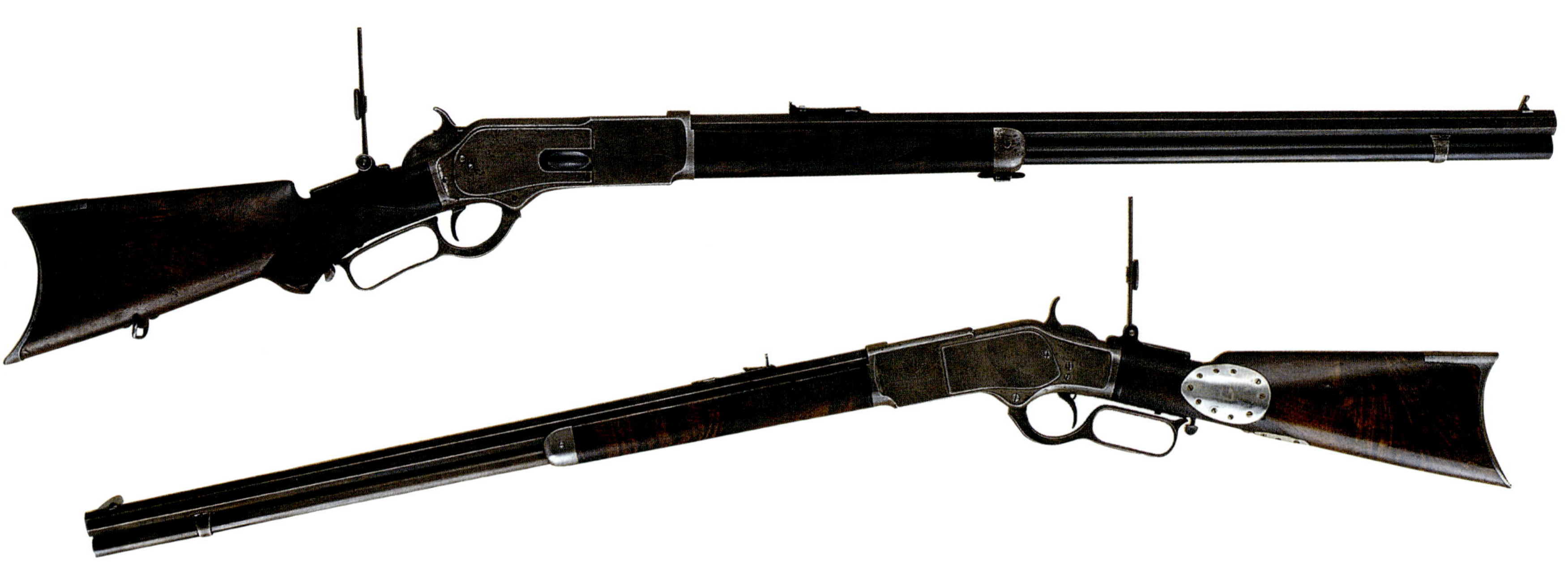

Page 138:

Tom Horn's Colt single-action army revolver (serial no. 168991), an early Fabrique Nationale–John M. Browning patent self-loading pistol (serial no. 56666), Horn's holster and cartridge belt signed by E. A. Meanea of Cheyenne, Wyoming, signed photograph of Horn, beaded Indian bag, leather holster rigs by E. A. Meanea, beaded Indian knife scabbard, and horsehair riding crop by Horn

Above, top to bottom:
Winchester Model 1876
"1 of 100" lever-action sporting rifle
Shipped from the Winchester factory November 15, 1877
Serial no. 711; .45–70 caliber
Walnut, brass, and steel
L. (barrel) 28 in.
Inscription: "One of One Hundred"

Winchester Model 1873
"1 of 1000" lever-action sporting rifle
Shipped from the Winchester factory, November 17, 1877
Serial no. 27140; .44–40 caliber
Walnut, brass, and steel;
German silver disk repairs
L. (barrel) 25 13/16 in.
Inscription: "One of One Thousand"

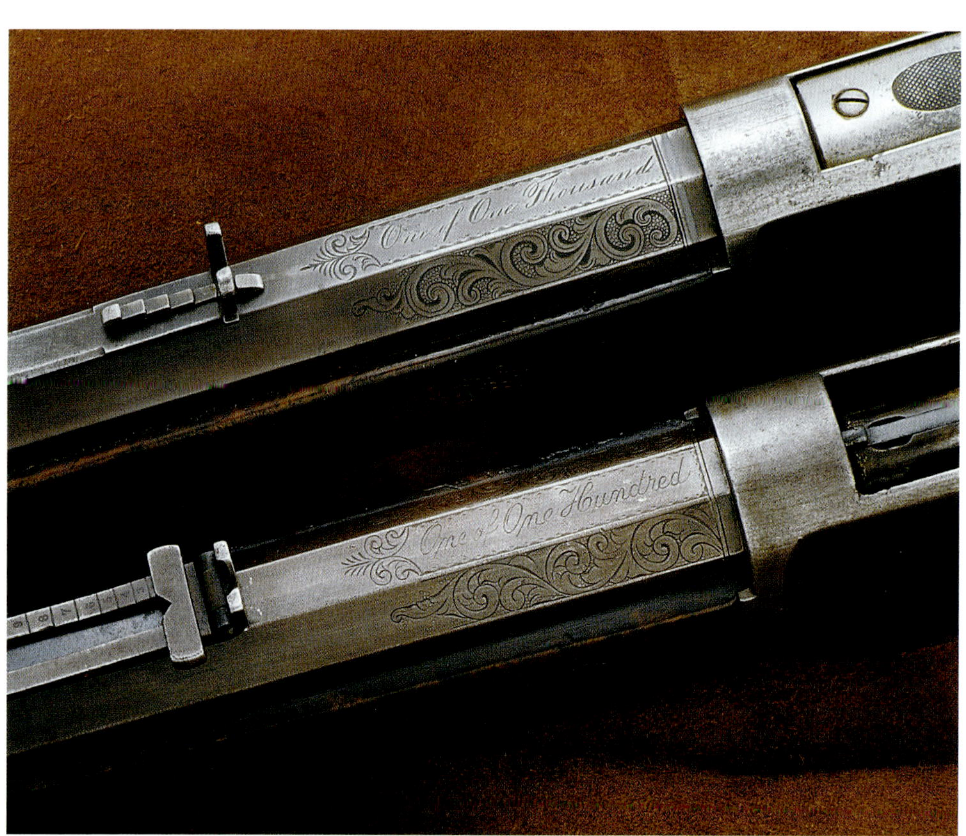

tain men, and cowboys. And he has collected artifacts with direct ties to such larger-than-life figures as W. B. "Bat" Masterson and Jesse James, Lt. Colonel Custer and Texas Ranger Captain William J. McDonald, and cowboy-outlaw-regulator Tom Horn, including historic and often embellished examples of the legendary Colt Peacemaker (pp. 142 and 144), the Winchester 1 of 100 and 1 of 1000 repeaters (p. 140), the Springfield officer's model rifle (right), and many others—the guns that won the West.

Complementing the arms in the Western Room are accessories and memorabilia: New Mexico Governor Lew Wallace's reward poster for Billy the Kid (p. 155), the bead belt and breast piece of Chief Sitting Bull (p. 146), an array of original family and campaign photographs of Custer (p. 155), gold and silver peace officer badges, outlaw handcuffs and leg irons, bowie knives, tomahawks and war hatchets, holsters and cartridge belts, ten-gallon hats and sombreros, spurs, branding irons and lariats, and Plains Indian beaded vests, dresses, war shirts, moccasins, and rifle and knife scabbards. They all evoke America's grand epic, the great West: an adventure, a way of life, a spirit, and a time and place—symbolized around the world by the noble native warrior and the daring frontiersman and -woman, and particularly by their weapons.

Koch's practice of collecting related artifacts along with the firearms, to tell their story more completely, is illustrated by his assemblage of Tom Horn's possessions (pp. 138 and 148). Horn was born in 1860 to a farm family in Memphis, Missouri. He held an assortment of diverse jobs, working as a tracklayer with the Santa Fe Railroad, a wagon freighter, stagecoach driver, night herder, and Spanish interpreter and scout for the U.S. Army at the San Carlos, Arizona, Apache reservation. Horn's career as scout lasted approximately ten years, and he is credited with playing a major role in the 1886 campaign to capture Geronimo.

When the last of the major Indian Wars concluded, Horn sought other lines of employment. In service of the Pinkerton Detective Agency, in Denver, from 1890 to 1894, he pursued train and bank robbers in Wyoming and Colorado. He claimed to have killed as many as seventeen men in those assignments but ultimately quit the Pinkertons, declaring that the work was too tame for him. He moved on to employment with cattle barons who operated forcefully, and often aside from legal niceties, in dealing with small ranchers and homesteaders who were prone

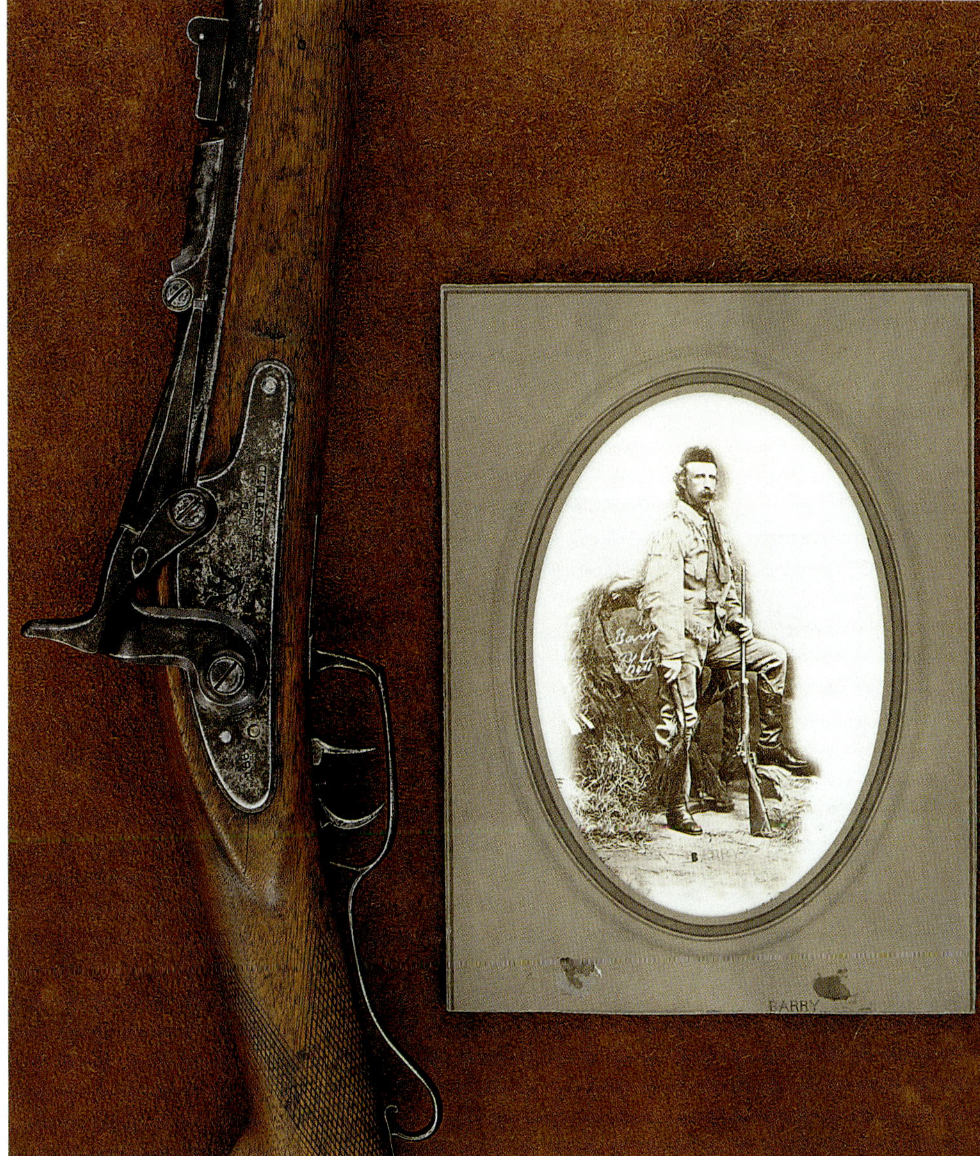

U.S. Springfield sporting rifle that belonged to Lt. Colonel George Armstrong Custer
Made in Springfield, Massachusetts, about 1872
.50–70 caliber
Steel, walnut, and tin
L. (barrel) 30⅛ in.

Studio picture of Custer in custom deerskin suit holding the Springfield Sporter, taken after royal buffalo hunt
Photograph by D. F. Barry, West Superior, Wisconsin, about 1872
Oval photograph on pasteboard mat
6 x 9 in.

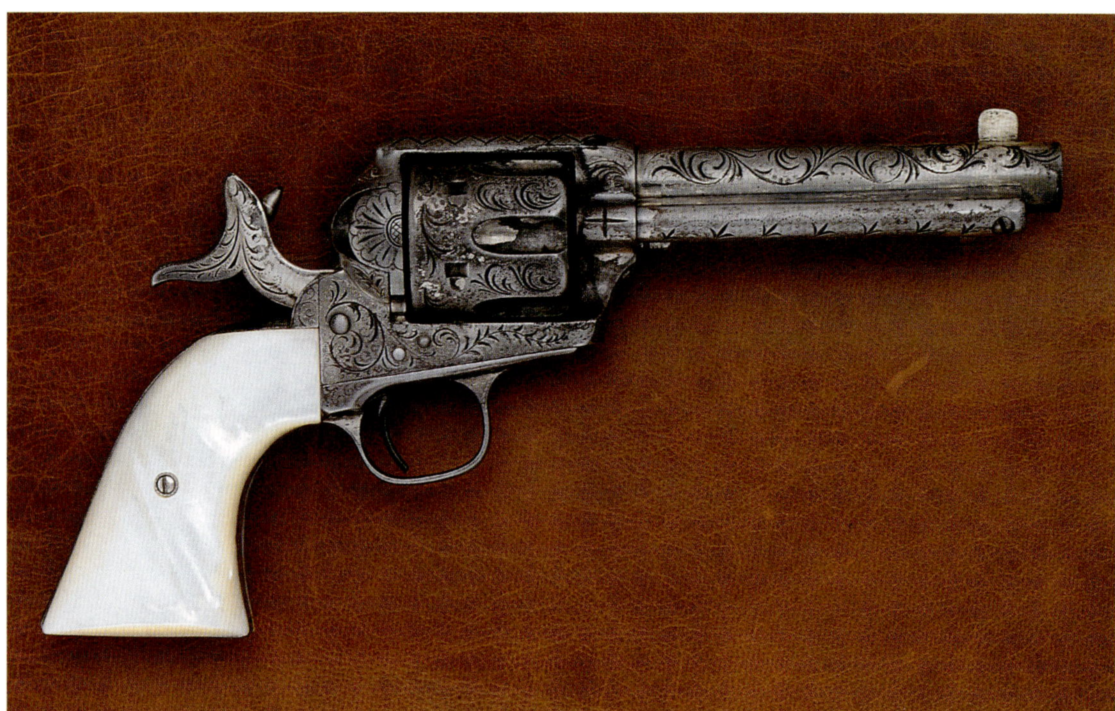

Custom-made Colt single-action army revolver that belonged to W. B. "Bat" Masterson
Made in Hartford, Connecticut, 1879
Serial no. 53684; .45 caliber; 6 shots
Steel and carved mother-of-pearl
L. (barrel) 5 in.; cut down from 7½ in.
Inscription on backstrap: "W. B. MASTERSON"

Opposite: *Smith & Wesson New Model No. 3 single-action revolver that belonged to Robert Ford*
Made in Springfield, Massachusetts, about 1878
Serial no. 3766; .44 S&W caliber; 6 shots
Steel and molded hard rubber
L. (barrel) 6½ in.
Inscription on side-plate: "BOB FORD / KILLED / JESSE JAMES / WITH THIS REVOLVER AT / ST. JOSEPH, MO. 1882"

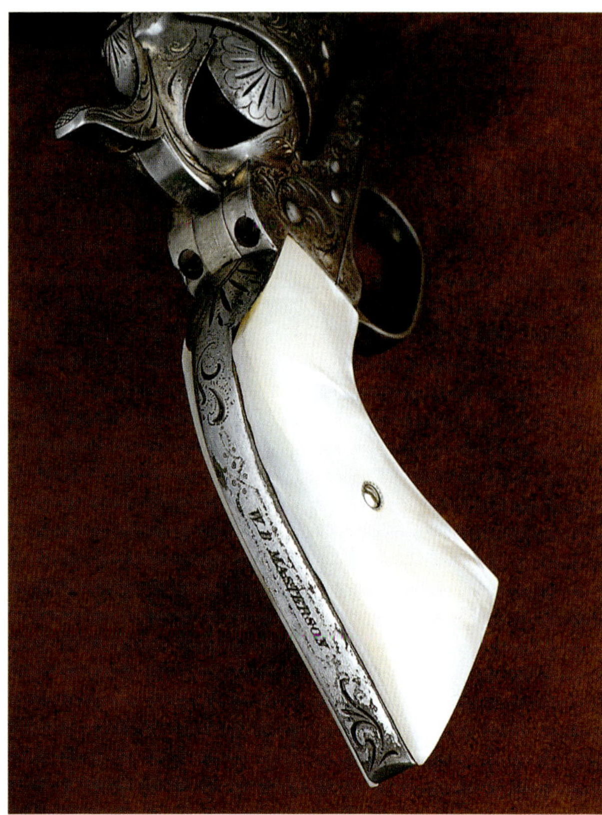

to trespassing and, sometimes, rustling cattle. Horn's charges included carrying out shootings, as well as hiring and training gunmen.

After a brief interlude as a mule packer to Theodore Roosevelt's Rough Riders during the Spanish American War, Horn returned to Wyoming and killing for hire. He was soon in trouble as the prime suspect in the murder of fourteen-year-old Willie Nickell in an ambush on July 19, 1901. When Horn became intoxicated during the investigation and bragged that the Nickell shooting was his work, he was arrested and charged with first-degree murder. A celebrated trial followed, resulting in a guilty verdict and a sentence of death by hanging.

While in prison, Horn and his cell mate, Jim McCloud, concocted an escape scheme. On August 9, 1903, they overwhelmed Deputy Sheriff Richard Proctor and forced him, at gunpoint, to open the safe that held the jail keys. At the same time, Proctor grabbed his FN-Browning patent Model 1903 semiautomatic pistol and opened fire. The prisoners wrestled him to the floor and seized the weapon, but Proctor had managed to slide the safety switch on the newly designed handgun, preventing firing.

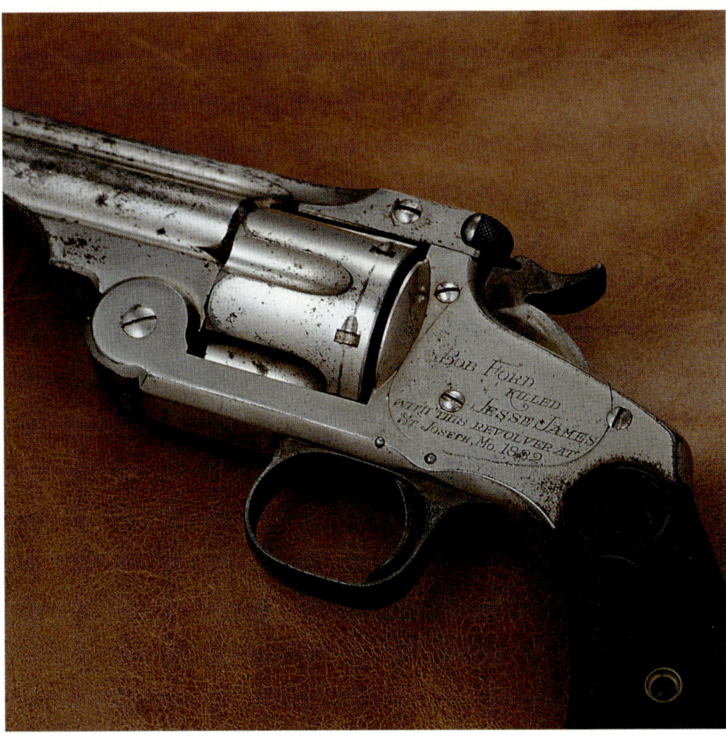

Horn charged into the street but was unfamiliar with how to make the pistol work. In effect unarmed, he was chased down by local citizens, who pummeled him with sticks and clubs until he was rescued by Proctor. Horn accepted the inevitability of his sentence and spent his final weeks weaving horsehair quirts and ropes, including the rope for his own execution. On November 20, 1903, he went to the gallows calmly, asking Proctor to place the noose over his head. Ironically, although responsible for several frontier shootings, Horn was likely innocent of Nickell's murder.

Horn's final letter to Proctor expressed appreciation for his friendship and for "the many little kindnesses you have done for me during my confinement under your charge.... Only your desperate courage kept me from escaping." The doomed adventurer also presented Proctor with his Colt six-shooter, a handmade horsehair riding crop, and a beaded knife scabbard and bag—all of which Bill Koch has managed to acquire, memorializing Horn's story.

A gun known to have consistently served on the side of law and order is the Colt .45 single-action revolver owned by Bat Masterson (p. 142). Masterson has been celebrated in fact and legend as a close friend of Wyatt Earp and other renowned frontier figures, and as a man of innumerable adventures: buffalo hunter, U.S. Army scout, railroader, saloon keeper, policeman, deputy sheriff and sheriff, deputy U.S. marshal, city marshal, gambler, gunfighter (then known as "shootists"), newspaperman, and journalist. Despite his adventurous lifestyle, he outlived all the great frontier heroes except Wyatt Earp, who died in 1929; Masterson died peacefully at his desk at the *Morning Telegraph*, a New York City sporting newspaper, in 1921. The author and columnist Damon Runyon eulogized him as "one of the most indomitable characters this land has ever seen [and] . . . a 100 percent, 22-karat real man." Runyon later drew on his close friend as the colorful character Sky Masterson in the long-running Broadway show and hit film *Guys and Dolls*.

The venerable frontiersman's six-shooter was made to order and shipped from the Colt factory on October 23, 1879: engraved, inscribed, silver-plated, enameled, and fitted with carved mother-of-pearl grips. It is the most historic handgun documented in the Hartford gunmaker's records of its line of products used in the West. The revolver was Masterson's constant companion for several years, until he eventually presented it to a cousin. The original grips were broken about 1950 but have since been replaced.

Perhaps even more legendary—indeed, maybe the most notorious gun in Koch's collection—is the Smith & Wesson New Model No. 3 single-action revolver that Robert Ford used to kill the outlaw Jesse James. The side-plate inscription, engraved by the Smith & Wesson factory, documents Ford's role in the assassination of James at St. Joseph, Missouri, April 3, 1882: "BOB FORD / KILLED / JESSE JAMES / WITH THIS REVOLVER AT / ST. JOSEPH, MO. 1882." The gun is accompanied by a signed and notarized letter by Colonel Corydon F. Craig, to whom Ford presented the gun shortly after the shooting, as well as an article from the January 2, 1904, *Baltimore Morning Herald* that details its history. By acquiring this documentation, as well as the revolver, Koch ensured that the story of the gun's heritage will be preserved. The *Herald*'s account of the infamous events reads as follows:

> When Jesse James was shot by Bob Ford he was living in St. Joseph under the assumed name of Howard. Colonel Craig's father, Capt. Enos Craig, was sheriff of the town. For eight

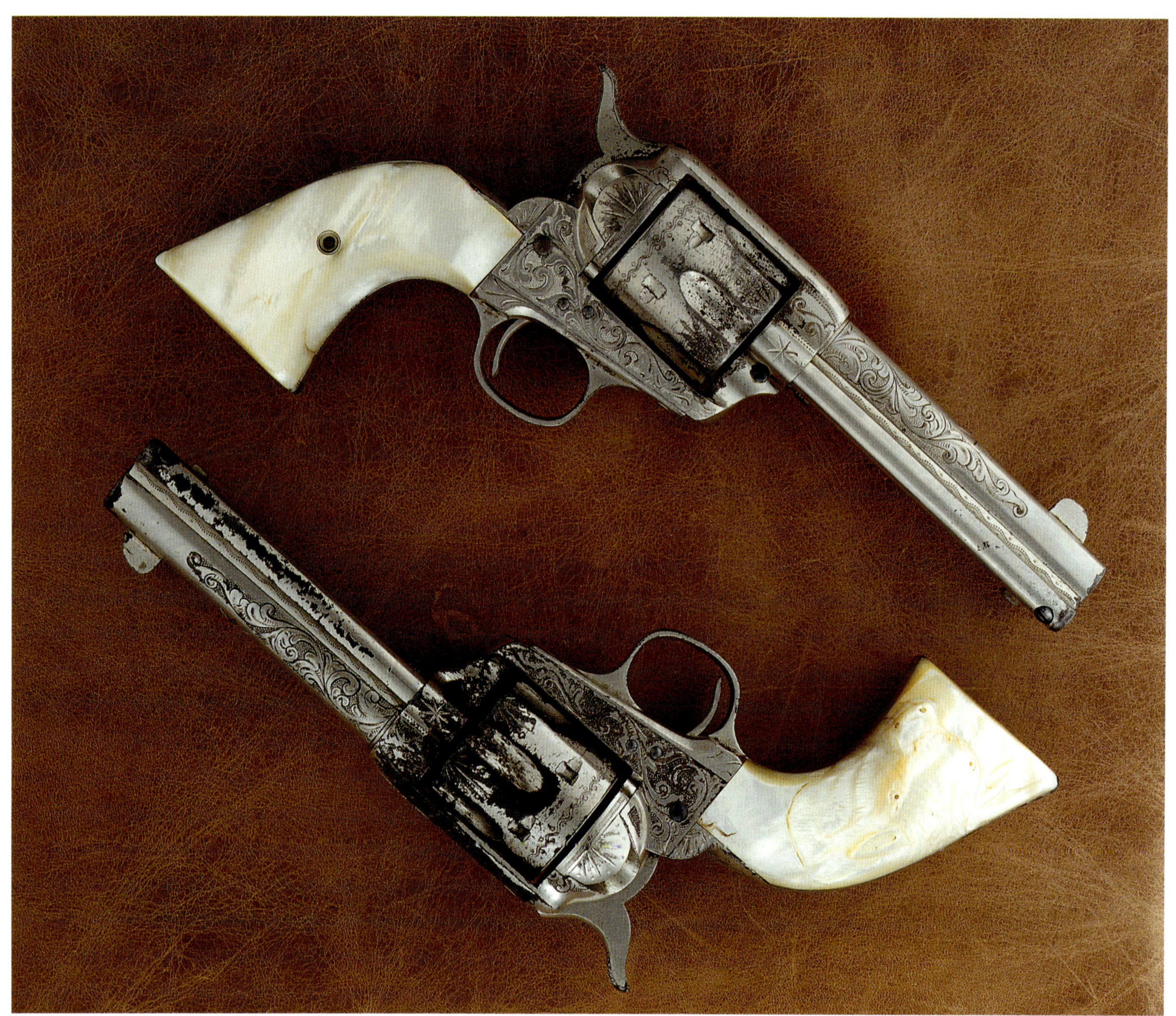

Colt single-action army revolvers that belonged to Captain William J. McDonald
Both engraved by Cuno Helfricht, or his shop, at the Colt factory, Hartford, about 1903
Serial nos. 244523 (top) and 244538; .45 caliber; 6 shots
Nickel-plated steel and mother-of-pearl
L. (each barrel) 4¾ in.
Inscription on backstrap of 244523: "CAPT WJ McDONALD"

months James lived in seclusion, and the residents were not aware of the fact that the noted bandit was among them. Governor Thomas T. Crittenden had offered a reward of $10,000 for the capture of Jesse, alive or dead. The Ford brothers, Charlie and Bob, decided to earn this reward, even if they had to kill their man. They were former pals of Jesse and knew he was hiding in St. Joseph.

They went to the small house where the bandit was living and represented themselves to be friendless and penniless. James took them in and gave them food and shelter. They began a long, drawn-out period of waiting to get the drop on their man. In constant fear of capture the outlaw was always heavily armed. Night and day his pistols were within reach. At last after eight months of waiting he relaxed his vigilance and the opportunity presented itself to Bob Ford to fire the fatal shot. One warm summer's day in 1882 Jesse entered the house and threw off his pistol belt. He climbed on a chair to dust a picture. Bob Ford drew the revolver Colonel Craig now has and shot the bandit in the back. After the shooting Bob went to a telegraph office and wired Governor Crittenden the facts of the shooting. He then surrendered to Colonel Craig's father, Sheriff Enos Craig. During his imprisonment he was befriended by Colonel Craig, who gave him literature, tobacco and other small necessities.

Ford was indicted, tried, sentenced to be hanged and afterward pardoned by Governor Crittenden. When he regained his freedom he presented the revolver from which he fired the fatal bullet to Colonel Craig, together with a few 44-caliber cartridges.

Ford tried to capitalize on his notoriety and occasionally sold other revolvers he claimed to have used in the assassination. But "the dirty little coward," as he is called in the song commemorating the event, was haunted by his betrayal of Jesse and was never able to claim the $10,000 reward. Instead, the brothers received a paltry $500. And in an extreme example of frontier justice, Bob was cut down by a shotgun blast at the hands of shootist Ed O'Kelley, in Creede, Colorado, in 1892. The deed was executed partially in revenge for the murder of Jesse James.

The heroic role of the Texas Rangers in western lore is highlighted in the Koch collection by two Colt .45s owned by Captain Bill McDonald. In January 1891 Governor James P. Hogg appointed McDonald Captain, Company B, Frontier Battalion, Texas Rangers. He soon became one of the most respected and feared lawmen in Texas.

Among his innumerable adventures, McDonald survived several pitched gun battles and served as a hunting guide for President Theodore Roosevelt and as a bodyguard to President Woodrow Wilson. On arrival by train to a Texas town, in response to authorities pleading for help to quell a riot, McDonald was asked where the other Rangers were. His answer became a classic of Texas lore: "Well—you only got one riot, haven't you!" The captain's Colts reveal the predilection of not a few Old West luminaries for engraved six-shooters with fancy grips and finishes.

The Native American side of the Wild West story is also represented in Koch's arms collection, by items such as the bead belt and breast piece worn by Chief Sitting Bull at the Battle of the Little Big Horn. The best known of American Indians, Sitting Bull distrusted the influence and encroachment of European-Americans. He was selected as the first chief of all the Teton Indians, also known as the Dakota Sioux. His fighting edge was honed in battles and skirmishes with other tribes, giving him a well-earned reputation for fearlessness. As much a medicine man and visionary as a war chief, Sitting Bull predicted the rain of white men on the largest encampment of not only Sioux but also Cheyenne and Arapaho at the Little Big Horn. His vision became reality with the attack led by Custer. The fearsome battle saw Custer and five troops of the Seventh Cavalry annihilated.

Despite breaking up into small bands and escaping to Canada, by 1881 Sitting Bull and many of his followers had surrendered to U.S. forces, moving onto reservation territory. In 1885 he was allowed to tour with Buffalo Bill's Wild West show, where he was often jeered, was sometimes cheered (at least in Canada), and sold his autograph to curious white audiences. On December 15, 1890, Sitting Bull, his teenage son, and six of his bodyguards were killed by Indian police, despite efforts by Buffalo Bill Cody to intervene and prevent bloodshed. Items such as the belt and breast piece serve as reminders of his courageous life.

A recent acquisition by Koch that integrates decorative arts with firearms is the custom-built matched pair of gold-plated and deluxe-engraved Colt officer's model match revolvers of the matinee idol and superstar Tom Mix. These elaborate pistols also represent the flamboyance common to most of the post–Old West characters, creators of the new

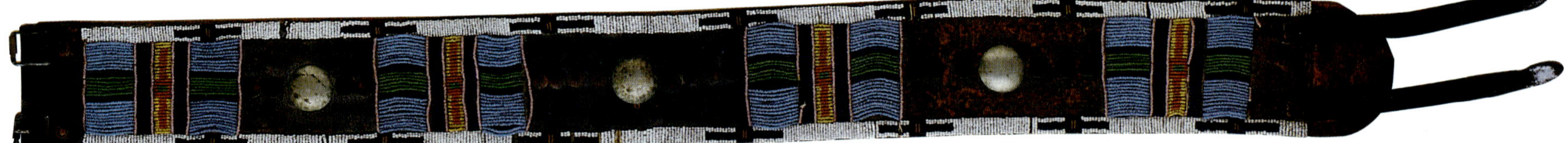

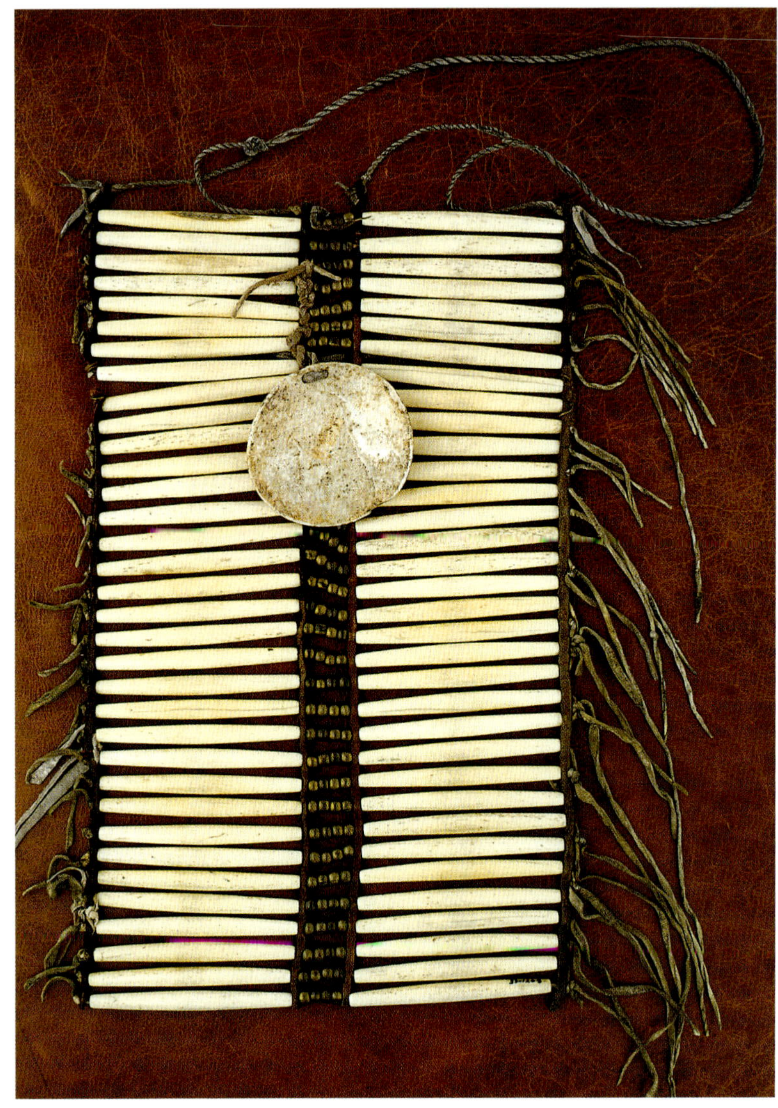

Sitting Bull's
Bead Belt and Breast Piece, worn by
him at the battle of "THE LITTLE
BIG HORN," where Gen. Custer and
his men were massacred.—
Presented to Major M. A. Reno, of the
7th U.S. Cavalry and in turn Given to
his nephew, R. A. Ross, 2nd of New Cumber-
land, Pa.
Affirmed and subscribed before me this 22nd day of February 1916.
J. C. Eichinger
My Commission Expires First Monday in January 1922 JUSTICE OF THE PEACE
R. A. Ross

Bead belt and breast piece worn by Chief Sitting Bull at the Battle of the Little Big Horn, about 1870
With documentation dated and notarized 1916
Bone, deerskin, brass, and cloth
L. (belt) 45 in.; (breast piece) 15 x 9½ in.

Deluxe Colt officer's model match double-action revolvers that belonged to Tom Mix
Made in Hartford, Connecticut, about 1926 and 1930
Serial nos. 567346 (top) and 532107; .38 caliber
Silver panels on mother-of-pearl grips
L. (each barrel) 6 in.
Inscription: "TOM MIX"

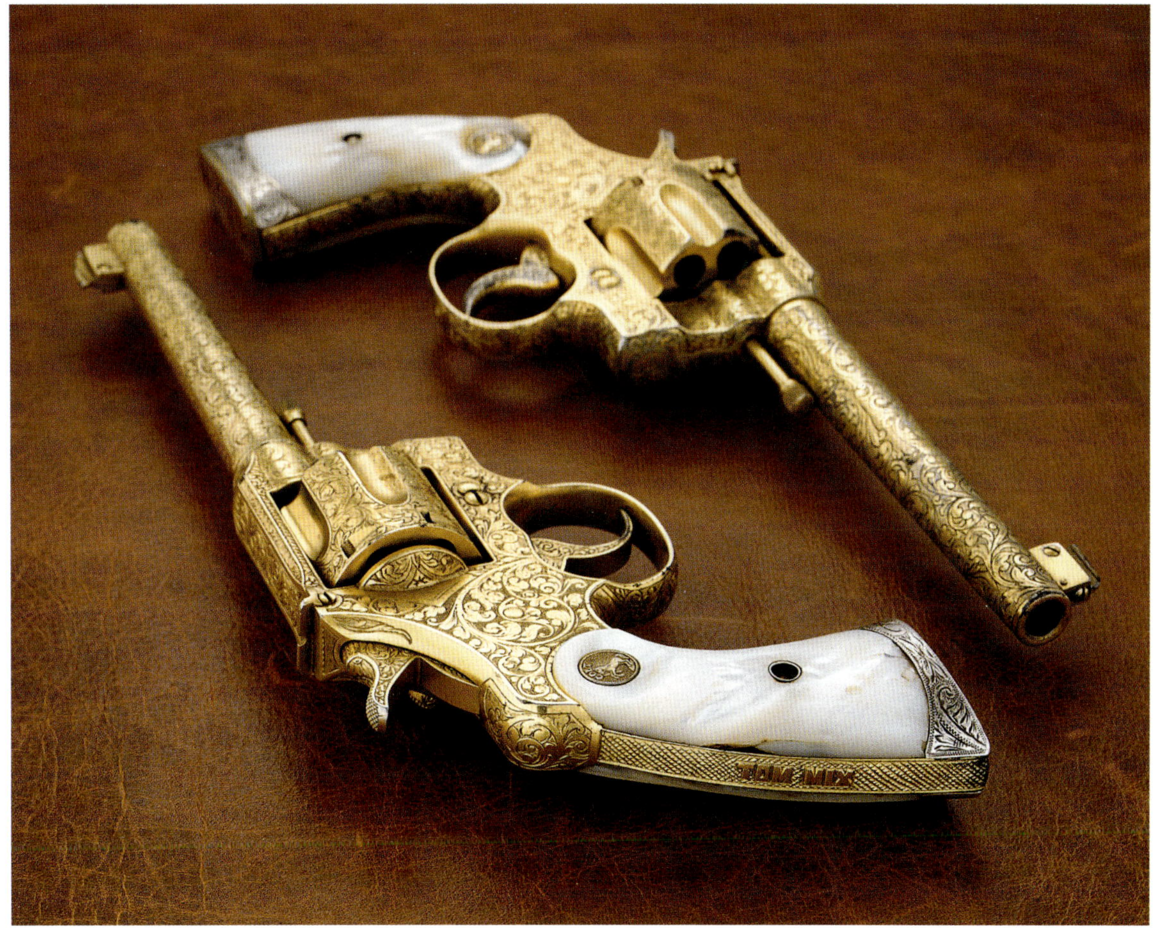

West presented by Hollywood on the silver screen and later magnified for a colossal television audience. Mix, an authentic cowboy, Wild West–show performer, rodeo champion, and his own stuntman, wryly observed that it was easier for a cowboy to become an actor than for an actor to become a cowboy. Like Gene Autry, Roy Rogers, John Wayne, and today's Tom Selleck, Mix was himself a keen collector of firearms.

As these stories illustrate, aficionados of firearms share a rich heritage—both in the objects collected and in the pedigrees of past and present collectors. By understanding the time-honored and historic connection between all the arts and antiquities and the field of weapons, and by integrating his Western Room with his other collections, Bill Koch continues the traditions of the past and inspires the grand collectors of future generations.

—R. L. WILSON

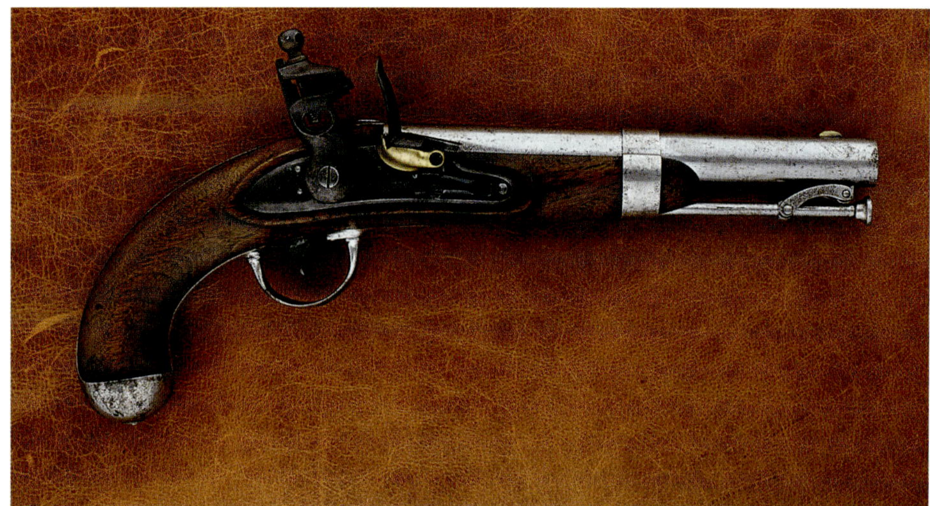

U.S. military Model 1836 flintlock pistol
Made by Asa Waters, Millbury, Massachusetts, dated 1838
.54 caliber smoothbore
Walnut, steel, and brass
L. (overall) 14 in.

Colt single-action army revolver that belonged to Tom Horn
Made in Hartford, Connecticut, about 1897
Serial no. 168991; .38–40 caliber; 6 shots
Steel and molded hard rubber
L. (barrel) 5½ in.

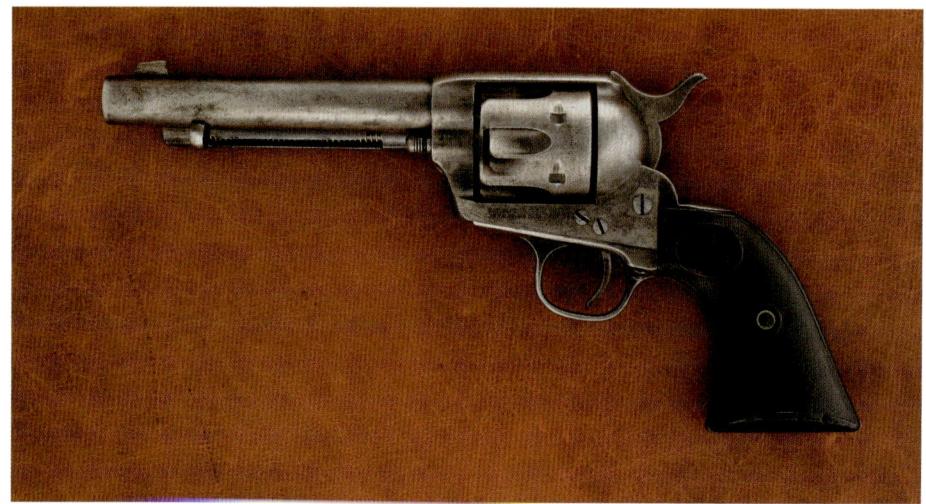

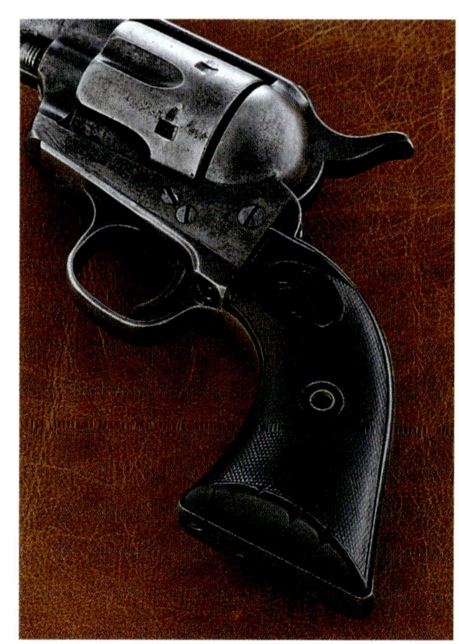

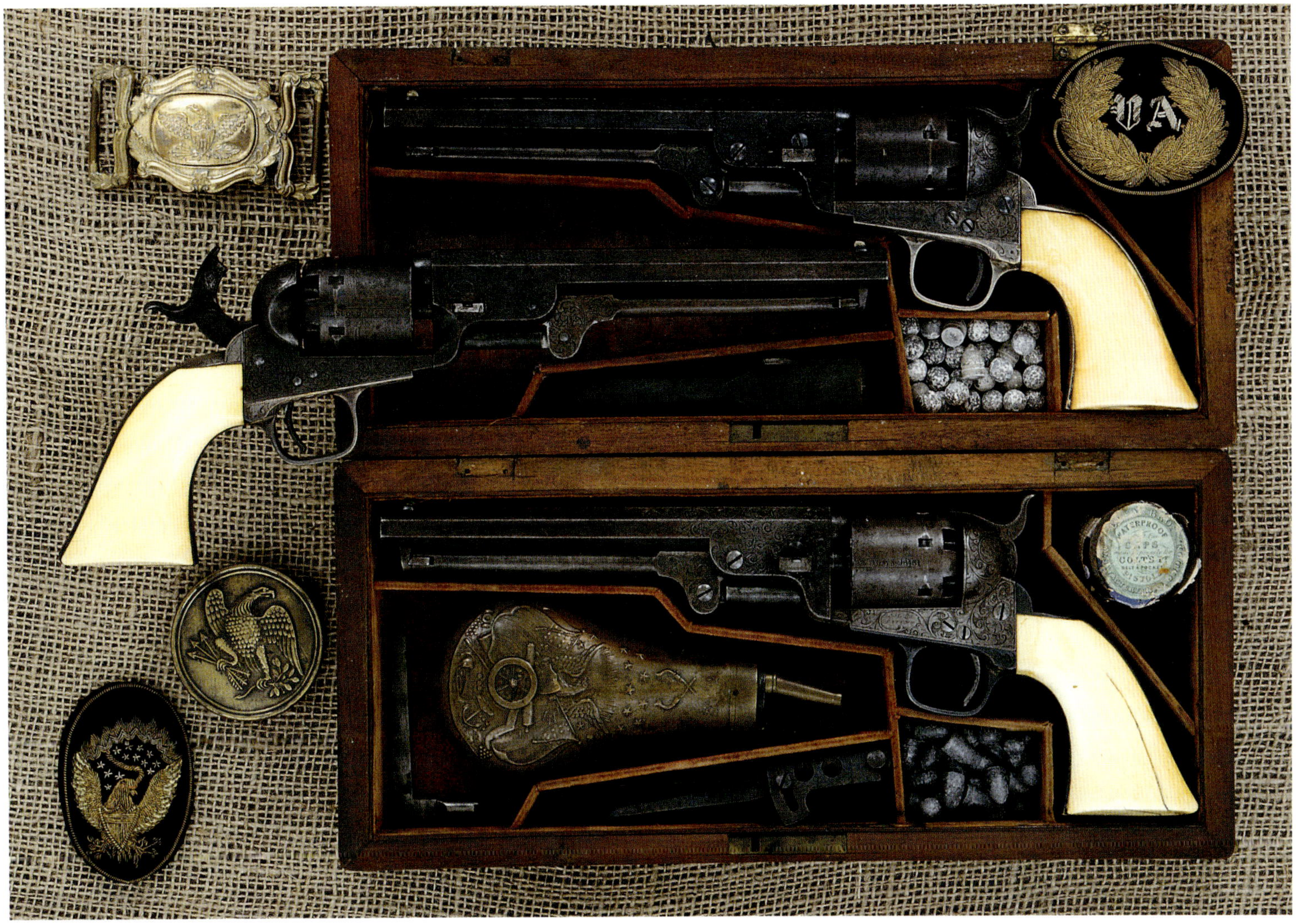

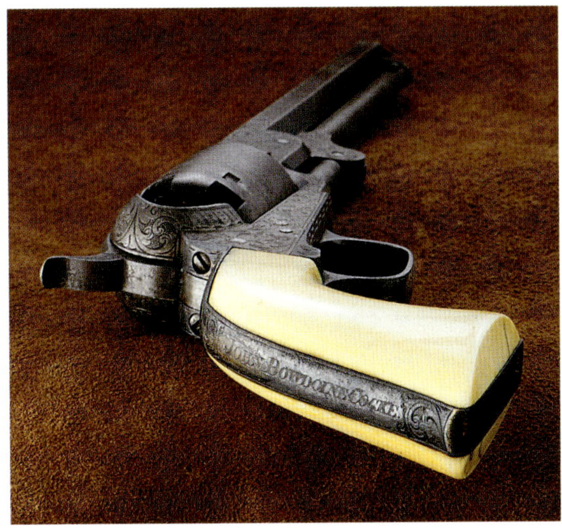

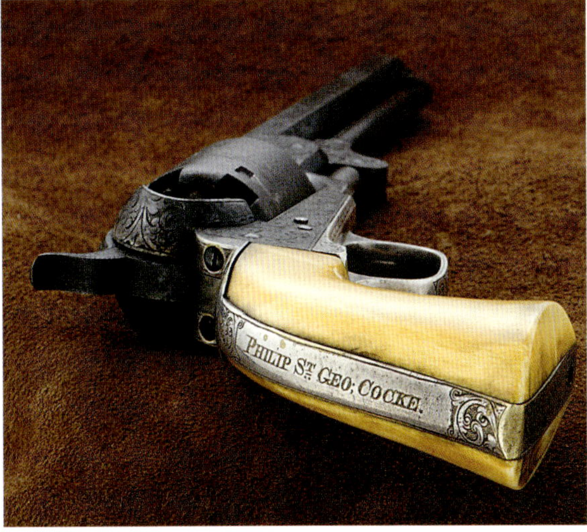

Top to bottom:

Pair of Colt Model 1851 navy percussion revolvers that belonged to Brigadier General Philip St. George Cocke
Serial nos. 93242/. and 93235/.; .36 caliber

Matching navy revolver that belonged to the general's son, John Bowdoine Cocke
Serial no. 96461/.; .36 caliber
Steel and silver-plated brass with ivory grips; mahogany cases
L. (each barrel) 7½ in.
Inscription: Owner's name

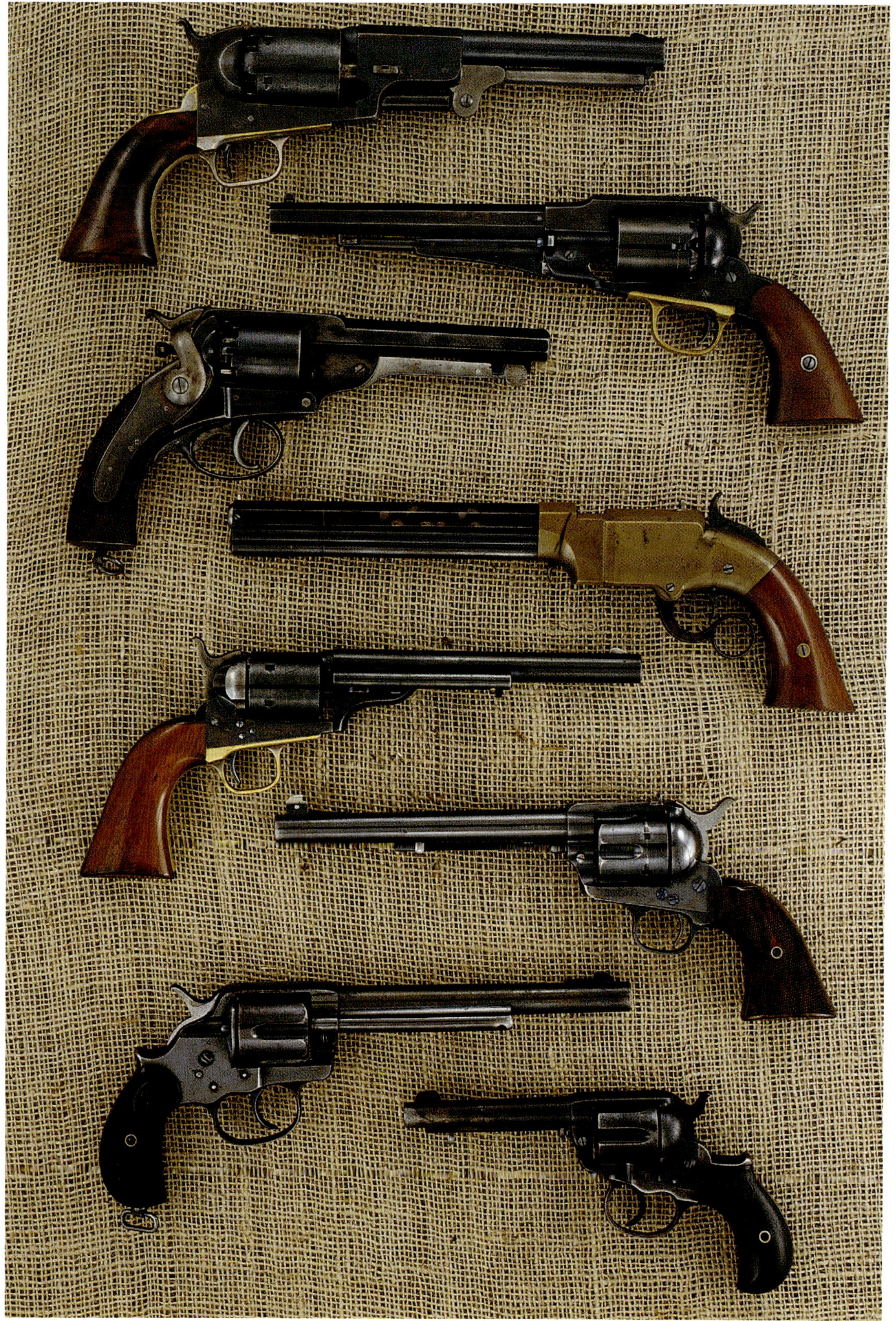

Top to bottom:

Colt third model dragoon or old model army percussion revolver
About 1853
Serial no. 13686; .44 caliber; 6 shots
Steel, brass, and varnished walnut
L. (barrel) 7½ in.

Remington new model army percussion revolver
Made in Ilion, New York, about 1863
Serial no. 106702; .44 caliber; 6 shots
Walnut, steel, and brass
L. (barrel) 7½ in.

Kerr's patent double-action percussion revolver
Made in England, about 1860
Serial no. 859; .54 caliber; 5 shots
Walnut and steel
L. (barrel) 5¾ in.

Volcanic navy model lever-action repeating magazine pistol
Made in New Haven, Connecticut, about 1855
Serial no. 2176; .38 caliber; 10 shots
Walnut, steel, and brass
L. (barrel) 8 in.

Colt Model 1871–72 open-top single-action revolver
Made in Hartford, Connecticut, 1871–72; shipped to J. C. Grubb Co., Philadelphia, Pennsylvania, November 1, 1872
Serial no. 943; .44 rimfire caliber; 6 shots
Walnut, steel, and brass
L. (barrel) 8 in.

Colt single-action army flattop target revolver
Made in Hartford, Connecticut, about 1893
Serial no. 149569; .44 S&W caliber; 6 shots
Walnut and steel
L. (barrel) 7½ in.

Colt Model 1878 frontier double-action revolver
Made in Hartford, Connecticut, about 1883
Serial no. 9539; .45 caliber; 6 shots
Steel and molded hard rubber
L. (barrel) 7½ in.

Colt Model 1877 lightning double-action revolver
Made in Hartford, Connecticut, about 1900
Serial no. 120097; .38 caliber; 6 shots
Steel and molded hard rubber
L. (barrel) 4½ in.
Inscription on backstrap: "Am Exp Co 586"

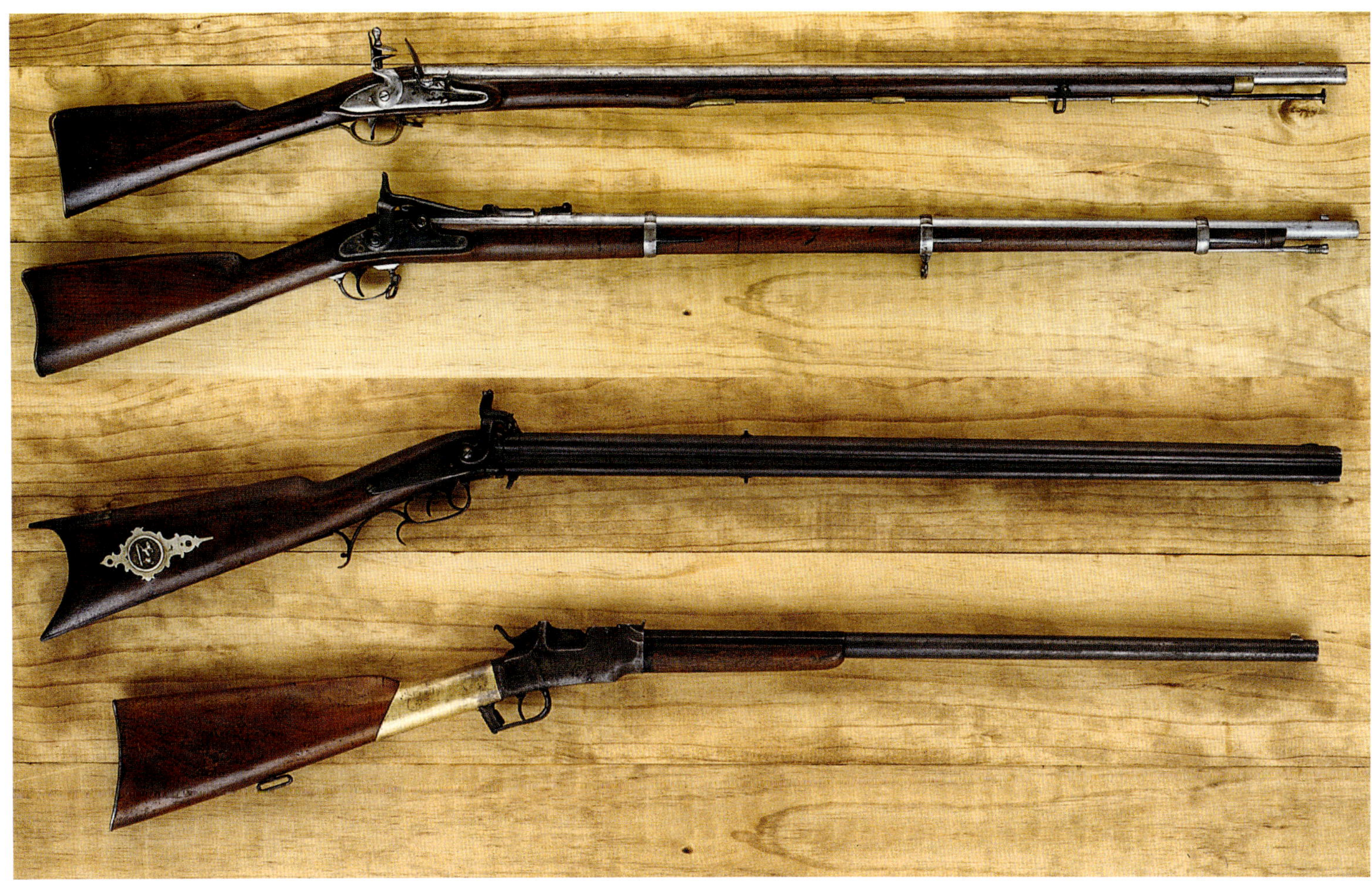

Top to bottom:

British Brown Bess flintlock musket
Made in London, England, about 1775
.74 caliber smoothbore
Walnut, steel, and brass
L. (barrel) 39 in.

U.S. Springfield Model 1866 conversion of percussion Civil War Model 1863 musket
Made in Springfield, Massachusetts, 1864; converted 1866
.50 centerfire caliber
Walnut and steel
L. (barrel) 40 in.
Inscription on lockplate: "1864"; on left side of stock: "HSH" U.S. ordnance inspector cartouche

Four-Barrel Wender or turn-over rifle/shotgun combination by Henry Parker
About 1860
.44 caliber rifle barrels on one side; .36 gauge shotgun barrels on other
Walnut, German silver, and steel
L. (barrels) 29¼ in.
Inscription on right side of stock: "THIS WAS MAHLON I PAXSN GUN IN / 1910 IN CO F 75 IND RIGAMENT / NO 1"

Allen & Wheelock drop-breech single-shot sporting rifle that belonged to Robert Hawkey, alias "Antelope Bob"
Made by Ethan Allen & Co., Worcester, Massachusetts, about 1860
Serial no. 73; .38 rimfire caliber
Walnut and steel with brass reinforced stock at wrist
L. (barrel) 26 in.

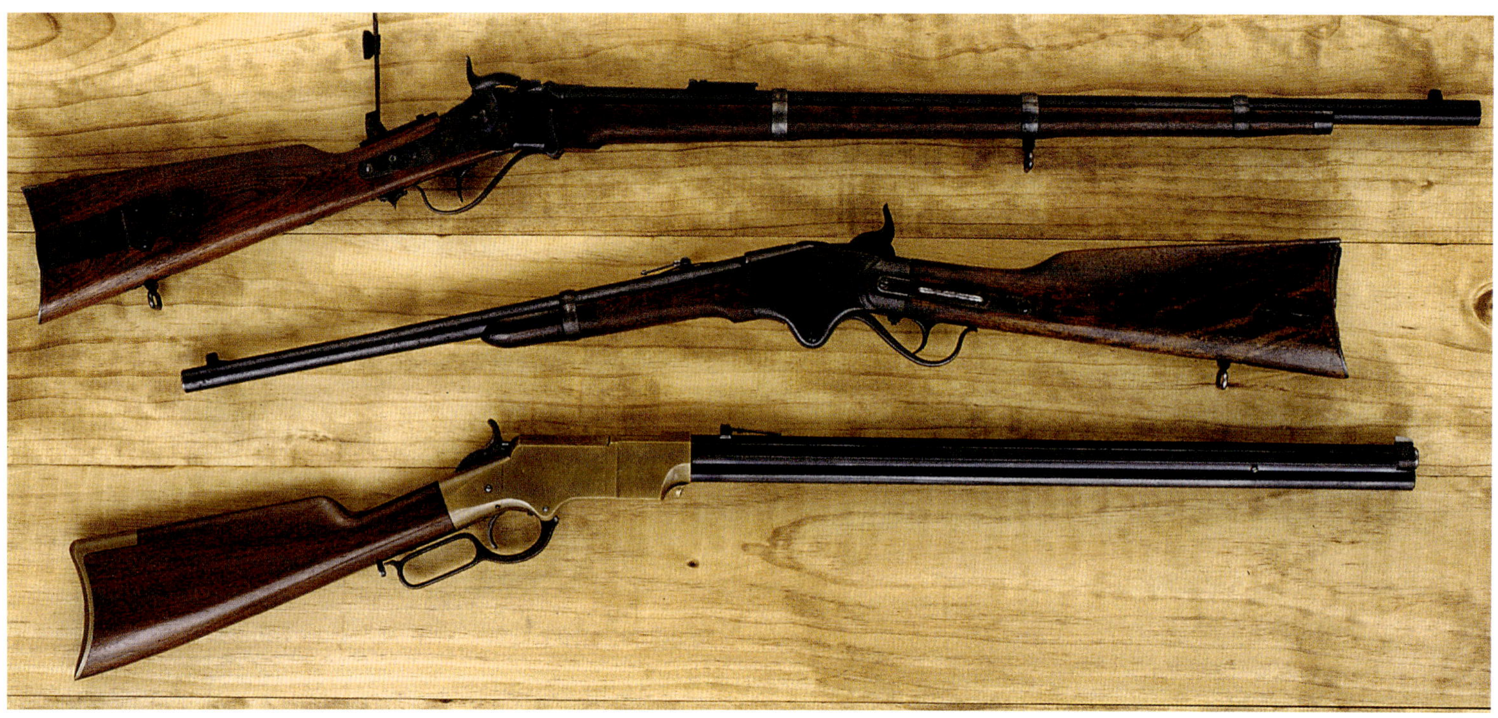

Top to bottom:

Sharps single-shot breechloading military rifle
Made by Drovel Tool Manufacturing, Inc., Farmingdale, New York, about 1990 (replica)
Serial no. D1037; .50 2½ caliber
Walnut and steel
L. (barrel) 30 in.

Spencer breechloading repeating rifle, with U.S. Colorado territory stock markings
Made by Spencer Repeating Rifle Co., Boston, Massachusetts, about 1868
Serial no. 20347; .52 rimfire caliber
Walnut and steel
L. (barrel) 22 in.
Inscription on left side of buttstock: "U.S. / COL. TER"; on left side of stock at wrist: "GC" and indecipherable U.S. ordnance inspector markings

Henry's patent repeating rifle
Made by New Haven Arms Co., New Haven, Connecticut, about 1861
Serial no. 1998; .44 rimfire caliber
Walnut, brass, and steel
L. (barrel) 22 in.

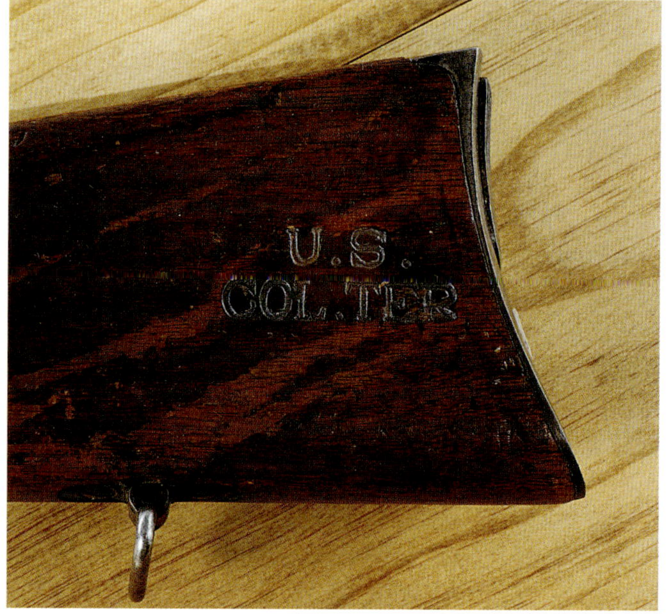

Top to bottom:

Winchester Model 1866 lever-action sporting rifle
Made by Winchester Repeating Arms Co., New Haven, Connecticut, about 1870
Serial no. 43069; .44 rimfire caliber
Silver-plated brass, steel, and walnut
L. (barrel) 24 in.
Inscription on left side of frame: "WELLS FARGO & CO / SAN FRANCISCO"

Winchester Model 1873 lever-action sporting rifle presented to Ute Chief Ouray
Made by Winchester Repeating Arms Co., about 1880
Serial no. 81505; .44–40 caliber
Walnut, brass, and steel
L. (barrel) 24 in.
Inscription on left side of frame: "Presented by / Winchester Repeating Arms Co"

Whitney-Burgess-Morse lever-action sporting rifle presented to Emmett L. Blood
Made by Whitney Arms Co., Whitneyville, Connecticut, about 1878
Serial no. 604; .45–70 caliber
Walnut and steel
L. (barrel) 28 in.
Inscription on left side of frame: "Presented to / EMMETT L. BLOOD / by / PHILIP KROHN, D.D."

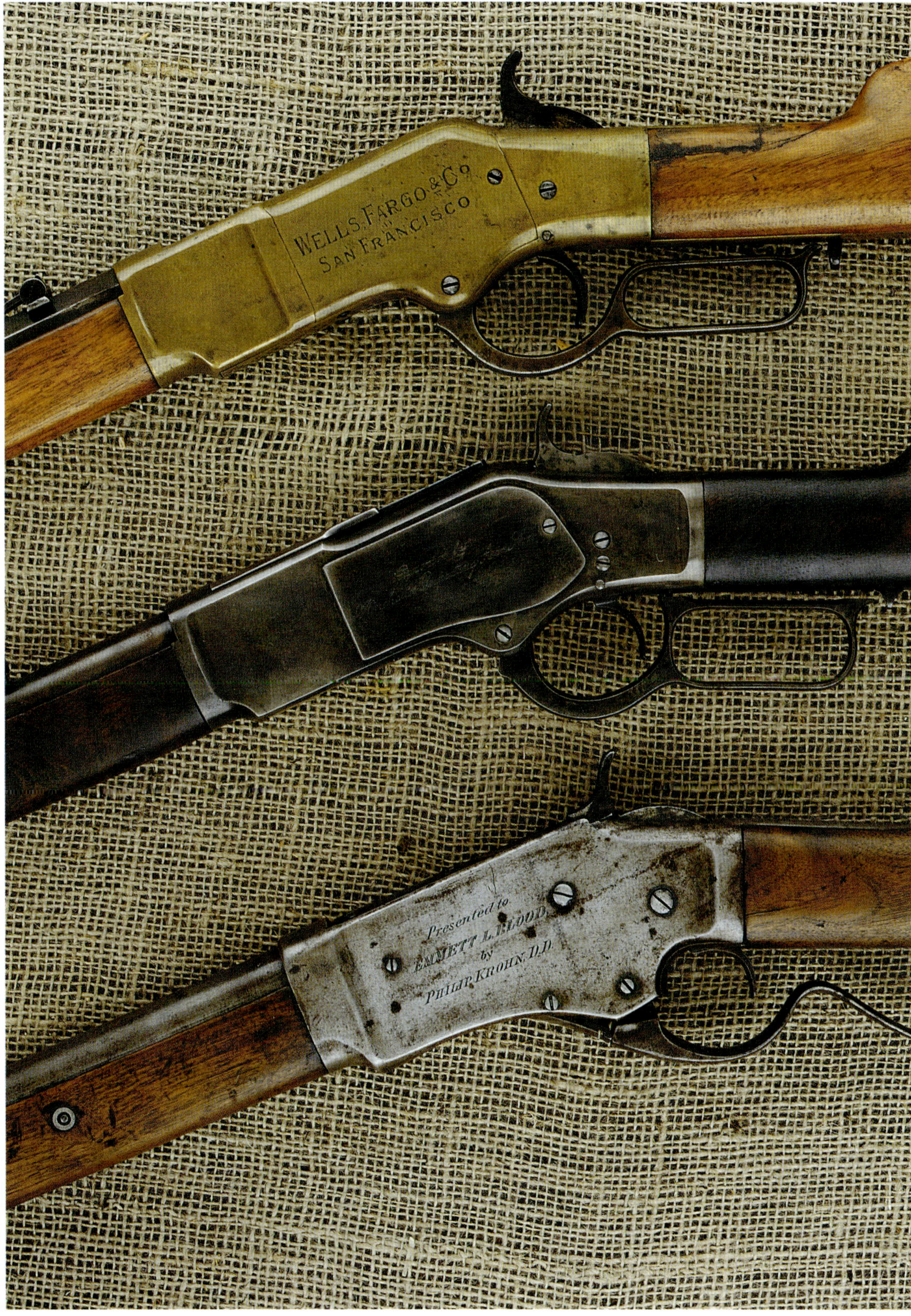

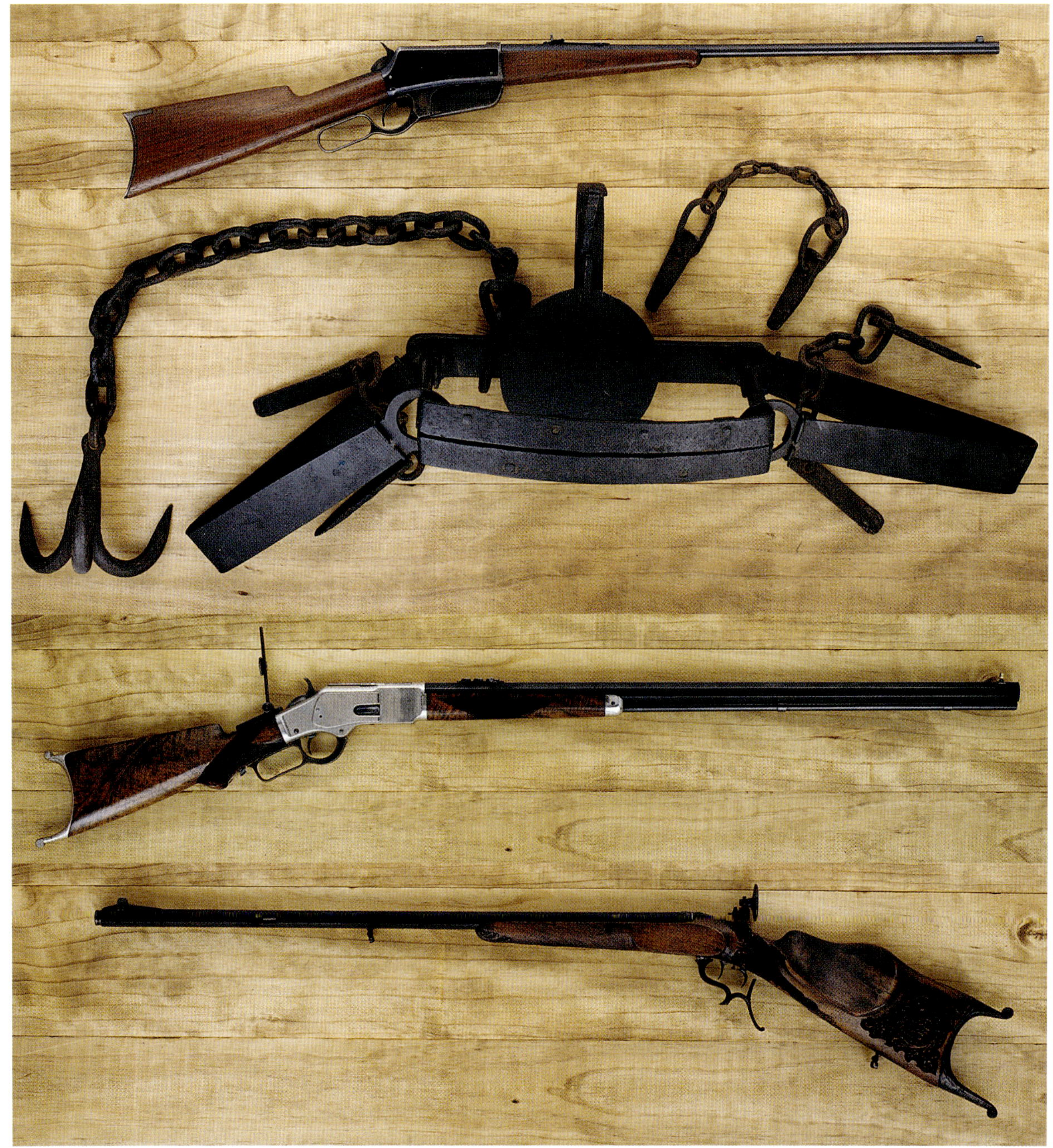

Top to bottom:

Winchester Model 1895 flat-side lever-action sporting rifle
Made in New Haven, Connecticut, about 1896
Serial no. 3107; .38–72 W.C.F. caliber
Walnut and steel
L. (barrel) 26 in.

Bear trap that belonged to Art Jackson
Chain, hand-forged metal wedges, iron, and wood
W. (jaws) 16¾ in.

Custom-made Winchester Model 1873 lever-action sporting rifle
Made in New Haven, Connecticut, about 1884
Serial no. 173887; .32–20 caliber
Walnut and steel
L. (barrel) 32 in.

Breechloading Scheutzen target rifle
Made by F. Ernst, Nurnberg, dated 1893
.17 caliber
Walnut and steel
L. (barrel) 29¾ in.
Silver inlay on top of barrel: "F. ERNST / EHRENGABE ZUM IX MITTELFRANCHISHEN BUNDE-SCHIESSEN 1893 IN ZIRNDORF / VOM ZIRNDORFER RADLERKLUB 'ALTE FEST'"

Custer with grizzly bear, Colonel William Ludlow, a third hunter, and the scout Bloody Knife
Photograph by William H. Illingworth, August 7, 1874
Stereoscope view
3⅜ x 6⅞ in.

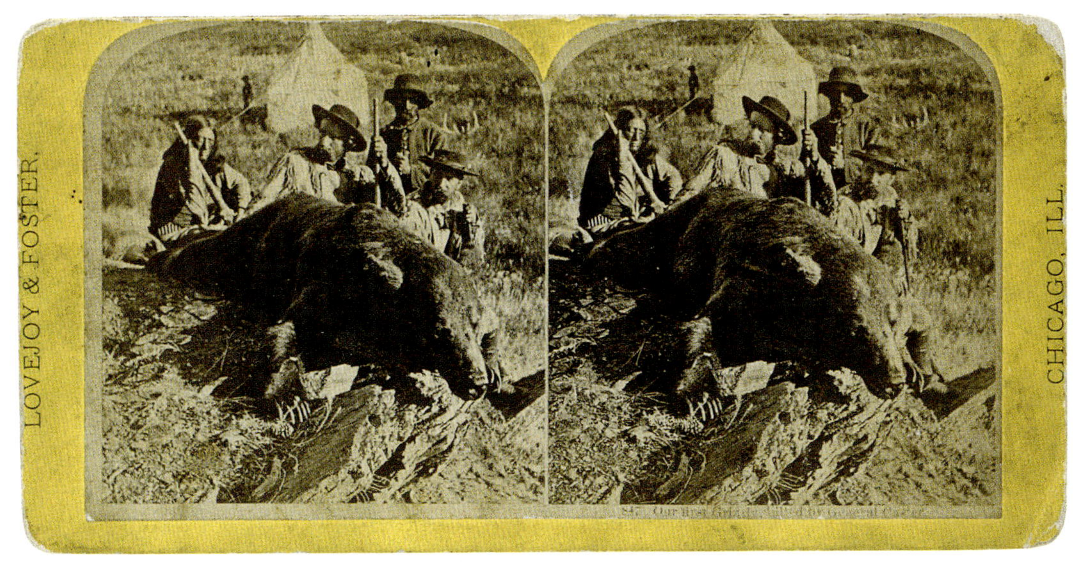

Custer with Remington rolling block single-shot rifle and "King of the Forest" elk during Yellowstone expedition
Photograph by William I. Pywell, September 6, 1873
Albumen print
6 x 9 in.

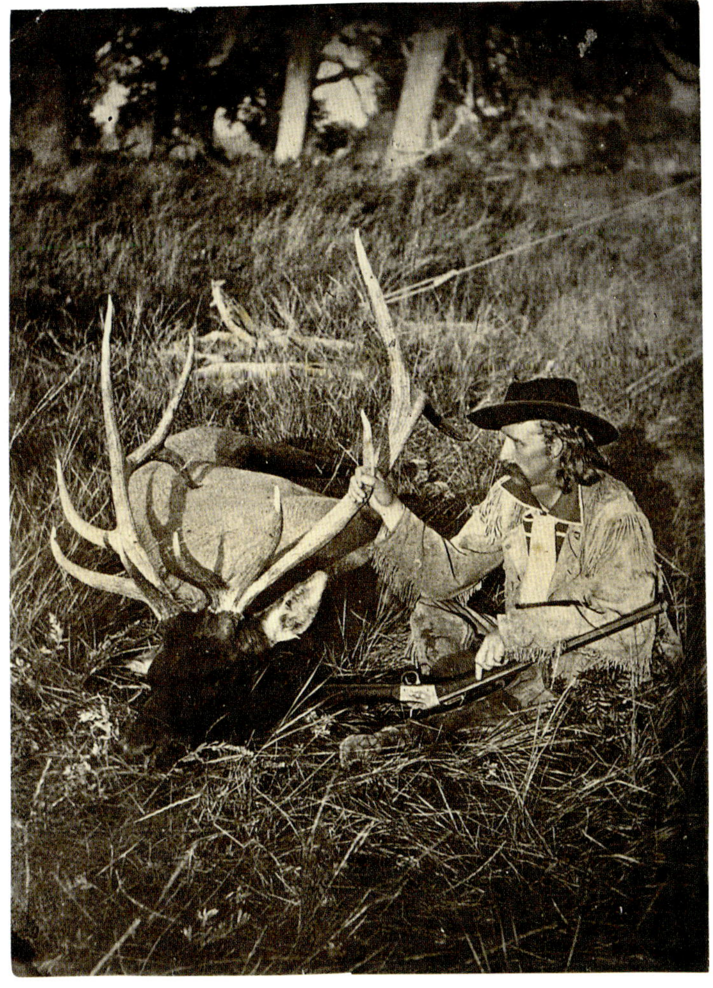

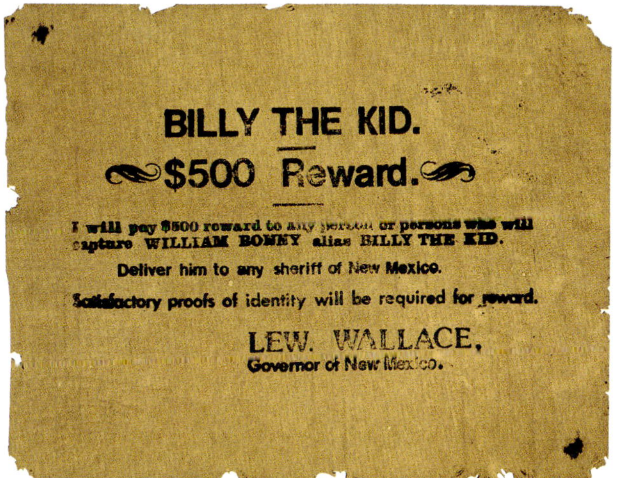

BILLY THE KID.

$500 Reward.

I will pay $500 reward to any person or persons who will capture WILLIAM BONNY alias BILLY THE KID.

Deliver him to any sheriff of New Mexico.

Satisfactory proofs of identity will be required for reward.

LEW. WALLACE,
Governor of New Mexico.

Reward poster for capture of Henry McCarty, alias William Bonney, alias "Billy the Kid"
Issued by Governor Lew Wallace, New Mexico, about 1880
Letterpress with ink on paper
9 x 12 in.

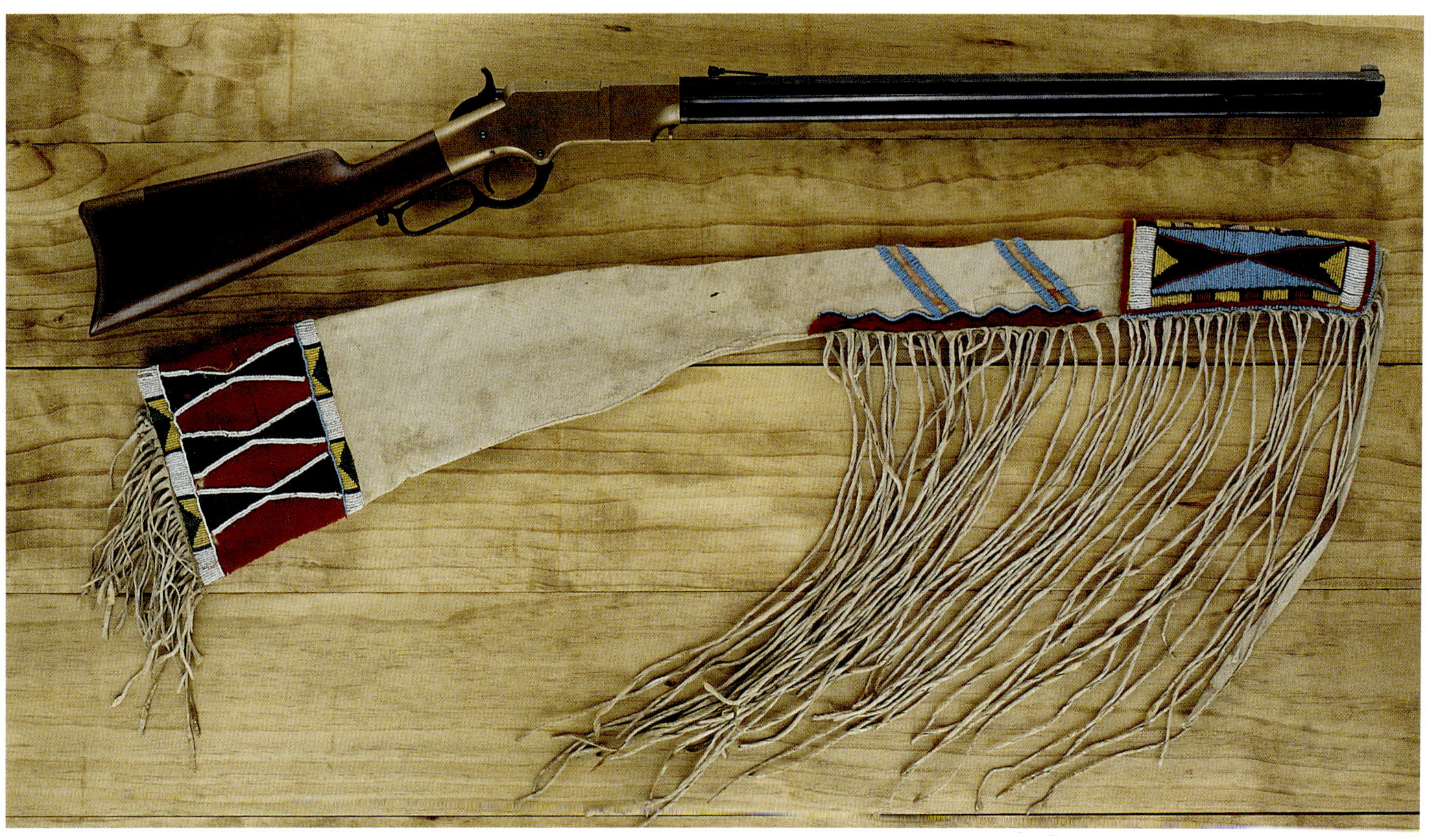

Henry rifle
Made by New Haven Arms Co., New Haven, Connecticut, about 1861
Serial no. 1642; .44 rimfire caliber
Walnut, brass, and steel
L. (barrel) 22 in.

North American Indian
Beaded deerskin scabbard, about 1865–70
Deerskin and glass beads
L. (overall) 42 in.

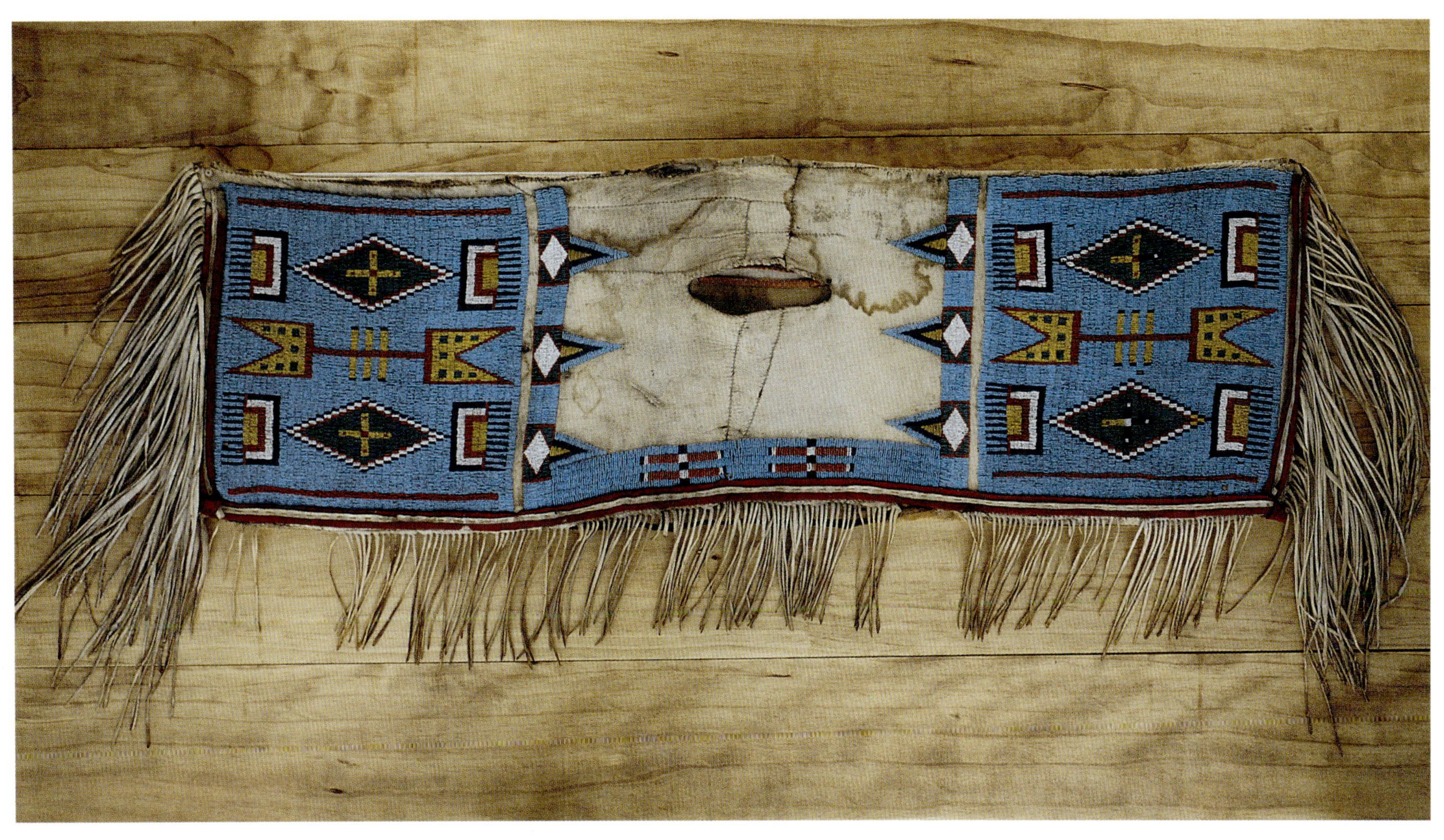

North American Indian
Beaded saddle throw, about
1870–80
Fringed buckskin, with glass beads
W. 48 in.

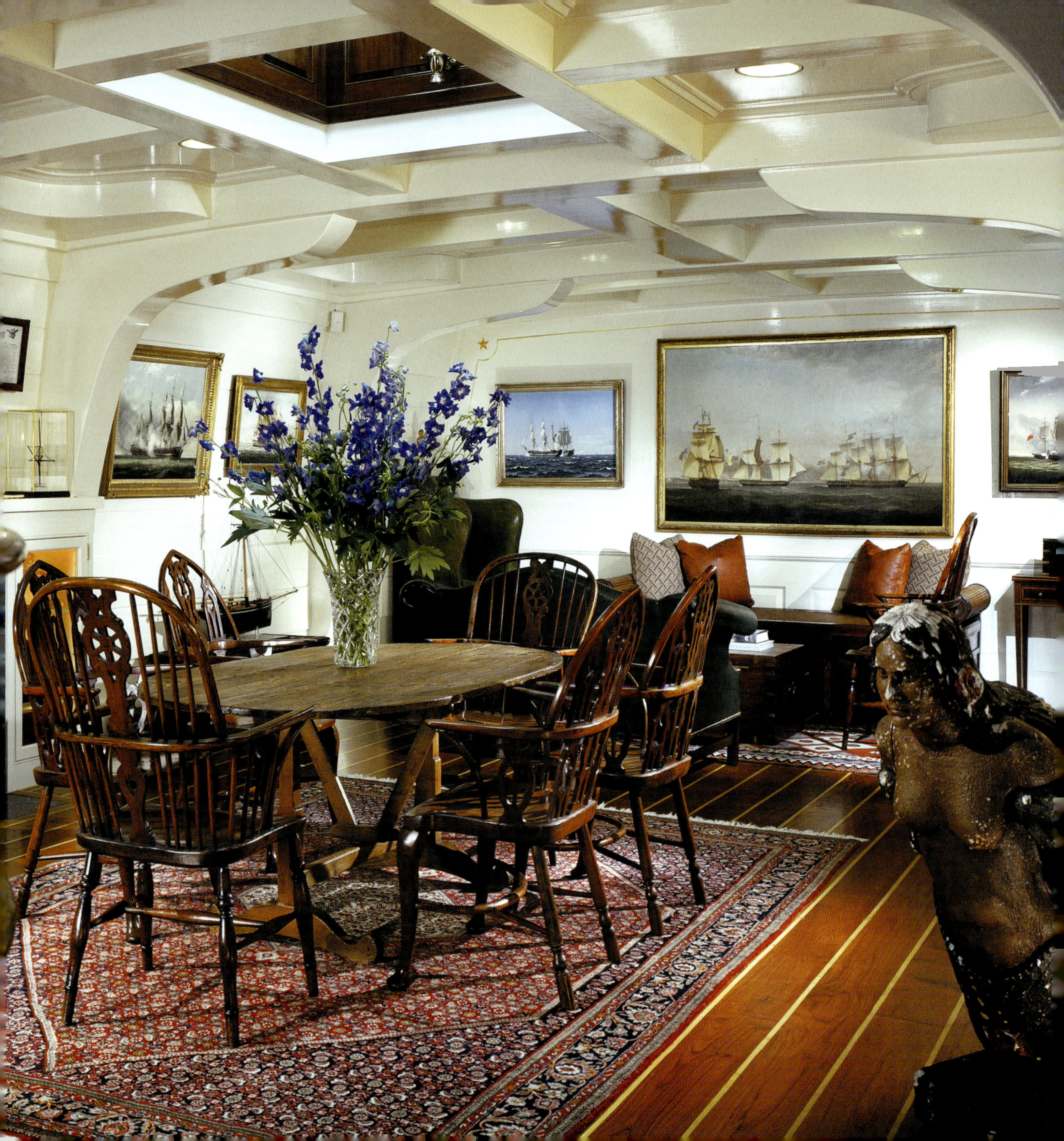

MARINE

* * * * *

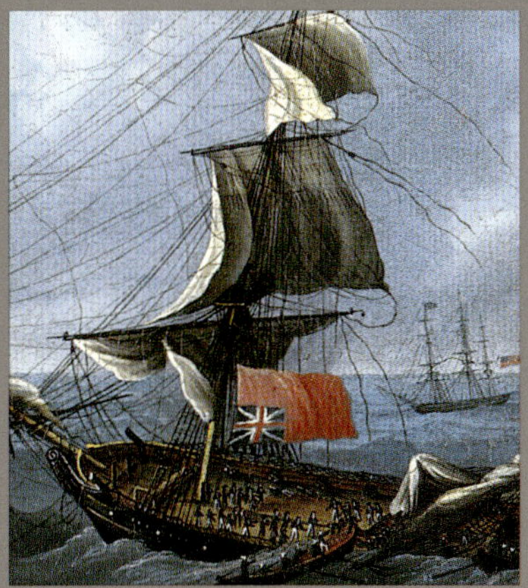

Fig. 25. The Ship's Room at Osterville, Cape Cod, based on the captain's quarters of the USS *Constitution*

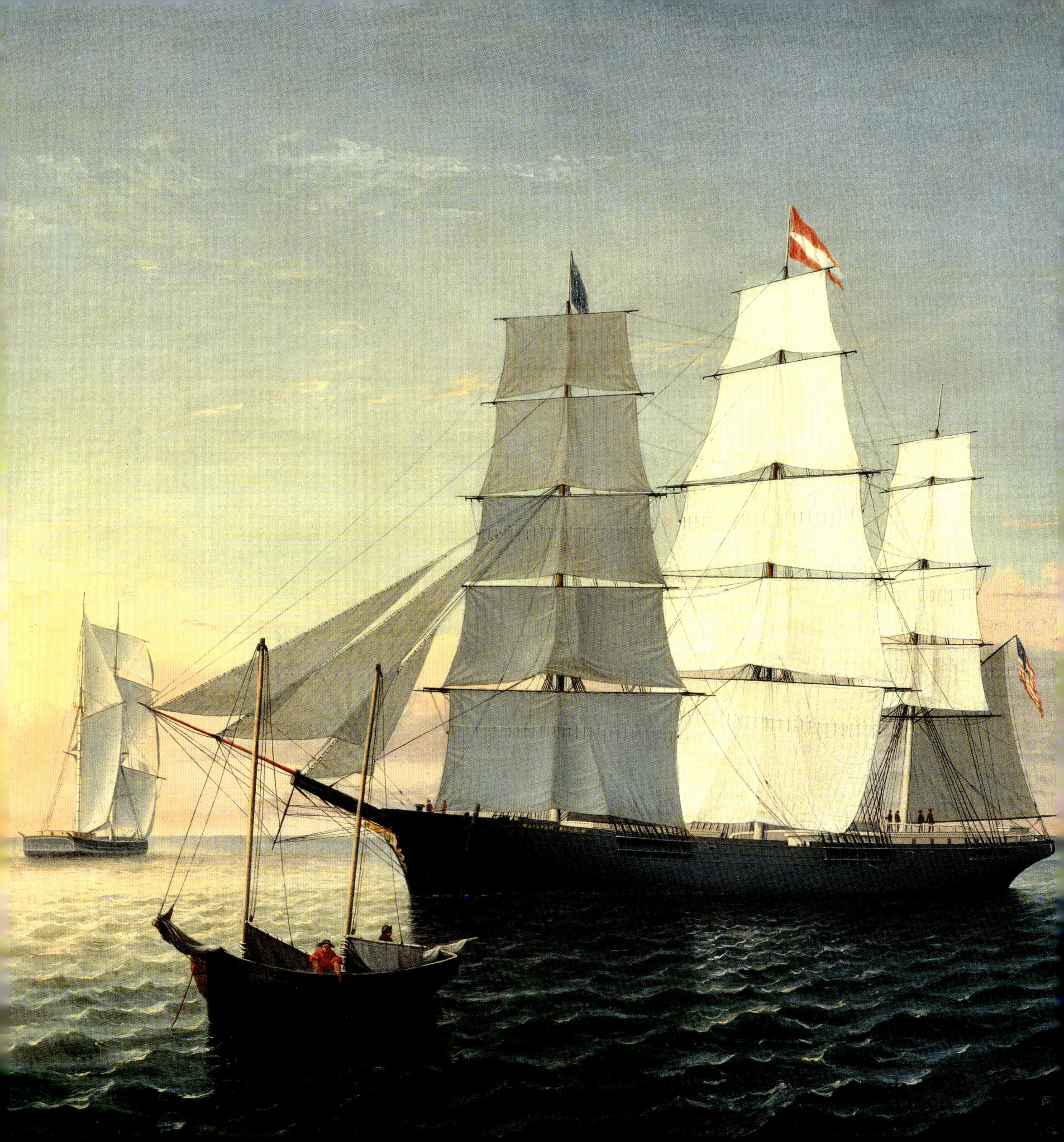

MARITIME ART

* * * * * * *

When Bill Koch purchased his first marine paintings in 1983, he was already a sailor himself and would soon begin racing competitively. Initially guided by his love of the sea and family lore, he quickly began to approach collecting with the same intensity he brought to racing. The marine paintings in his houses are displayed salon style, with outstanding works by leading marine artists covering the walls almost from top to bottom. As fine and decorative arts dealers, we have become familiar with Koch's collection and have even played a role in forming it. In our view, his paintings can be grouped naturally into three great categories of maritime activity: warfare (naval art), commerce (merchant art), and pleasure (yachting art). The first of these is perhaps the most personal portion of Koch's marine art collection, because it involves a family link to a heroic figure in American naval history: Captain James Lawrence, an ancestor on Koch's mother's side.[1]

Captain Lawrence had built a successful career in the U.S. Navy by the time he was placed in command of the eighteen-gun brig-sloop USS *Hornet* in 1811. He had served as second in command to Lieutenant Stephen Decatur during the dramatic 184 raid to board and burn the captured frigate *Philadelphia* under the walls of Tripoli during the Tripolitan War. After war with Great Britain was declared in 1812, Lawrence was sent to cruise off the coast of Brazil, blockading the port of Bahia and provoking the British man-of-war *Bonne Citoyenne.*

Lawrence was an ambitious seaman and yearned for an engagement that could bring him honor. A large, muscular man, he was described by contemporaries as a "colossal figure" who towered on the quarterdeck, with a "handsome, manly face and dark hair with side whiskers combed up."[2] His contemporary portrait by an unknown artist shows him in full uniform with his sword at his side, a hint of ruddiness in his cheeks, and one hand exposed (p. 172). Lawrence appears in the full compass of his glory, exuding a stoic pride—a passionate and heroic American naval officer who would go on to give his life for his country.

By chance, in mid-afternoon on February 24, 1813, off Demerara, the eager Lawrence spotted a vessel on the horizon that proved to be the equally matched eighteen-gun brig-sloop HMS *Peacock* under the command of Captain William Peake. Lawrence managed to weather his opponent and tack, and the two vessels exchanged broadside fire at short range. The *Peacock* attempted to wear, but Lawrence ran down her starboard quarter and poured in such a devastating and precise storm of fire that the *Peacock* was driven to surrender within fifteen minutes. The stunning victory over an equally armed opponent was the result of Lawrence's tactical superiority and seamanship.

Captain Peake lay dead on the deck, the *Peacock* began to sink, and her first lieutenant raised the ship's ensign upside down as a distress signal. The Italian émigré artist Michele Felice Cornè depicted the victorious *Hornet* with her sails lowered and two American flags fluttering, and the destroyed and sinking *Peacock* with her mainmast blown away in the foreground (p. 173). Lawrence sent men over to assist the desperate crew, but the *Peacock* sank quickly, and most of her men were lost.

Word of Lawrence's victory spread immediately. It was later immortalized in *The Naval Monument,* the popular publication in which Cornè's painting appears as a wood engraving. In an anonymous broadside printed in 1814 glorifying the action, *The Peacock Stung by the Hornet,* Lawrence is enshrined in the realm of myth: "And long shall gallant LAWRENCE'S name / Rank high upon the page of Fame, / For every true Columbian tar, / Will hail him HERO of the WAR."[3] When Lawrence returned home after the battle, he was greeted as a hero, promoted to captain, and given command of the frigate *Chesapeake.*

Lawrence's reputation soared with his victory, and he suddenly became known along the eastern seaboard as the legendary "Captain Jim." However, the crew of his new vessel, the *Chesapeake,* was green and mutinous; dissatisfied with their Navy pay, they wanted to become privateers. Lawrence

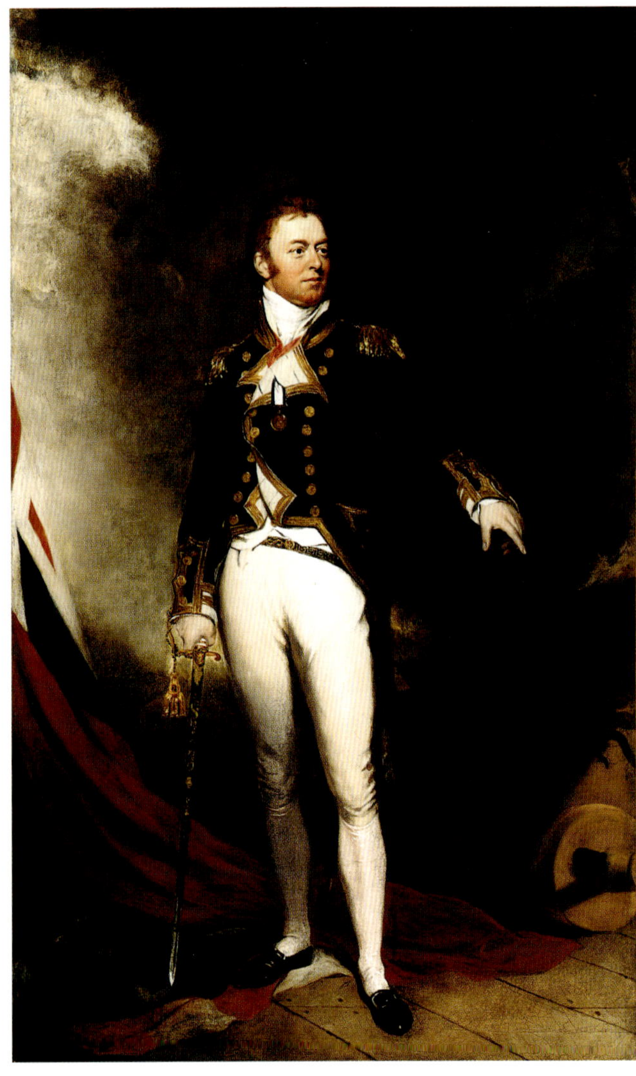

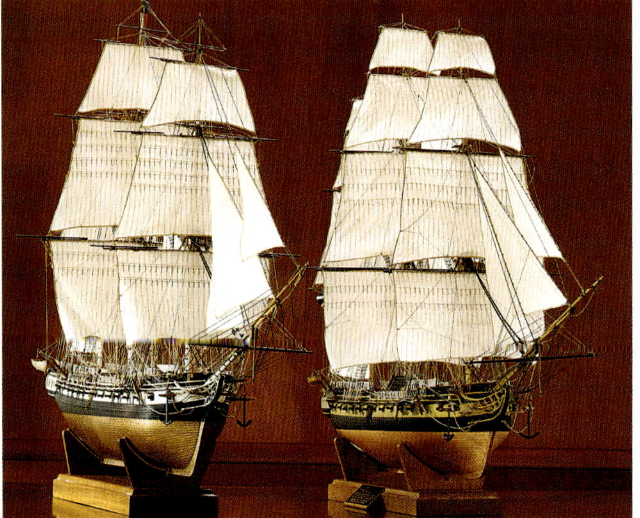

soon received orders to head to sea but was prevented from doing so by the presence of the British blockade off Boston Harbor. Captain Philip Bowes Vere Broke of the British thirty-eight-gun frigate HMS *Shannon* sailed into the mouth of Boston Harbor and then returned to sea, attempting to provoke Lawrence into a fight.

Captain Broke was an innovator in Nelson's navy, no mere stuffed shirt, but an officer determined to put Nelson's teachings into practice. He believed in "powder practice," or regular gun drills, and was reputed to have the best-trained crew in the Royal Navy. Four years Lawrence's senior, Broke had been in command of the *Shannon* for six years at the time of the battle. His full-length portrait, attributed to Samuel Lane (left), shows an energetic, candid commander gesturing with the index finger of his outstretched left hand, standing on the quarterdeck of a ship with his right foot on the American flag.

The *Chesapeake* was a thirty-eight-gun frigate, like the *Shannon*. Two ship models of the rival frigates (left, below) show them equally matched, worthy adversaries in what would become a historic battle. After two weeks of waiting, Broke finally sent Lawrence a letter stating, "Sir, As the *Chesapeake* appears now ready for sea, I request that you will do me the favour to meet the *Shannon* with her, ship to ship, to try the fortune of our respective flags. To an officer of your character . . . I assure you that what I write I pledge my honor to perform."[4] The gallant Broke also promised that no other British ships would be laying in wait. In spite of his poorly trained crew, Lawrence accepted the challenge.

On June 1, 1813, Lawrence ran out to meet the *Shannon* and sighted her sailing slowly toward Gloucester, as Broke did not want to fight off Boston where there was great anti-British sentiment. A view of the two vessels by John James Harwood (p. 163) shows them on the approach, trimming their sails in preparation for battle. The *Chesapeake* sailed into battle flying the "Free Trade and Sailors' Rights" flag, representing America's prewar grievances against British practices of unlawful boarding and seizure of ships. In the early going, Lawrence had a narrow chance to rake his opponent but demurred, choosing instead to run his port broadside against Shannon's starboard battery.

About 6 p.m., the ships exchanged broadside fire, as depicted in Thomas Luny's *Action between HMS* Shannon *and USS* Chesapeake (p. 174), but *Shannon*'s opening guns hit hard, inflicting severe damage on the *Chesapeake*'s quarterdeck and killing many of her officers. As the action progressed, the

JOHN JAMES HARWOOD
English, 1813–1871
The Shannon *and the* Chesapeake
Oil on canvas
42 x 66¼ in.

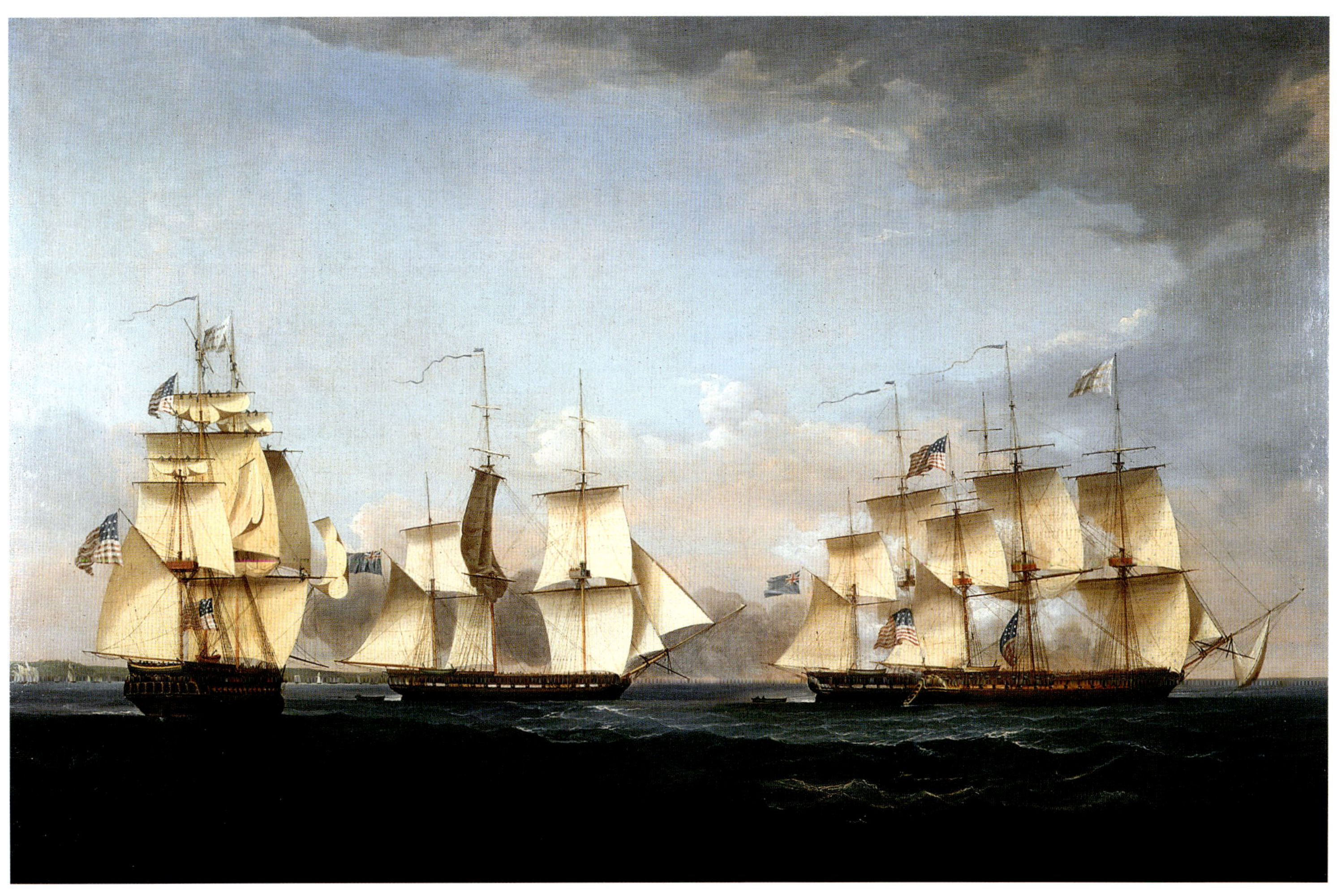

Opposite:
SAMUEL LANE
English, 1780–1859
Portrait of Captain Philip Bowes Vere Broke, about 1813
Oil on canvas
94 x 58 in.

Full rig maritime models of USS Chesapeake *and HMS* Shannon, 2000/2001
L. 53 in., w. 19 in., d. 37 in.

British guns continued to pound the *Chesapeake,* and her condition worsened, as can be seen in three separate depictions of the battle at its height by marine artists William John Huggins (p. 174), George Ropes (p. 175), and Thomas Whitcombe (p. 177).

Broke quickly realized that the *Chesapeake's* crew was badly hurt and gave the orders to board. His men swarmed aboard the *Chesapeake,* led by their daring captain, a moment dramatically captured in Thomas Hemy's *The* Shannon *and the* Chesapeake, *Close Quarters* (p. 176). Broke stands poised for victory, leading the charge with his sword drawn high in the air, as sailors armed with cutlasses and pistols clamber over the yards, and snipers stand ready in support.

During the boarding, Lawrence was struck and mortally wounded by small arms fire. He was taken below and was reported to have said, "Tell the men to fire faster and not to give up the ship; fight her till she sinks!" The boarders countered the fierce but disorganized resistance of the *Chesapeake's* crew successfully, but Captain Broke, too, was badly wounded in the attack. The *Chesapeake* was captured, and the British flag was raised as a sign of victory in the smoky aftermath of the battle, as depicted in Miles Walters's *Engagement between* Shannon *and* Chesapeake (p. 175).

Captain Lawrence's heroic death soon became the substance of legend. His final order, "Don't Give Up the Ship," was quickly circulated in reports of the action. Lawrence's body was restored to the United States by the victors and escorted to Salem's India Wharf, where the hero's cortege was received with "melancholy bells" and great ceremony. His remains were eventually buried in state in Trinity Church Yard, New York City, where a monument commemorating the captain's bravery and fortitude was erected. The *Chesapeake* was brought back from Nova Scotia to England, where it was studied by the British Navy. After the war, it was broken apart and its timbers were used to construct the Chesapeake Mill, which still stands in Wickham, England. Lawrence's last words became the motto of the entire U.S. Navy, and John Haley Bellamy, the most important carver of American eagles, used the phrase to adorn some of his famous hanging wall eagles (p. 177).[5]

Koch's collection of paintings dealing with naval subject matter also includes two fine scenes by the prolific British émigré marine artist James E. Buttersworth. Buttersworth is admired for his skill in rendering the moods of the sea and for his dramatic narrative style in the portrayal of vessels of all kinds under various weather conditions, positions, and states of sail. Although better known for his yachting scenes, he painted a significant number of canvases showing naval action. He achieved a familiar dramatic scene in *A Naval Incident between an American Frigate and a Spanish Cutter* (p. 165), depicting an unidentified American gunship unleashing her starboard cannon upon a fleeing Spanish cutter. The swells and crests of the deep-blue waves rise up to join the banks of gun smoke pouring out in the line of fire between the two vessels. A more placid scene is presented in *American Naval Vessel off Palermo* (p. 178), which shows an American frigate, a second, two-masted vessel, and a dinghy just outside Palermo Harbor, Sicily. The cliffs and hills of Sicily rise up out of the ocean like an enchanted island.

Koch's marine paintings not only are important examples of marine art, they are also significant historical documents. The era of the Civil War marked a new epoch in the life of the U.S. Navy, sundering brother from brother and ushering in some of the most remarkable innovations in fighting seacraft in centuries. A prime example of the revolution in naval warfare was the Confederate raider *Merrimack,* later renamed the CSS *Virginia,* the first of the ironsides. *Merrimack* was originally a U.S. Navy vessel built in Boston and stored in Gosport Yard in Norfolk, Virginia, where it was seized by Confederate forces at the outbreak of the war. Rebuilt by Confederate engineers with a two-inch layer of iron, a 1,500-pound iron ram on her bow, and six nine-inch Dahlgrens, *Merrimack* was the first ocean-worthy ironclad constructed in the United States.

In one of her first engagements, *Merrimack* encountered the 1,700-ton wooden USS *Cumberland* and the USS *Congress* sailing into Hampton Roads. Xanthus Russell Smith's *The Attack of the* Merrimack *on the U.S. Ships* Congress *and* Cumberland, *the Latter Sinking* (p. 183) shows the battle that ensued and the demise of *Cumberland. Merrimack* exchanged broadsides with *Cumberland,* whose fire from twenty-two nine-inch smoothbores bounced off the ironside's armor. The captain of *Merrimack* sent a message to the captain of *Cumberland,* demanding that she strike her colors. *Cumberland's* captain answered back, "Never! We will sink with our colors flying." *Merrimack* then rammed *Cumberland,* exploding her gun bow and strewing her with broadside fire

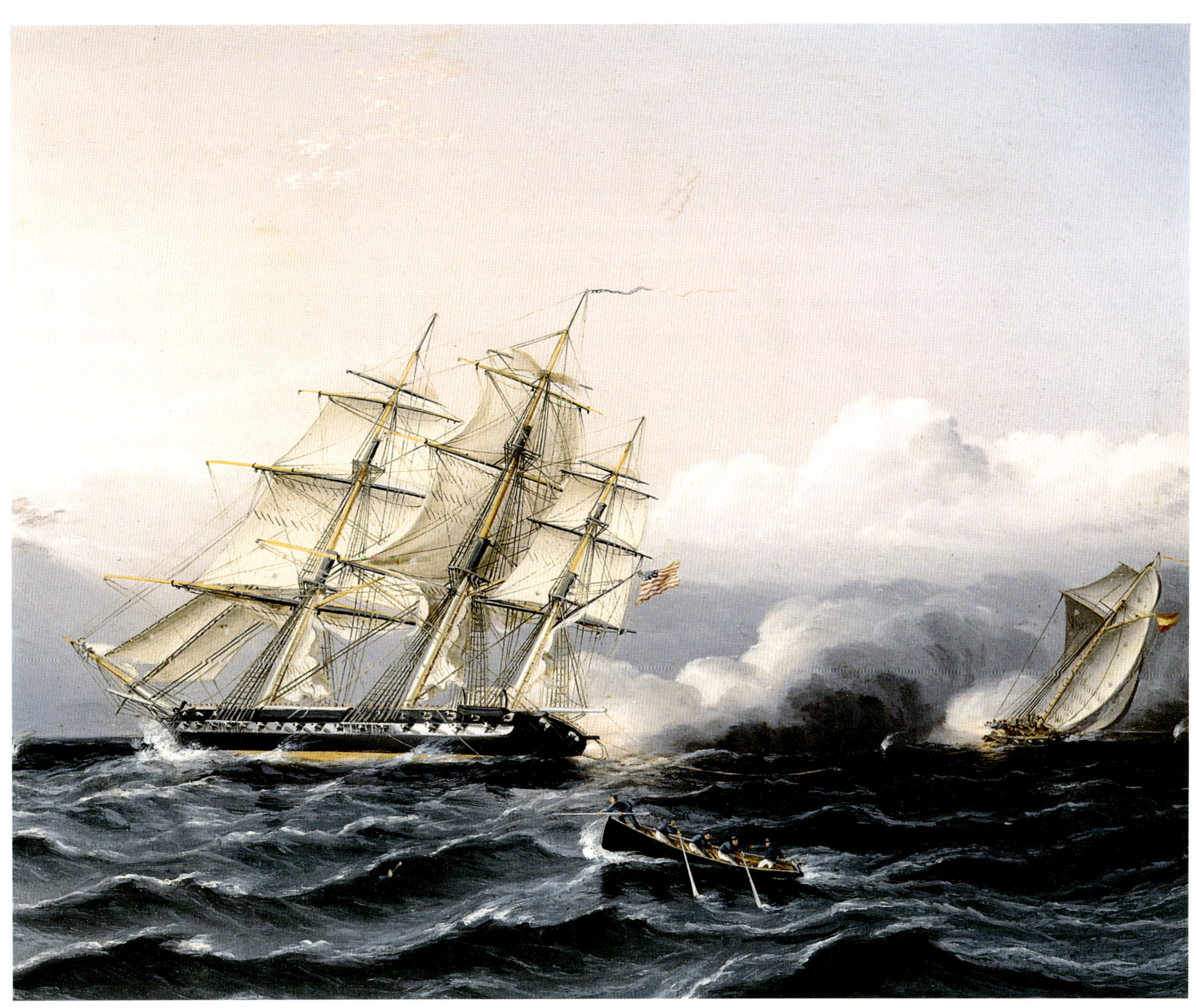

JAMES EDWARD BUTTERSWORTH

English, worked in America, 1817–1894
A Naval Incident between an American Frigate and a Spanish Cutter, 1860
Oil on panel
12 x 8 in.

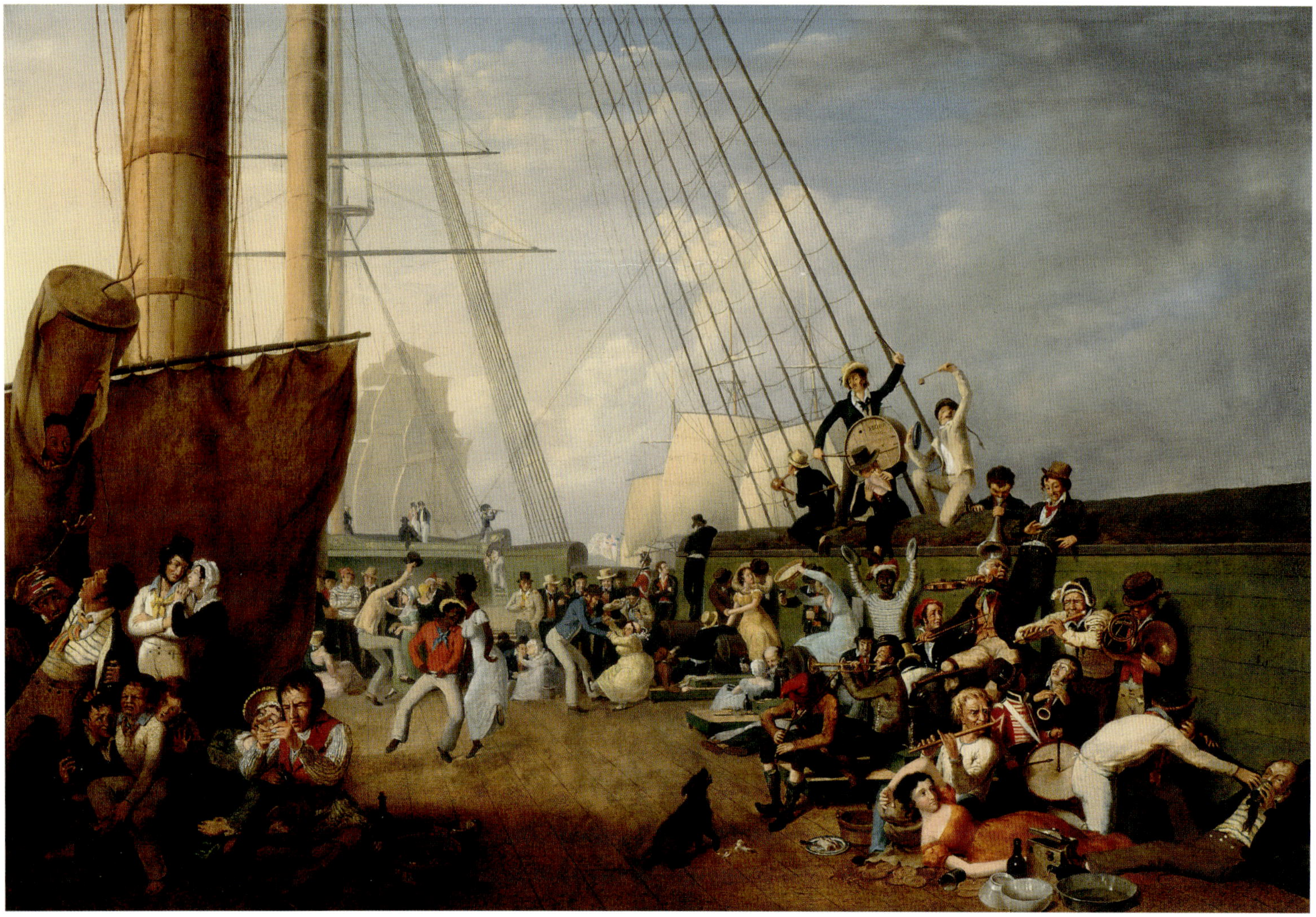

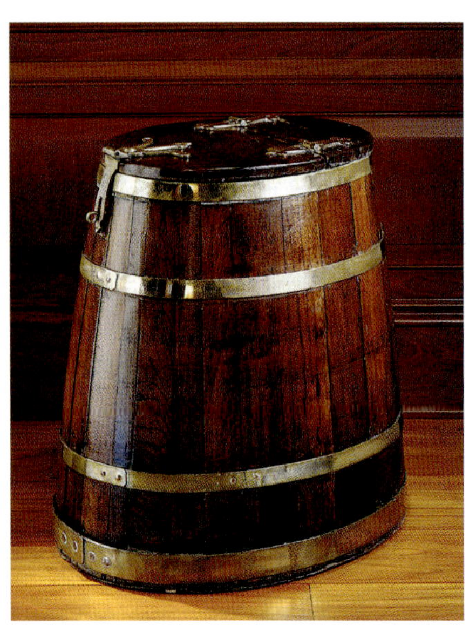

JOHN ALEXANDER GILFILLAN

Scottish, 1793–1864/66
Shipboard Celebrations before Departure,
1825
Oil on canvas
26¼ x 37¾ in.

Georgian brass-bound oak rum barrel
Oak and brass
H. 29 in., w. 20½ in., d. 15¾ in.

as she began to go under. The commander of *Merrimack,* Flag Officer Franklin Buchanan, went on to pursue *Congress* and ordered her to be thoroughly shot through. In the aftermath of their stunning success, Xanthus Smith wrote that the revolutionary ironsides "Swept England's wooden walls from the seas."[6]

In addition to the clashes and heroism of naval conflict, Koch's collection contains a group of paintings portraying the colorful and varied world of merchant shipping. One of the more boisterous aspects of merchant life was the shipboard celebration that took place before leaving port. It could lead to some remarkably Hogarthian scenes of merriment and debauch, fueled by the ever-prevalent shipboard beverage of rum, or the rum-and-water mixture known as "grog," rationed out from rum kegs (p. 166). The Scottish artist J. A. Gilfillan captured one such occasion in his painting *Shipboard Celebrations before Departure* (p. 166), showing the main deck of a West Indiaman turned into a spectacle of music, dance, and flowing drink. In the distance, the towering sails of two square-riggers are seen ghosted along the horizon, a reminder of the journey that awaits.

Another popular occasion for celebration was the opening of a new dockyard, which often inspired the whole community to attend and to enjoy the spectacle of "dressing ship" in a refurbished harbor. Typical of the industrial age, dockyard openings celebrated the promise of technology and commerce in communities connected by water. The English artist Mark Thompson produced a stunning panorama, *The Opening of the Sunderland Dockyard, 20th June, 1850* (p. 182). A brilliant crowd gathers before a host of steam- and sail-powered vessels, including side-wheelers, two brigs awaiting a load of coal, tugboats, and various spectator craft. The painting expresses all the expectation generated by the rebuilt forty-seven-acre dock, the groins of which gave out into Hendon Bay and the North Sea.[7]

Robert Salmon's *View of Liverpool from Cheshire* (p. 184) is a characteristically lively scene showing the Liverpool shoreline with working windmills, docks, warehouses, and landmarks such as St. Paul's Church and St. Nicholas, the city's parish church. The English-born marine painter emigrated to America in 1828 but continued to produce paintings of shipping in English and Scottish ports from memory in his new-found country. In this view, Salmon included a colorful foreground waterfront on the Cheshire side, a square-rigger cutting through the darkened middle ground, and a host of large merchant vessels and smaller craft in the pale background, traveling beneath a sky of creamy, gold-tinctured clouds. These kinds of lighting effects were extremely influential on the generation of American painters that would follow and learn from Salmon.

The most famous of Salmon's colleagues and epigones was the American marine painter Fitz Henry Lane. The son of a sailmaker, Lane was a largely self-taught artist who received some training in the Boston lithographer William S. Pendelton's studio, where he probably met the recently migrated Robert Salmon. Lane evolved a style of painting, later to be dubbed "Luminism," that at its finest expressed the transcendence and lucidity of moments of "stilled time."[8] The height of Lane's career in the 1850s coincided with the heyday of American sailing—the era of the great clipper ships. Lane painted many of the celebrated clippers of the period, setting them in delicate sunsets, surrounded by nearly motionless air, with sails hanging loosely in atmospheres of timeless, contemplative grandeur. One of the centerpieces of Koch's maritime collection is Lane's masterpiece of the clipper ship *The Golden Rule* (p. 185), which represents the culmination of the artist's development in the 1850s.

Golden Rule, owned by F. Nickerson and Co. of Boston, had a long career, sailing frequently to such distant ports as Calcutta, Valparaiso, and Shanghai and remaining in the American ship registers until 1900. Lane portrays her in a soft pink sky, with two schooners and a hermaphrodite brig in the background, and a small New England two-master in the foreground. Especially delicate is Lane's treatment of the clipper's sails, poised in contrasting pyramids of dark and light, with their very texture palpable to the eye. The striking shape of *Golden Rule*'s hull, an instance of "the imposing presence and modernity of the clipper ships,"[9] seems nearly to glow in sublime gray-white tones. The painting surpasses the genre of marine painting and is among the best nineteenth-century American paintings.[10]

Another familiar aspect of the golden age of sail was the advent of regular transatlantic crossings and the transport of celebrity personalities from continent to continent. Jenny Lind was a famous Swedish opera singer of the day, known as "the Nightingale," who had dazzled European audiences with her warbling cadenzas before she embarked for America aboard the Collins liner *Atlantic.*[11] Her two-year American tour was promoted by P. T. Barnum and included a performance at New York's Castle Garden. Lind's sojourn stateside created a lasting memory, and she became the subject of numerous engravings, as well as having two vessels named after her. The figurehead of one of these vessels, probably that of the square-rigger that ran Eagle Line's New York–Mobile, Alabama, route, is in Koch's collection (p. 187; the other is in the Mariners' Museum, Newport News, Virginia). Carved in the round and standing on scrolls, likely executed by a folk artist rather than a professional carver,[12] the figurehead of Jenny Lind shows off her corkscrew ringlets, tightly cinched waist, and simply carved but dramatic facial expression befitting a star of the stage.

Three other figureheads in the collection present splendid examples of carving from the nineteenth century. The figurehead of a female warrior with a helmet bearing a carved red plume is an exceptionally fine English carving dating from about 1830 that probably adorned the bow of a British naval vessel (p. 186). The figurehead of a young English Victorian gentleman (p. 169), which likely graced a merchant vessel, dates from about 1825–50. An oak carving in the form of a figurehead of a woman with flowing robes rates with the finest examples of nineteenth-century American ship carvings, and came from the collection of Nina Fletcher Little (p. 186).

The merchant section of the maritime art collection concludes with two paintings by Buttersworth. The first of these, *A Rescue at Sea* (p. 181), depicts two full-rigged American vessels attempting a dramatic sea rescue in rapidly worsening weather. The crew of the heeling ship can be seen boarding two rescue dinghies, while a third dinghy prepares to leave the sailer-steamer to assist the lost vessel. The second painting, *Ships off Gloucester Harbor* (p. 181), shows yachting vessels and a tea clipper being towed by a tugboat against the background of Gloucester Harbor, America's largest fishing harbor in the period, under a dramatically changing sky.

Although his prolific career spanned a wide range of subject matter, Buttersworth was renowned for his yachting scenes. From some of the earliest and best-known America's Cup depictions to paintings of the Great Ocean Race, Buttersworth produced a dramatic record of American yachting's glorious early years. Koch's success at the 1992 America's Cup with *America³* makes Buttersworth's America's Cup paintings a particularly meaningful part of his collection, but two paintings of the Great Ocean Race of 1866 record an equally famous moment of yachting history.

On December 11, 1866, the schooner yachts *Henrietta, Fleetwing,* and *Vesta* set out from New York to Cowes for a challenge with $9 in prize money that would become known as the Great Ocean Race. The three schooners, one centerboarder and two deep keelers, while not designed for open-ocean sailing, made the finish in under fourteen days, with *Henrietta* arriving victorious at the finish line of the Needles, Isle of Wight, on Christmas Day in a time of thirteen days, twenty-one hours, and forty-five minutes.

Buttersworth shows the three competitors at the start of the contest in *The Great Ocean Race* (p. 179). *Henrietta* is seen in the center background, with her blue flag flying from the peak of her mainmast. *Fleetwing* appears to the left flying a red flag, while *Vesta* can be seen on the right flying a white flag. All three vessels are sailing on the windward tack under full sail, flying a period-style square-sail spinnaker. They are approaching the red-hulled Sandy Hook Lightship at the very start of the race. Buttersworth captures the scene at the end of the race in *Racing Yacht off the Needles* (p. 180), in which a schooner identified as either *Henrietta* or *Fleetwing* is shown sailing past the Needles, with its familiar cliffs and lighthouse.[13] The Great Ocean Race concluded at 12:40 p.m. on Christmas Day, when *Henrietta* passed up the Channel, great cheers went out, and, as Buttersworth's painting depicts, "a sudden blaze of sunshine lit up the chalk cliffs of Old England."[14]

Another Buttersworth painting in the collection, *Racing off Sandy Hook Lightship* (p. 170), portrays an America's Cup race, probably the 1893 contest between *Vigilant* and *Valkyrie II.* In this scene, Sandy Hook Lightship is clearly visible in the background between the two vessels. The American defender *Vigilant* was the first of many Nathanael Herreshoff–designed vessels to race in the Cup and the first to employ the spoon-bow concept. In a remarkably close contest, the crew of *Vigilant* managed to perform some last-minute changes to her sails, replacing a working topsail with a club topsail and gliding by *Valkyrie II* to win by forty seconds. One commentator observed, "This race was one of the most thrilling of any ever sailed for the America's Cup and victory was achieved by the closest of margins."[15]

The Koch Collection also includes interesting items of yachting equipment. Whether engaged in competitive

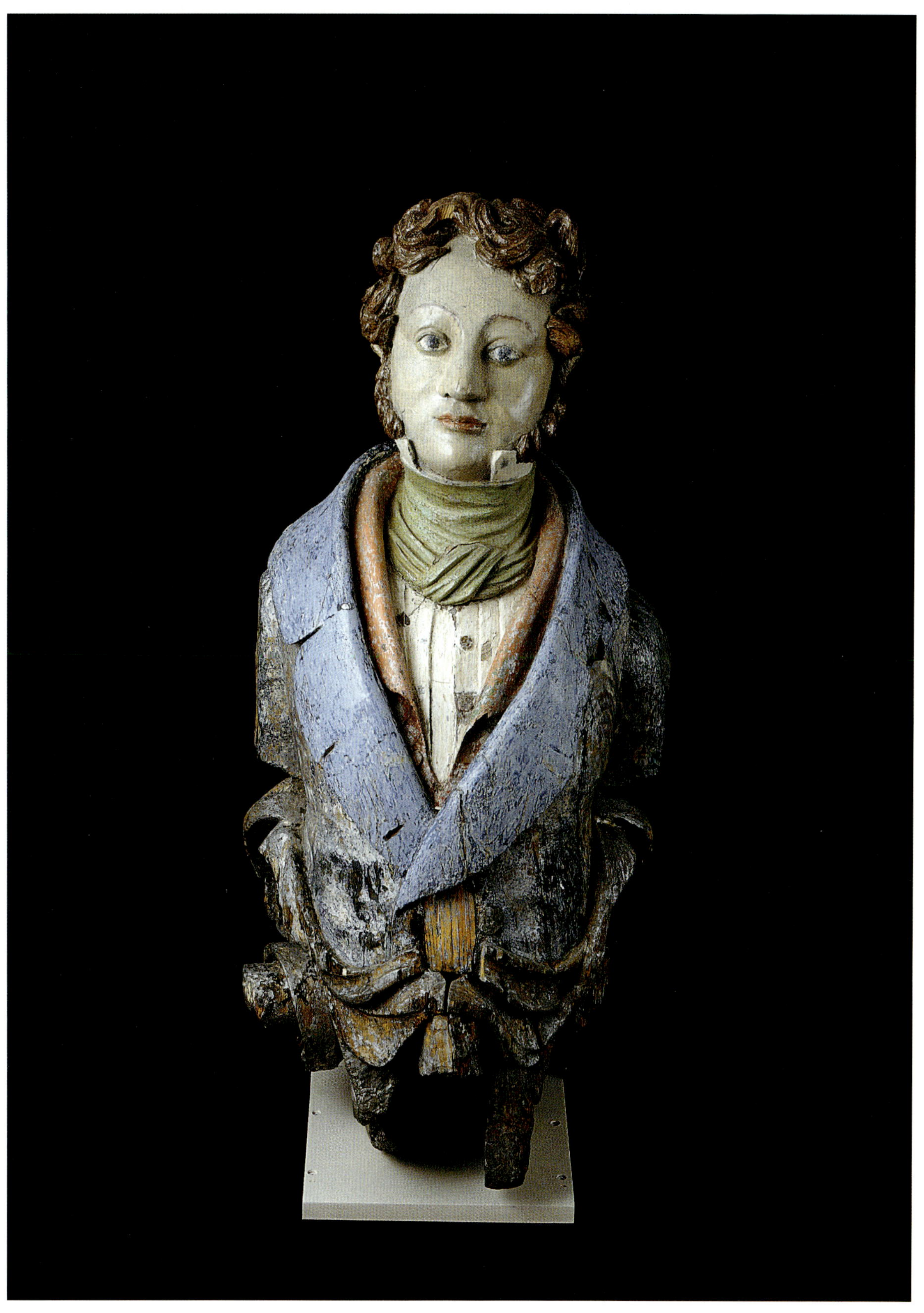

Figurehead of an English gentleman,
about 1825–50
Wood and polychrome
H. 35 in., w. 16 in., d. 15 in.

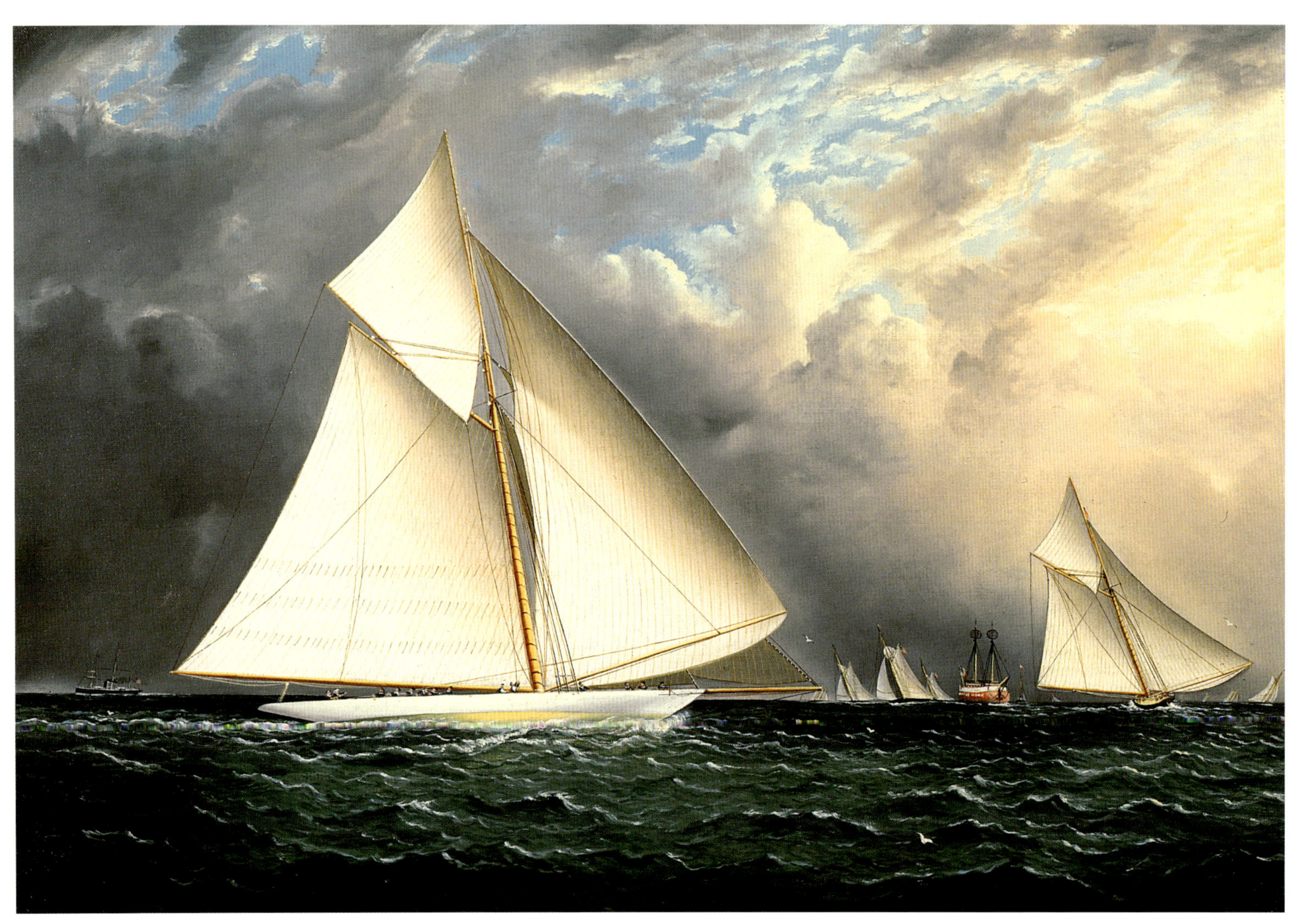

JAMES EDWARD BUTTERSWORTH

English, worked in America,
1817–1894
Racing off Sandy Hook Lightship, about 1893
Oil on canvas
20¼ x 30¼ in.

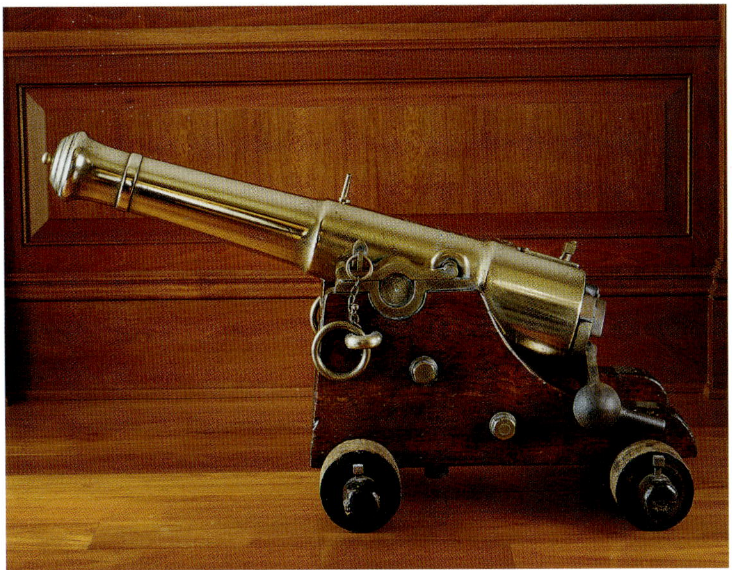

HOLLAND AND HOLLAND CO.
One of a pair of signal cannons from the yacht Valhalla
Brass, bronze, mahogany, and lignum vitae
L. (overall) 46 in., w. 24½ in

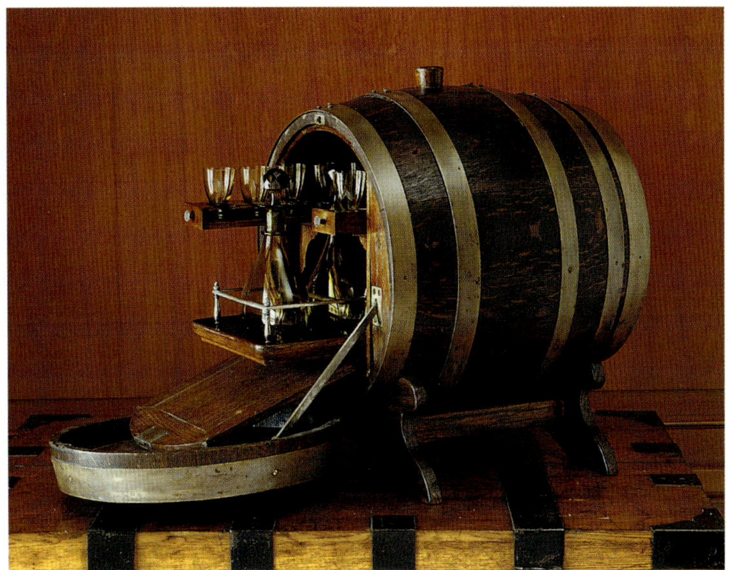

Yachting liquor set
Wood, brass, and glass
L. 17 in., diam. (center) 15½ in.

racing or deployed for cruising, yachts often carried signal cannons to mark their arrival and departure. Cannons are still used at Cowes and elsewhere for starting races. Koch owns an exceptionally rare pair of signal cannons (above, left) built by the premier makers of the day, Holland and Holland Co. Yachtsmen also enjoyed their periods of leisure alongside the intensity of competitive racing, and yachts were typically equipped with custom-designed liquor sets. One such set in Koch's collection pulls out of a brass-bound open keg (above, right). The keg can be conveniently closed when the yacht is not engaged in festivity, and just as easily opened to reveal the spirits sequestered within.

As these examples illustrate, Koch's collection of maritime arts spans the full range of life on the water. From his childhood years hearing naval stories of his heroic ancestor, to his victory in the America's Cup in 1992, Koch has had a long-lasting passion for the sea, an interest that is evident in the objects and artworks he has acquired.

—ALAN GRANBY AND JANICE HYLAND

1. Col. Carroll Peeke, *The Lawrence Lineage of the Kip Family* (N.p.: Privately printed, 1976).
2. Peter Padfield, "The Great Sea Battle," *American Heritage* (April 1969): 38.
3. Peters et al., *A Personal Gathering,* 176.
4. See Padfield, "The Great Sea Battle," 40.
5. See Yvonne Brault Smith, *John Haley Bellamy: Carver of Eagles* (Hampton, N.H.: Portsmouth Marine Society, 1982), 67.
6. Quoted in Peters et al., *A Personal Gathering,* 180.
7. Peters et al., *A Personal Gathering,* 148.
8. John Wilmerding, *A History of American Marine Painting* (Salem, Mass.: Peabody Museum of Salem, 1968), 158.
9. *Christie's: Catalogue of Important American Paintings, Drawings and Sculpture, May 25, 2000* (New York: Christie's, 2000), 68.
10. Wilmerding, *A History of American Marine Painting,* 165.
11. Paul Forsythe Johnston, *Steam and Sea* (Salem, Mass.: Peabody Museum of Salem, 1983), 70.
12. Peters et al., *A Personal Gathering,* 156.
13. Another Buttersworth of a similar size and composition titled *Vesta off the Needles* is plate xv in Rudolph Schaefer, *J. E. Buttersworth: Nineteenth-Century Marine Painter* (Mystic, Ct.: Mystic Seaport, 1975). It is also presumed to depict one of the three yachts completing the Great Ocean Race.
14. D. A. Rayner and Alan Wykes, *The Great Yacht Race* (London: Peter Davies, 1966), 152.
15. Robert F. Patterson, as quoted in Schaefer, *J. E. Buttersworth,* 218.

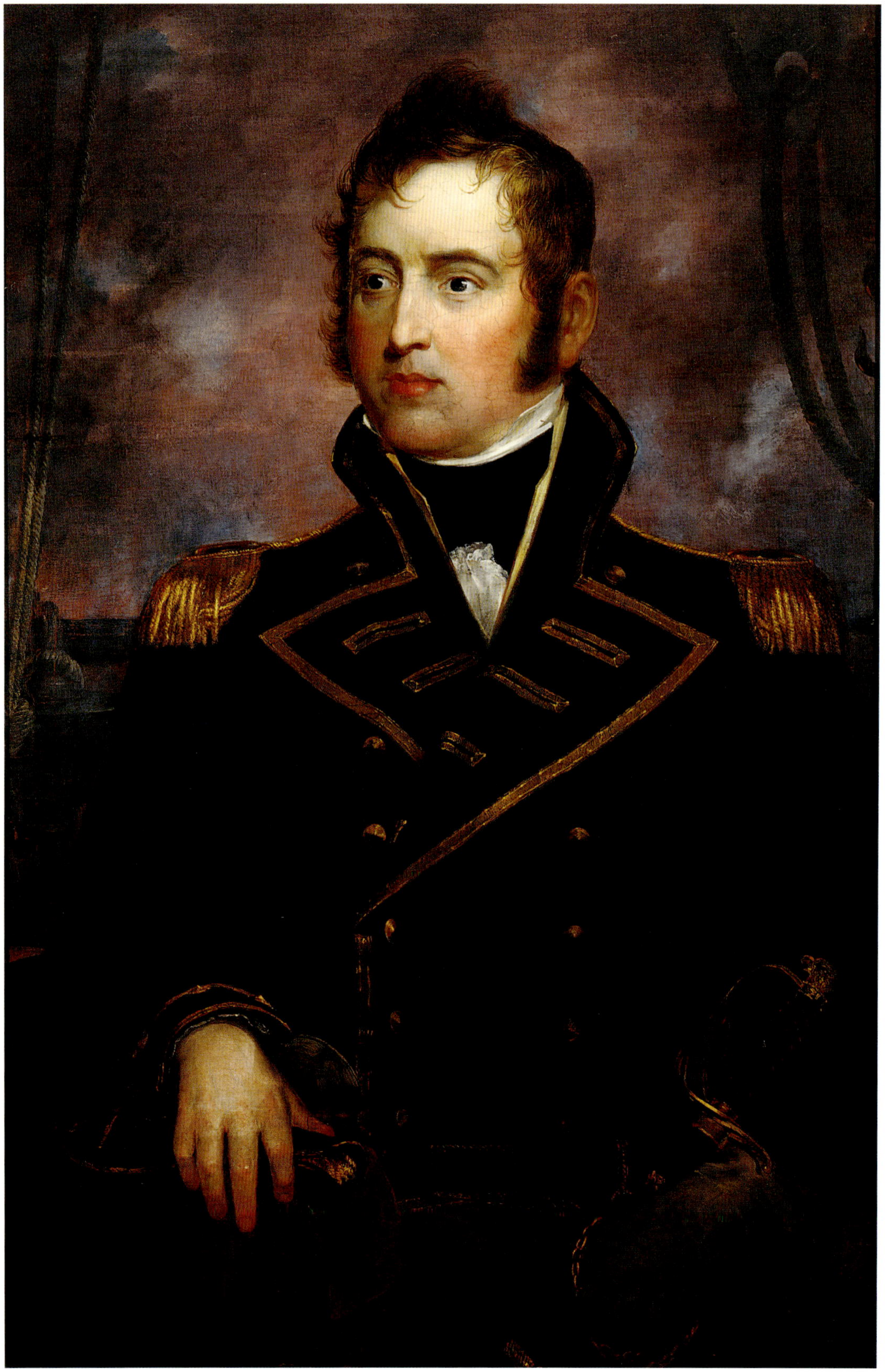

Captain James Lawrence
Oil on canvas
42 x 27½ in.

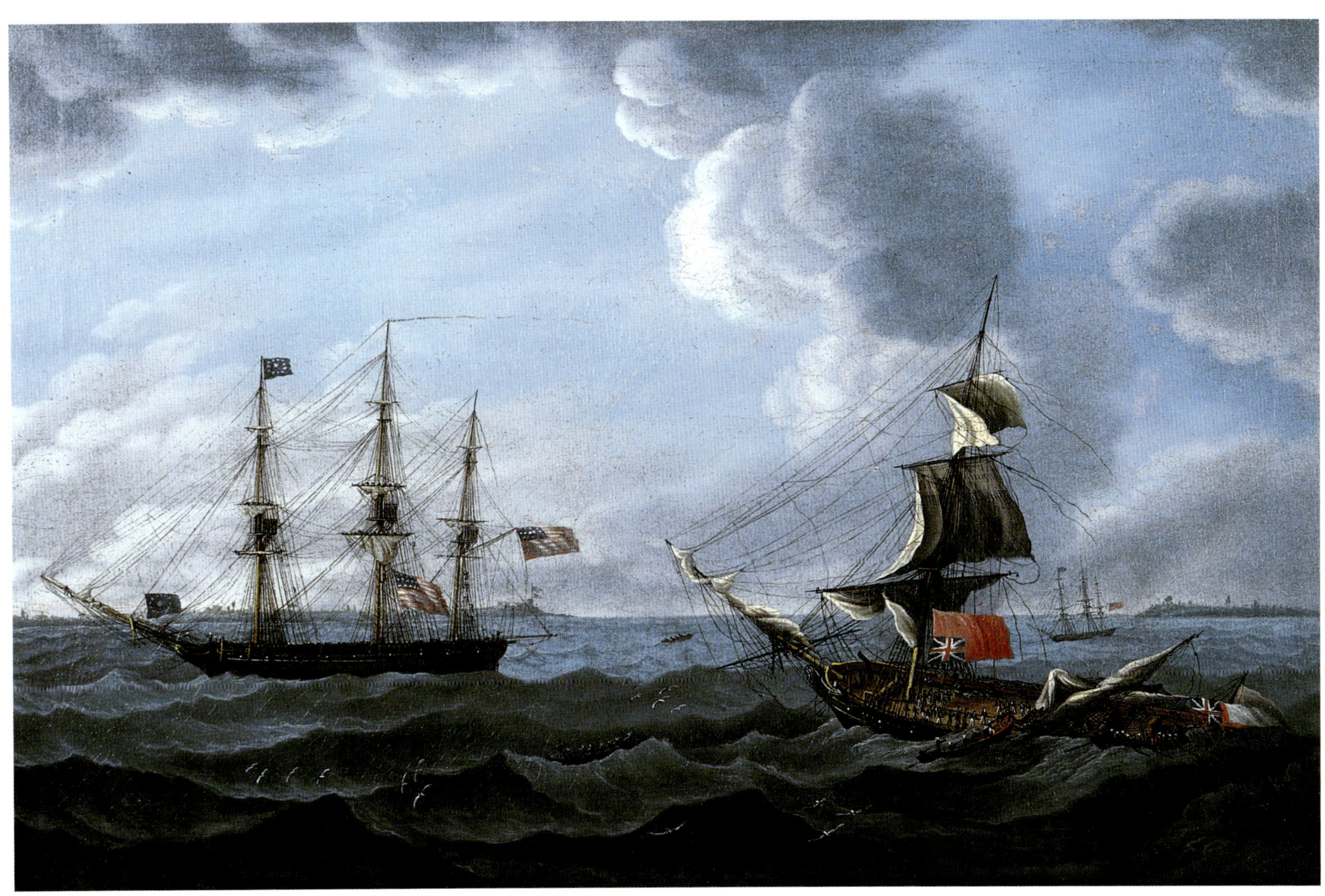

MICHELE FELICE CORNÈ

Italian, worked in America,
1752–1845
USS Hornet *Sinking HMS* Peacock,
about 1813–16
Oil on canvas
24½ x 38½ in.

THOMAS LUNY

English, 1759–1837
Action between HMS Shannon *and USS* Chesapeake
Oil on canvas
17¼ x 23 in.

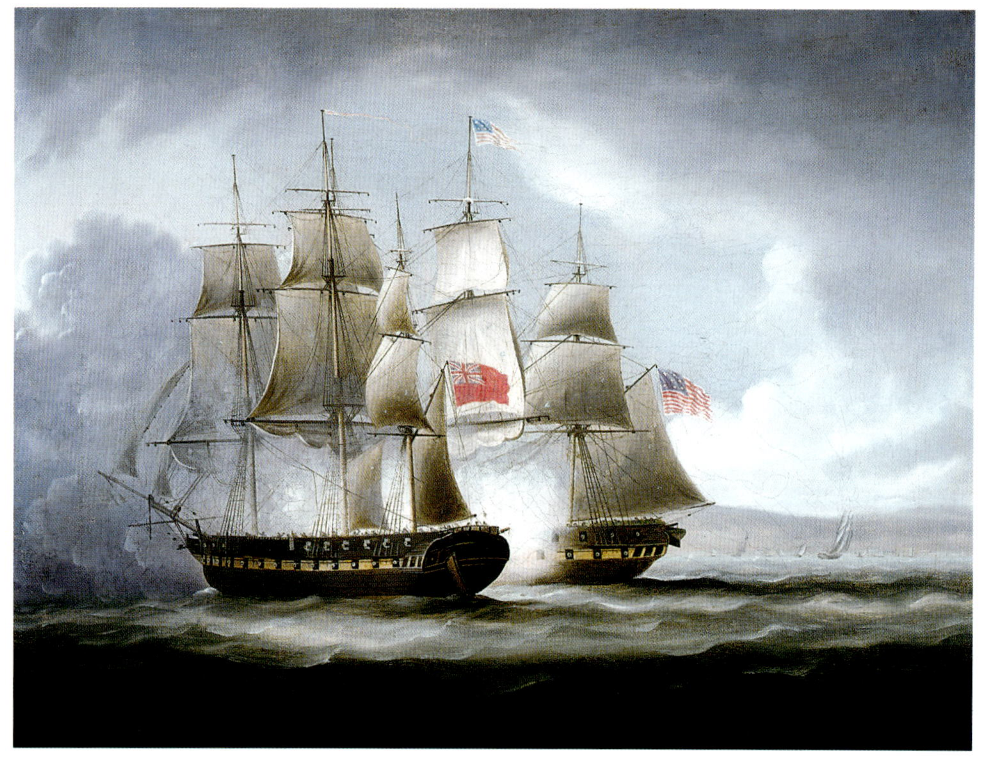

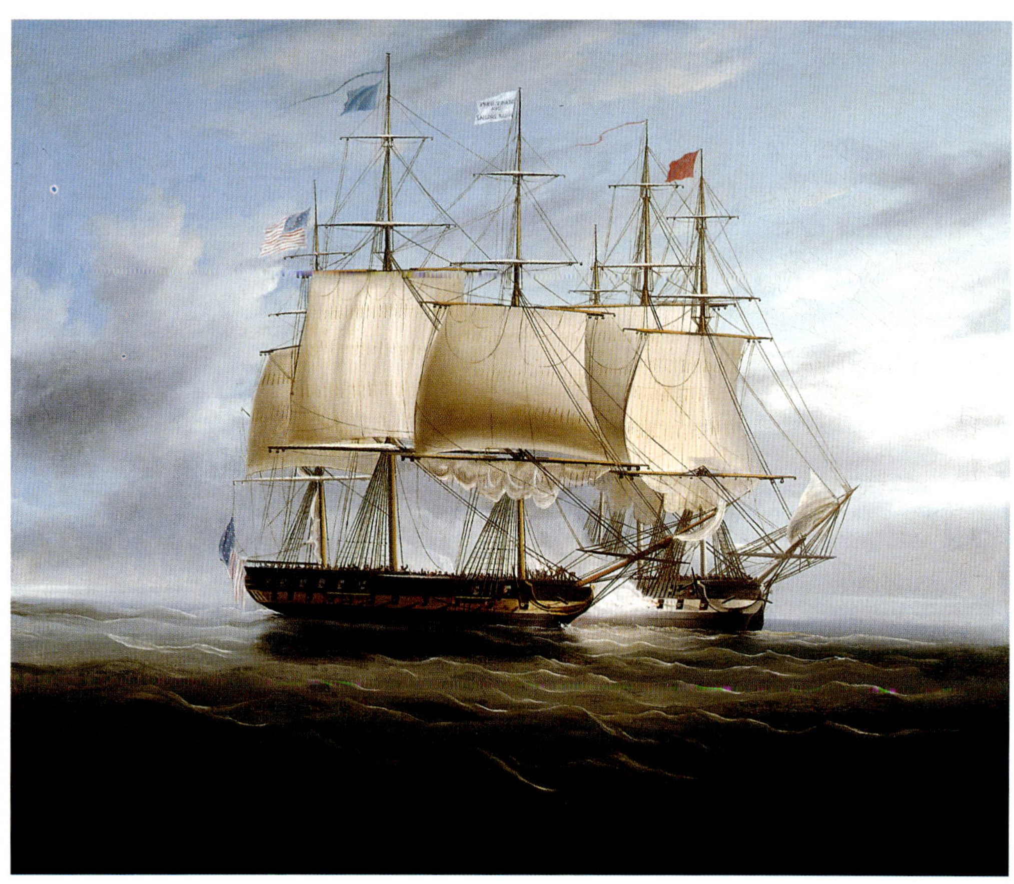

WILLIAM JOHN HUGGINS

English, 1781–1845
HMS Shannon *and USS* Chesapeake, *1st of June, 1813*
Oil on canvas
50¼ x 63 in.

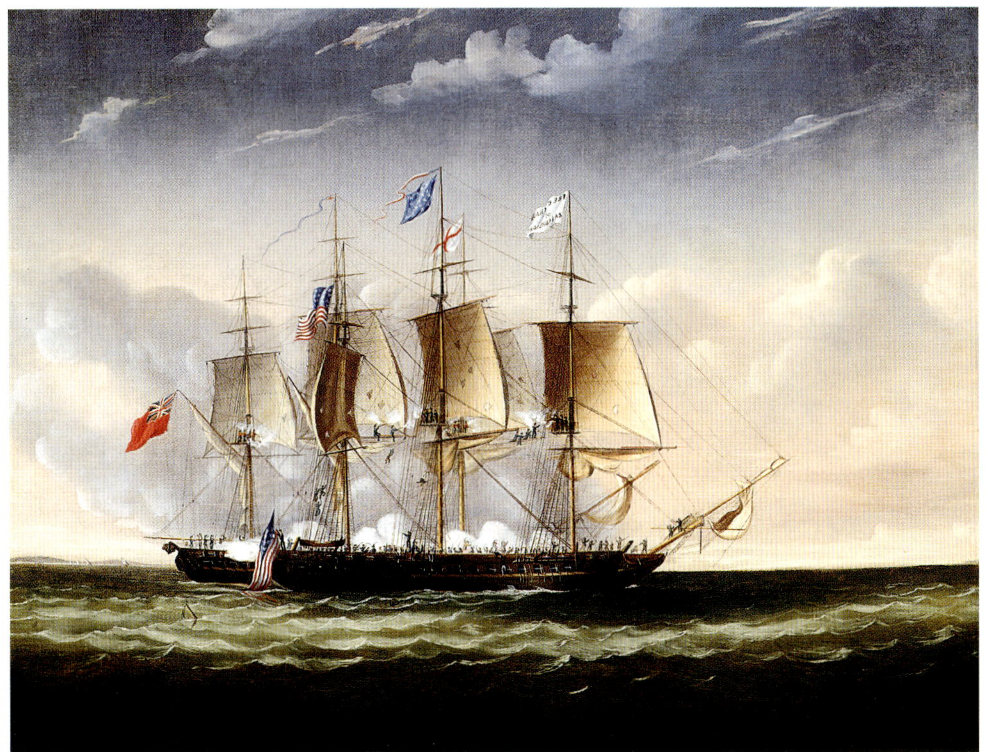

GEORGE ROPES

American, 1788–1819
Action between Shannon *and* Chesapeake
Oil on canvas
22 x 31¾ in.

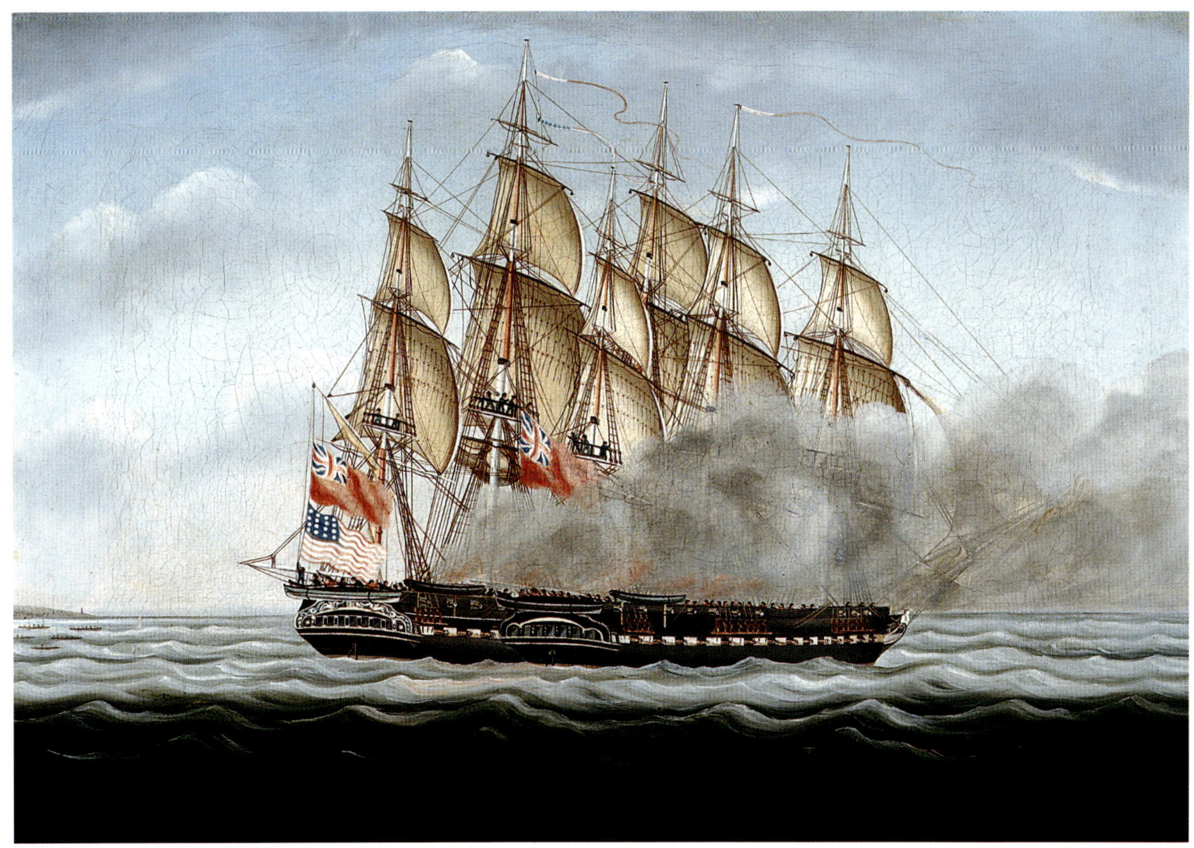

MILES WALTERS

English, 1774–1849
Engagement between Shannon *and* Chesapeake, 1826
Oil on canvas
15¾ x 23⅜ in.

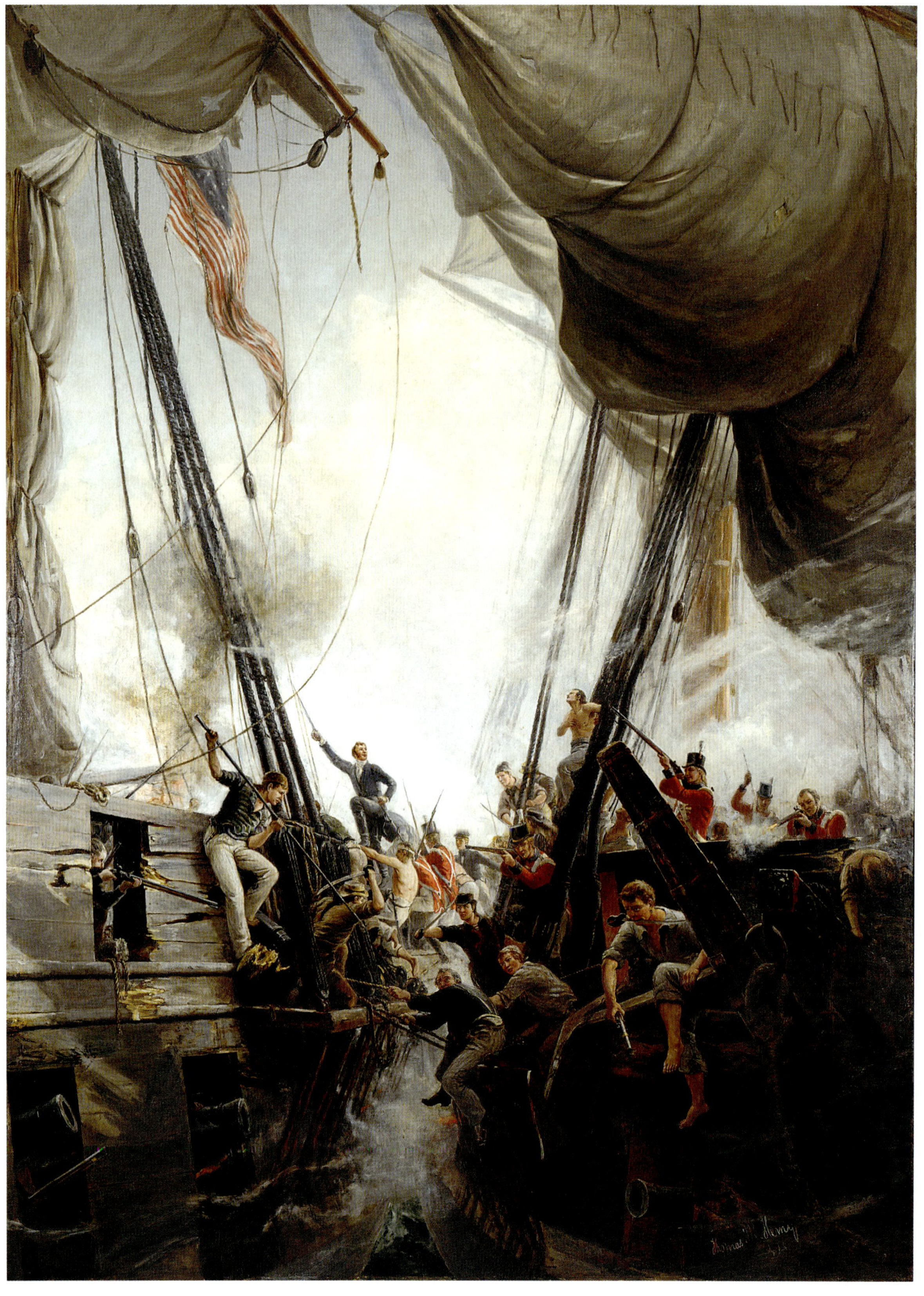

THOMAS HEMY

English, 1852–1937
The Shannon *and the* Chesapeake, *Close Quarters*, 1895
Oil on canvas
110 x 80⅜ in.

THOMAS WHITCOMBE

English, 1760–about 1824
Engagement between the USS Chesapeake *and the HMS* Shannon, *1813*
Oil on canvas
22½ x 28 in.

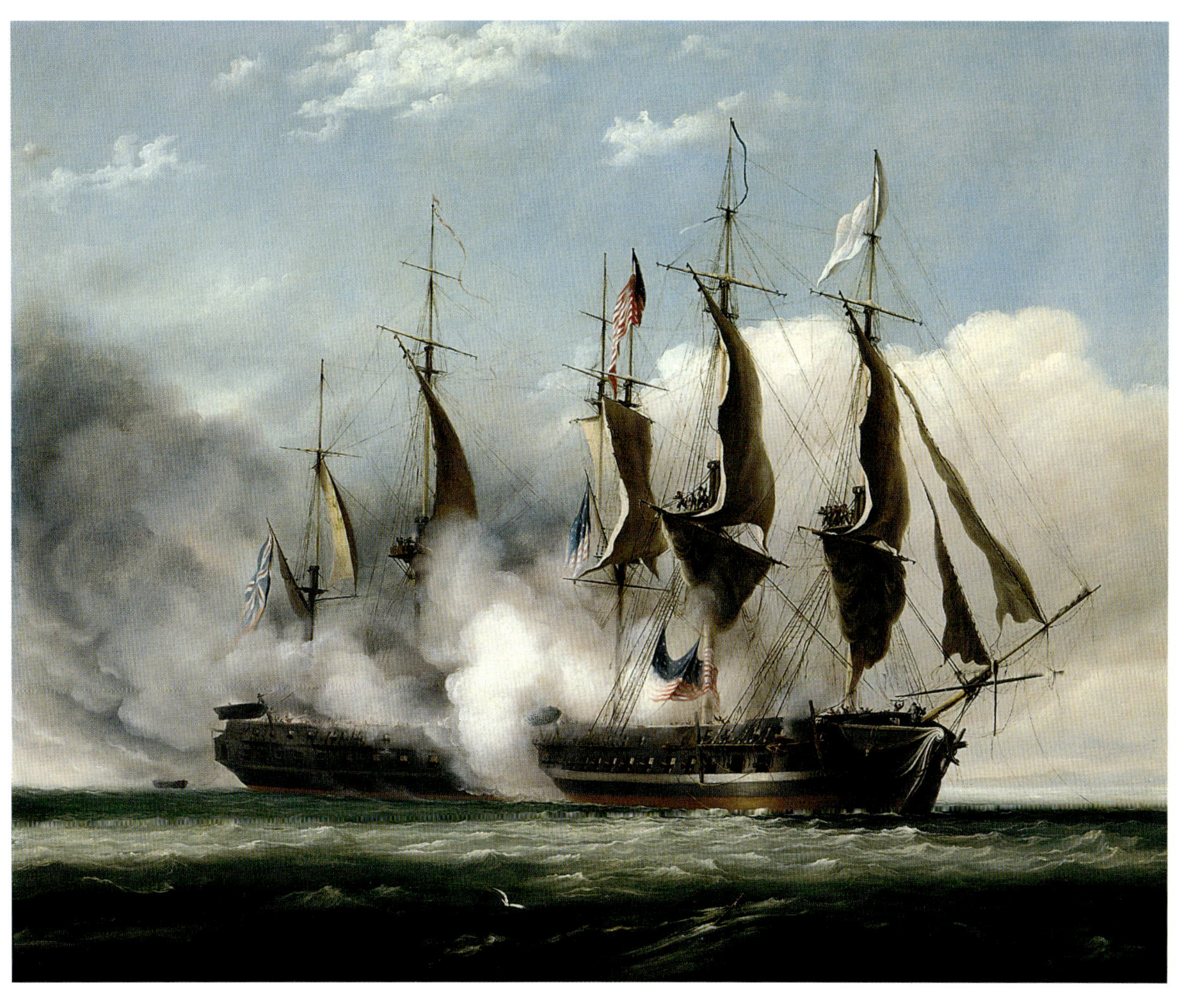

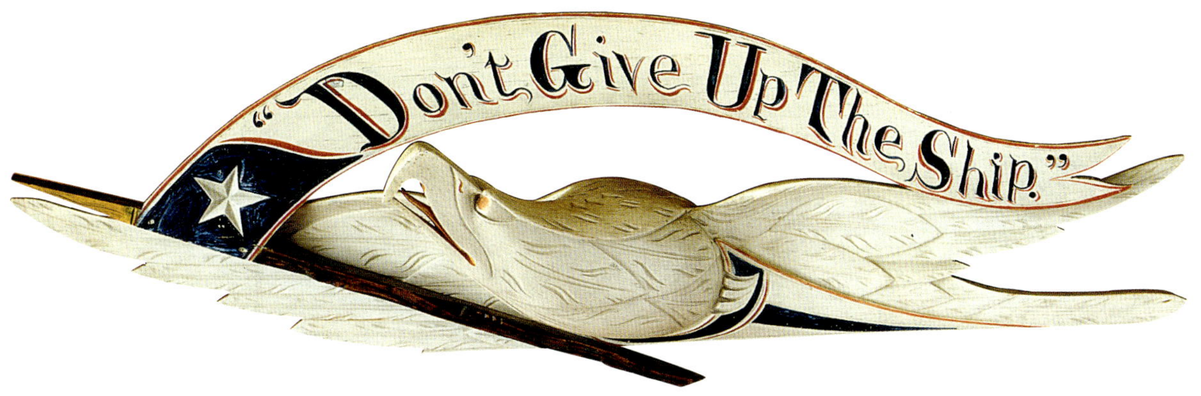

JOHN HALEY BELLAMY

American, 1836–1914
Bellamy spread eagle wall plaque, late 19th century
Carved and painted wood
H. 7½ in., w. 26 in.

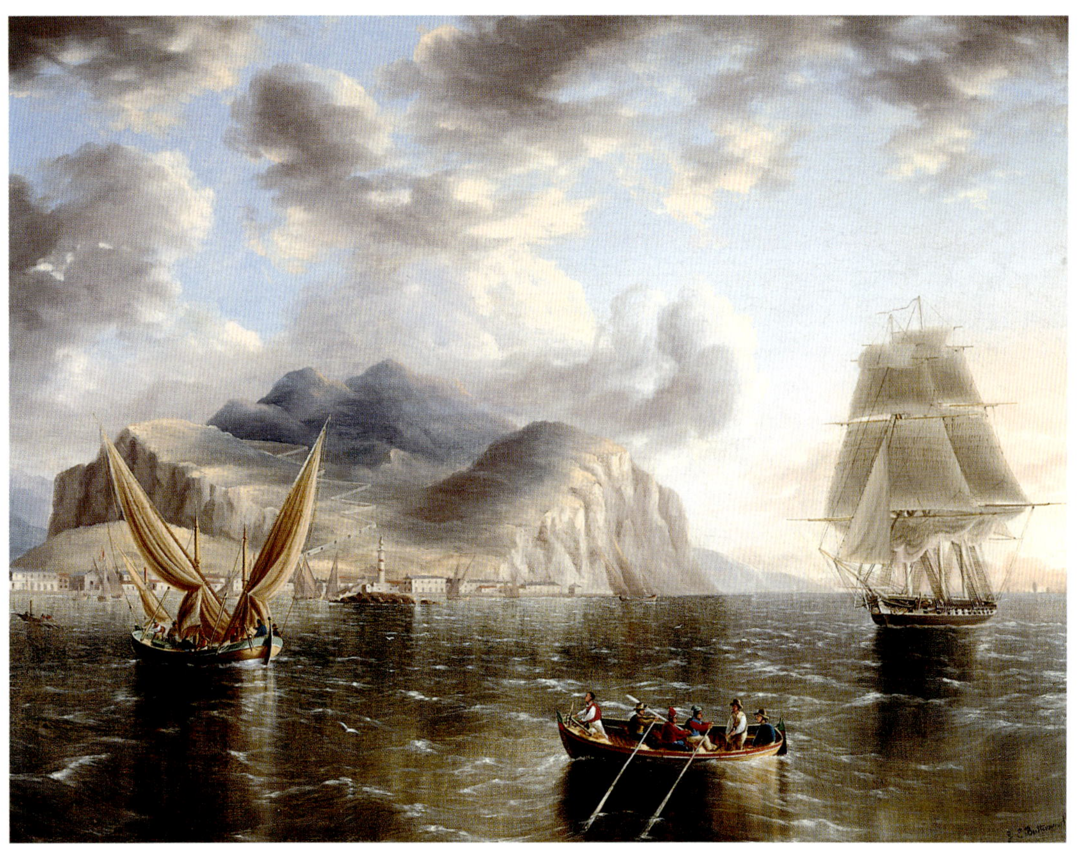

JAMES EDWARD BUTTERSWORTH

English, worked in America,
1817–1894
American Naval Vessel off Palermo,
1860
Oil on canvas
18 x 24¼ in.

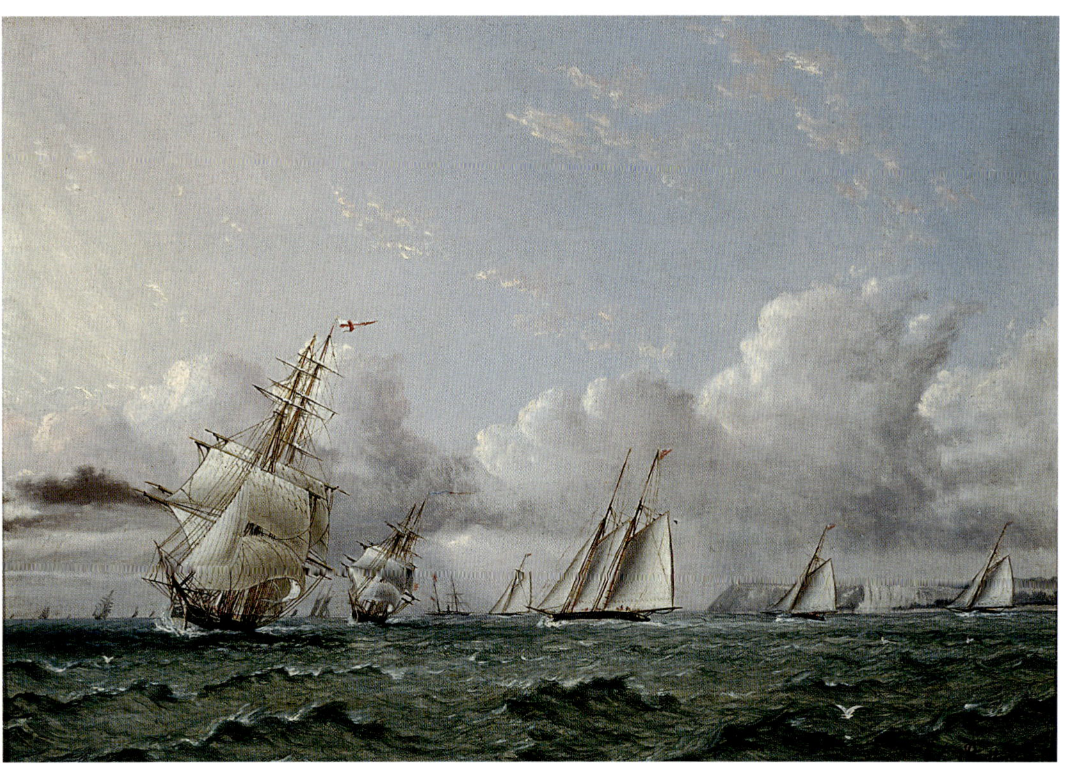

JAMES EDWARD BUTTERSWORTH

English, worked in America,
1817–1894
Racing off the Coast
Oil on board
7½ x 11½ in.

JAMES EDWARD BUTTERSWORTH

English, worked in America, 1817–1894

Offshore, Belem Castle, Tagus River Entrance to Lisbon, Portugal

Oil on canvas

8½ x 16½ in.

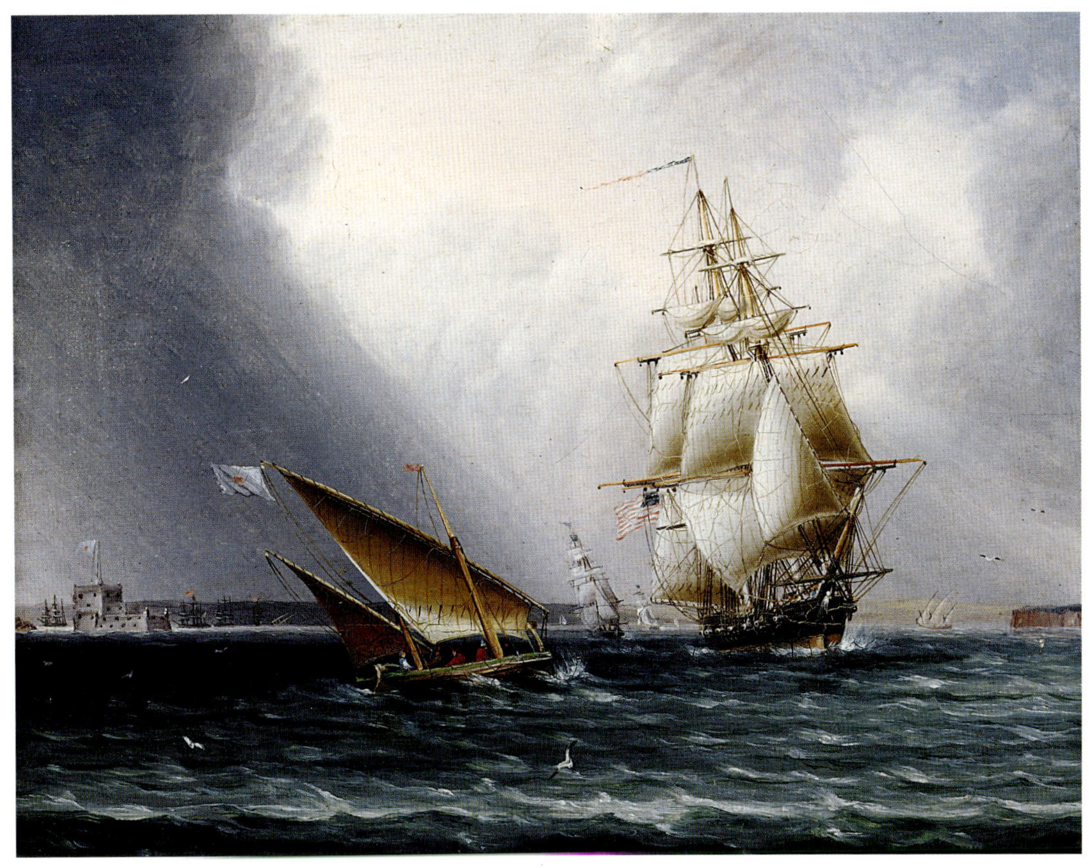

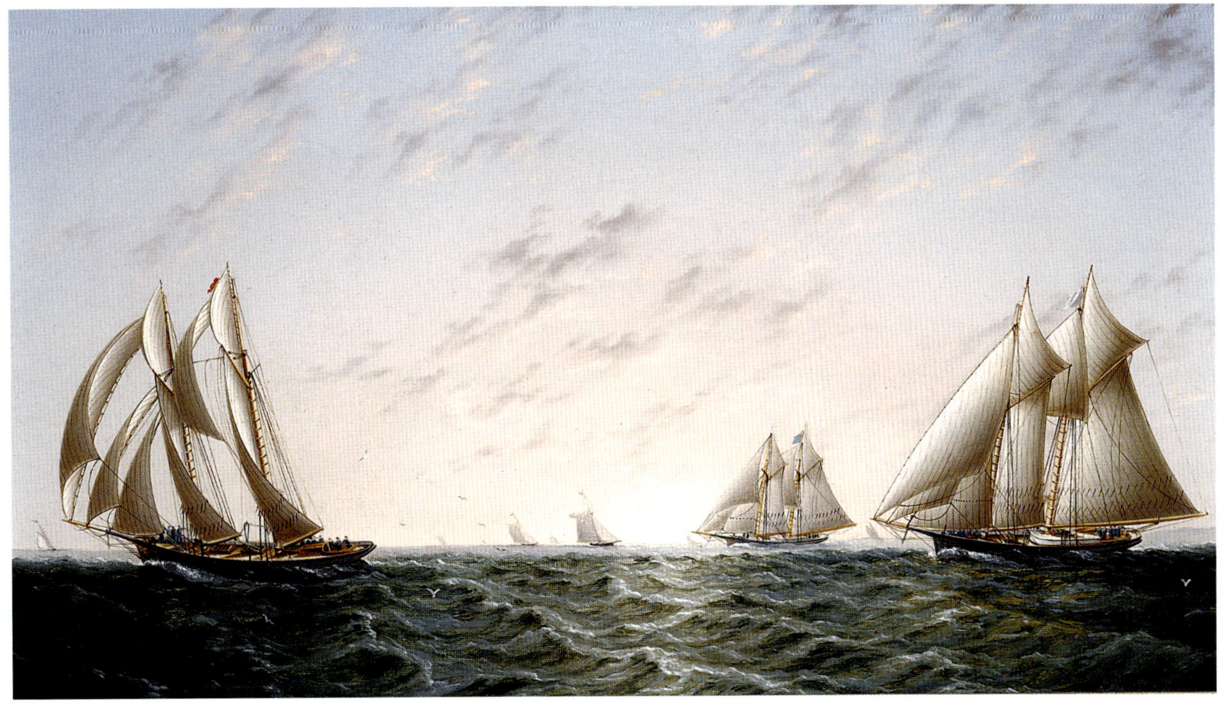

JAMES EDWARD BUTTERSWORTH

English, worked in America, 1817–1894

The Great Ocean Race

Oil on canvas

10 x 18 in.

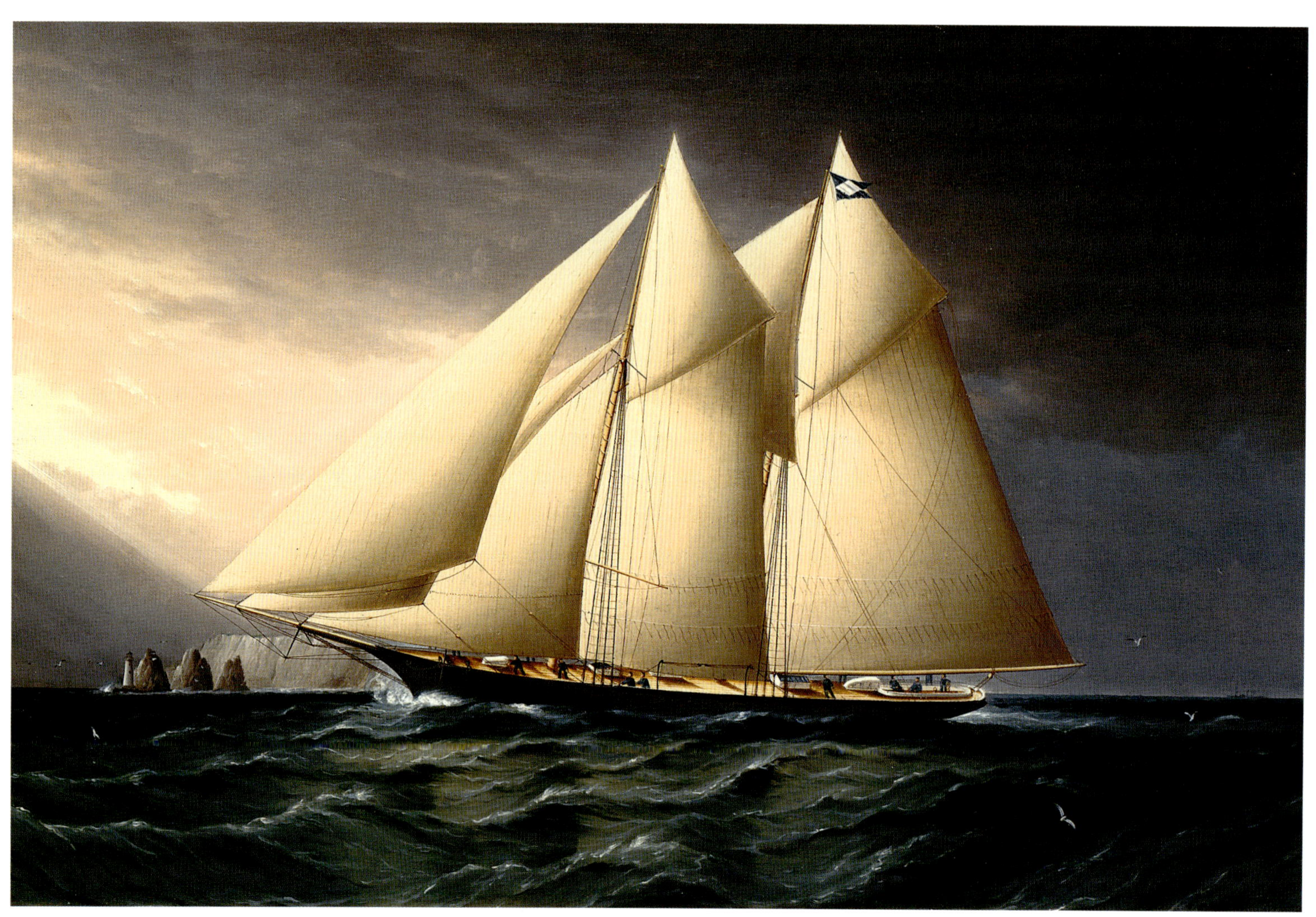

JAMES EDWARD BUTTERSWORTH

English, worked in America,
1817–1894
Racing Yacht off the Needles,
about 1865–79
Oil on canvas
21⅛ x 32 in.

JAMES EDWARD BUTTERSWORTH

English, worked in America, 1817–1894

Ships off Gloucester Harbor, about 1860s–70s

Oil on canvas

12 x 24 in.

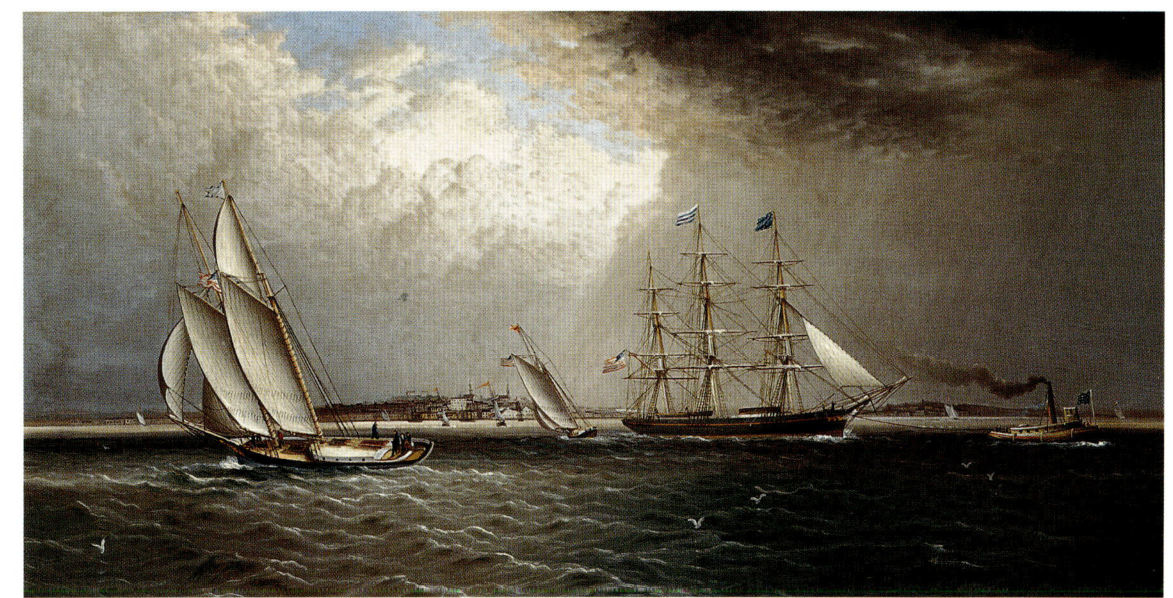

JAMES EDWARD BUTTERSWORTH

English, worked in America, 1817–1894

A Rescue at Sea, 1850s–60s

Oil on canvas

14 x 24¼ in.

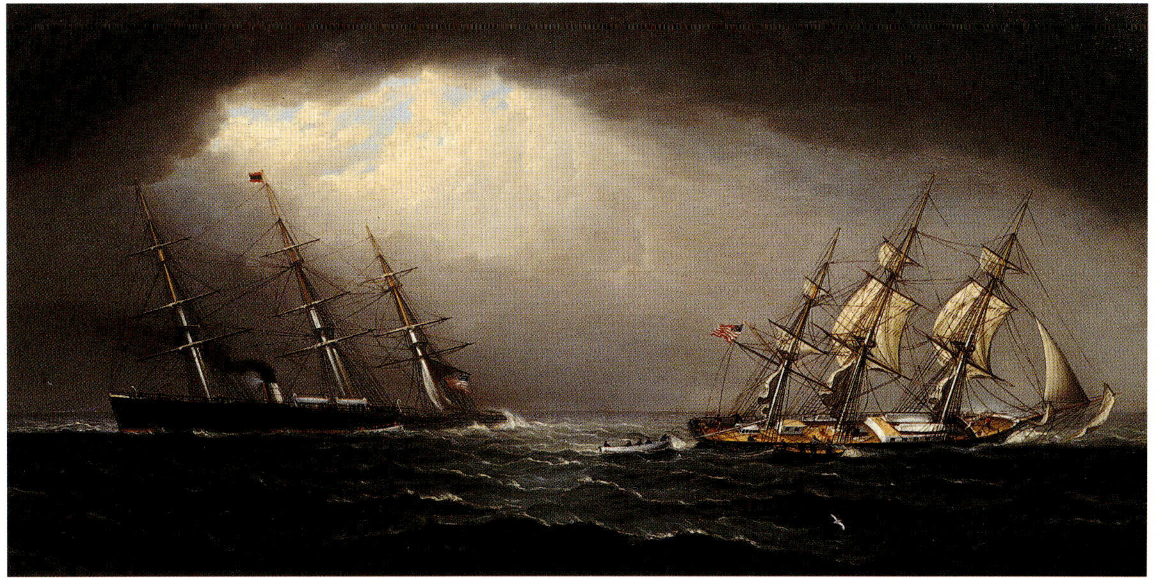

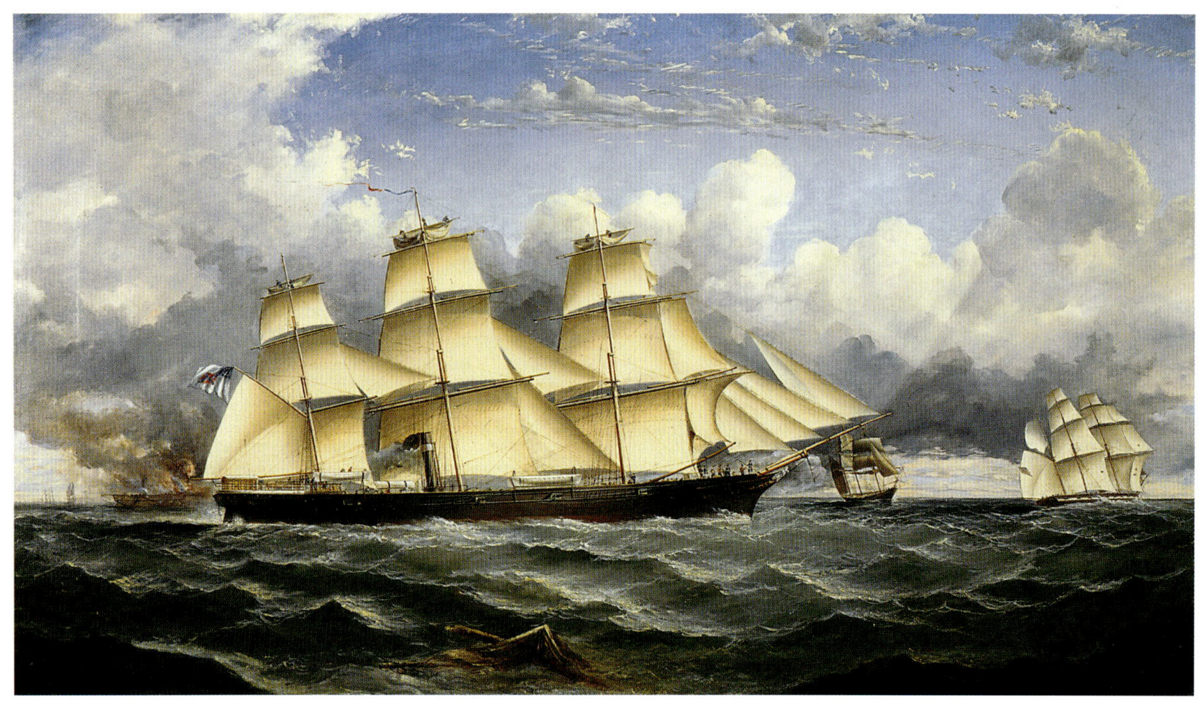

GEORGE ALEXANDER NAPIER

Scottish, 1827/28–1869
Confederate Armed Forces,
Shenandoah, 1865
Oil on canvas
35½ x 64 in.

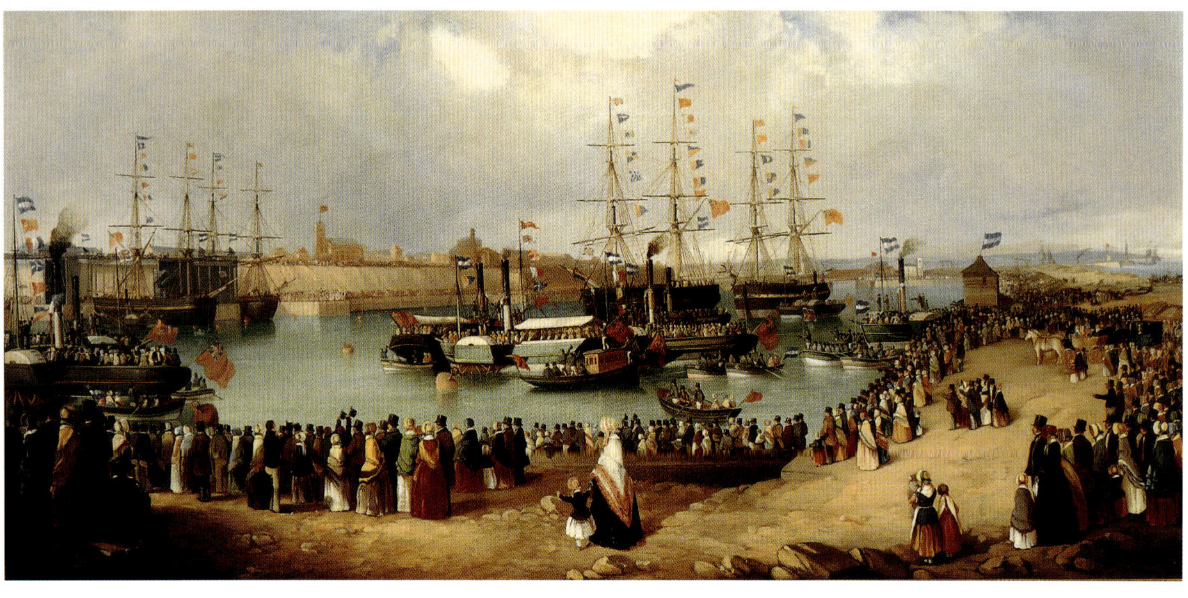

MARK THOMPSON

English, 1812–1875
The Opening of the Sunderland Dockyard, 20th June, 1850, 1851
Oil on canvas
25⅝ x 54¾ in.

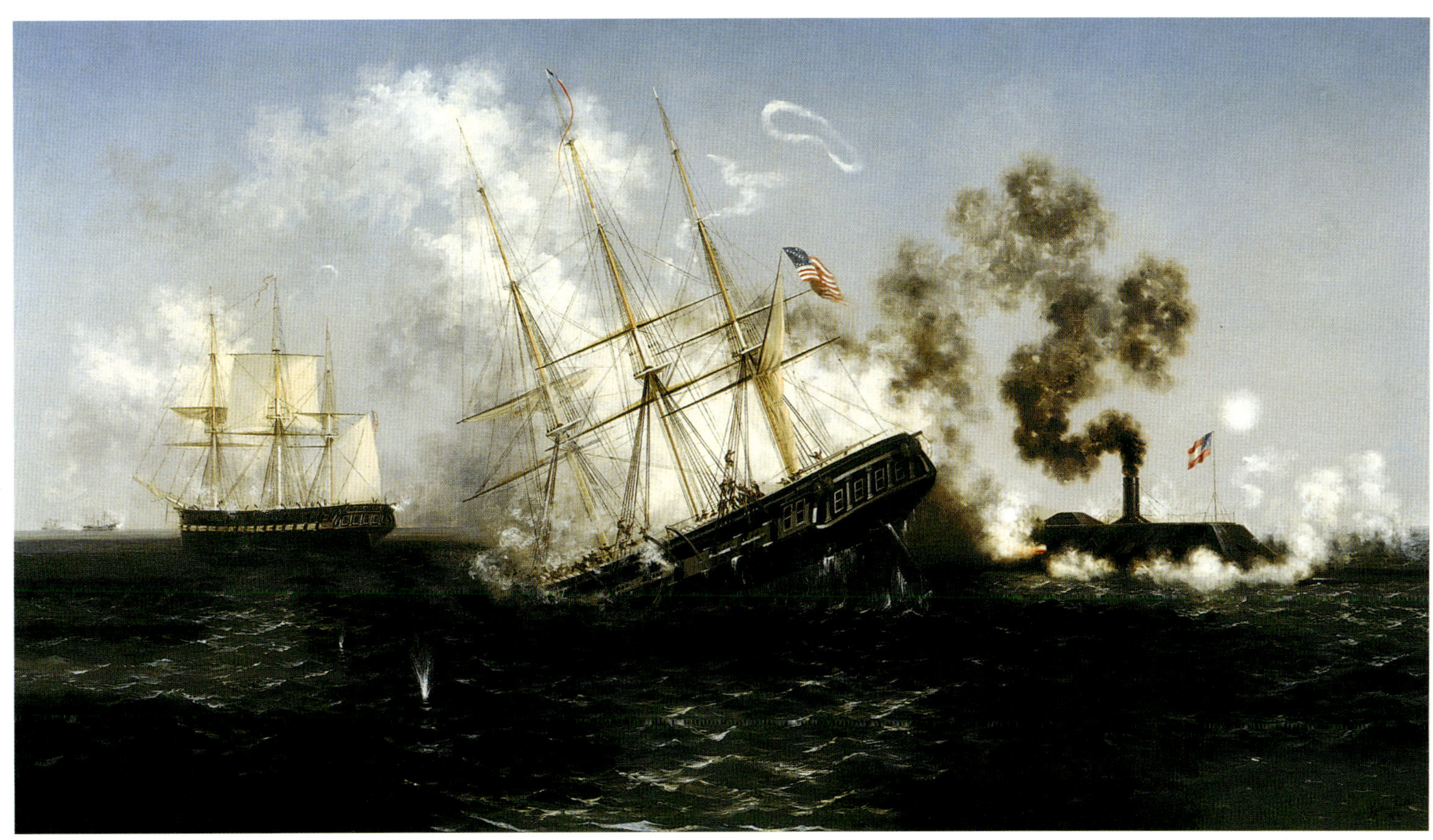

XANTHUS RUSSELL SMITH

American, 1838–1929
The Attack of the Merrimack *on the U.S. Ships* Congress *and* Cumberland, *the Latter Sinking,* about 1872
Oil on canvas
36½ x 67 in.

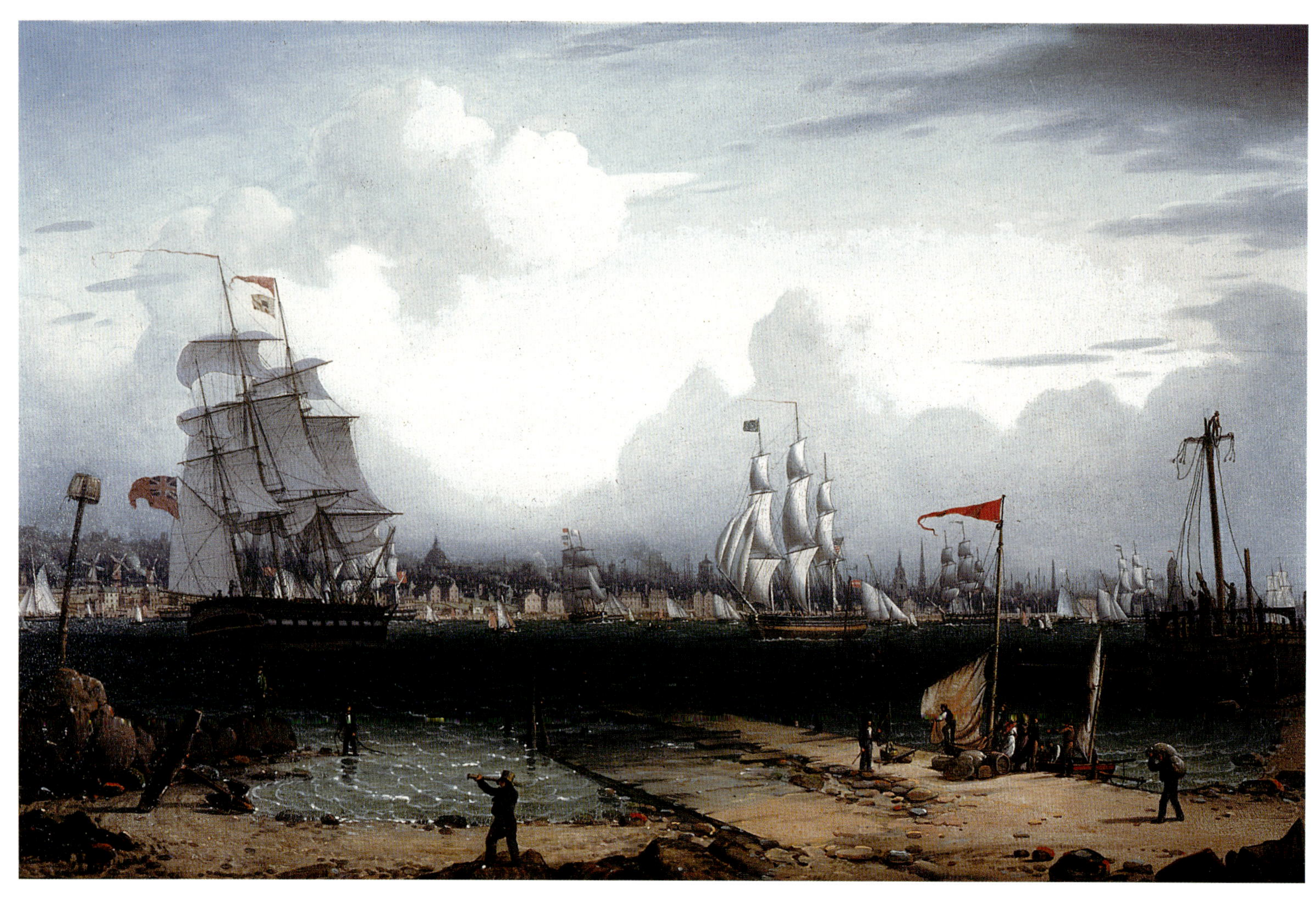

ROBERT SALMON

English, 1775–about 1845
View of Liverpool from Cheshire, 1835
Oil on panel
16½ x 26¾ in.

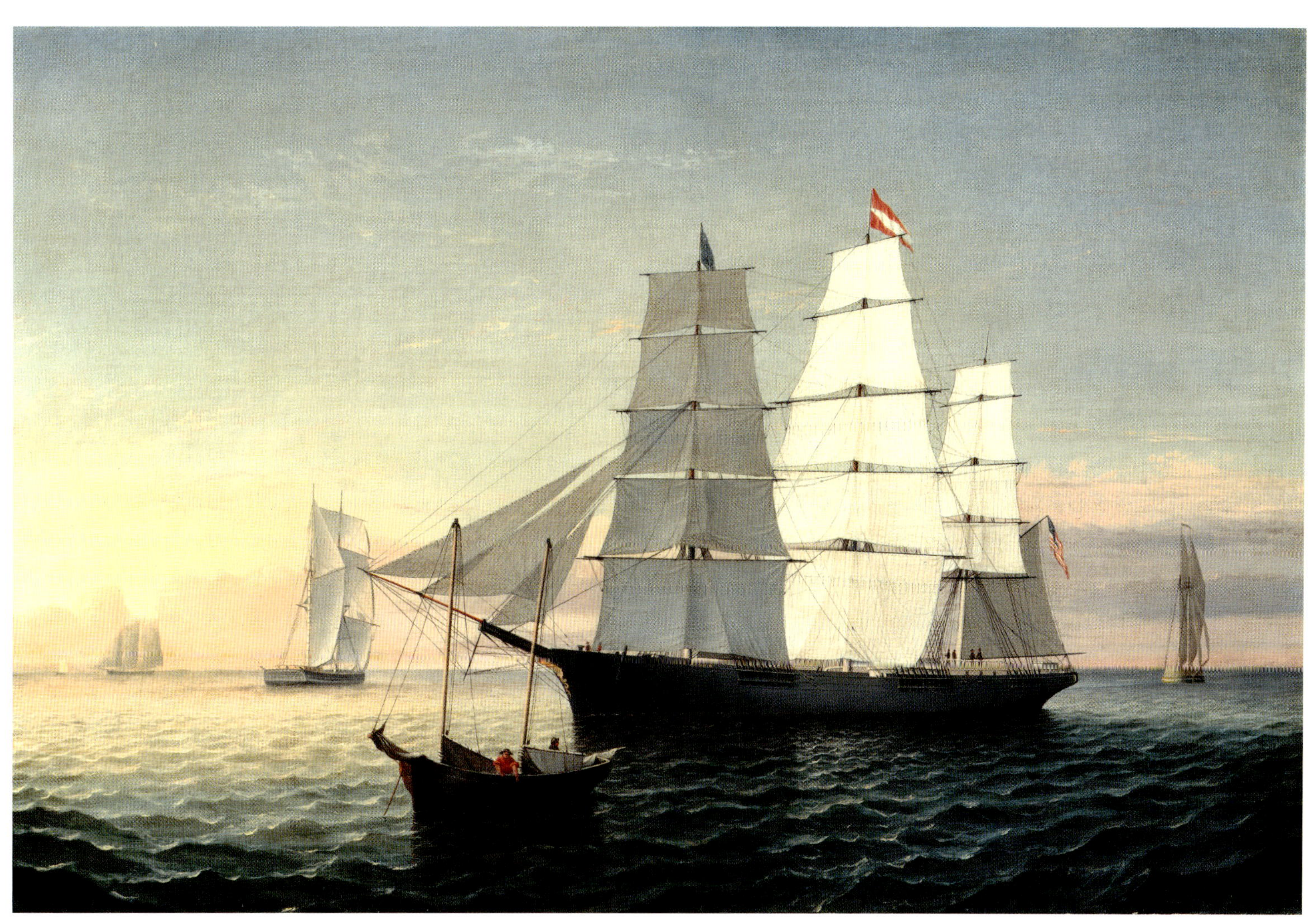

FITZ HENRY LANE

American, 1804–1865
The Golden Rule, about 1855
Oil on canvas
24¼ x 36¼ in.

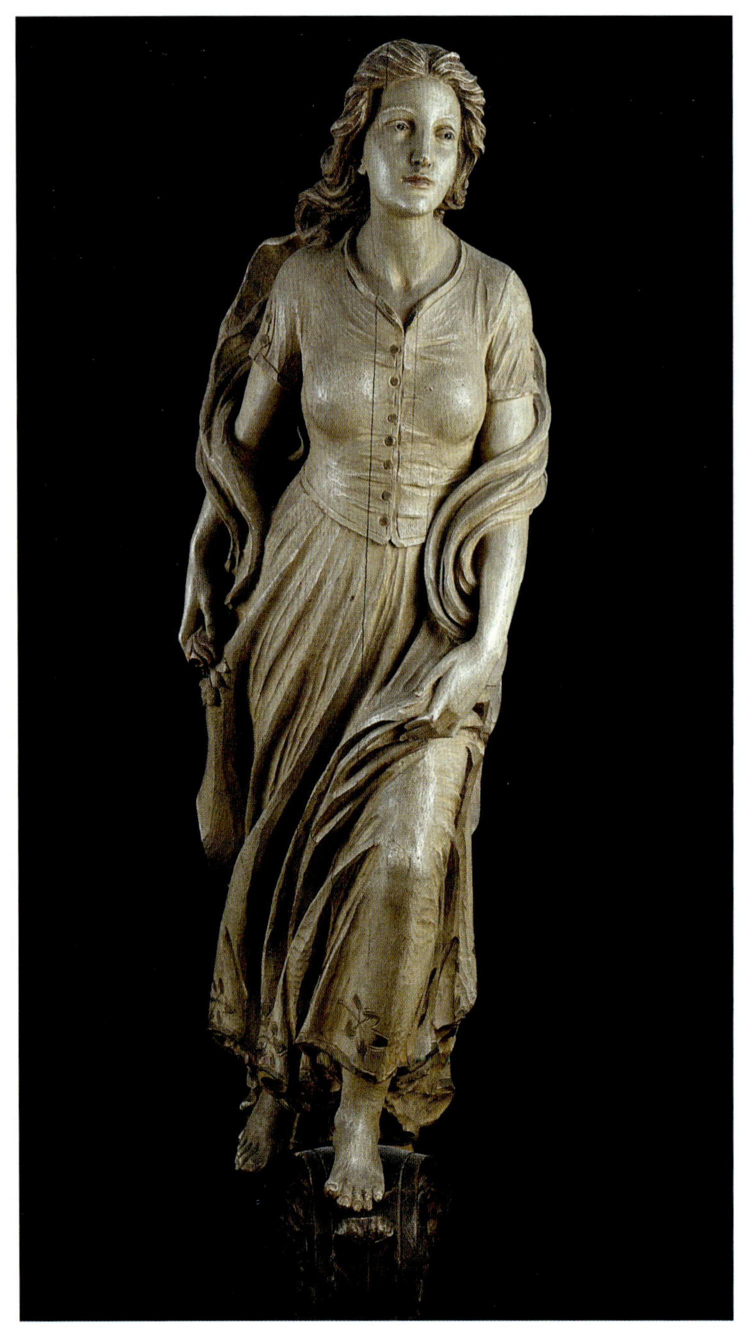

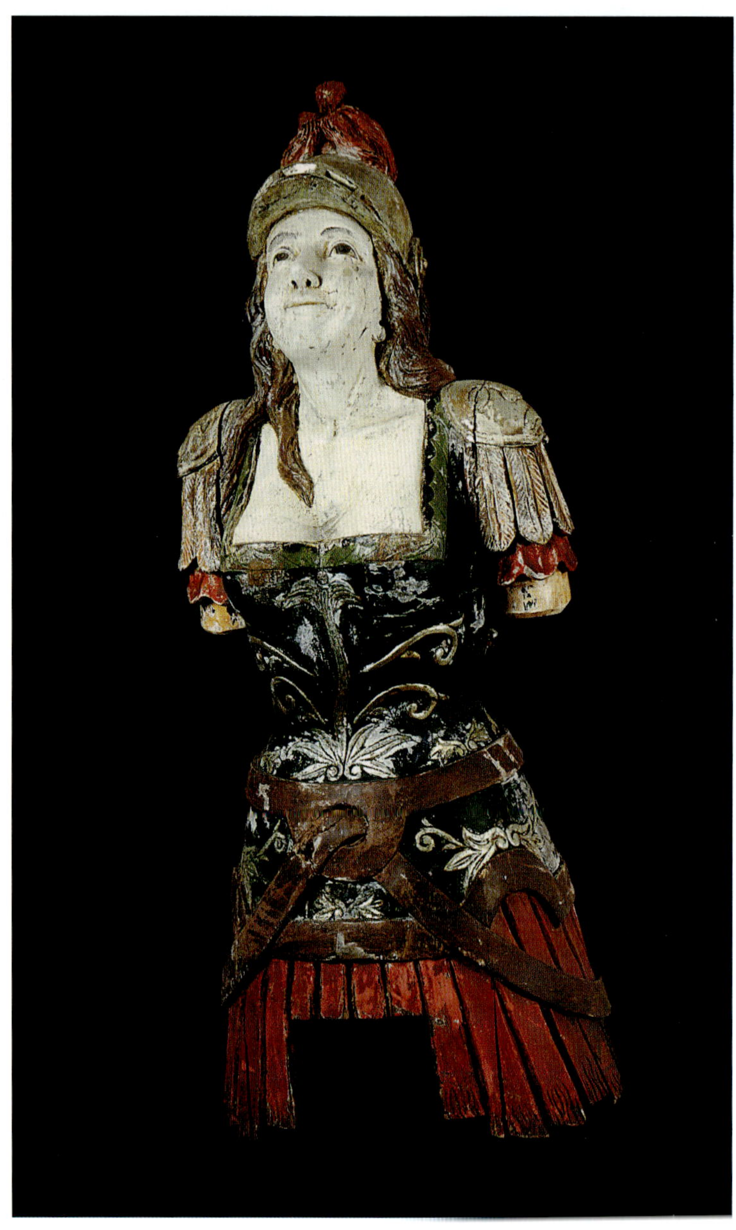

Carving of a woman in the form of a ship's figurehead, late 19th century
Wood and polychrome
H. 66 in., w. 15 in., d. 20 in.

Figurehead of a female Roman warrior, about 1830
Wood and polychrome
H. 53 in., w. 22 in., d. 16 in.

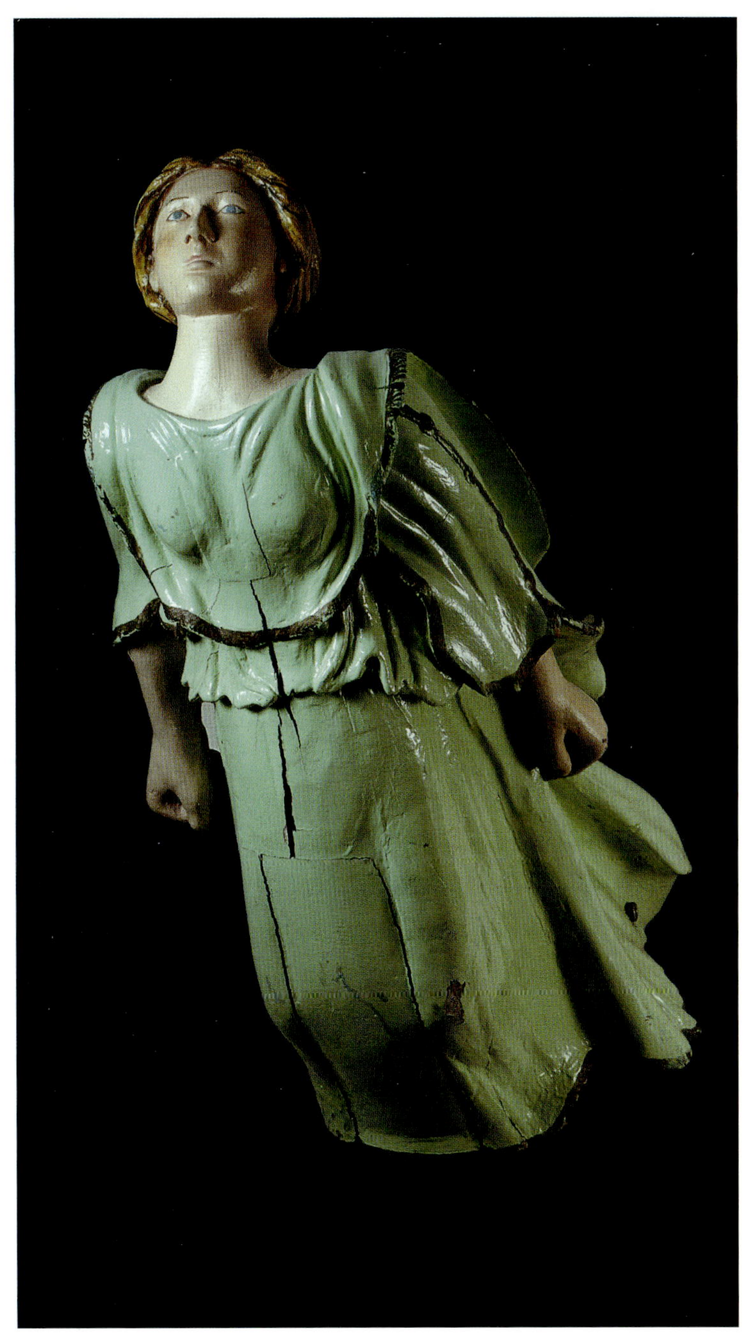

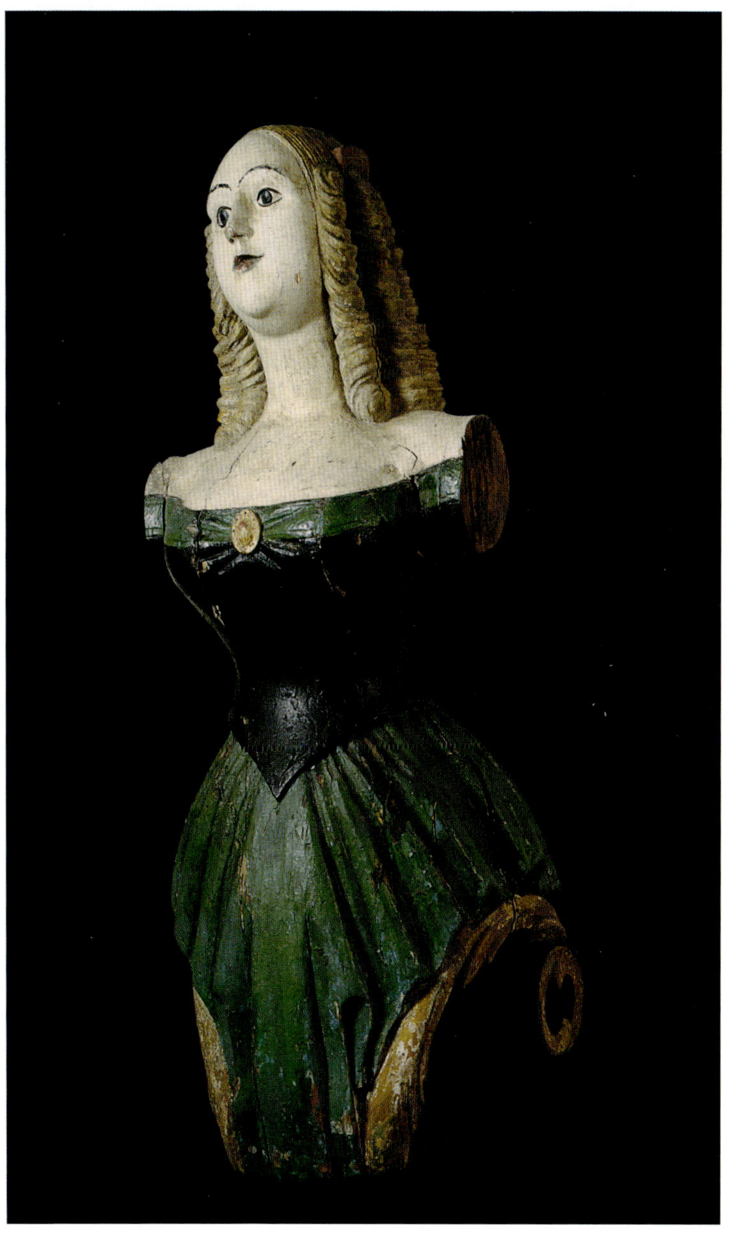

Figurehead of a woman (angel)
19th century
Wood and polychrome
H. 38 in., w. 28 in., d. 18 in.

Figurehead of Jenny Lind,
about 1850–60
Wood and polychrome
H. 38 in., w. 15 in., d. 16 in.

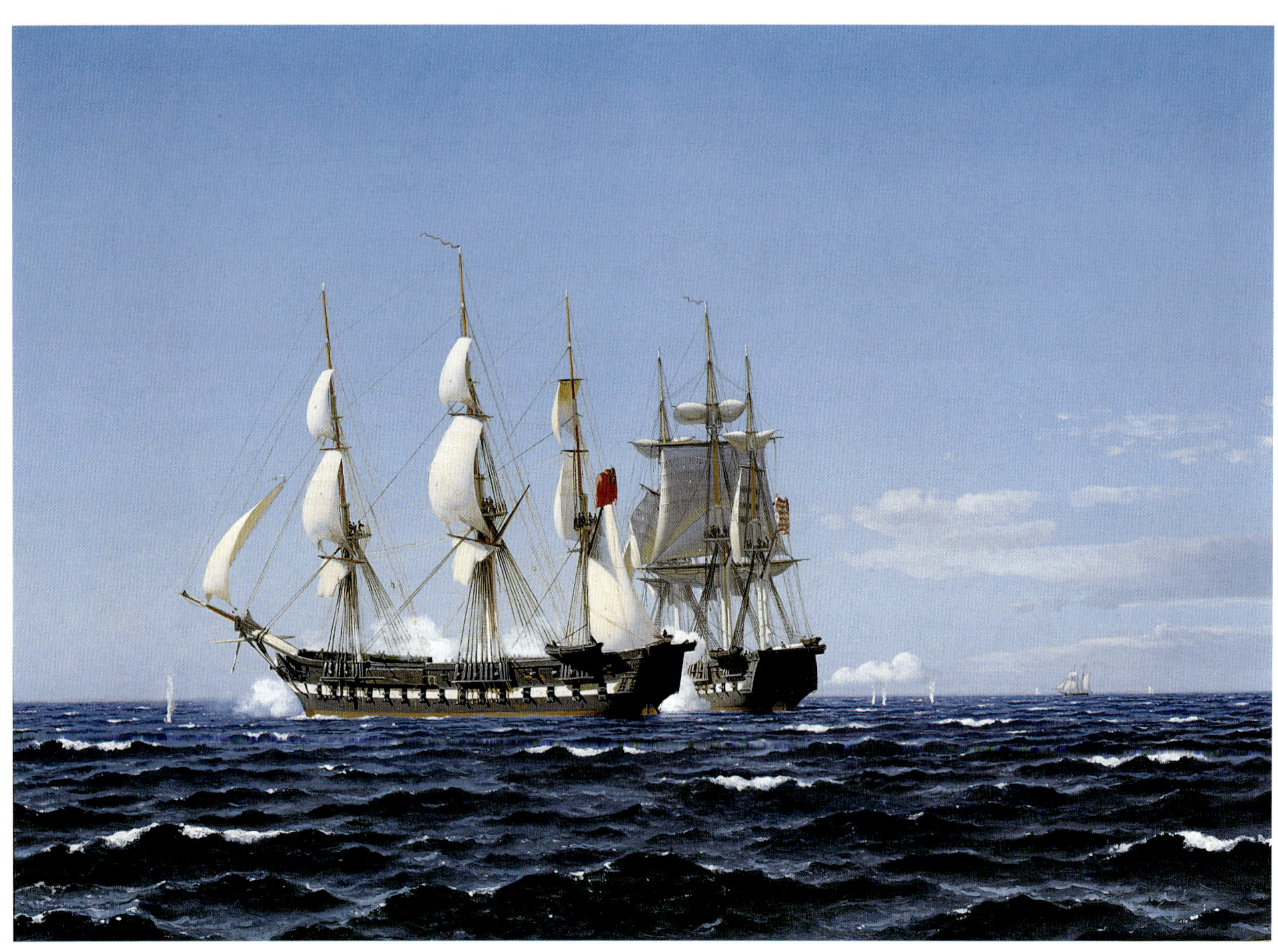

CHRISTOFFER WILHELM ECKERSBERG

Danish, 1783–1853
The Chesapeake *and* Shannon *in Combat*
Oil on canvas
23 x 31 in.

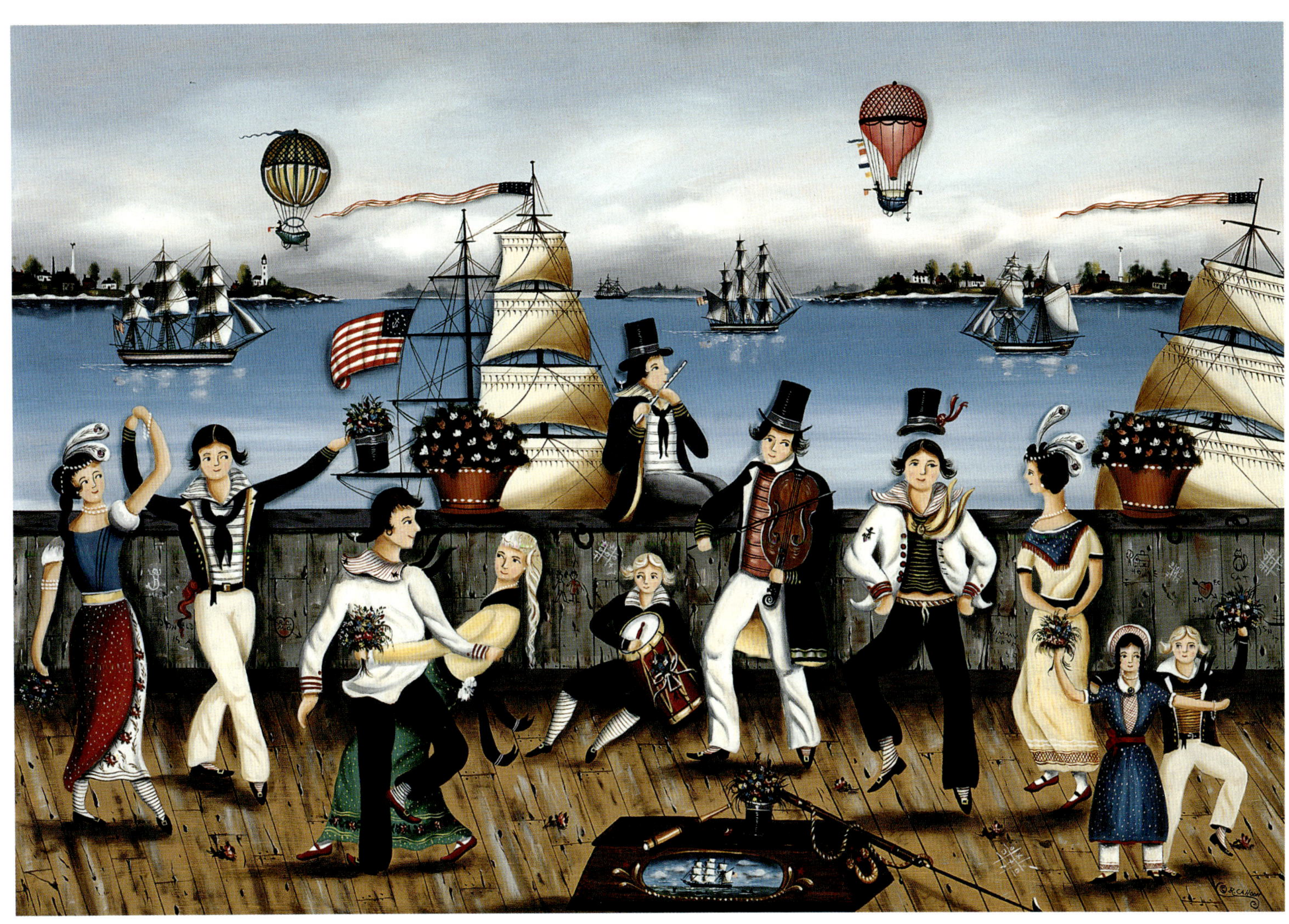

RALPH EUGENE CAHOON

American, 1910–1982
Sailor's Wedding
Oil on Masonite
28 x 42 in.

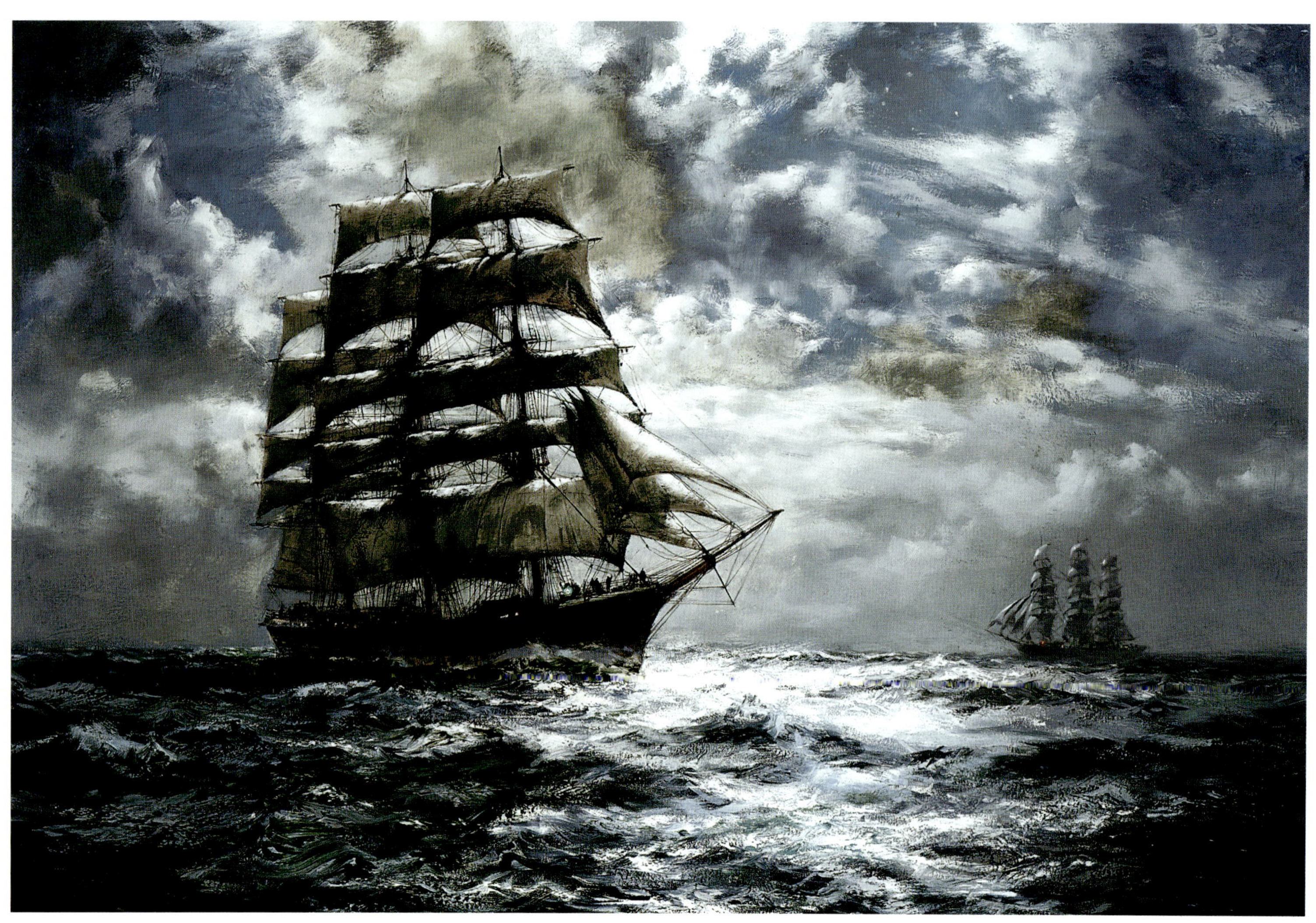

MONTAGUE DAWSON

English, 1895–1973
Moonlight Sonata—The Clan Macfarlane
Oil on canvas
28 x 42 in.

GUY CARLETON WIGGINS

American, 1883–1962
Beside the Wharf, about 1910
Oil on board
15⅝ x 12 in.

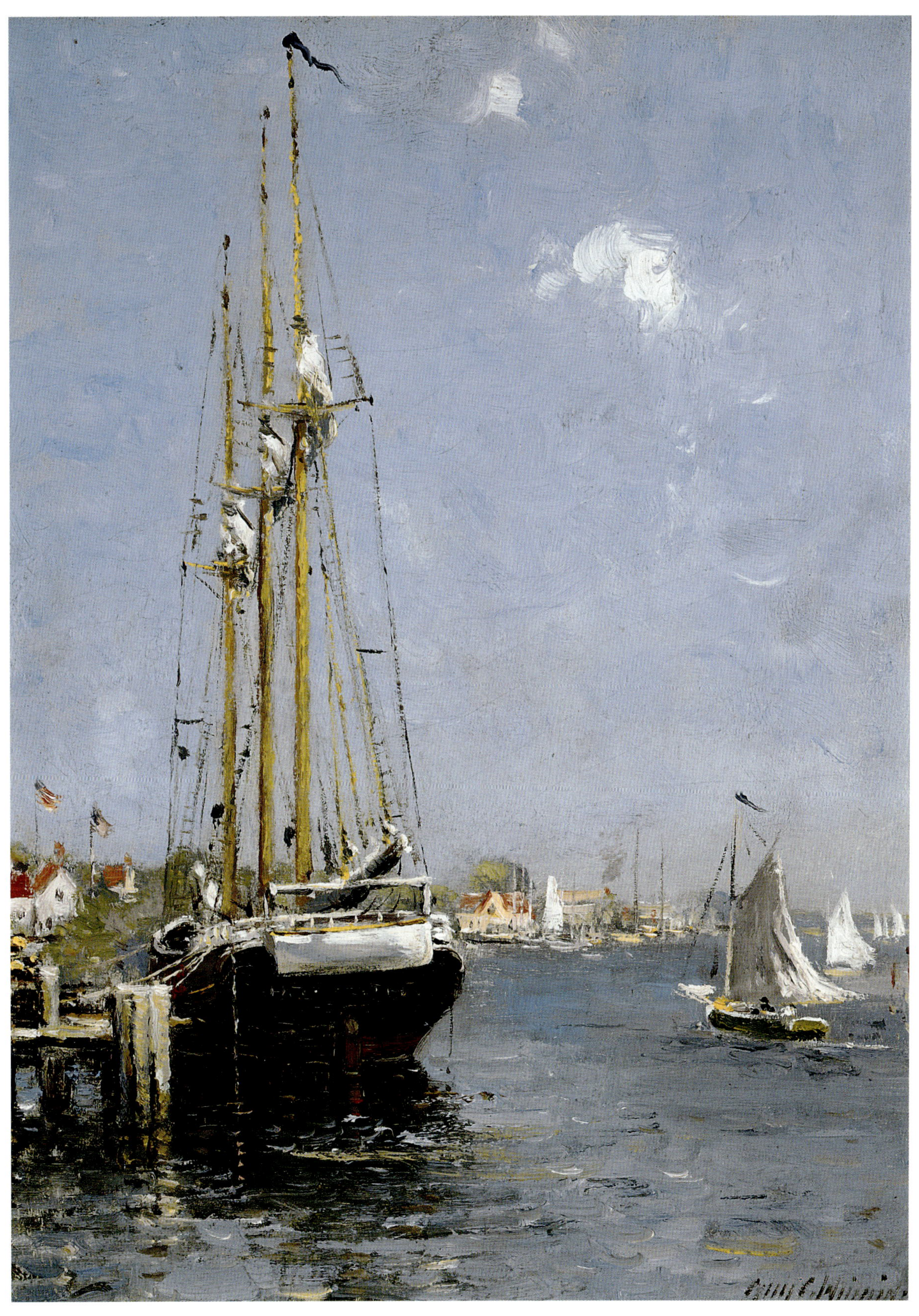

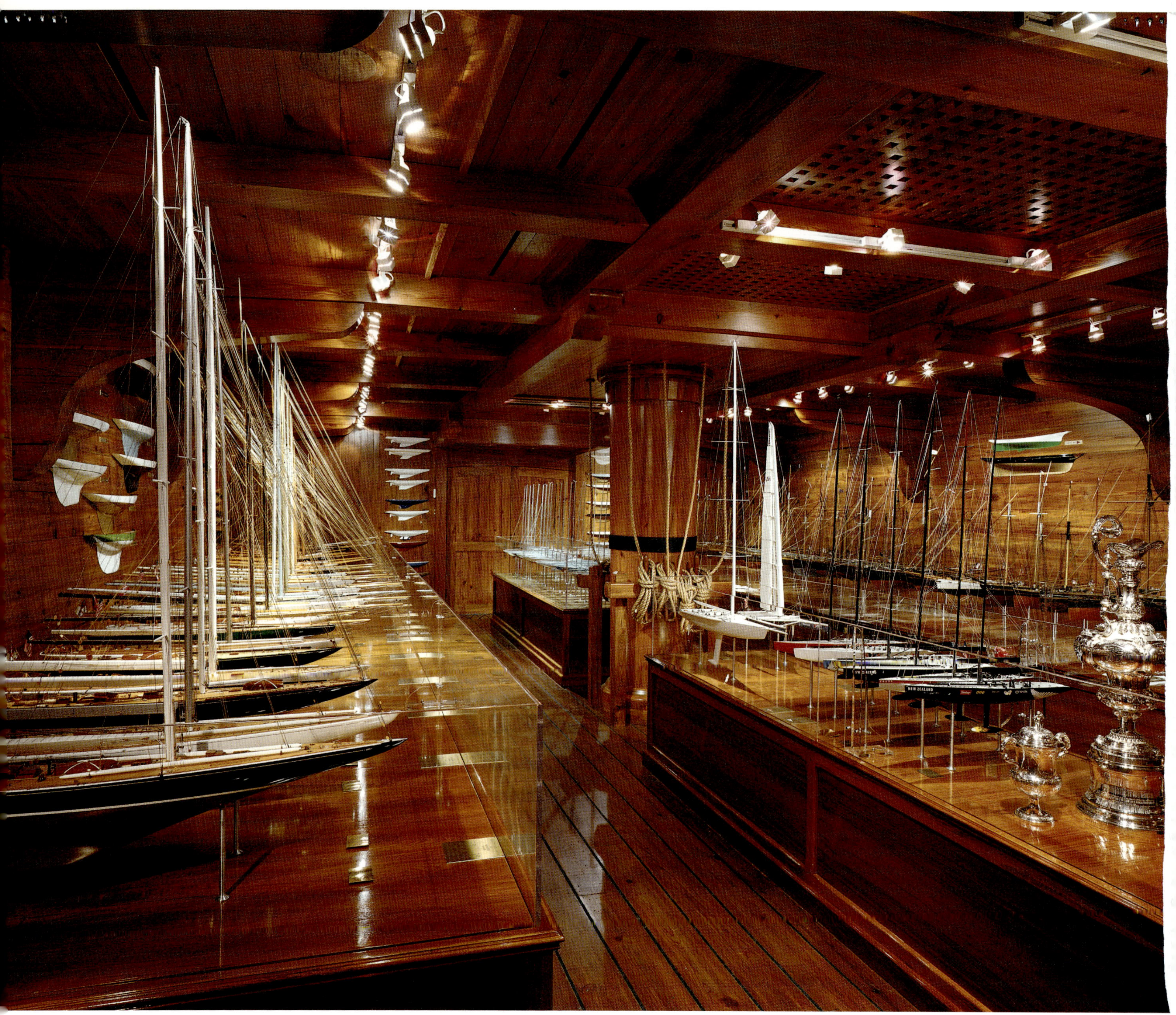
NEW ZEALAND

AMERICA'S CUP YACHT MODELS

* * * * * * *

Better known for his eclectic collection of art and artifacts, Bill Koch also owns models of all 102 yachts that have taken part in the America's Cup, from the first event in 1851, off Cowes, England, through the thirty-second in 2003, off Auckland, New Zealand. The largest existing collection of America's Cup models, it is housed in a wooden room that resembles the cargo hold of an old square-rigger in Koch's home in Palm Beach, Florida. All the models are built at the same three-eighths-inch-to-the-foot scale and set on the same waterline plane. They are carefully crafted to match, in miniature, the beauty of the yachts that have competed in an event that has brought both fame and shame to those involved in its 154-year history.

Ship models have now become decorative records of the craft they represent. When the America's Cup began, they held a much more practical purpose, being the only guide the yacht builder had of the designer's intentions. Nineteenth-century builders did not have the benefit of the detailed lines plans that naval architects supply today, or the computer-driven schedule of offsets to allow the lofting of the molds full-scale. Instead, they used a half model, similar to those that form the complementary collection Koch has assembled to provide greater understanding of the continuously changing world of yacht design over a century and a half.

Koch's collection shows the sheer beauty of these racing yachts as well as the evolution of yachting technology. The design of the boats was determined by the materials available for hull and sails, current construction techniques, the state of the science of aerodynamics and hydrodynamics, the creativity of the designers, the aggressiveness of the owner, and the confines of measurement rule, set generally by mutual agreement between the defender and the challenger. The collection also hints loudly at the colorful history of the Cup and its diverse and sometimes outrageous participants.

The America's Cup is the oldest sporting trophy in history. It was first won in 1851 by the yacht *America* for the New York Yacht Club, who held it for 132 years, the longest winning streak in sporting history.[1] The club successfully defended the Cup twenty-four times but lost it to Australia in 1983. The NYYC skipper who lost it, Dennis Conner, won it back in 1987 for the San Diego Yacht Club. The SDYC successfully defended it twice, but then lost it to New Zealand in 1995. New Zealand, in turn, successfully defended it once but lost it to the Swiss in 2003.

Many millions of dollars have been spent in challenging for, and defending, the 134 ounces of sterling silver that was crafted in 1848 by Robert Garrard, the royal silversmith, into a baroque ewer of dubious function. In a bizarrely apposite move, Garrard fashioned this strange jug, of which a replica is part of the Koch Collection, as a bottomless vessel, thereby able to absorb the vast quantities of dollars that have been poured into it.

The saga of the America's Cup began when the schooner *America* (p. 194) was designed and built for a five-member syndicate of the NYYC who had an eye on turning a quick buck. They had gambled with the yacht's builder and obtained a one-third reduction in the quoted price, and they were confident that many wagers might further augment their investment.

When *America* first entered British waters and was met by *Lavrock*, one of the Royal Yacht Squadron's racing fleet, it was a temptation that the Yankee sailors could not resist. They lined up against *Lavrock* and sailed swiftly away from her on the short passage along the Isle of Wight coast to Cowes, thrashing her soundly. The Americans' offers of additional matches for substantial wagers were, rather naturally, rejected.

America was entered for the RYS regatta for a cup valued at one hundred sovereigns, in a race around the Isle of Wight on August 22, 1851. She severely outpaced fourteen British yachts of varied sizes and shapes—sloops, schooners, and even a 110-foot square-rigger outfitted with cannons.[2] There was, however, some controversy: *America* passed the Nab Light Ship to port, while the British yachts went the usual way and left the lightship to starboard.

Fig. 26. The Ship Model Room in Koch's Palm Beach home

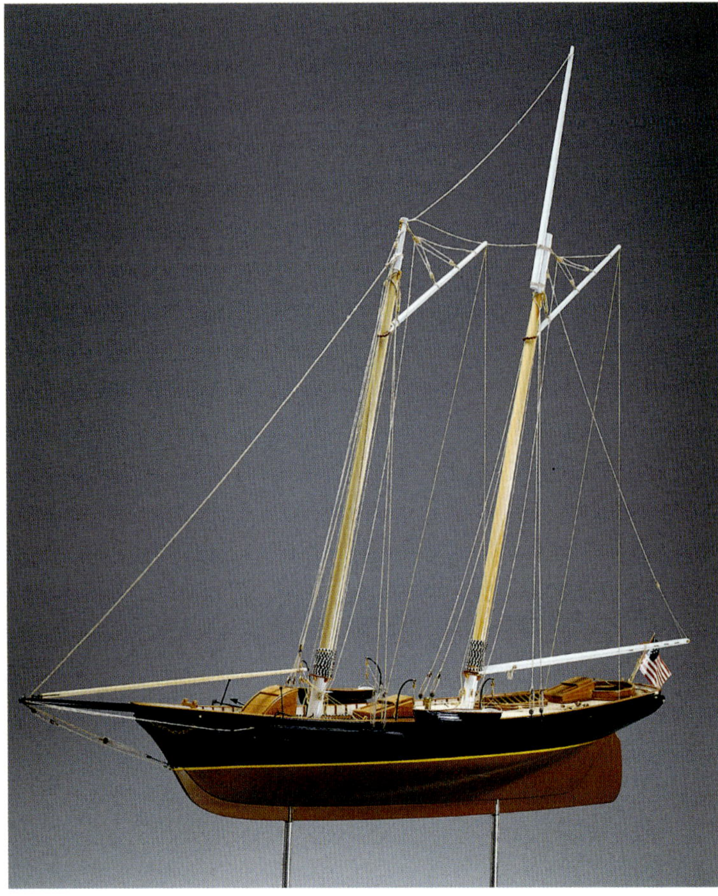

Model of America, *winner of 1851 America's Cup,* wood, h. 50 in., w. 13 in., d. 51 in.

The Earl of Anglesey, a tough old bird of eighty-three who had lost a leg at the Battle of Waterloo in 1815, examined the yacht's design in amazement, declaring, "I've learned one thing; I've been sailing my yacht stern foremost for the last twenty years." Comparison of the lines of *America*'s model and those of the British yachts would show how his words ring true. *America* had a radical hull design, swept back masts, and state-of-the-art sails of Egyptian cotton.

The last surviving syndicate member, George L. Schuyler, donated the Cup to the NYYC as a perpetual trophy "for friendly competition between foreign countries" with a deed of gift on July 8, 1857. The deed stated that unless the competitors could reach mutual consent on the terms of the match, the minimum and maximum length of the boats should meet the specified conditions, six months' notice should be given of the challenge, and the races should be sailed on the usual course for the defending club's annual regatta.

In 1870 a Brit, James Ashbury, challenged with *Cambria.* Son of a wheelwright, Ashbury wanted to enhance his potential candidacy for the English Parliament by a sporting gesture. The NYYC raced seventeen boats against him, and *Cambria* finished eighth. In 1871 Ashbury challenged again with his boat *Livonia,* and this time the NYYC agreed to race only one boat against the British schooner but reserved the right to change boats in between races depending upon the weather. The club won four to one. After the Cup, Ashbury moved to New Zealand to farm sheep, went broke, moved back to England, and committed suicide.

From 1881 to 1887 the boats raced were 67-foot to 100-foot gaff-rigged sloops. The most beautiful of these were *Puritan* (p. 196; designed by Ned Burgess and owned by General Charles Paine, both of Boston) and *Genesta* (p. 196), who raced in 1885. *Puritan* was a fairly typical American sloop, steered by a wheel, and eight feet wider and five feet shallower than her opponent, a standard narrow English cutter steered by a lengthy tiller. *Puritan* won two races to none.

The next year William Henn brought his "country cottage" *Galatea,* the first boat built out of steel, from England to New York to challenge for the Cup. His yacht, fully furnished even down to a fireplace and a leopard skin rug, could not compete with General Paines's *Mayflower.* Mrs. Henn, who sailed with her husband, kept a small menagerie aboard—several dogs and a monkey called Peggy.[3]

In 1887 the Scottsman James Bell challenged with *Thistle.* Much secrecy surrounded *Thistle,* and when she was launched on the River Clyde a tarpaulin covered her entire underbody from the waterline down. It was the first time a "security skirt" had been used, a tactic that wasn't repeated until Alan Bond made it fashionable ninety-six years later with *Australia II,* hiding her winged keel from prying eyes.

The era of 1889 to 1903 was one of monster boats ranging in size from 117 to 143 feet. *Defender,* a 123-foot sloop, was the first NYYC boat without a centerboard. She had magnesium and bronze bottom plating, aluminum topsides, steel frames, and bronze and steel fastenings. The materials induced electrolysis, and she was in effect a floating battery. She easily beat *Valkyrie III,* owned by the Earl of Dunraven, who is held as the worst sportsman in America's Cup history.[4]

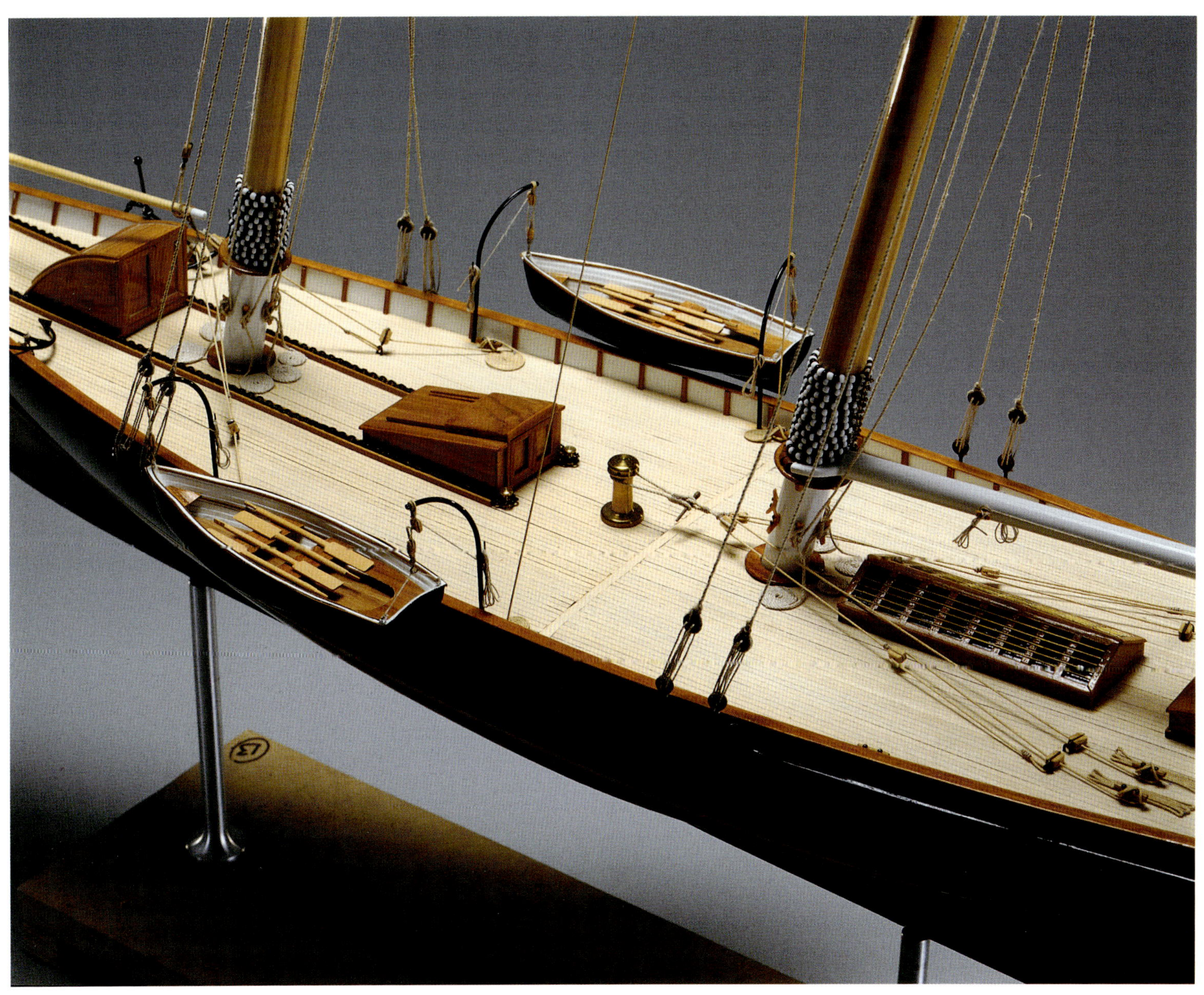

Detail view of *America*'s deck

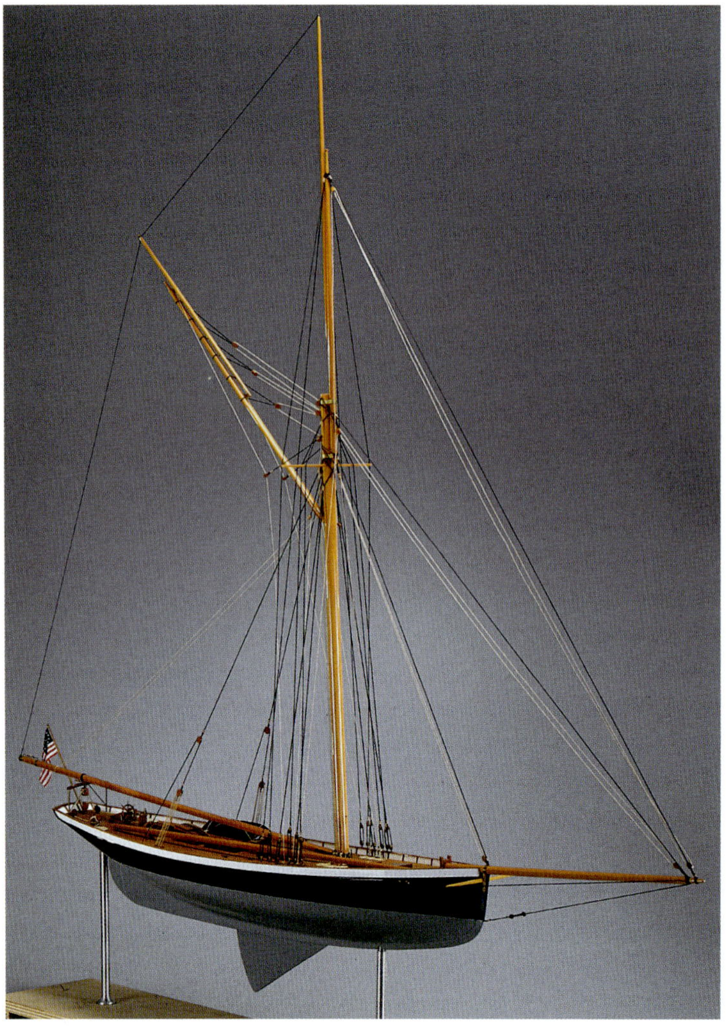

Model of Puritan, *winner of 1885 America's Cup*, wood, h. 58½ in., w. 10 in., d. 55½ in.

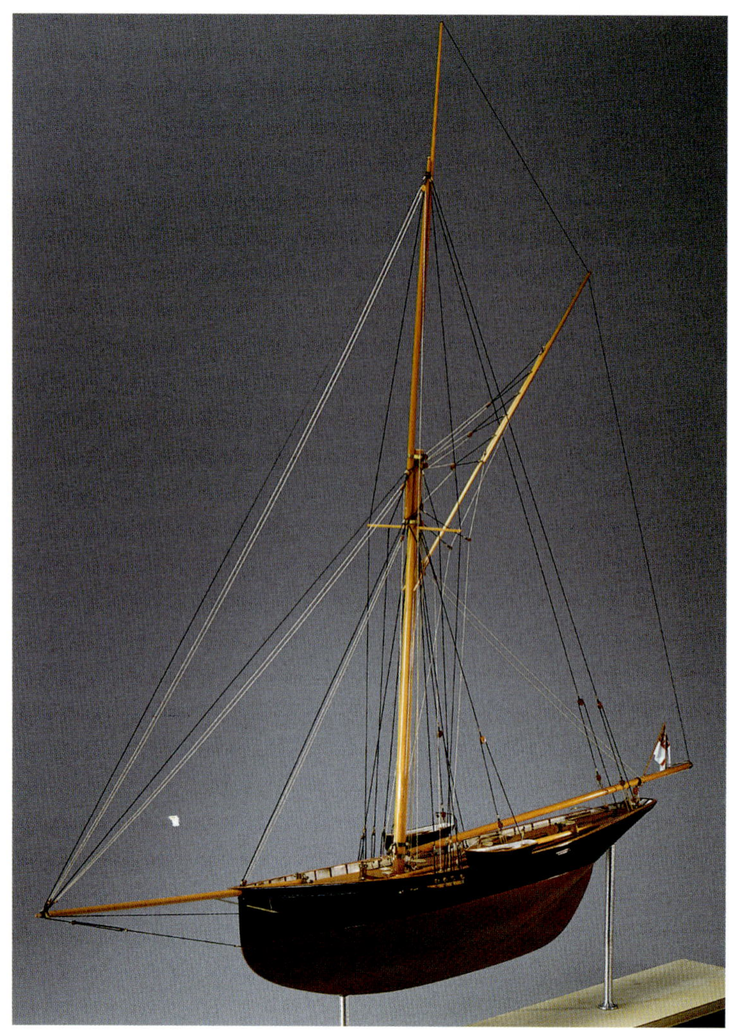

Model of Genesta, *challenger in 1885 America's Cup*, wood, h. 59 in., w. 9½ in., d. 56 in.

Losing was a gracious habit of Sir Thomas Lipton, who challenged on five occasions between 1899 and 1930. He came up against formidable opposition in the form of the designer Nat Herreshoff (a former engineering student at MIT who had a record seven winning yachts to his designs) and skipper Charlie Barr, who won nine races in a row in three defenses (a record that stood until Russell Coutts broke it in 2003). Barr's third defense was with *Reliance*, backed by a Rockefeller and a Vanderbilt, which at 202 feet from the tip of her bowsprit to the end of her main boom was the longest boat ever used in the Cup races (p. 199). *Reliance* beat Lipton's *Shamrock III* easily three to zero.

In 1930 Lipton mounted the first challenge in the now-legendary J-class boats, with *Shamrock V*, but deferred to the greater speed of Harold "Mike" Vanderbilt's *Enterprise* four to zero, in the first races to be held off Newport, Rhode Island.[5] The J-class era lasted eight years. These utterly elegant yachts were considered the most beautiful of all the boats. They were the first with a triangular mainsail and were made of steel or, in the case of the seven built in America, bronze. Only eleven J-class boats were built.[6]

Sir T. O. M. Sopwith, the creator of the Sopwith Camel, claimed to his dying day that he was cheated out of the Cup in 1934 by misinterpretation of the rules. His *Endeavour* was fast enough to go two to zero up then lost the next four races, including one on a spurious protest. The result of the protest committee's decision led to the quip that appeared in the press: "Britannia rules the waves, but America waives the rules."

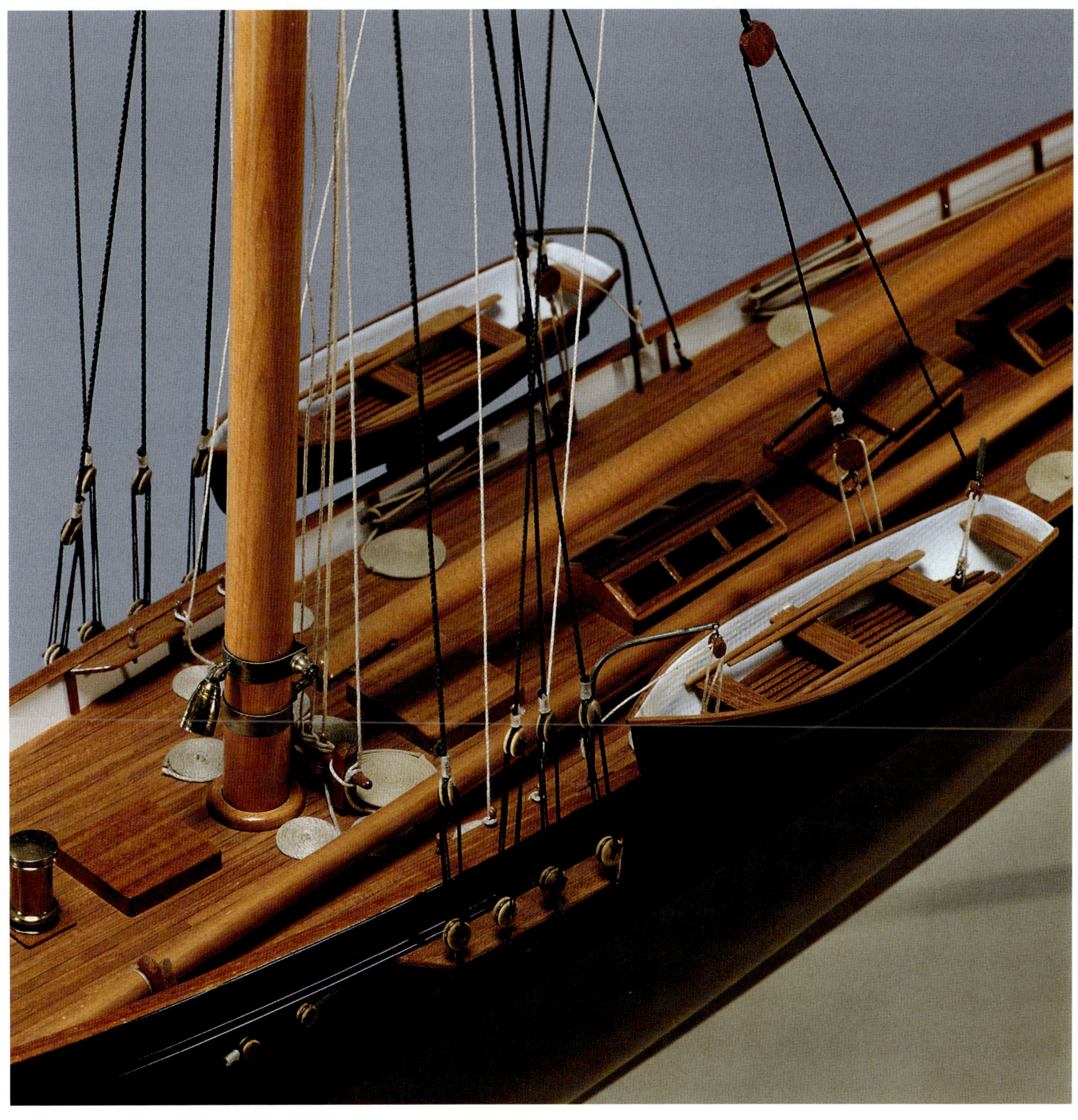

Detail view of *Genesta*'s deck

Ranger (p. 199), the 1937 J-class boat in which Olin Stephens shared the design with Starling Burgess, at 135 feet proved to be the "super boat" of her day and had no problem defeating Sopwith's *Endeavour II* four to zero. *Ranger* was made all of steel with a welded hull. She was a product of testing first at the Stevens water tank and then at the Navy water tank in Washington, D.C.

World War II temporarily halted racing. Following the war, in 1956, the regulations in the Cup's deed of gift were amended to allow the 12-Meter class to be used. The smaller boats lowered the costs of competition, resulting in the democratization of the Cup. They also introduced what many believe was the golden age of racing, the era when the game changed from the gaiety of Corinthianism to the fiercely competitive professional approach to sport.

The 12-Meter era lasted from 1958 to 1987. It involved not only great advances in technology but also some of the more colorful characters. In 1962 *Weatherly*, skippered by Bus Mosbacher, who would become Richard Nixon's chief of protocol, narrowly beat *Gretel*, owned by the Australian publishing magnate Sir Frank Packer. In 1964 *Constellation* easily beat the British challenger *Sovereign* four to zero. For the next two Cups, in 1967 and 1970, Olin Stephens for the NYYC came up with a super yacht, *Intrepid*, built of wood. He separated the rudder from the keel, put the grinders below deck, and lowered the boom to improve the airflow on the mainsail. *Intrepid* easily beat *Dame Pattie* of Australia four to zero.

In 1970, for the first time, the NYYC opened the challenge to multiple yachts. *Intrepid* defended again in a close series with *Gretel II*, Packer's second try. Packer was defeated four to one in the series. After losing several protests, including one over a toilet door, Packer moaned, "An Australian skipper complaining to the NYYC Committee is like a man complaining to his mother-in-law about his wife."

Two well-known characters came into the Cup competition in the 1970s: Ted Turner, who would become quite famous in the Cup and elsewhere; and Baron Bich, the promoter of the Bic ballpoint pen. Bich became addicted to the 12-Meter class and the Cup. He tried four times, but he won only one race—in 1980, in the challenger trials.

In 1974 12-Meters were allowed to be made of aluminum. Olin Stephens designed *Courageous* to match *Southern Cross*, a first challenge from the outspoken Australian Alan Bond using an unknown designer, Ben Lexcen. The NYYC played musical chairs with helmsmen before choosing Ted Hood of Marblehead, Massachusetts, as skipper of *Courageous* with Dennis Conner as tactician, and putting Turner, the "Mouth from the South," on the bench. *Courageous* won four to zero. Turner came back with a vengeance in 1977. He bought *Courageous*, improved her, and swept Bond's *Australia*, which had a new extruded aluminum mast, in four straight close races.

Turner was back in 1980 but was efficiently dispatched by Conner, whose "no excuse to lose" attitude saw him spend three hundred days a year for two years practicing with a two-boat program. Bond was also back again, but this time he had a flexible mast copied from the British that allowed him to shape his mainsail more efficiently. Nevertheless, Conner beat the Australians with *Freedom*, four to one.

Bond and Conner returned for 1983. Dennis built three boats, while Bond had a secret weapon, a winged keel, which he kept under strict cover. His boat, *Australia II* (p. 200), defeated six other potential challengers, winning forty-eight races and only losing five.[7]

The NYYC America's Cup Committee, led by a spiteful Bob McCullough, sought to prove that the "secret" winged keel of *Australia II* was improper. It claimed that Dutch scientists from the testing tanks at Wageningen were responsible for its design, not the Australian Ben Lexcen. What happened next became "The Race of the Century." *Liberty* won the first two races, as a result of gear failure on *Australia II*. *Australia II* won the third, but Conner won the fourth. The score was three to one. Alan Bond declared, "Don't count us out," and *Australia II* won the next two races, tying the score. Then Conner changed his boat configuration. *Liberty* led around the course, until the last downwind leg, where she failed to cover *Australia II* and was passed. The Australian had come from three to one down to win four to three, breaking the 132-year winning streak of the NYYC. Bond commented, "All the money in the world can't win the Cup."

The Royal Perth Yacht Club took the America's Cup to Fremantle, Australia, for the race in 1987. Thirteen challengers showed up, and there were four potential defenders.[8] Conner had an even more rigorous training program, in Hawaii, and three boats. Bond did not make the Cup; he was beaten by *Kookaburra III*, backed by Kevin Perry, an Australian retail and mining magnate who would have financial troubles. Bond was starting to have his own legal problems, which ended in bankruptcy and a four-year stint in prison for income-tax evasion.

Conner, in *Stars & Stripes*—the result of a design team rather than an individual designer, and computer modeling plus tank testing—survived an intense elimination series. At the beginning of the challenger finals, *Stars & Stripes* had a record

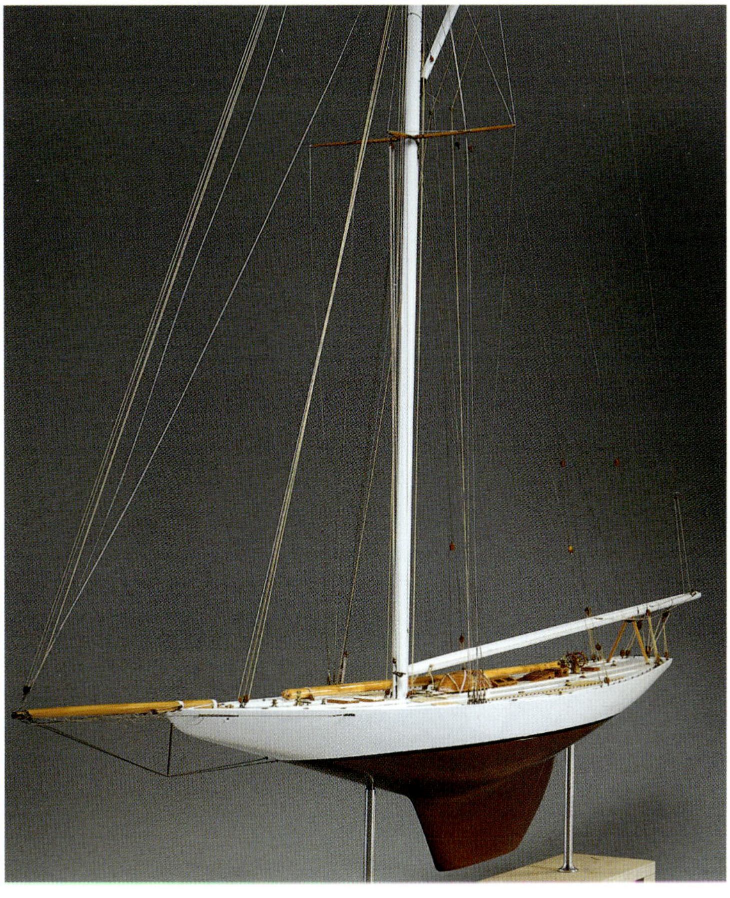

Model of Reliance, *winner of 1903 America's Cup,* wood, h. 76½ in., w. 13½ in, d. 73½ in.

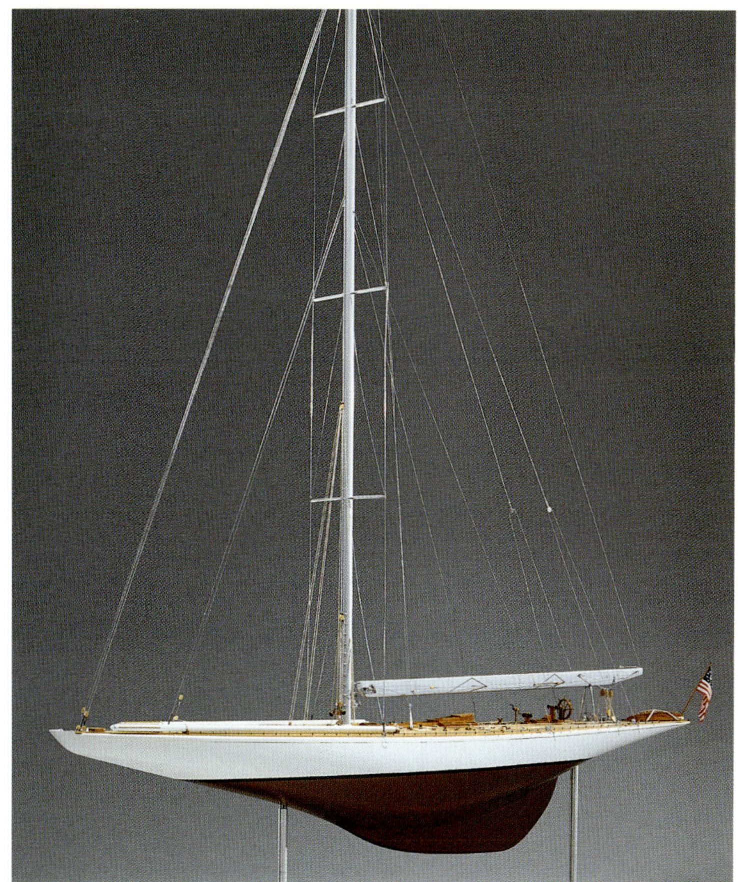

Model of Ranger, *winner of 1937 America's Cup,* wood, h. 71 in., w. 9 in., d. 55 in.

of thirty-one to seven, and *Kiwi Magic,* a record of thirty-seven to one. *Kiwi Magic* belonged to Michael Fay, a thirty-seven-year-old merchant banker from Auckland whose team had thought outside the box and built three boats, two identical for on-the-water testing, out of fiberglass.[9] *Stars & Stripes* beat *Kiwi Magic* four to one. (Koch bought *Kiwi Magic* in 2003 and currently sails her in 12-Meter regattas off Martha's Vineyard, Nantucket, and Newport). Conner beat *Kookaburra III* four to zero and took the Cup to San Diego.[10]

Every once in a while there is a hiccup in the best of plans. When the San Diego Yacht Club failed to make a decision about where, when, and in what boats the next Cup would be raced, it left itself open to a challenge under the deed of gift. As there was no other valid challenge, one came from Fay, with a ninety-foot waterline boat, *New Zealand.* The SDYC answered with another *Stars & Stripes,* a sixty-foot catamaran with a fixed wing instead of a sail. It was a walkover: *Stars & Stripes* won two to zero. Fay sued, claiming the use of a catamaran did not satisfy the deed's requirement for a match (it was more of a mismatch), and the Cup spent eighteen months in court until it was decided the defense was legal.

There was a need for a new class of boats, and twenty leading designers, constructors, engineers, and sailmakers gathered in Southampton, England, to formulate the International America's Cup rule allowing new technology and materials. The shift of technology appealed to Bill Koch, who holds a doctorate of science from MIT. Even though he began racing only seven years before the 1992 Cup, he could start level with everyone by applying a scientific and sophisticated management approach emphasizing teamwork. His forty-six-person design and technical team tested sixty-five hull designs in a water tank and 150 keel designs in a wind tunnel, invented a new sail material using carbon fiber, and built four boats, eventually improving their speed around the racecourse by 5 percent, or about 6.5 minutes for each race.[11]

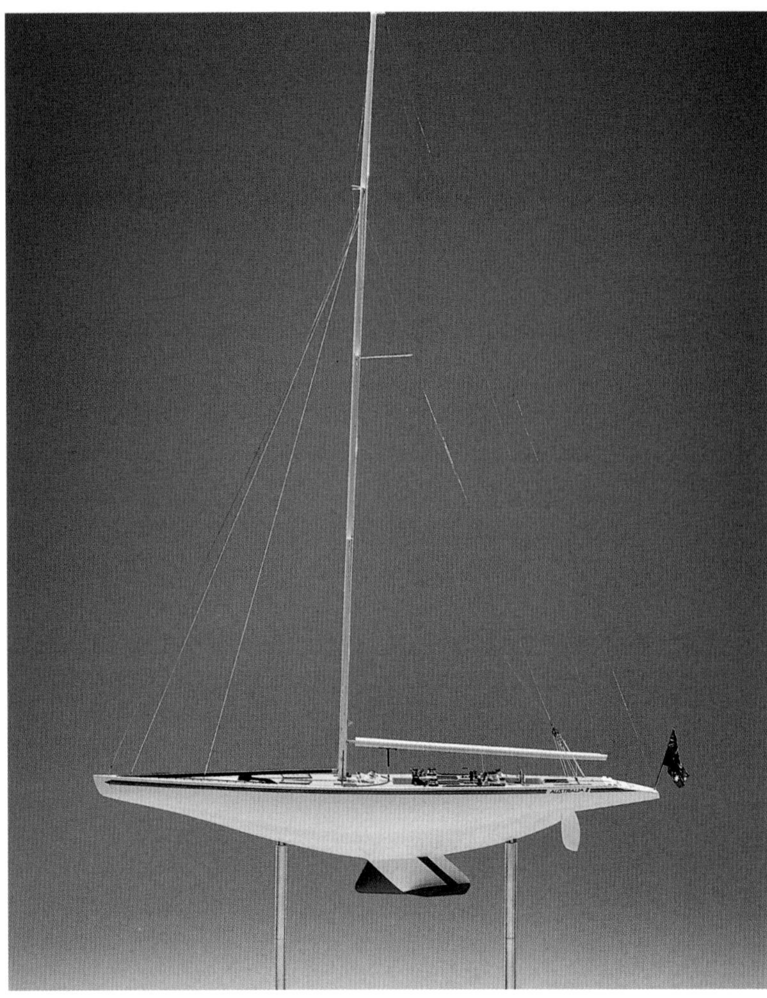

Model of Australia II, *winner of 1983 America's Cup,* wood, h. 43½ in., w. 5½ in., d. 27 in.

Koch insisted on skippering his own boat, *America*^{3} (p. 201). The Las Vegas odds were one hundred to one against him, yet his team beat Conner on his home waters to take on the challenge of *Il Moro di Venezia,* backed by Raul Gardini and skippered by the American sailor Paul Cayard. *America*^{3} won four to one, and her single loss was by the thinnest victory in America's Cup history, just three seconds. The 1992 Cup was the most expensive ever; the competitors spent more than $500 million. Gardini alone spent $238 million and Koch $68.5 million, of which $25 million went toward research and development. Gardini returned to Italy, to a torrent of legal problems, and shot himself within a year.

The designs of *America*^{3} and *Il Moro* provide an interesting comparison. *America*^{3} has seven additional inches in overall length, the same waterline length, a beam one inch narrower on deck, a quarter-inch deeper draft, thirty square feet less sail area, the same 110-foot mast, and 4,300 pounds more weight. A closer look at the boats shows that *America*^{3}'s hull is narrower and deeper and her bulb is more streamlined. This combination, plus her Cuben Fiber sails, was the main reason for her success.

The Cup in 1995 was another strange affair.[12] There were three defenders, including *Young America* and *Mighty Mary,* a women's team backed by Bill Koch. Conner was out of the competition until the three syndicates agreed upon a three-way final. Conner came from four minutes behind in the last race and passed *Mighty Mary* to become the defender. He borrowed *Young America* to defend the Cup. During a challenger selection race in over twenty knots of wind, *OneAustralia,* skippered by the 1983 Cup winner, John Bertrand, and believed to be the fastest of the challengers, hit a big wave and broke in two, becoming the first boat to sink in the America's Cup. The Kiwi boat, *Black Magic*—skippered by Russell Coutts, who ran a low-profile, efficient, low-cost campaign—swept the challenger series.[13] *Black Magic* won the Cup five to zero, in what became known as "slaughter on the water."

The Kiwis took five years to mount the Cup in 2000, and there was only one defender, *Team New Zealand.* Intense competition among the eleven challengers propelled the fashion house Prada's boat, *Luna Rossa,* to the front; but *Team New Zealand,* skippered by Coutts, won easily five to zero. In the 2003 Cup, *Team New Zealand* defended and there were nine challengers. Ernesto Bertarelli of Switzerland, with *Alinghi* (p. 201), had cleverly hired Coutts and ten other Kiwi sailors. *Alinghi* won the challenger series after many close races and swept the Cup, beating *Team New Zealand* five to zero. *Team New Zealand* had lost its magic.

After winning the Cup, *Alinghi,* having no access to an ocean from landlocked Switzerland, put the venue for the 2007 Cup up for bid. Valencia, Spain, won. Coutts left the *Alinghi* campaign as a result of a dispute with Bertarelli, and the high cost of a competitive campaign—now about $150 million—caused Conner to bow out. It will be fascinating to watch both the onshore and offshore developments leading up to the race.

Some say that the Cup is a curse, or a poisoned chalice;[14] others, that it is the most noble, glorious, and beautiful of all trophies. Whatever it is, it brings out the worst and the best in people. America's Cup yacht development has always mirrored the availability of technology and materials, and the competition stimulated by rival crews has ensured that this evolution continues unabated. The models in Bill Koch's collection display the pace of this development in the constant pursuit of speed.

—BOB FISHER

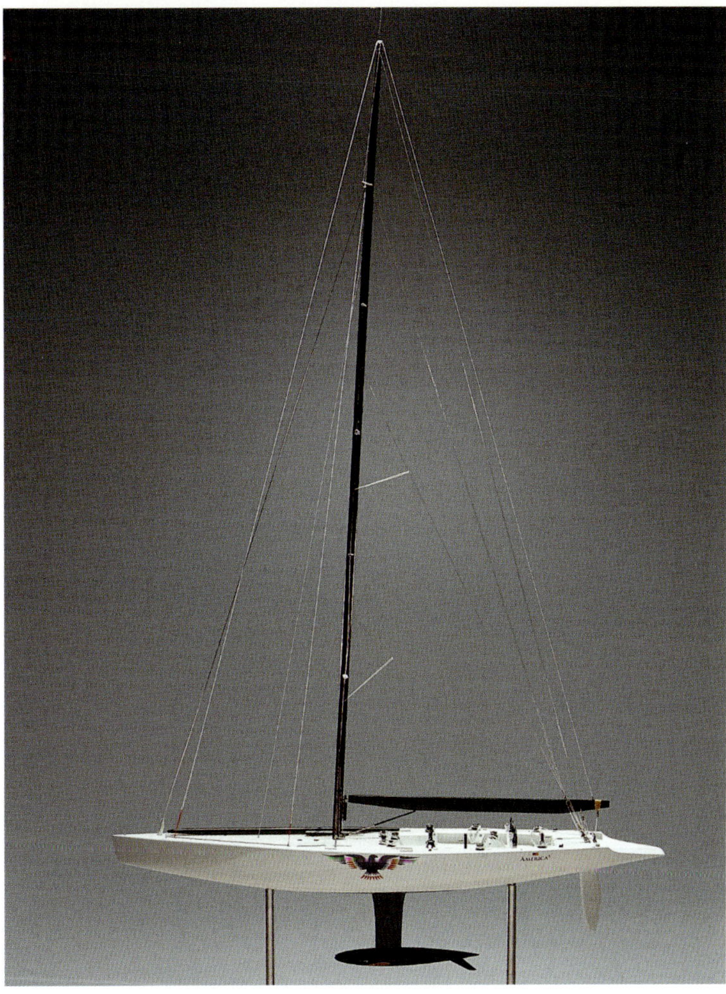

Model of America^3, *winner of 1992 America's Cup*, wood, h. 54 in., w. 7 in., d. 29½ in.

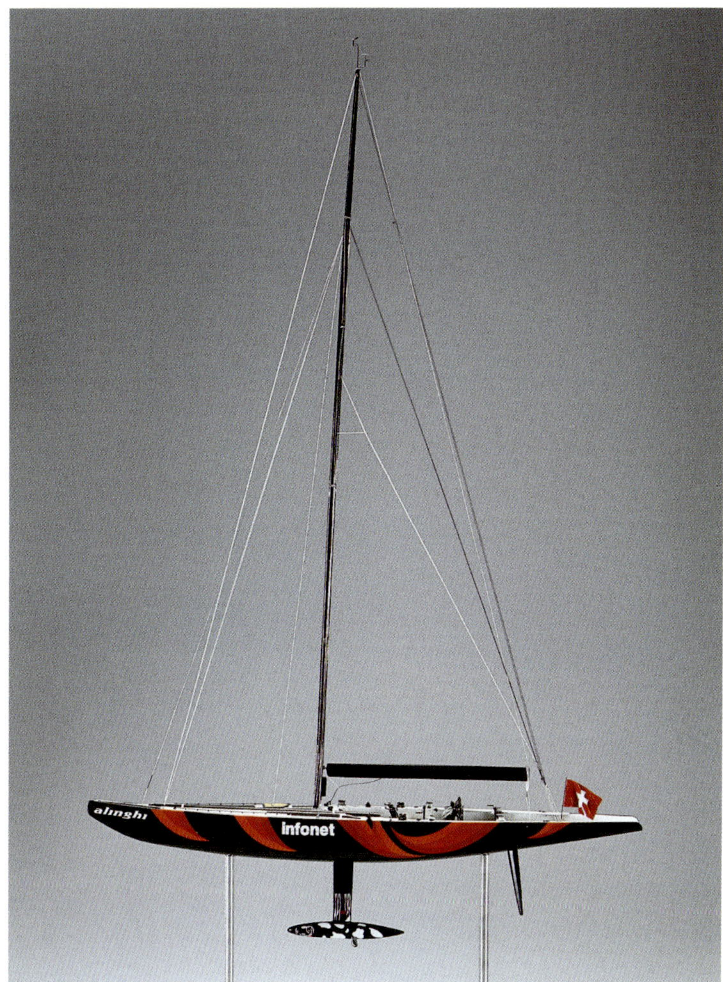

Model of Alinghi, *winner of 2003 America's Cup*, wood, h. 50 in., w. 5 in., d. 31 in.

1. The fullest possible description of the first race for the Cup is found in Winfield M. Thompson and Thomas W. Lawson, *The Lawson History of the America's Cup* (Boston: Published privately, 1902), xxi.

2. Francois Chevalier and Jacques Taglang, *America's Cup Designs, 1851–1886* (Paris: Auteurs Editeurs, 1987), 38.

3. John Rousmaniere, *America's Cup Book, 1851–1983* (London: Pelham Books, 1983), 41.

4. Doug Riggs, *Keelhauled: Unsportsmanlike Conduct and the America's Cup* (Newport, R.I.: Seven Seas, 1986), 49.

5. Harold S. Vanderbilt, *Enterprise: The Story of the Defense of the America's Cup in 1930* (New York: Charles Scribner's Sons, 1931), is the only book written about a defense by the owner/skipper of the winning boat and provides a complete exposé of what is required for success.

6. One of the boats, *Velsheda*, was built by Bill Stephenson, the chairman of Woolworth's, solely to race in Britain and with no thoughts of challenging for the America's Cup.

7. John Bertrand, the skipper of *Australia II*, recalls the difficulties faced and explains how the problems were overcome in "The Summer Rampage of Australia II," chap. 12 in *Born to Win: A Lifelong Struggle to Capture the America's Cup*, by Patrick Robinson and John Bertrand (New York: Hearst Marine Books, 1985), 176–94.

8. Full details of all thirteen challengers and four defenders can be found in "And then there were two. . . ," chap. 1 in *The America's Cup 1987: The Official Record*, by Bob Fisher and Bob Ross (London: Aurum, 1987), 21–68.

9. Alan Sefton, *The Cup Down Under* (Stamford, Conn.: Longmeadow Press, 1987), 49.

10. Dennis Conner and Bruce Stannard, *Comeback: My Race for the America's Cup* (New York: St. Martin's Press, 1987), contains a complete description of the masterful victory by *Stars & Stripes*.

11. Paul C. Larsen, *To the Third Power: Bill Koch's Winning Management of the 1992 America's Cup* (New York: America^3 Foundation, 1994), 425.

12. Full coverage of the twenty-ninth defense of the America's Cup can be found in Bill Center, *America's Cup '95: The Official Record* (Del Mar, Calif.: Tehabi Books, 1995).

13. Russell Coutts and Paul Larsen give detailed accounts of the Cup races from the New Zealand perspective in *Russell Coutts: Course to Victory* (Auckland: Hodder Moa Beckett, 1996).

14. Warren St. John, "Pursuit of the America's Cup Can Be Fulfilling and a Curse," *New York Times*, February 2, 2003.

CONTRIBUTORS

****

ELLIOT BOSTWICK DAVIS is the John Moors Cabot Chair, Art of the Americas, at the Museum of Fine Arts, Boston. She has lectured and published on a variety of nineteenth- and twentieth-century topics, including Mary Cassatt, Winslow Homer, and Fitz Henry Lane. Her upcoming projects include exhibitions on Edward Hopper and Japonisme in American art.

BOB FISHER, a sailor himself, regularly writes about the sport for England's *Guardian* and *Observer* newspapers and a plethora of sailing magazines internationally. Fisher has authored thirty-one books on sailing matters and is currently engaged on a definitive history of the America's Cup.

ALAN GRANBY received his bachelor's degree from Clark University in 1970. He obtained his next two degrees from Boston University, the last being a doctorate in media and technology. Granby serves on the Fine Arts Committee of the New York Yacht Club. He recently completed a book on marine art entitled *A Yachtman's Eye.*

JANICE HYLAND received three degrees from Boston University, including a doctorate in library science in 1974. In 1978 Hyland, along with her husband, Alan Granby, founded Hyland Granby Antiques, which specializes in maritime antiques of the eighteenth and nineteenth centuries.

CHRISTINE KONDOLEON is the George and Margo Behrakis Senior Curator of Greek and Roman Art at the Museum of Fine Arts, Boston. A specialist in Roman art, she has written and lectured widely on mosaics and domestic arts. Her most recent publications include *Games for the Gods: The Greek Athlete and the Olympic Spirit* and *The Arts of Antioch.*

GEORGE T. M. SHACKELFORD is Chair, Art of Europe, and the Arthur K. Solomon Curator of Modern Art at the Museum of Fine Arts, Boston. A specialist in Impressionist painting and graphic arts, he has written and lectured extensively on the art of the nineteenth and early twentieth centuries. His most recent projects include *Van Gogh: Face to Face, Impressionist Still Life, Impressions of Light,* and *Gauguin Tahiti.*

R. L. WILSON is the author of forty-five books and some three hundred articles on firearms. For twenty years he was consultant on American arms to Christie's. A member of the Visiting Committee, Department of Arms and Armor, The Metropolitan Museum of Art, New York, Wilson also consults for various other museums and collectors.

PHOTOGRAPHY CREDITS

* * * * * * *

The photographs in this catalogue have been provided as follows:

pp. 2–3, 8, 22, 29, 32, 34–35, 38, 62, 158: Kim Sargent. © Sargent Architectural Photography.

pp. 10–13, 15 (bottom), 17, 24, 27, 49–53, 55 (bottom), 60, 67 (left), 69, 78, 88 (bottom), 106–7, 109, 115 (right), 124–26, 128, 131, 163, 170, 173, 180, 181 (bottom), 182 (top), 184–85: Courtesy of William I. Koch. All rights reserved.

pp. 14, 15 (top), 16, 18–19, 44, 67 (right), 72, 73 (right), 74, 76, 79 (bottom), 81, 85, 90, 92–95, 97–98, 113, 116 (left), 119–23, 127, 129–30, 132–38, 140–44, 146–57, 162, 165, 166 (bottom), 169, 171–72, 174–79, 181 (top), 182 (bottom), 183, 186–92, 194–97, 199–201, 204: C. J. Walker Photography. All rights reserved.

pp. 20–21, 31, 43, 46–48, 54, 55 (top), 56–59, 61, 64, 66, 68, 71, 73 (left), 75, 77, 79 (top), 80, 82–84, 86–88 (top), 89, 91, 96, 103–5, 112, 114, 115 (left), 116 (right), 117–18, 166 (top): The Photo Studios, Museum of Fine Arts, Boston. © Museum of Fine Arts, Boston.

p. 28: Daniel Forster. © Daniel Forster.

p. 102: Courtesy of the Gerald Peters Gallery. All rights reserved.

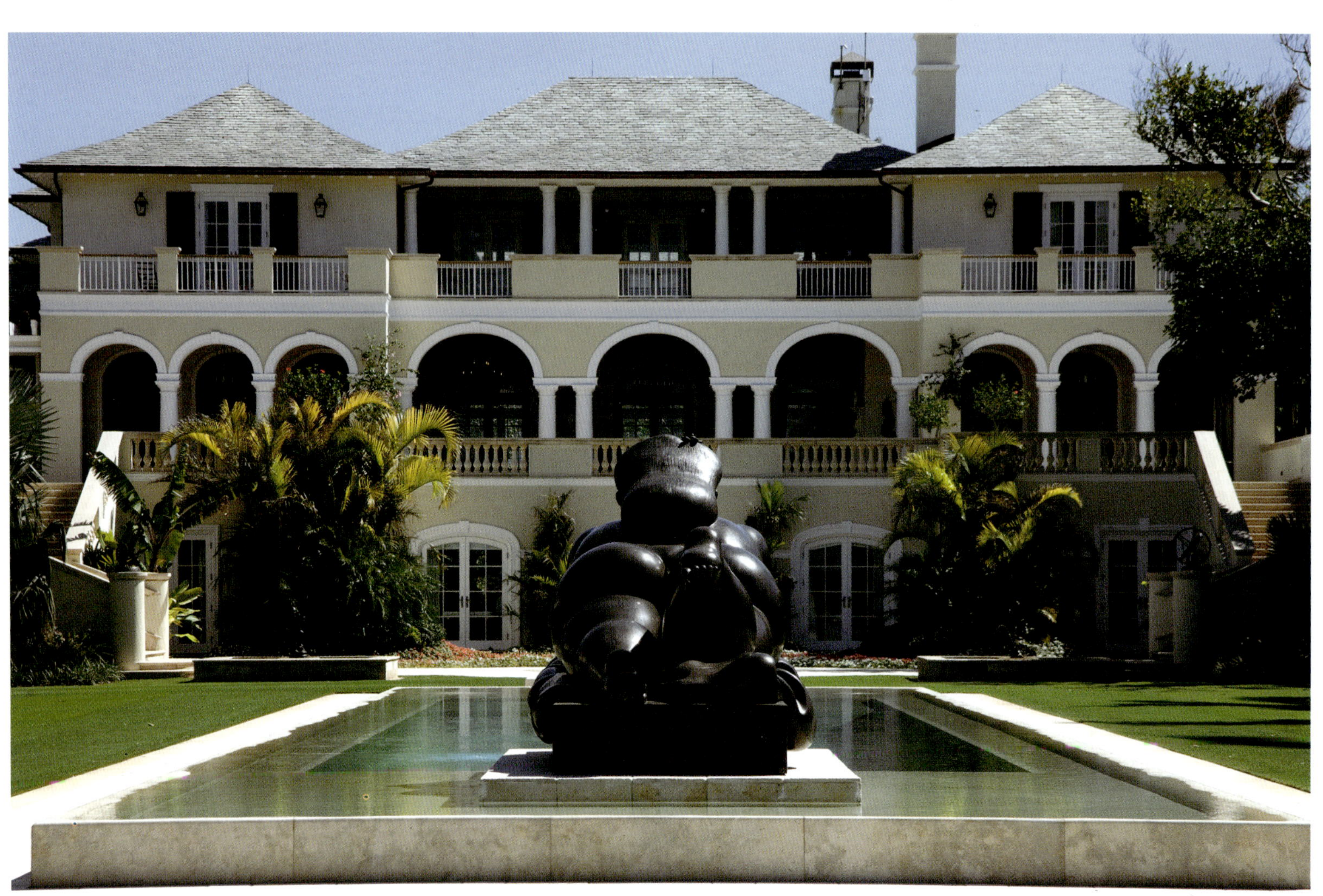

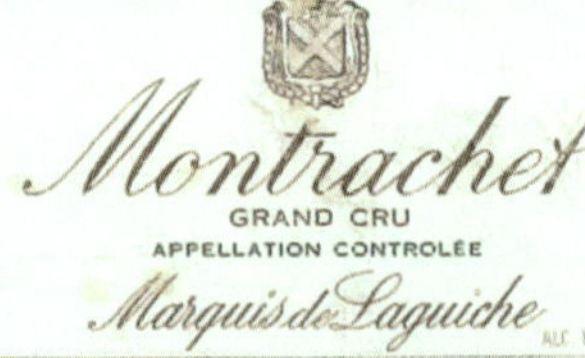
Joseph Drouhin
Montrachet
GRAND CRU
APPELLATION CONTROLÉE
Marquis de Laguiche

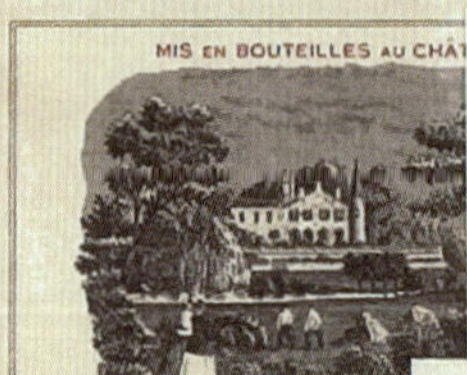

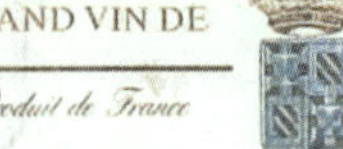
GRAND VIN DE
BOURGOGNE

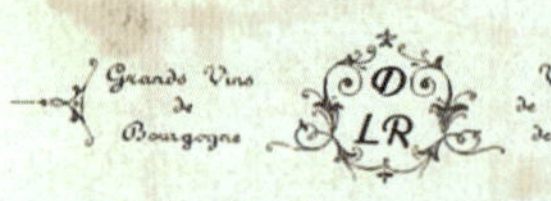

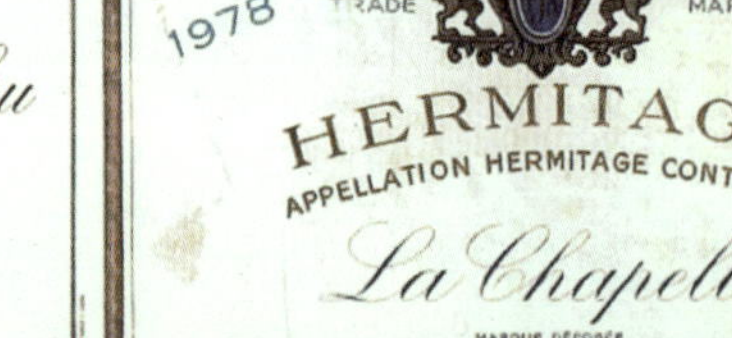
PRODUCE OF FRANCE
CONTENTS 75 CL
1978
1978
HERMITAGE
APPELLATION HERMITAGE CONTROLÉE
La Chapelle